# UNSETTLING THE WEST

E. FARNHAM G. KIRBY

# UNSETTLING THE WEST

*Eliza Farnham and Georgiana Bruce Kirby in Frontier California*

JoAnn Levy

*foreword by* KEVIN STARR

SANTA CLARA UNIVERSITY, SANTA CLARA, CALIFORNIA
HEYDAY BOOKS, BERKELEY, CALIFORNIA

*Library of Congress Cataloging-in-Publication Data*

Levy, Jo Ann, 1941–
    Unsettling the West : Eliza Farnham and Georgiana Bruce Kirby in
frontier California / JoAnn Levy ; foreword by Kevin Starr.
        p. cm. — (California legacy book)
Includes bibliographical references (p.  ) and index.
        ISBN 1-890771-83-x (pbk. : alk. paper) — ISBN 1-890771-85-6
(hardcover : alk. paper)
    1. Women pioneers—California—Biography. 2. Women social
reformers—California—Biography. 3. Feminists—California—Biography.
    4. Farnham, Eliza W. (Eliza Wood), 1815-1864. 5. Kirby, Georgiana
Bruce, 1818-1887. 6. Frontier and pioneer life—California. 7.
California—Gold discoveries. I. Title. II. Series.
    F865.L675 2004
    979.4'04'0922—dc22
                                        2003023487

Cover design: Rebecca LeGates
Interior design: Philip Krayna, PKD

Cover art: "View of San Francisco Taken from Telegraph Hill," April 1851. Courtesy
of The Bancroft Library, University of California, Berkeley (Banc Pic 1963:002:1495-
FR). Portraits (cover and preceding page): Eliza Wood Burhans Farnham. From the
*Burhans Geneaology* by Samuel Burhans Jr. (New York: 1894). Georgiana Bruce Kirby.
Courtesy of the Society of California Pioneers (CO22513).

Printing and binding: Phoenix Color, Hagerstown, MD

Orders, inquiries, and correspondence should be addressed to:

Heyday Books
P.O. Box 9145, Berkeley, CA 94709
(510) 549-3564, fax (510) 549-1889
www.heydaybooks.com

Printed in the United States of America
10 9 8 7 6 5 4 3 2 1

# Contents

EDITOR'S NOTE: Quoted material is reproduced exactly as it appears in original sources except for minor editing of spelling and punctuation for the sake of comprehension.

## ⸻ ILLUSTRATIONS ⸻

# Foreword

*by* KEVIN STARR

With the exception of the most privileged, American women of the nineteenth century led difficult lives—physically, emotionally, intellectually. Even among the middle classes, they worked long, hard hours, cooking, cleaning, washing, and caring for husbands, children, surviving parents, and other relatives. Even the simplest tasks constituted energy-draining chores. Emotionally, women were forced to endure the loss of their children at alarming rates. Their own inner landscapes, moreover—their dreams and aspirations and hopes for personal fulfillment—were constantly at the beck and call of others and frequently disregarded altogether. Intellectually, women were frequently denied education beyond the most rudimentary grades, whatever their talents might be. All women, even the most brilliant and educated, were denied the simple right to vote or, in most states, to own property in their own names. By the standards of today, then, it can almost be argued that most mid-nineteenth-century American women of ordinary circumstances lived exhausting and constrained lives, structured by neglect and disappointment.

The frontier compounded these difficult conditions. Frontier women, by the very nature of their existence, worked longer hours at more exhausting tasks, stood in danger of a suppressed inner life, lost more children, enjoyed fewer consolations of home and good company. In this regard, the frontier of 1850s California—remote, harsh, undeveloped, almost totally masculine in population and tone—perhaps offered an even greater burden for the women who found themselves living there.

All this makes the careers of Eliza Farnham and Georgiana Bruce Kirby even more remarkable. In Eliza Farnham's case, orphaned at an early age, she was in every sense a physically and emotionally abused child. While not as desperate, Georgiana Bruce Kirby's early years were comparably challenged. Yet each of these young women, with next to nothing given to her, managed to maintain her integrity and, even more, make connection with a finer self. In Eliza Farnham's case, this meant connecting with the values of her almost lost Quaker heritage. They went to school, however briefly, where they mastered the arts of reading and writing; and in so doing, they established citadels within themselves: citadels of thought and imagination that a harsh and uncaring world could not destroy. They became intellectuals and writers, social activists and reformers. Even more impressively, they never repudiated their female identities, despite the second-class life that women were then forced to live. They married. They brought children into the world. They gloried in motherhood while, simultaneously, struggling against the shackles that bound women to unceasing cycles of childbirth and domestic labor.

Eliza Farnham's life is especially dramatic in this context of struggle and achievement. She married a lawyer-writer and brought a physically challenged child into the world. Her husband, the well-known travel writer Thomas Jefferson Farnham, died, leaving her a young widow with a sickly and dependent child. Rather than withdraw into herself, however, she—along with her lifelong friend Georgiana Bruce Kirby—made a creative connection with the women's movement, as exemplified by the great Margaret Fuller, who was then living in the reformist commune Brook Farm in West Roxbury, Massachusetts.

Securing the position of Women's Warden at Sing Sing prison in 1844, Farnham, with the help of her friend Georgiana Bruce, embarked upon a program of reform that in and of itself would have earned her a place among notable American women in the mid-nineteenth century. She lifted the no-talking rule and sponsored reading lessons. She established a prison library. Above all else, she encouraged inmates to regard themselves as women, imprisoned perhaps, but still possessed of the awesome power and role nature had assigned the female half of the human species. It was at this point, perhaps, while serving as Women's Warden, that Eliza Farnham discovered the grand theme and motif of her life. It was the role of women to redeem society: not only to free themselves from social, political, and cultural restraints but, once freed of these, to redeem society through high-minded activism and motherhood. Despite the constraints of nineteenth-century American marriage, Eliza Farnham never lost faith in the redemptive work of women in society through the moral leavening of the whole and the care of the particular child. Perhaps because she herself was devoted to her wounded child, she had thought through this position in a most personal and anguished manner.

This is why she organized a group of marriageable women to emigrate to California so as to upgrade the tone of society. For various reasons, this enterprise failed, but as statement, as gesture, as moral philosophy, it was an outstanding success. California would never amount to anything until it bypassed its good-old-boy frontier phase and began, under the encouragement of women, to care for the things that truly matter in society. This faith in marriage makes it doubly, even triply, tragic that Eliza Farnham, settling in Santa Cruz in the 1850s alongside her friend Georgiana Bruce Kirby, chose, in marrying for the second time, an alcoholic—a man of talent and charm, perhaps, but a demon when in his cups—whom she eventually divorced. Of the four children she brought into the world through these marriages, only one would survive into adulthood. She believed in marriage, but had no husband. She believed in motherhood, but her children were taken from her.

Fortunately, her friend Georgiana married a more stable and mature man, brought beautiful children into the world who survived, and lived on into the 1880s, an ardent feminist-reformer as well as—by then—the prosperous wife of a successful businessman. Eliza Farnham was gone by then, having died in 1864 at the age of forty-nine—but not before writing many fine books, lecturing extensively on both coasts, nursing the wounded on the battlefield of Gettysburg, and lobbying and arguing, in season and out, for not only a better role for women in America, but an even higher conception of their own destiny in society among women themselves.

How wonderful, how consoling, that Eliza and Georgiana enjoyed a lifelong friendship. How wonderful that they could keep company with each other in that far-flung frontier, talking together, when the work of the day was done, of books, going on picnics in the company of Georgiana's beau, walking beneath the redwoods of the Santa Cruz peninsula, and talking, as they walked, of that better life that women would one day enjoy in California and the rest of the United States.

Mrs. Kirby left behind her diary. Eliza Farnham left behind a series of books that are only now becoming appreciated for the role they played in forging a new consciousness among American women. Mrs. Kirby lived long and comfortably. Mrs. Farnham did not. How typical of her—she who never counted the cost of anything she did—to have shortened her life, as is most likely the case, through infections gained while nursing wounded soldiers at Gettysburg. Thanks to JoAnn Levy, the lives of these two pioneer reformers—so inextricably bound up with each other through the lifetime gift of friendship—stand revealed as important chapters in the story of nineteenth-century American women. For all its suffering, that story—the Eliza Farnham story, the Georgiana Bruce Kirby story—bears within itself a sustaining, compelling, heroic, and utterly beautiful message of hope.

FOR GLADYS TILDEN (1900–1995)
—who recognized a singular woman
when she found one.
Here she is, Miss Tilden,
—rest in peace.

The mission of the Reformer can scarcely be identified with that of other individuals. He is placed in a position where the soul is moved and the actions governed by the most pure and disinterested motives. There is for him no selfish object to be gained, like those which attract the groveling mass. His reward is not outward—he acquires not wealth, nor honor, nor ease. His path is not one on which the sunshine may long rest—the frowns, reproaches, and heartlessness of men cast shadows upon his soul. A spirit of self-sacrifice and devotion to humanity can alone prompt and sustain his efforts. He must feel amid the darkest clouds of persecution, the majesty and power of Truth. The inward rather than the external—the spiritual more than the material, must be made the basis of his trust....The Reformer should be regarded as an instrument in the hands of angels and of God, to impel man onward to an exalted destiny. A halo of glory surrounds his brow, though he feels but the crown of thorns. The reward of interior approbation and spiritual guidance is his, though he feeds upon the husks of poverty, or dwells amid the shadows of earthly sorrow.

—Russell Perkins Ambler,
"The Mission of the Reformer,"
*Spirit Messenger and Harmonial Guide* (Springfield, Mass.),
December 28, 1850

I do not care so particularly that the biographer of the sage, poet, hero, or lover, should furnish me with the dates of the great events in his life; and even the events themselves have less interest than a week's daily journal of this man's doing and being—as, how he lived; in what sort of house; his gardens and fruits, and the care he gave them; how he entertained and repelled his children; his joy at their birth and his grief at their death; how he talked with his friends; how he was related to his wife, and wherefore he chose her. These items, and such as these, would bring us nearer to that soul, which is now become only a name and a thought to us, than the knowing when a certain book was written; whether at thirty or forty; when a victory was won, or a defeat nobly sustained....It is the life we crave, not the record of its outward doings. It is the soul-life that appeals to our soul: and hence the great charm of those few, rare biographies, and rarer autobiographies, which melt the heart before us.

—Eliza Farnham

# Preface

The praising of famous men occupies biographers wonderfully. Readers enthusiastically welcome a new book on Lincoln or Twain, a new look at Hemingway or Patton, curious to know what minuscule fact has newly surfaced, what current interpretation sheds new light on familiar deeds. Brand names sell. The lives of public women likewise attract attention. Whatever new might be added to Eleanor Roosevelt's story, or Susan Anthony's, an audience awaits. Because the names are familiar, because we already know them, we want to know more.

Eliza Farnham is a stranger's name. So is Georgiana Kirby. They ring no bells. If they were important, we reason, surely we would have heard. Kirby, born in England, died in Santa Cruz in 1887, her name enduring only in the small California city she influenced for thirty-five years. Farnham, a New Yorker, died in 1864, at forty-nine. In her time, the public knew her name—it made the newspapers on both coasts regularly for a quarter century—but eventually it slipped from memory and out of fashion, and into few history books. Thus do many remarkable lives escape recognition, become unknown, unsung. The book before you, it is hoped, both provides the proof to that pudding and corrects the record for two of them.

Every biography contains two beginnings. Foremost, of course, is the subject's birth and consequent achievement of celebrity or notoriety sufficient to engage a reader's interest. The second beginning belongs to the writer: a birth of decision, the moment in which one chooses to devote a portion of one's own life to reconstructing another's. I made that decision subconsciously the day I discovered Eliza Farnham at the Los Angeles Public Library, in the book she wrote about California as she found it, in the midst of the gold rush. In that moment, and I remember it well though two decades have since elapsed, I fell under her spell. The force of her personality was such that she resurrected herself and walked off the page of her life and into mine.

I took her home with me from the library, in chapters photocopied from her rare book—and within its pages met her friend, Georgiana, the dearly beloved Geordie.

The book, *California, In-doors and Out; or, How We Farm, Mine, and Live Generally in the Golden State*, is a record—albeit seriously deficient—of Eliza's adventure in gold rush California, starting with a voyage in which the ship's captain intentionally abandoned her in Chile and sailed off with her children aboard. And that was just the introduction. The story grew even better when she reached Santa Cruz. What I also had from her book, besides an astonishing tale, was a sense of the person who wrote it. I thought she was extraordinary from the first words on the page. And that was *before* I discovered she'd written four other books, including a two-volume treatise on the superiority of women; *before* I learned she'd addressed the Woman's Rights Convention of 1858; *before* I learned she'd lectured widely on phrenology and Spiritualism; *before* I learned she'd been at Gettysburg *and* Sing Sing prison.

Eliza Farnham begins her California book with an "Explanatory," her preface, "To my few particular friends, if I have any such, which the general reader has permission to pass by, if he hope for something better further on." That's her first sentence, elegantly crafted, slightly droll, simultaneously invitational and dismissive. Interesting to me in time was her recognition in that preface that the reader might find "discrepancies between the early and later pages." She lays it off to having written much of the book in 1851 and the remainder a few years later. True enough, but hardly an explanation for the bleak, detached, sermonizing tone of the latter half, a jarring contrast to the vivid and witty early pages. Eventually I discovered the true reason for the "discrepancies," and I was stunned by what she failed to mention regarding her California experience. Now when I read those last chapters, their solemnity and detachment conjure images of her abusive second husband, the drunken William Fitzpatrick, plunging his knife into her books, and the terror of her young son Charles hiding in the cornfield with his new baby sister. Just two in a long list of staggering omissions. Every bit as turbulent and adventurous as the story she told is the one she didn't, in the blanks she left. It's been my great pleasure and privilege to fill them in.

Eliza Farnham's life cannot fully be told without Georgiana Kirby's. Margaret Fuller introduced them, and in 1844 they worked together at Sing Sing prison. Later, Georgiana joined Eliza in California, where they lived together, farmed together, and relied upon one another for intellectual and emotional sustenance. They had their differences, on women's rights, on how to run the farm. Occasionally they criticized each other. Eliza married a man Georgiana abhorred. Georgiana married well. There was a falling out, but even then Georgiana confided to her journal, "I love Mrs. F in spite of the trouble and anxiety she has caused...." To Georgiana, Eliza declared, "I rejoice in you as it is rarely given to one woman to rejoice in another." Georgiana wrote, "I hear that Mrs. F will not return to Cal[ifornia]....What then am I to do? How can I live?"

This then is a biography of two friends, two remarkable women bypassed by fame—I've come to praise them.

J. L. L.
Sutter Creek, California

*Californians eager for news from "the States" lined
up at San Francisco's Clay street post office.*
From Annals of San Francisco *by Frank Soulé et al., 1855*

# ONE

# This Singular Woman

Mrs. Farnham, the celebrated matron of the Sing Sing Prison, is going to Boston this week on an enterprise her circular will explain. She is, of all women ever created (within my knowledge of God's works), the fittest for the enterprise. She has nerves to explore alone the seven circles of Dante's Hell. She has physical strength and endurance, sound sense and philanthropy, earnestness, and a coolness that would say 'I know!' if an angel were sent to tell her the secrets of the upper world....I have promised her a letter to Mrs. Minot, who I know will be pleased to see so rare a specimen of womanhood, and who...will appreciate this singular woman.
—Catharine M. Sedgwick, New York, February 5, 1849

MRS. FARNHAM'S ASSOCIATION FOR CALIFORNIA.—Mrs. E. W. Farnham has just returned to the city, after visiting the Eastern States for the purpose of making up her company of migrating ladies, who, having no husbands to engage their attention here, are desirous of going on an errand to the golden land. The mission is a good one, and the projector deserves success. The enterprise in which Mrs. F. has engaged is one which evinces moral courage. Her reward will be found in the blessings which her countrymen will invoke for her when the vessel in which the association is to sail shall have arrived in California with her precious cargo. May favoring gales attend the good ship Angelique.
—*New York Herald*, April 12, 1849

The infant city of San Francisco welcomed notice of eastern events twice monthly, courtesy of the Pacific Mail Steamship Company's side-wheelers. Their arrival was announced atop Telegraph Hill by two raised boards hinged to a pole, the appearance of which invariably threw the populace into a veritable paroxysm of anticipation. Long lines immediately formed in front of the post office on Clay street, where more than one opportunistic frontier entrepreneur pocketed a ten-dollar gold piece by selling his window position to an anxious latecomer.

That Eliza Farnham's name and fame preceded her to California constitutes no small achievement in 1849, when communication consisted of conversation, handwritten letters, and newspapers composed from type trays. The speed with which news traveled from the East to the West depended upon prevailing winds and the seaworthiness of vessels. Local distribution relied upon feet, two or four, usually both: the carrier's and his horse's.

Californians eager for the latest advice from the East paid as much as five dollars a copy for New York and Baltimore newspapers hawked on San Francisco street corners, and local editors liberally reprinted in their own publications the reports others contained, however dated. San Francisco's *Alta California* informed its readers on June 28 that "Mrs. Farnham...is now busily engaged in making final preparations for the departure of her expedition on the ship Angelique"—with the vessel and its famous passenger then already more than a month at sea.

San Franciscans impatiently awaited the *Angelique*'s arrival. For months the city had been abuzz over the astonishing intention of Mrs. Farnham, a thirty-three-year-old New Yorker, mother of two young sons, and newly widowed. They had read all about it in the *New York Tribune* of February 14:

> A NEW CALIFORNIA EXPEDITION.—A lady of this State, well known for her labors in many a philanthropic cause, is about forming a benevolent expedition to California, which cannot but prove of great public benefit, in the present unsettled condition of that region. Aided by several gentlemen of wealth and liberality, she proposes to purchase a vessel, to be freighted with every article necessary for the aid and assistance of the sick or disabled, including the frame of a building intended for a hospital. She is now engaged in raising a company of intelligent and respectable females, to accompany her in this mission of charity, each of whom shall contribute something toward the purchase of the vessel and cargo, and assist in the humane object of the enterprise. None will be taken who have not attained the age of twenty-five years, and can also produce sufficient testimonials of character. A part of the freight is to consist of articles to furnish a store, in which a part of the women may be employed, and in material for clothing, to be made up according to orders on the spot.
>
> This plan, the great utility of which will be seen at a glance, may be ranked among the most truly Christian enterprises of the day. Of the thousands of inexperienced emigrants now on their way to the land of promise, large numbers must feel severely the hardships and privations of their new mode of life, and their situation, without the

**SHIP ANGELIQUE.**

# CALIFORNIA ASSOCIATION OF AMERICAN WOMEN.

NEW YORK. FEBRUARY 2D, 1849.

THE death of my husband, THOMAS J. FARNHAM, Esq., at San Francisco, in September last. renders it expedient that I should visit California during the coming season. Having a desire to accomplish some greater good by my journey thither than to give the necessary attention to my private affairs, and believing that the presence of women would be one of the surest checks upon many of the evils that are apprehended there, I desire to ask attention to the following sketch of a plan for organizing a party of such persons to emigrate to that country.

Among the many privations and deteriorating influences to which the thousands who are flocking thither will be subjected, one of the greatest is the absence of woman, with all her kindly cares and powers, so peculiarly conservative to man under such circumstances.

It would exceed the limits of this circular to hint at the benefits that would flow to the growing population of that wonderful region, from the introduction among them of intelligent, virtuous and efficient women. Of such only, it is proposed to make up this company. It is believed that there are hundreds, if not thousands, of such females in our country who are not bound by any tie that would hold them here, who might, by going thither, have the satisfaction of employing themselves greatly to the benefit and advantage of those who are there, and at the same time of serving their own interest more effectually than by following any employment that offers to them here.

It is proposed that the company shall consist of persons not under twenty-five years of age, who shall bring from their clergyman, or some authority of the town where they reside, satisfactory testimonials of education, character, capacity, &c., and who can contribute the sum of two hundred and fifty dollars, to defray the expenses of the voyage, make suitable provision for their accommodation after reaching San Francisco, until they shall be able to enter upon some occupation for their support, and create a fund to be held in reserve for the relief of any who may be ill, or otherwise need aid before they are able to provide for themselves.

It is believed that such an arrangement, with one hundred or one hundred and thirty persons, would enable the company to purchase or charter a vessel, and fit it up with every thing necessary to comfort on the voyage, and that the combination of all for the support of each, would give such security, both as to health, person and character, as would remove all reasonable hesitation from the minds of those who may be disposed and able to join such a mission. It is intended that the party shall include six or eight respectable married men and their families.

Those who desire further information will receive it by calling on the subscriber at

ELIZA W FARNHAM.

The New-York built Packet Ship ANGELIQUE has been engaged to take out this Association. She is a spacious vessel, fitted up with state rooms throughout and berths of good size, well ventilated and provided in every way to secure a safe, speedy and comfortable voyage. She will be ready to sail from New-York about the 12th or 15th of April

WE, the undersigned, having been made acquainted with the plan proposed by Mrs. FARNHAM, in the above circular, hereby express our approbation of the same, and recommend her to those who may be disposed to unite with her in it. as worthy the trust and confidence necessary to its successful conduct.

| | |
|---|---|
| Hon. J. W. EDMONDS. Judge Superior Court | W. C. BRYANT, Esq. |
| Hon. W. T. McCOUN, Late Vice Chancellor. | SHEPHERD KNAPP, Esq. |
| Hon. B. F. BUTLER, Late U. S. Attorney. | Rev. GEORGE POTTS. D. D. |
| Hon. H. GREELEY. | Rev. HENRY WARD BEECHER. |
| ISAAC T. HOPPER, Esq. | Miss CATHARINE M. SEDGWICK. |
| FREEMAN HUNT, Esq. | Mrs. C. M. KIRKLAND |
| THOMAS C. DOREMUS, Esq. | |

NESBITT. PRINTER.

*Mrs. Farnham's circular.*
*Courtesy of The Bancroft Library, University of California, Berkeley*

aid thus furnished, must be indeed deplorable. We trust the originator of this expedition may meet with abundant support. There
are certainly enough of enterprising and benevolent women in this
part of the country to second her in the work.

It was a plan as bold as the woman who proposed it.

Famed novelist Catharine Sedgwick's endorsement of Mrs.
Farnham as the "fittest for the enterprise" echoed that of the
dozen influential intellectuals who had appended their illustrious
signatures to the circular advertising the formation of the California Association of American Women. Supporters attesting to their
confidence in Mrs. Farnham and the worthiness of her proposal
included such luminaries as Henry Ward Beecher, Quaker philanthropist Isaac Hopper, former U.S. Attorney Benjamin F. Butler,
Superior Court Judge John W. Edmonds, and *New York Tribune*
editor Horace Greeley.

Mrs. Farnham's laudable enterprise proposed, at least in part,
to offset California's widely reported evils of drunkenness and
gambling, such vices inevitably arising in the absence of the civi-
lizing influence of good women. "Among the privations and deteriorating influences to which the thousands who are flocking
thither will be subjected," she wrote, "one of the greatest is the
absence of woman, with all her kindly cares and powers, so peculiarly conservative to man under such circumstances."

"Flocking thither" put it mildly. When President Polk
announced in his December 1848 address to Congress that
"recent discoveries render it probable that these mines are more
extensive and valuable than was anticipated," thousands of
impetuous young men promptly deserted the East for the West,
galvanized by gold and fevered by greed. From the Atlantic
seaboard those intent on the fastest passage launched themselves
in anything seaworthy—and much that was not. More than ninety
vessels departed New York in January of 1849. By the close of that
year, an estimated thirty-nine thousand argonauts had reached
San Francisco's port, joined in California by some thirty thousand
emigrants who had herded themselves across the continent in covered wagons in pursuit of the golden promise. In 1850, California
would welcome another fifty thousand from the overland trail,
with thirty-six thousand more arriving by sea.

In February of 1849, when Eliza Farnham published her audacious proposal, eastern newspapers already overflowed with the latest advice from the mines, accounts of deprivations and riches in equal proportion. A letter in the *Boston Journal* described California's tumultuous state of affairs:

> Half of the houses in Monterey are empty, and at least two thirds of those in San Francisco. The hotels and stores have all been closed, and many farms have no occupants whatever....strangers arriving, and officers stationed here, some days hardly know where to get anything to eat, even without the necessary comforts....Many families are without a single servant....towns in the lower part of Upper California must soon share the fate of San Francisco and Monterey, as the whole population are going crazy—old as well as young, are daily falling victims to the gold fever....Every woman who chooses can now find ready employment in making up clothing for the gold diggers, and at a great price. The market now contains nothing whatever, and it is with great difficulty that we can get anything, even the common necessaries of life....If people ever suffered from an overplus of this precious metal, we now suffer, for it has deranged every one, and forced everything out of its proper channel.

An opportunity to offset evil *and* to "find ready employment" in a country beset by an "overplus" of gold contained such certain appeal that Mrs. Farnham anticipated a full subscription to her association. She had already contracted for the packet *Angelique* and set its sailing date for April. Her personal circumstances necessitated that she undertake the journey as soon as possible, as she announced in her circular:

> The death of my husband, Thomas J. Farnham, Esq., at San Francisco, in September last, renders it expedient that I should visit California during the coming season. Having a desire to accomplish some greater good by my journey thither than to give the necessary attention to my private affairs, and believing that the presence of women would be one of the surest checks upon many of the evils that are apprehended there, I desire to ask attention to the following sketch of a plan for organizing a party of such persons to emigrate to that country.

The unexpected death of her husband, noted travel writer Thomas Jefferson Farnham, compelled a journey Mrs. Farnham had long anticipated, but to far different purpose. Years before the discovery of gold at Sutter's mill, before the urgent fever now infecting the nation, the Farnhams had determined to make their home in California, on two thousand acres adjacent to the mission of Santa Cruz. Tom had gone ahead, in 1846, to prepare for the family's eventual emigration. Unfortunately, in September of 1848, while still in California, he had contracted a fever and died.

The distressing news had reached Eliza in Boston, at Dr. Samuel Gridley Howe's school for the blind, where she had been employed for several months as matron and teacher—after overcoming Dr. Howe's reluctance to hire her.

She was, after all, as Dr. Howe well knew—as did everyone who had regularly read a newspaper in Massachusetts, Maryland, New York, or Pennsylvania during the summer of 1846—the infamous matron of Sing Sing prison.

# TWO

# Sing Sing Prison

Mrs. T. J. Farnham of this city has been appointed Matron of the Female Department of the State Prison at Sing-Sing....We hope the time is not distant when Women, and Men too of the highest character will be selected to preside over all our receptacles for criminals, animated by an abiding faith in the power of Goodness and Love to subdue the most depraved and sinful.

—*New York Tribune*, March 18, 1844

The papers of...the city of New York have teemed for the past year with comments upon the outrageous conduct at the Sing Sing Prison. The Rev Mr. Luckey, a clergyman of the Methodist persuasion, who had held his post as Chaplain through various Administrations has been removed under circumstances which reflect the highest discredit upon the Inspectors, and in his expose to the public, he casts imputations upon the Matron, which if true, (and they have not been disputed) show that she is wholly unworthy the station she fills. It appears that books are introduced and placed in the hands of the male and female convicts of the most licentious and demoral-izing character, and because the Chaplain objected to this system of debauchery he was unceremoniously thrust out, and not even favored with an explanation for such uncalled for and unheard of treatment.

—*Hudson River Chronicle*, December 22, 1846

Abolitionism, women's rights, social philosophies, penal reform—the 1840s banged a drum for a parade of desired improvements to American culture. Mrs. Farnham energetically lent her voice to reform through a series of lectures she delivered in New York City, impressing John W. Edmonds, chairman of the New York State Prison Board of Inspectors. Edmonds and the board also possessed reformist inclinations, more particularly since a recent uprising among the women prisoners at Sing Sing. There had been:

> a sort of rebellion among the convicts, or among some of the most daring, who had deliberately refused to conform to the rules of the prison, or to perform the duties assigned them. They tyrannized

over and maltreated the weaker and more docile of their fellows, and made night hideous by singing blasphemous and obscene songs....The [Prison] Board, on making a visit to the prison, had been met by shouts of derision and insolent defiance, and they had to make a hasty exit to escape the kids (a wooden tub, holding about a quart, used in place of plate and saucer for the rations) flung at them by the rioters.

The criminal mind fascinated Mrs. Farnham, who confessed to possessing an "intense curiosity to penetrate the innermost centre of the stained soul, and observe the mysterious working of that machinery by which so fatal a result was produced." Although that inclination and her admiration for the work of English penal reformer Elizabeth Fry constituted the whole of Eliza Farnham's qualifications for the Sing Sing appointment, Horace Greeley roundly applauded her selection: "She brings to the arduous duty she has undertaken lofty intellectual and moral qualities, and we anticipate the most auspicious results from her efforts, which we are sure will be ardent and untiring."

Eliza's husband remained in New York, writing the next installment of his *Travels in California*, when she and their three-year-old son, Charles, took up residence in the west end of the Mount Pleasant Women's Prison, an impressive white marble building with imposing Doric columns. The fitting but ironic name attached from the prison's beautiful location above the Hudson river. Despite this official designation, both the female prison and the main prison were known generally as Sing Sing, the name of the adjacent town, a charming village with graceful, winding streets.

The interior of the women's prison consisted of three galleries of cells, twenty-four cells to a gallery, seventy-two cells in all. Stoves placed in the corridors provided warmth. At the eastern end of the building a raised platform served as a chapel, reading room, and lecture hall.

Mrs. Farnham immediately hired four assistants, including Georgiana Bruce, a young Englishwoman fresh from Brook Farm, a cooperative living experiment near Boston distinguished for its transcendentalist philosophy—the spiritual and intellectual conviction that God is immanent in nature and individual intuition.

At Sing Sing, Georgiana Bruce identified her colleagues:

Mrs. Mary Anne Johnson, a lady admirably suited for the position, Sarah Mallory, a handsome, dignified girl of twenty-two, from Connecticut; an evangelical sister, a hard-worked sempstress, past middle age, whose narrow views and general illiteracy made her a greater hindrance than help; and I, were the four assistant matrons.

Mrs. Farnham was only twenty-eight years old, but her grave face, with its high, impressive brow, made her appear much older. I could hardly believe that she was but three years my senior....She had a creative intellect, large benevolence, a keen sense of humor, but was deficient in external perception, and so had to depend on Mrs. J. and myself for quick observation, which is eminently necessary to a person having charge of those unaccustomed to speaking the truth.

Mrs. Farnham knew Mary Anne Johnson as the wife of journalist Oliver Johnson, employed by Horace Greeley on the *Tribune*. Georgiana Bruce was indirectly a Greeley connection, too. The famed intellectual Margaret Fuller had lately taken residence with the Greeley family, and there Miss Fuller introduced Mrs. Farnham to a young woman known to her from Brook Farm.

Whether Eliza or Georgiana, upon meeting, felt the portent of their eventual profound friendship and shared destiny, neither recorded it.

Eliza Farnham devoutly believed that humanity was a higher obligation than discipline, and reformation a nobler object than punishment. Her first action as the new matron was to address the women prisoners and tell them she would, as far as the law permitted, make their situation comfortable. As she was "so evidently fearless, and at the same time so gentle in manner and speech," according to Miss Bruce, she soon secured order and respect from the formerly rebellious inmates.

When word of her quick success reached Horace Greeley, he enthusiastically provided his *Tribune* readers a progress report of Mrs. Farnham's new employment:

Although less than two weeks have elapsed since she entered upon the duties of her office we learn from sources entitled to implicit confidence that she has done much to reform previously existing abuses, and that the effects of her firm and dignified yet kind and benevolent deportment are already strikingly manifest in the establishment of wholesome disciplines and the increased comfort and happiness of prisoners. This is no more than was anticipated by all who knew Mrs. F, and must afford high satisfaction not only to her immediate friends but to all who are interested in the moral welfare of the unfortunate criminals under her care.

The prison reform measures instituted by "Mrs. F" included abolishing the "no-talking" rule; substituting kindness for punishment; providing books to those who could read and reading instruction to those who could not; offering opportunities for work; and presenting musical events and lectures by such luminaries as Margaret Fuller. Unfortunately, in less enlightened circles than those orbiting around Horace Greeley, these reforms elicited constant criticism. The general opinion on punishment endorsed torture, not tenderness. The pulley, for example, remained a popular disciplinary device: the convict was obliged to stand on one leg while the other limbs were raised by ropes. Stocks and chains had been a favored punishment for women prisoners at Sing Sing, as was wrapping a misbehaving woman in a blanket and leaving her, head exposed, handcuffed, and chained to the floor, at the head of the stairs for everyone to see. And it had been almost a daily occurrence for women prisoners to be tied up by the arms with their toes just reaching the floor and left in this painful posture for an hour or more. Prisoner Phoebe Spires, sentenced for manslaughter, testified to Mrs. Farnham's success:

> When Mrs. F came she had to punish as there were constant attempts after she had been here a day or two to subvert her authority. But after that there was very little punishment. We have received instructions....Several have been taught to read...Mrs. F has lectured to us...And if the prison had been as it is now many women who have gone out of prison would have been reformed. But it used to be that women were absolutely corrupted by being here. Mrs. F has read very interesting books...She got maps for us and gave us lessons in geography.

Nonetheless, the prison board received steady condemnation for their reformist views, with John Edmonds accorded particular censure for observing the nation's celebration of independence by sending flowers to the women prisoners. Georgiana Bruce recorded the occasion:

In New York friends of the new *regime* had united in buying a quantity of good, fresh meat for women prisoners on Fourth of July, sufficient to satisfy every one....Judge Edmonds also sent the required number of bouquets, among which were two, much larger than the others, which were to be given to the most amiable among the prisoners. The matrons were to nominate one person and the women the other. These flowers and the meat, indicating a kind thought for their welfare on the part of friends, had a most salutary effect. Ripe currants and candy purchased by the matrons had been placed in the cells while the voting was going on in the shops, and while Judge Edmonds' address was being read by Mrs. Johnson.

At 8 a.m. they returned to their cells for the whole day, during which they kept perfectly quiet, only anxious that the lady in charge should have no trouble whatever.

Some may consider these proceedings an evidence of false sentiment for criminals. If such people, however, could see the low, narrow cells, and the unvarying salt-junk and pork, and picture to themselves the long years of imprisonment to which so many were doomed who treasured the belief that they were the born enemies of society, which in its turn entertained for them only a feeling of hate and contempt—not only the kindness but the policy of such acts will become apparent. Punishment with adults is seldom reformative.

In consequence of such practices, Eliza Farnham for nearly four years found herself hopelessly embroiled in the political tug-of-war waged between prison reformers and their critics. The noisiest voices raised against her belonged to clerics.

In residence for several years at Sing Sing was the Reverend John Luckey, a Methodist minister whom Georgiana Bruce dismissed as "a well-meaning, tight-skulled little chaplain." Luckey, whose views occupied a narrow compass, claimed as his especial province both the chapel and the prison library—and so was doomed to feel doubly imposed upon by the new matron.

The prison library, Mrs. Farnham discovered upon inspection, consisted of seventy-five copies of one book, *Call to the Unconverted Sinner*. Nothing in the universe of this self-educated intellectual aroused more insistent devotion than books. And, due to an irreligious upbringing, almost nothing in the world interested her less than the noisily righteous. As a youth, "Religious, praying people I always heard denounced as fools or hypocrites....All my teaching had brought me to disdain prayer, and despise those who offered it."

Although Eliza's attitude softened with experience, and she embraced spirituality (but never a church) as an adult, her religion was books.

Mrs. Farnham's clash with Mr. Luckey, all but foreordained, commenced with the acquisition of new books for the library—books of instruction, books of philosophy, and most odious of all, novels. Adding insult to injury, Mrs. Farnham proceeded to read these books to the prisoners—in the chapel. Miss Bruce, charged with the responsibility of library solicitations, witnessed the engagement of battle:

> Instead of spending half an hour each morning on Bible-reading, Mrs. F read "Oliver Twist," and similar books aloud, hoping to lead the women's thoughts into healthier channels, and to awaken good resolutions....I need not assure the reader that a howl against such infidel proceedings was at once set up by the churches of the place, and we were designated "a set of wantons" by the more pious.

The "howl" heightened to uproar, forcing Eliza to defend her actions:

> If contact with, and the example of elevated and enlightened minds are profitable to those who have never fallen into crime, how much more essential to those who have all their lives been abandoned to it? If books, and other means of mental culture are requisite to the advancement of the well disposed, how much more to the reformation of those who have not only been reared in ignorance, but under the dominion of the baser propensities?
>
> Believing thus, I have sought every possible means of presenting to those under my charge the fact that they are endowed with other faculties, capable of affording them enjoyment, besides the passions whose abuse have wrought their degradation. This is a new truth to most of them, and to the better class one of deep interest....
>
> Let the cultivated or the unacquainted, who have been accustomed to regard these unfortunate persons as totally lost, and unworthy of effort, sneer at the supposition that they have susceptibilities such as move other hearts. The little ray of humanity is not quenched. By judicious, patient, and trusting effort, it may, perchance, even within the walls of a prison, be kindled into brighter and clearer light than ever before shone in the benighted bosoms of those whose lots have been cast here.
>
> It should be observed...that the state makes almost no provision for the instruction of convicts in this prison. Even the books we have

now in use are the fruit of private liberality; the only officer provided by law from whom any thing but gratuitous effort at instruction or moral suasion can be expected is the Chaplain; and his time is so arduously and incessantly employed with the male convicts that his visits to us are confined almost exclusively to the hours of public service, on the Sabbath.

...But with all the disadvantage under which the reformation, commenced in April last, has been thus far carried forward, such manifest improvement is confessed on all hands, that those who have laboured in producing it are encouraged to persevere....

In the result of our labours, therefore, arduous and uncongenial though they be, we find much cause for congratulation and hope. To be able to redeem one of these unfortunate beings from the ruin to which, without such effort, they seem inevitably destined, would be a reward for labours even more exacting than ours.

Despite such impassioned beliefs and intentions, Mrs. Farnham failed to find popular support and for the next three years battled increasingly hostile critics. This was indeed a trying time for Eliza, who, in February 1845, gave birth prematurely to a son, Edward Hallock Farnham, afflicted with a crippling spinal injury. From this misfortune and the mounting difficulties of her prison administration, Eliza took refuge in her pen, recalling happier times, reliving again in memory the five years she and her husband had spent in Illinois. Quite likely inspired by her husband's success with *Travels in the Great Western Prairies*, Eliza Farnham vividly captured an early Illinois. Published in 1846 by Harper & Brothers, *Life in Prairie Land* received the *Tribune's* commendation:

Mrs. F. wields a vigorous pen and describes what she sees with remarkable fidelity. Many of her pictures of Western scenery and domestic life are beautiful, and the whole book is adapted to impart clearer impressions of the state of society in the places through which she has traveled. It will no doubt find many readers who will prize it no less for the instruction it conveys than for the amusement it cannot fail to supply.

*Life in Prairie Land* was barely off the presses before Mrs. Farnham offered the public a second book, in a quite different vein.

Mrs. Farnham's belief in phrenology—the popular idea that the contours of one's head revealed one's character—provided the bedrock of her reformist measures and inspired her to edit, and otherwise improve for American publication, *Criminal Jurisprudence Considered in Relation to Mental Organization,* first published in 1841 in London by Marmaduke Blake Sampson, an English journalist and reformer. In 1846 Mrs. Farnham reissued it through New York's D. Appleton & Company as *Rationale of Crime and its Appropriate Treatment.* The book advanced the theory of phrenology as a basis for understanding the criminal mind, and the new edition included Mrs. Farnham's liberal notes as well as engravings of prisoners' heads, the work of a young daguerreotypist whose photographic chronicles of a war still fifteen years in the future would bring him enduring fame. "My acknowledgments are due....Mr. Brady, to whose indefatigable patience with a class of the most difficult of all sitters is due the advantage of a very accurate set of daguerreotypes."

To the phrenologist, criminal behavior resulted from a pathological imbalance of cerebral faculties, classified as "propensities" and "sentiments." Among propensities, for example, was "acquisitiveness," considered a primordial quality promoting survival in a hostile environment. Left unbalanced by countervailing sections of the brain, however, the impulse was believed to enkindle thievery.

While today phrenology may prompt amusement and the presumption that only eccentrics accepted its tenets, it was, in its time, as serious a discipline as present-day psychology, embraced by many eminent nineteenth-century scientists, educators, and physicians. It was also an important cultural influence. Testifying to the subject's popularity was the *Phrenological Almanac's* 1846 circulation figure of ninety thousand.

The *Phrenological Almanac* was the work of Orson and Lorenzo Fowler and their sister Charlotte's husband, Samuel Wells. Visitors to the New York City offices of Fowler and Wells, 131 Nassau Street, heard lectures on phrenology; inspected, in the Phrenological Cabinet, plaster casts of famous skulls collected from around the world; received a hands-on lesson, costing twenty-five cents, on the different temperaments; or submitted to an analysis by one of the Fowlers, with a written report of the findings available for three dollars. Among those offering their heads for examination were the dancer Fanny Essler, Horace Greeley, social reformer Lucretia Mott, the Poughkeepsie clairvoyant Andrew Jackson Davis, and

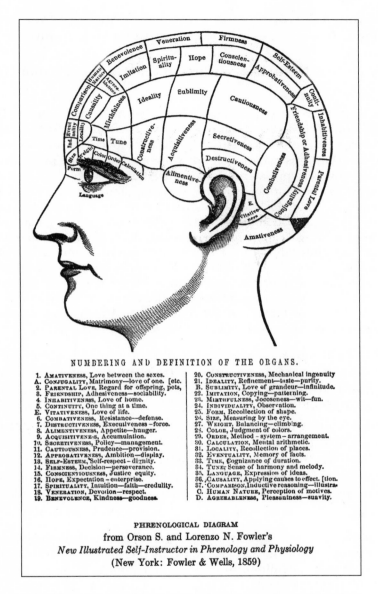

## NUMBERING AND DEFINITION OF THE ORGANS.

1. AMATIVENESS, Love between the sexes.
A. CONJUGALITY, Matrimony—love of one. [etc.
2. PARENTAL LOVE, Regard for offspring, pets,
3. FRIENDSHIP, Adhesiveness—sociability.
4. INHABITIVENESS, Love of home.
5. CONTINUITY, One thing at a time.
E. VITATIVENESS, Love of life.
6. COMBATIVENESS, Resistance—defense.
7. DESTRUCTIVENESS, Executiveness—force.
8. ALIMENTIVENESS, Appetite—hunger.
9. ACQUISITIVENESS, Accumulation.
10. SECRETIVENESS, Policy—management.
11. CAUTIOUSNESS, Prudence—provision.
12. APPROBATIVENESS, Ambition—display.
13. SELF-ESTEEM, Self-respect—dignity.
14. FIRMNESS, Decision—perseverance.
15. CONSCIENTIOUSNESS, Justice equity.
16. HOPE, Expectation - enterprise.
17. SPIRITUALITY, Intuition—faith—credulity.
18. VENERATION, Devotion—respect.
19. BENEVOLENCE, Kindness—goodness.

20. CONSTRUCTIVENESS, Mechanical ingenuity
21. IDEALITY, Refinement—taste—purity.
B. SUBLIMITY, Love of grandeur—infinitude.
22. IMITATION, Copying—patterning.
23. MIRTHFULNESS, Jocoseness—wit—fun.
24. INDIVIDUALITY, Observation.
25. FORM, Recollection of shape.
26. SIZE, Measuring by the eye.
27. WEIGHT, Balancing—climbing.
28. COLOR, Judgment of colors.
29. ORDER, Method - system – arrangement.
30. CALCULATION, Mental arithmetic.
31. LOCALITY, Recollection of places.
32. EVENTUALITY, Memory of facts.
33. TIME, Cognizance of duration.
34. TUNE, Sense of harmony and melody.
35. LANGUAGE, Expression of ideas.
36. CAUSALITY, Applying causes to effect. [tion.
37. COMPARISON, Inductive reasoning—illustra-
C. HUMAN NATURE, Perception of motives.
D. AGREEABLENESS, Pleasantness—suavity.

### PHRENOLOGICAL DIAGRAM
from Orson S. and Lorenzo N. Fowler's
*New Illustrated Self-Instructor in Phrenology and Physiology*
(New York: Fowler & Wells, 1859)

*Mrs. Farnham based her prison reform measures on phrenology, a controversial belief that a pathological imbalance of cerebral faculties governed criminal behavior. Illustration from* Rationale of Crime, *reprinted from Fowler's* New Illustrated Self-Instructor in Phrenology and Physiology *(New York: Fowler & Wells, 1859)* abolitionist John Brown (Orson's analysis survives: "You are too blunt and free-spoken—you often find that your motives are not understood").

Eliza's new book, like her first, received support from Horace Greeley:

> We cannot too earnestly commend its facts and its reasonings to the attention of those on whom rests the responsibility of framing and administering our laws. The disposition to decry in advance and without fair investigation every new theory that may be proposed is unhappily too prevalent; but Truth ultimately vindicates itself against all opposition, however contemptuous, unreasonable or malignant. That the doctrines advanced by Mr. Sampson are perfectly sound, we do not now affirm; we only ask for them a fair and candid hearing. If they must be rejected, let it be done dispassionately and under the influence of reason, not in a tempest of obloquy and passion. One thing only will we say at this time, and that is that in our judgment the assailants of Phrenology have hitherto been singularly unfortunate in the issues they have raised as well as in the tone and temper of their arguments. We shall see whether they will meet the conclusions of this work in a better spirit.

Eliza Farnham's arguments for phrenology outraged clerics. If behavior emanated from inborn traits and propensities rather than free will, then criminals need feel little guilt for transgressions prompted by nature, not evil.

Chief among her detractors was the unfortunate Reverend Luckey, whose long tenure at the prison impressed the prison board less than his Old Testament convictions about sin and punishment, with which they generally disagreed. Rumors that the board planned to replace him reached the ears of J. B. Swain, editor of the local *Hudson River Chronicle,* which derisively reported:

> Some say that...Mr. Luckey, the Parson, will have an indefinite leave of absence granted....Others assure us the matron of the female prison will be permitted to take another ramble through "Prairie Land," minus $800 salary. The prison pot is bubbling furiously, but it is difficult to tell how much scum will be thrown off.
>
> For some time there has been a kind of secret warfare going on between Hiram [Harman Eldridge, principal keeper] and the Parson on one side, and the "allied powers" of Phrenology, Animal Magnetism and Fourierism combined in the modern Joan of Arc,

LIFE

IN

PRAIRIE LAND.

BY

ELIZA W. FARNHAM.

" Dear Nature is the kindest mother still."—*Childe Harold.*

NEW-YORK:
HARPER & BROTHERS, PUBLISHE
82 CLIFF STREET.
1846.

*Title page of* Life in Prairie Land. *Mrs. Farnham published her first book, an account of her five years in Illinois, while at Sing Sing. The* Hudson River Chronicle's *editor vilified her and her staff in his newspaper, writing, "It is a pity the whole bag and baggage are not trotted off to 'Prairie Land.'"*

*Title page of* Rationale of Crime. *During her tenure as matron at Sing Sing, Mrs. Farnham edited and reissued the work of English journalist and reformer Marmaduke Sampson, adding daguerreotypes made for her by Matthew Brady of prisoners' heads.*

RATIONALE OF CRIME,

AND ITS

APPROPRIATE TREATMENT;

BEING

A TREATISE ON CRIMINAL JURISPRUDENCE

CONSIDERED IN RELATION TO

CEREBRAL ORGANIZATION.

BY M. B. SAMPSON.

FROM THE SECOND LONDON EDITION.

WITH NOTES AND ILLUSTRATIONS

BY

E. W. FARNHAM,
MATRON OF MOUNT PLEASANT STATE PRISON.

Embellished with numerous accurate Portraits of Criminals and
other Persons.

NEW-YORK:
D. APPLETON & COMPANY, 200 BROADWAY.
PHILADELPHIA:
GEO. S. APPLETON, 148 CHESNUT-STREET.
MDCCCXLVI.

who rules the females. Hiram goes for governing the prison upon the principles heretofore practiced—while she would bring to his aid the science of bumpology.

The prison board did indeed deprive the Reverend Luckey of his position as chaplain, affronting both the cleric and the *Hudson River Chronicle*'s editor:

> THE PRISON HOUSE.—"In spite of lamentations here or elsewhere," our friend, the Parson did get the sack. We almost feared such would be the case, although we hoped much from his known ability as a tactician. The particular reasons assigned for his discharge, we are not familiar with....
>
> It is a pity that the whole bag and baggage were not trotted off to "Prairie Land."

The chaplain responded to the prison board's decision by refusing to vacate his post. Eliza Farnham—who rarely felt constrained to withhold her opinions—wrote John Bigelow (her chief defender on the prison board after John Edmonds resigned to accept a judgeship):

> The Parson remains and I understand has expressed a determination to do so until the Board compel him to leave his place. What a delightfully shrinking sensitive yielding body of gentlemen he must esteem you to be. I hear all your sins in this regard are charged to me. Poor man! he little knows how many times I have defended him—with more sincerity than I could now exercise in the same cause.

Things proceeded downhill from there. The press boiled over with the scandal. Luckey aired his opposition to the prison board and his objections to Mrs. Farnham's multiple offenses, at considerable length, in various newspapers. When Mrs. Farnham read the allegations against her in the local paper, she wrote John Bigelow with uncharacteristic distress:

> You have seen the *astonishing disclosures* which Mr. L has made, I suppose....Do you think the circumstances altogether demand anything of me, for I confess I am at a loss to decide....I cannot consent to undertake a formal contradiction of the rumors that have gone forth nor of those miserable & pointless sayings of his....Whatever is said should be said quickly. I should not wait a month before I gratified the public curiosity to see me in a ridiculous position, not

even to follow the example of so illustrious a defender of evangelical religion as my worthy & now distinguished assailant.

Then another local cleric, the Rev. B. C. Morse, prevailed upon the local newspaper to publish more humiliating accusations, intimating that:

> Mrs. Farnham is herself a woman of ill fame; that she permits or has permitted improper intercourse to be carried on between the male and female convicts; and that persons have had access to the female prison for a like purpose, at improper hours of the night, with her consent.

John Bigelow replied in Mrs. Farnham's defense, and the Reverend Mr. Morse defiantly responded by writing Bigelow:

> Do not entertain the idea that any number of letters addressed either to the Clergy or other citizens will render us silent on a subject that cries so loud for redress.
> I will not vouch that there will not be an improvement in the morals, both of the Matron and culprits, after a free use of "Fowler's Sexual Intercourse," and such like *virtuous* books.

An investigation was called for and commenced; the Reverend Luckey declined to appear and sent his wife instead; and the local newspaper declared that the "prison is a sink of pollution."

Had Eliza's husband been even as close as New York City, he might have lent support. But Thomas Jefferson Farnham, in a puzzling marriage distinguished by his absence, had gone west again to California. And alas for Eliza, her most sympathetic associate, Georgiana Bruce, had resigned her prison position in the spring of 1845. It would be five years before they would meet again, in far-off California, tumultuous years for Eliza, adventurous ones for Georgiana.

But the young Englishwoman was no stranger to adventure.

# THREE

# A Restless Woman

I must be glad to see you thrown so completely on yourself, both as to outward and inward life; thus shall you learn; thus shall you teach. But it seems
to me you are too restless.

—Margaret Fuller to Georgiana Bruce, July 1844

The reputation of Brook Farm for brilliancy, wit, and harmless eccentricity
was seriously compromised. The joyous spirit of youth was sobered. The
outside community henceforth regarded the enterprise as a mechanical
attempt to reform society, rather than a poetic attempt to regenerate it.

—Georgiana Bruce Kirby

Georgiana Bruce had devoted "a whole year to the unfortunates":

> My passion for sympathizing, for putting myself in another's place,
> and, where necessary, advising, warning, comforting, and, as far as
> might be, taking the burden on myself, had had free play at Sing
> Sing. Much practice had made me skilful in that line, and never
> before had I found such large opportunity for the exercise of my
> gift....it had pleased us to love these low-down children of circum-
> stances less fortunate than our own.

But she "had drawn too steadily" on her "nervous force." It was
time to leave. From Sing Sing, Georgiana headed for Cincinnati,
where her young stepbrother, Edmund, discontented with life at
Brook Farm, had found work in an Ohio printing office and was
waiting to join her.

Georgiana's journey from New York to Cincinnati must have
seemed but a hop, skip, and jump to a woman who, at fifteen, had
left Bristol for Paris, gone from there to London, and then crossed
the Atlantic for the backwoods of Canada. In less than three years
she had returned to England, where she had promptly turned
around and gone to Boston. Three years there as a domestic had
preceded return trips to Canada and Massachusetts, a year at

Brook Farm, and a year in New York at Sing Sing. Georgiana was not one to gather moss.

Now, in 1845, Georgiana aimed her arrow at a teaching position, an occupation in which she was as abundantly experienced as she was at travel:

> At fourteen I taught my brothers and three children of about their age whose parents had been living a few doors from us all the summer. The children were dear little ones of eight, five and a half, and four....Three such loving and lovely children were a guaranty for every thing that was kind and honorable in the parents, and I was half afraid to believe in my good fortune when, after a few months' acquaintance, they offered to take me with them to France as governess to the children.

Possessed of a quick mind and a love of books, Georgiana had received an unhappily brief education. Her mother slid from property to poverty after the death at sea of Captain Francis Bruce; the fortune he left his wife, an educated woman proud of her noble French lineage, was soon lost:

> When I was in my fifth year, my mother made an unfortunate second marriage, which...was the cause of my spending the succeeding six without any education, in a home without order or repose. For my step-father undertook "gentleman" farming on a considerable scale with my mother's capital. As his knowledge of agriculture, however, was confined to fox-hunting, it took less than two years to dissipate the funds invested.

The remainder of the family's affluence disappeared "through the failure of my godfather....the lawyer into whose well-meaning but incapable hands my mother had unadvisedly entrusted the better half of her fortune."

Under such circumstances, and despite her tender years, Georgiana's departure for France as governess to the Charles Spencer family meant one less mouth to feed at home. Although Georgiana received no money for her services, the Spencers treated her as one of the family, her clothes were bought for her, and she enjoyed a freedom and leisure denied at home. After the Spencers returned to England, Georgiana stayed on with them. When, after a year and a half in London, Spencer decided to try his luck at

farming in Canada, all agreed the young governess must come
too:

> As the white cliffs of Dover and the Needles of the Isle of Wight
> seceded from view, I began to realize what a fair page of life was
> spread out before me....The voyage was varied by storms and calms,
> by meeting a vessel whose crew was starving whom we promptly
> relieved, by the burial of two steerage passengers, by glorious sun-
> sets and splendid moons....We passed Quebec...went by boat to
> Nicollet and the sorry little village at Port St. Francis, where we
> could scarcely get any thing to eat but sour ryebread....to a place in
> the interior named Melbourne.
>
> The journey occupied three long days, which were delightful
> notwithstanding the fact that the carts were springless and the roads
> new and rough....Our progress was slow on account of the wretched
> horses, but I enjoyed every hour of it.

An adventurer had been born.

In Quebec, Spencer undertook farming by purchasing, "on the
installment plan," a large property with a dwelling less attractive
than its lovely river view:

> The house was a mere shell provided with eight large window
> frames, and not a single pane of glass; a fire-place and stone chim-
> ney with a conspicuous slant; a hole beneath the kitchen for a cel-
> lar, into which you descended by a ladder through a trap-door.
> Planks were laid across the rafters for ceiling, and their board parti-
> tions divided the space into apartments....our numerous trunks
> served for tables and shelves. We were young, healthful, and hope-
> ful, and inconveniences were only food for mirth.

The family's adventures proved more mirthful than skillful,
and the amateur pioneers soon abandoned the farm in favor of
the village, where Spencer briefly taught at the district school
before giving up on Canada entirely and returning the family, and
Georgiana, to England.

It was 1837. Georgiana, now eighteen years old, resumed
teaching:

> But four months sufficed to cure me of any lingering desire I might
> have to live in my native land while my living had to be earned....So
> I overpowered my mother's fears and arguments, and started for
> New York...with a small sum of money in my pocket. England, I had

concluded, was the very best place in the world for a rich person, and the very worst for a poor one.

On the voyage to New York, the young governess met the Reverend Ezra Stiles Gannett, of Boston, traveling with his wife and infant, "but no nurse." Prevailed upon, Georgiana accepted the position, soon concluding her prospects were "decidedly gloomy." In Boston, her place was clearly that of a domestic servant. Mrs. Gannett expected her to do laundry and treated her as hired help. "It did not take long for me to learn that the caste spirit in Boston was harder, more insensitive than in the mother-country."

Fortunately, Mr. Gannett "had little, if any, of this frigid exclusiveness." And his generous instincts included bringing from England, as "sole passenger in a British bark," Georgiana's fourteen-year-old stepbrother, Edmund. Georgiana had seized on the suggestion, but found the reality of her stepbrother's presence "tied me hand and foot."

After a time, with her added responsibility in tow, Georgiana left Boston in hopes of teaching at the district school in the Canadian village she'd departed from two years previously:

> How old memories thronged back as we approached the…village, with half of whose inhabitants I had been on quite intimate terms! Alas, it soon became apparent that either they or I had greatly changed!….The district school had languished and finally given place to a private one of inferior grade, in which the church catechism was in order Wednesdays and Saturdays. If I would consent to abide by the new rules I could be put in as teacher at once. But I was not given to mental reservations. The catechism was a condensed statement of the Christian mythology, and I would have nothing to do with it.

Georgiana returned with Edmund and her uncompromised opinions to Boston, where Gannett sympathetically suggested to the two wanderers an acceptable alternative to service in his family: Brook Farm.

In 1841, at nearby West Roxbury, Unitarian minister George Ripley had established an experimental farm, based on cooperative living, in which members agreed to share manual labor in the interests of self-sufficiency. The membership included several recognizable names, among them the novelist Nathaniel Hawthorne and noted journalist Charles A. Dana. Their prominence, and that of such renowned and distinguished supporters as Ralph Waldo Emerson, Horace Greeley, and Margaret Fuller, all advocates of the literary and philosophical movement known as transcendentalism, greatly elevated Brook Farm's standing, if not its accomplishments. Ultimately, the community's school proved substantially more successful than the farming part of the venture, as Georgiana observed firsthand:

> It is proverbial that clergymen are ignorant on the subject of land and horses. They should have called on some bent old farmer for an opinion, before purchasing that much gravel. But the mistake was not discovered immediately, and we,—the younger converts to the association, found the pine-woods, the river-side, and brook a pleasant framing for the wealth of our social felicity, even though they were not profitable....Democracy and culture made the animus of the association. Had the world denied you opportunity for education? Here your highest needs should be satisfied. Able scholars were at your service....What a heavenly world this was getting to be!

And endlessly interesting. Brook Farmers eagerly adopted such "novel propositions" as Mesmer's "discoveries regarding clairvoyance, hypnotism, and somnambulism." A young woman named Cornelia found that she "possessed genuine magnetic power." And when two women at the community became converts to hydropathy, the belief that water cured most ills and ailments, nearly everyone at the Farm was soon taking the "pack":

> We were wrapped in a wet sheet and then in four or five blankets, looking like modern mummies after the operation. As soon as any moisture was visible on the patient's forehead a drink of water was allowed. When the sweating became profuse the patient was assisted off the bed and scuffled in slippers to the large bath-tub filled with cold water. Into this she plunged the instant the blankets were unswathed, remained in it only a minute or two, while the "pack" may have lasted three or four hours. Then followed a breakfast of brown bread, baked apples, mush and cream, or similar diet, after which came a walk of several miles. At least from seven to ten miles must be accomplished during the day, leaving intervals for a sitz-bath and the drinking of innumerable goblets of water.

Unfortunately for the members, insufficient capital and the slim profits derived primarily from the school and the sale of milk eventually doomed their enterprise. And they encountered other problems in their earnest application of community principles:

> It had even been found necessary to call a meeting to settle the question of griddle-cakes or no griddle-cakes, since those eating their breakfasts declared that they could not enjoy the hot cakes while oppressed by the thought of two or three friends leaning over the stove cooking them. It is true that the vote taken on this occasion was in favor of that diet, the best *cuisinieres* insisting that the sight of the golden brown cakes made the trouble a pleasure.

In 1844, after three years of quaint disputes and the headiness of intellectually invigorating association with many of the day's most brilliant and original minds, Georgiana, leaving Edmund at Brook Farm, "decided on a fresh migration":

> On withdrawing, I did not leave behind one iota of my belief in the present necessity for a reorganization of society, on a just basis. I only felt that nothing of further moment with regard to it would occur at the "Community." I could not see how the change was to come about, how it was to begin, but I was certain that it was only a question of time. If the wave of generous and just feeling which had lately swept over the enlightened few, moving them to attempt reform from above, had expended itself, the millions would surely rise up, and amend their status themselves.

And so Georgiana, with Margaret Fuller's intercession, went to Sing Sing, stayed a year, and then was off to the West to join her stepbrother. Edmund had, after Georgiana's departure from Brook Farm, grown discontented; nearly eighteen, he had moved on to Cincinnati, where he found work in a printing office. Georgiana intended to take him with her to St. Louis, but a thief aboard her steamboat found the money she had brought for her stepbrother's passage. Meeting Edmund in Cincinnati, she assured him she could earn more money and would send for him, but before she could accomplish her aim, the boy fell ill of an "inflammation of the lungs" and died:

> He had been dead a week before I knew any thing of his illness, as there was neither railroad nor telegraphic communication then. It was a terrible blow, and it seemed especially hard that he should die alone among strangers. He had been more of a child than a brother to me....When he had left me, all motive seemed to have dropped out of my life, and I could not rouse myself to exertion.

*Margaret Fuller, journalist, critic, teacher, lecturer; author of*
Woman in the Nineteenth Century *and* Summer on the Lakes;
*editor,* The Dial; New York Tribune *foreign correspondent;*
*and a leading intellectual of her time. Fuller befriended the young*
*Georgiana Bruce at Brook Farm and corresponded with her frequently.*
*Courtesy of the Library of Congress (LC-USZ62-70956)*

Margaret Fuller wrote her condolence:

It seems very hard that this grief should come, and thoughts of the poor child's lonely death be your companions, just as there was a chance that free nature and new impressions should bring you refreshment....My dear Georgiana, invite every peaceful thought that shows any willingness to come, and live on courageously as you can, for us who cherish and the many who will yet need you. I can say no more; this is all the consolation I have been able to find for myself at certain dark periods of my life, yet have lived after to beautiful moments, and successive daybreaks of glorious light.

Indeed, Georgiana would live on to see many, many "successive daybreaks." In 1845 she accepted a position as substitute teacher at the Monticello Seminary. The school, built of stone and embowered with trees, accommodated one hundred female students and a devoted faculty of four lady professors to instruct them in math, Latin, French, European history, English composition, and a "critical knowledge of the most noteworthy passing events."

In contrast to this elevating academic experience, students and faculty periodically endured the addresses, and occasional rants, of hired preachers. Georgiana's acquaintance with Sing Sing's resident chaplain, the Reverend Mr. Luckey, little warmed her to the breed. The 1846 commencement address of the Reverend Mr. Todd of St. Louis to the Monticello Seminary graduates likely cemented her disdain:

That gentleman used this occasion to fire volley after volley of insolent invective against women in general and these young women in particular. They should remember that woman was not endowed with the solid intellect that had been bestowed on man by his Creator....Women should never forget that their mother Eve had caused the downfall of the race. This fact should engender humility. Running through the Old Testament he cited the case of every notable and faulty female character. Let them remember these women, who when they attempted to be strong were inevitably wicked, and enter on their new path with becoming humility.

This tirade occupied the allotted three quarters of an hour, during which we looked at one another in disgusted astonishment, indignant that the bright graduates should be treated with such contempt.

"And to think that we shall have to pay that villifier of the sex for insulting us all," Miss Fobes whispered to me, as we rose and tried to draw a long breath once more. "It goes against my sense of right to ask him to eat with us."

Two years later, in Seneca Falls, New York, women courageously voiced, at the first Woman's Rights Convention, objection to their discounted status in society. Georgiana, who ardently embraced the fight for women's equality, would, in California, become influential in its cause. But first, in Illinois, a more immediate injustice required objection.

In Alton, Georgiana made her home with the family of Moses Atwood, president of the Illinois Mutual Fire Insurance Company—and concealer of escaped slaves:

> Alton was only twenty-three miles from St. Louis, where the pro-slavery sentiment was hellish. There is no other word that would express it....It was a Southern city, with whipping-posts, slave-pens, and auction-blocks. Gangs of manacled human beings might be seen any day threading their way through its streets to the steamboat and the New Orleans market.

Her teaching position in Alton being temporary, Georgiana in 1847 sought new employment. She found it in Missouri:

> Why did I go into a slave State to teach? For the reason that...the salary offered was large; I could return easily at any moment, and Captain David H., of Bonne Femme, who urged me to this step, was a polished gentleman...determined that his children should not suffer for the want of teaching.

At Bonne Femme, about seven miles from Columbia, Georgiana's school proved satisfactory in every respect but one.

> Never were children more studious, while the parents were exceedingly kind, polite, and hospitable. I was invited first to one home, then to another, and tried to be sympathetic with all. But there was always a shadow between us. I could not like a person who was polite and generous to me, if they were discourteous and unjust to others. When a gentleman, after making himself extremely agreeable to me, would go out and talk to a slave as no one but a brute would speak to a horse, I felt repelled and miserable....The constant sense of restriction and sad faces of the house-servants, which were a continual reproach to me, made me decide on leaving.

Georgiana returned to Alton, placed an advertisement in the *Anti-Slavery Standard* that she wished to teach at a "colored school," and quickly received an offer from Columbus, Ohio:

On arriving at the capital I was much disconcerted by learning that the State school fund could only be used for the benefit of children who were three fifths white (I believe that was the proportion). If I accepted this position I should have to keep a card stained the approved shade, test the complexion of each applicant for admission, and reject those of too dark a color. No exposition of the good I might do to mezzo tints or quadroons could reconcile me to the half-way right.

She engaged instead at an independent school in Ohio but within a month was informed that a committee had discovered various personal objections to her:

One disapproved of a "Garrison Abolitionist"; another urged that I must be a Fourierite, *having been with Mrs. Farnham at Sing Sing;* a third cited my acquaintance with Theodore Parker, and my unsoundness regarding the Trinity; while the fourth expressed dispraise equally absurd.

There was nothing to be done with the West but abandon it for the East. There she accepted a teaching position at a public school in West Chester, Pennsylvania, then left it in 1848 to serve as governess for the five children of Mr. Robert Purvis, in Byberry, Pennsylvania. Although she thought Byberry "an uncommonly stupid place," she greatly admired Robert Purvis, who was then president of the highly active Pennsylvania Anti-Slavery Society, and whose home served the Underground Railroad.

Georgiana Bruce had found at last a position that suited her. Meanwhile, Eliza Farnham had lost one.

*Perkins School for the Blind. Serving as matron, isolated and lonely, Mrs. Farnham wrote, "You cannot imagine how I long to see the dear old Hudson again." Courtesy of the Perkins School for the Blind*

# Valparaiso

The demand for an official inquiry into Mrs. Farnham's administration at Sing Sing resulted in the appointment of a three-member Committee of Investigation. Despite the committee's findings of "apparent order, quiet, and good government" within the prison, the cloud of controversy surrounding Eliza Farnham's administration failed to lift. Changing political winds unfavorable to innovative ideas swept her from her post, and 1848 found her without an income and the sole support of her two sons, six-year-old Charles and three-year-old Eddie, who, with his crippling birth defect, required an attendant.

Eliza moved back to New York City, dependent upon friends. One of them, Eliza Robbins, urged the notable Dr. Samuel Gridley Howe to hire her as matron for his New England Institution for the Blind (Perkins School for the Blind), in Boston:

> I have some hope that the situation may be suitable to Mrs. Farnham, late matron of Sing-Sing prison. By a recent overturn of authorities in the prison government Mrs. F and all her coadjutors have been superseded, and they, consequently, thrown out of employment.

Mrs. F, though she has a husband, now in California, derives no support from him, and is forced to provide for herself and two children. This urgent necessity makes her desirous of immediate occupation, even with small remuneration, and I have persuaded her to seek this for which I am interceding.

....Mrs. Farnham was treated in Westchester Co. with a measure of injustice and cruelty....The worst license of opinion and of meanness was imputed to her, and her whole course of discipline misrepresented; for one, I feel that I owe her all the sympathy and service that rectitude traduced, and consummate innocence abused, can demand from social justice. I know that she is upright and altogether without stain, and regard her as gold seven times tried.

Dr. Howe hesitated. The calumnies with which Mrs. Farnham had been charged concerned him sufficiently to seek reassurance of her character from the New York Prison Association. Corresponding secretary John D. Russ, who had chaired the Sing Sing investigation, replied:

Mrs F is in every way worthy and qualified for the situation of matron in any public institution....I think the confidence placed in her by the late Board of Inspectors of Sing Sing after a long and tedious investigation of charges made against her is entitled to much weight—....Those charges which affect her character as a virtuous woman seem to me to be the offspring of malevolence...I am disposed to think...that the worst thing that can be said against Mrs Farnham is that she is the Editor of the American edition of Sampson's Rationale of Crime.

Dr. Howe offered Mrs. Farnham the position of matron at an annual salary of three hundred dollars, plus board for herself and her children, and Eddie's attendant. Placing young Charles in school, she moved with little Eddie to South Boston, to the school located in a former hotel, Mount Washington House. She was grateful but not happy, lamenting to her good friend John Bigelow:

You cannot imagine how I long to see the dear old Hudson again. Even New York, little as I love it, begins to assert its claim upon my affectionate remembrance, and I think the day may not be very far distant when I could set foot upon its wharves with a thrill of genuine pleasure....My friends seem to have formed a conspiracy to be severe as possible, for I have not received a solitary letter, save those I found awaiting me....I know you are as pitiless as a man who associates much with gentle and pitiful females can be, but if I do not move you to say as much as "Poor Mrs Farnham"! or "The Lord help her"! I shall give you up forever.

The one bright spot in her new employment was teaching Laura Bridgman, a girl destined for fame as the country's first deaf-blind child to be systematically educated:

> The even vivacity of her disposition, with her fine organization, and sensitive temperament, is to me one of the most wonderful facts in nature. She is not indifferent to the great privations she lives under, but she seems to have in her loving heart a source of light and harmony that enables her to defy the outward darkness and silence to which she is doomed.

Mrs. Farnham "read" to Laura from *Life in Prairie Land* by spelling the words into the girl's palm, and their many hours together fostered an attachment Laura felt keenly: "I am extremely happy to think that she is one of my most droll & evident friends in the world." Eliza's departure from the school moved the girl to confide: "I hate to part with her for so long a time."

Mrs. Farnham's departure from the school was, of course, precipitous. Having received the distressing news that her husband had died in California, she returned at once to New York, where she proposed the grand plan announced in the *Tribune* on February 14, 1849.

In subsequent issues of the *Tribune*, however, the hospital and the store mentioned in the first notice of the enterprise disappeared. The lesser ambition of "rendering themselves useful" reflected Mrs. Farnham's reduced expectations for the women she hoped would accompany her to California. The response had been discouraging:

> My proposed expedition must be much smaller than I first desired to make it. It seems *probable* that it may now consist of from 30 to 50; it is *possible* that it may not number 20. There is much uncertainty with respect to almost anyone who proposes to go until they become members of the Assn by signature and payment. There are so many contingencies arising from the opposition of friends, the possible ridicule of acquaintances—the difficulty of controlling immediately the funds necessary for such an enterprise and the shortness of the

**LAURA BRIDGMAN,**
TEACHING OLIVER CASWELL TO READ;
BOTH BEING DEAF, DUMB AND BLIND.

*Laura Bridgman teaching Oliver Caswell to read. The famed
Laura Bridgman became greatly attached to Eliza Farnham at the
Perkins School for the Blind: "I am extremely happy to think
that she is one of my most droll & evident friends in the world."
Courtesy of the Library of Congress (LC-USZ62-84749)*

time for preparation, that one who has fully resolved in her own mind to go, may, without great weakness, be deterred at any time before she is constituted a member. I find however that the chief difficulty is that of getting money. There have been in New York and Boston at least 200 females who have made known to me their strong desire to be of this Assn. More than half of this number have been women highly qualified for such a mission—prepared by constitution and experience to scatter blessings to the inhabitants of that distant and homeless land. There they could sew, nurse the sick, provide household order and comfort for the parties of men whose neglected life now brings disease and death among them. All that women can do any where they can do in California with great profit to themselves and something better than that to those whom they serve. I hope that my few pioneers may open the way for hundreds of those who are crowding each other here to follow. They can do so with entire safety. The wants and means of the people to whom they go will be the best security that they will be provided for.

On May 19, 1849, the long-delayed packet *Angelique* cleared for San Francisco and sailed out of New York harbor with twenty-two passengers. Among them were a disappointed Eliza Farnham, her two sons, one spinster and two widows subscribed to the California Association of American Women—Miss Sampson, Mrs. Griswold, and Mrs. Barker—and a young woman hired to attend Eddie. In a conflict of news-making proportions destined to unfold aboard the *Angelique* and conclude dramatically in Valparaiso, that young woman would play a starring role.

But the first problem aboard the *Angelique* was bad water.

The passengers' agreement expressly stipulated that the *Angelique* would, on its southerly course, put in at St. Catherine's Island, a frequent stopping place for fresh supplies. Two days north of the island the captain, Phineas Windsor, announced his decision not to stop. Mrs. Farnham demanded he put in. Windsor refused. Mrs. Farnham insisted, for, "in consequence of the bad water, it was a hundredfold more necessary that he should do so." To bolster her protest, Eliza drew up a petition, obtained the signatures of all the passengers but one—most likely her newly love-struck servant, whose inamorato was the ship's steward—and placed the remonstrance upon the captain's desk.

Mrs. Farnham's successful demand that the captain put in at St. Catherine's, and her indifference to his resultant animosity, undoubtedly laid the foundation for his cruel trick upon her at Valparaiso. She recorded its details, briefly, as she did those of the stop at St. Catherine's. But of the great adventure of sailing around the Horn she wrote only a single sentence, summing tedium and complaint into a succinct dismissal of the subject:

> The voyage to California has been the beginning of suffering to thousands of quiet home-bred people, and the continuation of it to as many whose previous experiences had been more varied, so that having had no wonderful escapes, or startling adventures, it need barely be said of ours that it was commonplace enough in the early part—made wearisome by the slowness of our vessel, and insufferable by the dreadful quality of the water furnished us nearly all the time after the first few hours out of New York.

Eliza Farnham's failure to record, in any document as yet discovered, the details of her voyage is a loss, given her skill with words, but it is no surprise, given the impulse of her journey. Unlike the thousands of other argonauts of 1849, she sailed not with hopes and dreams, but with disappointment that must have bordered on despair. How could she rouse interest and energy to record her daily experiences when she was so weighted with discouragement by the failure of her plan to bring women to California, the humiliations of Sing Sing, the disappointment of Boston, the responsibilities magnified by the unexpected death of her husband?

And now she was en route to California aboard a ship whose captain galled her, and with the tedious responsibility of Margaret, the girl hired to tend Eddie:

> This person was a young woman, of about eighteen or nineteen, in whom, from her peculiar traits of character, and some circumstances in her previous history, I felt a strong interest. She was extremely ignorant of everything, which her own keen powers of observation, exercised in a very limited sphere, had not taught her....We were but a few days at sea, when the steward begged her to assist in laying and clearing the tables, etc.; and upon her asking my consent, I told her that when she could oblige them, without leaving her own work undone, I was quite willing she should do so. I did this, because it is a principle with me to train all young persons, and my own children as well, never to refuse to accommodate others when they can do so without neglecting a paramount duty.

But...the girl was gradually withdrawn, more and more, from my service and influence; her daily lessons, which Miss Sampson and myself were giving her, were soon neglected; and we had not, I think, been more than a month or six weeks at sea, when...the steward—a lazy, lying, worthless creature...proposed marriage to her. I expostulated very earnestly with her, but the captain...encouraged it to the utmost.

After rounding Cape Horn, California-bound ships frequently put in at Valparaiso, Chile, for wood and water. The stop, like the voyage that preceded it, received no mention from Eliza Farnham's pen. She recorded only that Margaret and the steward married there, in the house of the English consul, the Reverend Mr. Armstrong. Of the city itself, she wrote nothing.

Valparaiso was not likely to have impressed Mrs. Farnham, even had her emotional spirits been higher. Elizabeth Gunn, sailing aboard the *Bengal* in 1851, described the city as:

very hilly, with not a tree to be seen anywhere....In town the houses are close together, but outside they are scattered about the edges of the hills and in little groups. There are no trees about them except some round shrubs like evergreens. The hills are covered with grass and low bushes. The harbor is full of vessels; there are four men-of-war....Captain and Mr. Grover went ashore; they say the streets are like cow-paths.

At Valparaiso, Eliza hired a Chilean woman to take Margaret's place and complete the journey with her. Careful to inquire about whatever preliminary steps might be necessary, Eliza was twice assured by the acting consul that Chile's passport law applied only to men, for the protection of creditors, and never to women. And, since she already had arranged for the passage of a servant, she was not even required to notify Captain Windsor of her intention.

Nonetheless, Miss Sampson informed the captain of the new arrangement, and the day before sailing he saw the Chilean woman in Mrs. Farnham's stateroom. But then, just before the *Angelique* was to sail, he suddenly declared, to Eliza's astonished consternation, that he would not take the Chilean woman without a passport. When he remained unyielding to argument, Eliza said she would go ashore and get something from the consul equivalent to a passport. Windsor replied that he would not wait for her

*Valparaiso harbor. From Joseph Henry Jackson's* Gold Rush Album.
*Courtesy of The Mariners' Museum, Newport News, Virginia (LP469)*

if she were not back in time. She was not alarmed:

> I knew the depth of water the ship lay in, and what had been done to get her ready for sea; and, judging from what I had seen before, I knew that I could go to the consul's office and back twice before she would get under way in the ordinary manner. But, to be fully assured, I asked the mate, who entered the cabin as I was putting on my bonnet, how long it would probably be before the ship would get under way, to which he replied, "In two hours and a half or three hours." This was the time I had calculated on; and as I could do no more than step to the consul's office, state the case, and get something that would deprive him of the power to refuse taking her, I felt entirely safe in leaving the ship for the time it would take me to accomplish this....
>
> I passed hastily down the ship's side, and we pulled ashore. We stopped but a moment at the consulate, but long enough to get a note to the Intendente and learn that the miscreant had no authority whatever to demand any paper, and that the very moment before going into the boat to go off, he had promised Mr. Samuels [the acting consul] faithfully to do nothing to annoy us in regard to this matter.
>
> At the Intendente's office, which was directly in our way back, we were told that the captain had said that he hated me, and meant to

play this trick upon me; and although the gentlemanly official assured me, in broken English, that I had no business with a passport for the woman, he gave me a slip of paper written hastily upon, which procured it for me at an office two or three doors from his own; and when I had paid all and borrowed three or four dollars from the gentlemen who accompanied me, I had a single shilling left in my pocket.

Mrs. Farnham's errand consumed barely an hour, but upon returning to the harbor, she saw that the ship had sailed:

She stood before my straining sight, a phantom vanishing so swiftly and surely, with the fresh, steady breeze filling her hollowed sails, that the hope with which I first caught sight of her died out of my heart in a moment, and a sickening, terrible conviction that she was gone settled down upon me like the chill of death....I did not faint, for I am strong and resolute by nature; but my faculties seemed stunned and scattered.

For three days, disbelieving witnesses assured the distraught mother that Captain Windsor was playing another trick on her, that he would come back. Eliza knew better:

I never entertained it, and yet when they talked of its being so cruel and extraordinary a step, and said, again and again, that surely he never would go on, carrying little children away from their only parent to a country like California, I could not help hoping a little, and my eyes were often searching the distant waters for the gladdening sight. But she did not return...

# FIVE

# San Francisco

Our voyage was miserable, owing to the brutality of the Captain and the uninteresting character of the passengers. Except Mrs. Farnham, I had not one companion, and she, by a most flagrant act of the Captain, was left at Valparaiso. It is too long a story to go into the particulars....in not more than twenty minutes a brisk breeze was carrying us out to sea, leaving behind the mother; and it was truly a sight to try stout nerves to hear the children screaming and crying. Your friend, Mr. Shuchard, is the owner of the ship, and it would be a kindness to some unfortunate woman who might chance to be thrown in his power, if he never again could get a command; his treatment to me was cruel—to Mrs. Farnham brutal. She is urged to institute proceedings against him, and I think will.

—Letter, *Angelique* passenger, San Francisco, December 29, 1849

**D**ependent upon the kindness of strangers, Eliza Farnham saw Chilean homes and purses opened to her during the long month that elapsed before the *Louis Philippe,* a ship out of Baltimore and bound for San Francisco, put in at Valparaiso.

> To all the lady passengers on board that vessel, and many of the gentlemen, and especially her kind-hearted captain, I am indebted for innumerable mitigations of my weariness and sense of injury. If we did not sometimes encounter the evil side of human nature, we should feel less pleasure in the excellences that make the reverse.

When the *Louis Philippe* arrived at the famed harbor entrance to San Francisco, a dangerous fog prevented passage for nine long days, maddening for any passenger and agonizing for an impatient mother consumed with anxiety for children whose fate remained a mystery to her. On the evening of the tenth day of waiting, the *Louis Philippe,* in a translucent fog and a pouring rain, finally dropped anchor off North Beach. Not until past noon the following day did Eliza Farnham find her children, still aboard the *Angelique,* where Lucy Sampson remained with them. Eliza's joy

*San Francisco, as Mrs. Farnham saw it: "View of San Francisco Taken from Telegraph Hill," April 1851. Courtesy of The Bancroft Library, University of California, Berkeley (Banc Pic 1963:002:1495-FR)*

at their reunion, however, was "painfully qualified by dear little Eddie's feebleness, which had increased very materially since our parting." Eliza collected up her little family, including Miss Sampson, and took them ashore:

> if that could properly be called shore where tall men were wading to the tops of boots above their knees, and where the falling flood filled the atmosphere so, that floundering along with a strong man at each elbow, we seemed to be almost submerged, and felt thankful for so small a favor as having the upper portions of our persons bathed in a medium somewhat purer than that below.

The weather, ever a topic in San Francisco, was particularly remarked upon in the rainy season. Mary Jane Megquier, who also arrived by sea in 1849, exclaimed, "O the mud, it is dreadful, man and beast get stuck in the slush and cannot move it is like glue takes their boots off their feet it is a foot deep." A Frenchman announced indignantly, "This is not a town, it is a quagmire; it is chaos!...San Francisco literally floats on an ocean of mud." Margaret De Witt's husband came home from his store "with mud above the knees," and declared "he had been where there was no bottom."

Mrs. Farnham bravely toured the soggy city, not so much making observations as enduring them:

> At that period in the history of San Francisco, it was so rare to see a female, that those whose misfortune it was to be obliged to be abroad felt themselves uncomfortably stared at. Doorways filled instantly, and little islands in the streets were thronged with men who seemed to gather in a moment, and who remained immovable till the spectacle passed from their incredulous gaze. Bold-faced unfortunates, whose presence added infinitely to the discomfort one felt in those dreadful times, were occasionally to be seen in bar-rooms, or, perhaps, hatless and habitless on horseback in the streets, or the great gaming-houses that never were emptied of their throngs.

On a later visit to San Francisco, Eliza would admire the stylish French women decorating San Francisco's numerous gaming tables, but the distress and anxiety accompanying her initial impression of the city, worry for her children, and the lawsuit she had filed against the *Angelique*'s captain, deflected her attention:

> This, then, was California; but I was too much engrossed in thinking of my dear children, and what had been their fate since they were parted from me, to entertain a thought of the wonderful country whose emporium lay before me, like a young giant but half-conscious of his power, or a single speculation upon my own probable destiny in it.

As with her voyage around the Horn and her stay at Valparaiso, Mrs. Farnham, on her first visit to San Francisco, was little inclined to describe the sights. Not even evidence of San Francisco's great fire, which had devoured much of the city only three days before her arrival, elicited sufficient interest to remark it. She likely read all about the conflagration, however, in the *Alta California*, where the editor's heights of eloquence all but exceeded those of the flames:

> The glare grew bolder, the flames dashed from the windows, struggling with the heavy masses of smoke; they writhed and twisted about; they shot up into the air vindictively; they curled about corners; they licked the adjoining buildings with serpent-like animosity. Men rushed to and fro half bewildered...a confused roaring sound

of human voices rent the air, mingled with the crashing and crackling of the flames....The morning was still, scarcely a breath of air swerving the fiery volumes. Soon came thronging to the scene our affrighted citizens, and then commenced the din of a thousand voices, the crash of property, jingling of battered windows, the quick, sharp sound of axes, plied vigorously...and yet, above this the roar of the devouring element....Portsmouth Square, in front of the burning buildings, was crowded with anxious spectators, when an alarm was created of *stored powder* in the Parker House. A *stampede* of six thousand human beings then added to the terrors of the spectacle.

From descriptions of San Francisco prior to this conflagration, the reduction to rubble of several hotels, restaurants, stores, and saloons was likely not considered a loss by any but their owners. The infant city Eliza Farnham encountered late in December 1849 had received abundant delineation from other pens, there having been more than thirty thousand arrivals there that year from around the Horn and across the isthmus—and no one praised it.

San Francisco entirely failed to impress Mrs. Megquier: "There is nothing pleasant or comfortable now here, you would not enjoy it."

Franklin Buck, who arrived in August, declared:

I found things here just as I had heard with some few exceptions. The town is growing very fast. You can see it grow every night. It already contains streets and squares, several large hotels and any quantity of grog shops and gambling saloons. This is carried on with a perfect looseness, night and day. A large number of the houses and stores are merely frames covered with canvas.

Bayard Taylor, a *New York Tribune* correspondent, and thus paid to be at least as observant as he was inconvenienced, wrote of his arrival that year:

A furious wind was blowing down through a gap in the hills, filling the streets with clouds of dust. On every side stood buildings of all kinds, begun or half-finished, and the greater part of them mere canvas sheds, open in front, and covered with all kinds of signs, in all languages. Great quantities of goods were piled up in the open air, for want of a place to store them. The streets were full of people, hurrying to and fro, and of as diverse and bizarre a character as the houses.

When Methodist missionary William Taylor arrived, in September 1849, he found:

> not a brick house in the place, and but a few wooden ones, and not a wharf or pier in the harbor. But for a few old adobe houses, it would have been easy to imagine that the whole city was pitched the evening before for the accommodation of a vast caravan for the night; for the city now contained a population of about twenty thousand, and I felt oppressed with the fear that under the influence of the gold attraction of the mountains, those tents might all be struck some morning, and the city suddenly leave its moorings for parts unknown.

The California sights and experiences that failed to stir Mrs. Farnham's pen included her first California earthquake, but the shaking moved the *Alta California*'s editor to typically florid description:

> The combined influences of intemperance and miasmatic vapors could not have produced on the over wrought system of a San Joaquin gold digger such sensations as mother earth appeared to experience during the whole day and part of the evening of Wednesday last, yet the same character of disease appeared, which was downright, undisguised chill and fever; more commonly called the "shakes"....a silent retching, a terrible commotion in the deep bowels of the earth, in a word, the agitation or shock of an earthquake, which if not felt by all was experienced by a majority of our citizens. For a few seconds, at intervals throughout the day, the earth trembled violently, and we shall undoubtedly hear of an earthquake in some of the lower countries, probably South America, which has proved destructive to a considerable degree.

Mrs. Farnham's attention lay elsewhere—on the future, and women's opportunities in California:

> Women are more in requisition than gold or any thing else. Those who came out with me had immediately offers of employment at $75 and $100 per month. If there had been five hundred instead of five, they could all have engaged immediately on similar terms. They must be got here in considerable numbers before society can take any shape or assume any character. I hope that while our good brethren at home are bestirring themselves kindly to send out churches and clergymen, they will not forget that the best of all missionaries to such a population are resolute, virtuous, intelligent women.

One of the chief difficulties that were felt by the women who con-sulted me was the fear that they should not be protected against rudeness, or perhaps something worse. I reasoned them that it would not be so, but it was difficult to convince by argument. Therefore, let the *fact* be known to all who care to know it, that the utmost possible deference and care are shown to females....No woman need fear to come here who has the sense and energy to take care of herself elsewhere; and she will have, in her capacity for any occupation suited to her sex, a better capital than the gold of the mines. If there had 1,000 females sailed last May, they would, all who chose to, be profitably employed this day. Everything is scarcer here than gold.

She might have added, "including justice."

On January 18, in Judge Almond's Court of First Instance, Mrs. Farnham soon realized that her suit against the *Angelique's* Captain Windsor was a "foolish hope of obtaining some semblance of jus-tice for the outrage and wrong" she had suffered. Her attorneys presented her case as:

a breach of contract to convey plaintiff, her two children and servant from New York to San Francisco, and for ungentlemanly and unkind treatment of plaintiff and her children, and for countenancing and aiding her servant to marry the steward, a colored man, and for car-rying her children away and leaving her at Valparaiso.

Witnesses were called for both sides, and "considerable scandal introduced during the trial," in which it was only proven, as those sympathetic to Mrs. Farnham concluded, that she was "a little too much of an advocate for the rights of women, and had a penchant for climbing the rigging in unmentionables."

It was not until six o'clock that evening that the case went to the jury "without any remarks from counsel on either side." Judge Almond concluded that "from the intelligence of the jury he was perfectly satisfied to leave the case in their hands without any remarks from him."

Court was adjourned until nine o'clock the next morning. At the appointed hour Captain Windsor appeared, was declared not guilty by a jury of men, and boarded the *Angelique,* which cleared immediately and departed.

Mrs. Farnham's California disappointments were destined to form a long list. And her inherited *casa* was the next item on it.

*Santa Cruz, 1856, as it looked when Mrs. Farnham departed for
the East to publish the first book about California written by a woman.
Courtesy of The Bancroft Library, University of California, Berkeley
(California Mission Sketches by Henry Miller, 1856)*

# SIX

# Santa Cruz

It was not till twenty-two years after the first visit of the Spaniards...in search of Monterey bay, that Santa Cruz Mission was founded....It was on the 25th day of September 1791 that Fathers Alonzo Salazar and Baldomero Lopez arrived and pitched their tent on the hill on which the Catholic church now stands....It must have been rather lonely.

—W. W. Elliott, *History of Santa Cruz County,* 1879

DEED OF SALE.—Coleto, et al. to Thomas Jefferson Farnham, August 5, 1847—Bernardino Coleto, Pascual Coleto, Angel Coleto, Mariano Bassillo, Pedro Viejo, Fidel Viejo, Carlos Fidel, Andrea Viejo, Alandro Viejo.... Indians of the Mission of Santa Cruz...and...now the owners of the following described premises...for...the sum of Two Hundred Dollars...do hereby sell and convey in full ownership the following described lands to wit the Potrero lying north of the church of the mission aforesaid....containing two thousand acres more or less.

—*Santa Cruz County Book of Deeds*

On February 22, 1850, Mrs. Farnham and company—Charlie, Eddie, and Lucy Sampson—arrived by sea at Santa Cruz, where, there being neither wharf nor pier, they were "landed like bales of goods through the surf, partly in boats and partly in the arms of the seamen."

Eliza left Lucy Sampson to superintend the transfer of their several boxes and bales from ship to shore and, with Charlie at her side and Eddie on the shoulders of an accompanying friend, climbed the hill to her new home:

See us, after a walk of two miles...through clover and grass four inches high, borne down by the heavy dews that had fallen on the previous night, enter the casa of El Rancho La Libertad....The casa is not a cheerful specimen even of California habitations—being made of slabs, which were originally placed upright, but which have departed sadly from the perpendicular in every direction. There is not a foot of floor, nor a pane of glass, nor a brick, nor anything in the shape of a stove. The fire is made upon the ground, and the smoke departs by any avenue that seemeth to itself good, or lingers

in the airy space between our heads and the roof, which is beauti-
fully done in bas relief of webs....The dimensions of the entire structure are about twenty-five feet in length by fifteen feet in width at
one end, and diminishing, by beautiful convergence, to about ten
feet at the other. A partition of slabs, thrown across the narrow end,
rather divides the house than makes a room, of which the other
three walls are so imperfect that you may walk through them almost
where you will.

But the view was glorious. From the gentle height the "casa"
shared with the old mission buildings, sadly fallen into disrepair,
Eliza saw the San Lorenzo river emptying into the blue Pacific's
"endless waters" and heard the music of the surf rolling in and
breaking on the beach "in all varieties of tone, from the alto of
thunder to the sweet tenor of that gentle chime which, heard
through the deep solitudes of the night, soothes and charms the
soul." She was entranced:

> I had been told it was a beautiful place, but I was not prepared for
> the sort of impression it produced.
>
> It was one of those peerless days, such as only a California winter
> affords, with a cloudless sky above the head, and the earth piled with
> tenderest herbage under the feet. In the deep seclusion of La
> Libertad I enjoyed that silence and solitude which for a day one finds
> so welcome a change from bustle and annoyance, such as had been
> our previous lot in California. Only the song of birds, the bubbling
> of the stream over the roots of the trees whose tops embower it, min-
> gled with the gleeful shouts of the delighted boys, who are already
> deep in the mysteries of its most secret places, greet my ear. The beat-
> ing of the distant surf rather aids than breaks the silence, and by
> ascending a gentle slope to the right, I look out on a picture so filled
> with repose and beauty that while I gaze, the hateful stir of the world
> in which I have lately been mixed up seems to die out of the uni-
> verse, and I no longer remember it. For the hour, I forget that life
> subjects the spirit to jar or discord, and am only conscious of the har-
> mony that flows from the generous breast of nature into our own,
> when, for a happy moment, she gets undivided audience of it.

But the hour was soon up, and there was much to be done. The
boys were hungry, and their new home, such as it was, must be
made habitable. On the beach, Lucy Sampson waited amid the wet
privilege of their offloaded goods brought from San Francisco,
clothes and provisions now sopping bundles and baskets, bags and

boxes burst by the surf in landing—at a cost of twenty-five dollars for each boatload delivered.

Next day, a hired wagoner charged eight dollars per load to haul these things from the beach to the house. Eliza had the funds, but they were not limitless. She would worry about money later. First there was the unpacking and drying of wet goods and helping Miss Sampson create a "really elegant chamber" from a white tent a neighbor loaned them to make a bedroom. And then there was the stove to install, for bread must be baked and winter nights warmed.

The stove required assembling. Eliza assigned the task to Tom Russell, hired to help her transform her land into a paying farm. When Tom discovered that several stove parts were "fractured," damaged in delivery, Eliza, engrossed in "dragging out and exposing to the occasional sun gleams whole cases of wetted linen, muslins, and clothing," encouraged him to do the best he could. By nightfall Tom confessed defeat. The next day Miss Sampson tackled the project, with no better success:

> On the third day, it was agreed that stoves could not have been used in the time of Job, or all his other afflictions would have been unnecessary. But our spirits were now so thoroughly tamed by it, and our demands upon it so humbled, that we agreed to come to its terms without further parley, and abandon the use of the refractory rods, plates, etc., which before had been thought indispensable to its perfect action. No sooner was this done than the question was amicably settled; and it shows how, often, difficulties that seem insuperable are in truth more imaginary than real—that in an hour from this concession we had our stove well heated and its oven doing duty upon a generous pan of biscuit, very comforting to our eyes. This was a great triumph.

And only a shadow of that to come. The family needed a better house, a new house—and Eliza decided to build it herself. But first the farming must be launched, for it was nearly March and the ground must be turned, and a team acquired to do it, a costly undertaking:

> Having ample means legally deposited in the hands of a person in San Francisco, who had been some three years in the country, and knew this neighborhood well, we had, nevertheless, been prevailed

upon by him to come empty-handed to our undertaking, having his assurance that anything we needed was to be had on a hint, and that it would commend us far more to the hearts of our neighbors if we wanted occasionally some favor from them, than if we went among them too independent. This assertion bore a sort of brotherly-love air that commended it to me, and beside, seemed like probability in California, where money was more abundant than anything else man desired, and spent with a prodigality of which any description would convey but a faint notion to those who count sixpences at home.

So here we were, in that glorious state of dependence which was to be so happy a bond of union between us and those who were about us, wanting everything for putting in a crop, but seed, plow, and the labor of one man. Every day was important to us; but it took several days to canvass the settlement and get our wants supplied. At length, on the 10th of March, two horses and a mule having been furnished by the liberality of as many owners, the plow started.

Also lent to Mrs. Farnham was a fine saddle horse, placed at her disposal by her near neighbor, William Anderson. Any kindness he might offer Mrs. Farnham was as nothing compared to what he owed her late husband. Eliza appreciatively borrowed the horse to ride up to the Zayante grant that lay adjacent above her property, to call upon Isaac Graham. Graham and his partner had a sawmill there and lumbered the redwoods. And Graham, like Anderson, was indebted to Thomas Jefferson Farnham for his rescue, in 1840, from the Mexican jail at Monterey. Graham's gratitude likely assisted Farnham's purchase of the Indians' two thousand acres of mission land for the modest sum of two hundred dollars.

Thomas Jefferson Farnham had met Graham on the last leg of an adventure commenced in 1839 from Illinois, where he'd contracted a bad case of the westering fever then just beginning to infect the nation. Americans had been moving west ever since Plymouth Rock had lost its novelty, and in the late 1830s Oregon was all the rage.

Farnham had organized the Peoria Company, seventeen men, including himself, and departed for Oregon in May of 1839. After some excellent adventures, recorded in the first of several books he subsequently published with much success, Farnham arrived, on September 23, at Dr. Marcus Whitman's mission on the Wallawalla river. There he visited with Indians, under instruction of Christianity, and with Narcissa Whitman, destined to die with

*Thomas Jefferson Farnham, author of* Travels in the Great Western Prairies *(1841);* Travels in California *(1844);* History of Oregon Territory *(1844); and* Mexico *(1846). Portrait by unidentified artist, ca. 1845. Collection of The New-York Historical Society (24290)*

*"Old Graham the Hunter," engraved by W. G. Jackman. This romantic portrait, purportedly of Isaac Graham (and dismissed as "bogus" by historian Doyce B. Nunis Jr.), was the frontispiece for Thomas Jefferson Farnham's* The Early Days of California: Embracing What I Saw and Heard There, with Scenes in the Pacific, *an 1860 reprint of* Travels in California.

her husband for the presumption. On December 4, 1839, having toured Oregon and Fort Vancouver to his heart's content, Farnham departed. To get going, he apparently needed to slash his way through a veritable forest of exclamation points: "Lower Oregon! A verdant belt of wild loveliness!" "Seaward over the great Pacific! A spectacle of true grandeur!" "The shores of Lower Oregon! They rise so boldly from the sea!" "The Pacific! the Great South Sea!" At sea, in a storm pounding the ship *Vancouver:* "It is the Creator's great choir! Ocean tuned by His own hand, and swept by the fingers of His tempest!"

Farnham indulged inclinations he knew he possessed. A few years previously, a phrenologist had "read" his head and declared that the contours indicated "a pure poetical taste and great facility in literature," as well as "a love of traveling, natural scenery & the sublimities of Nature."

On December 25, 1839, the *Vancouver* dropped anchor at Honolulu. Farnham went ashore, made the acquaintance of King Kamehameha and the beautiful island, and stayed three months. Then, "To the sea!...bound for Upper California!" aboard Captain John Paty's ship, *Don Quixote.*

When the *Don Quixote* arrived at Monterey in April of 1840, Farnham discovered that the Mexican government had incarcerated several dozen Americans and Englishmen. His sympathy with their plight entangled him in what came to be called the "Graham affair," an event involving a horse race, a revolution, Mexican politics, and racial disharmony, and so knotted by discrepant reports as to defy ready unraveling. Farnham clearly admired the chief disputant, Isaac Graham:

> A stout, sturdy backwoodsman, of a stamp which exists only on the frontiers of the American States—men with the blood of the ancient Normans and Saxons in their veins—with hearts as large as their bodies can hold, beating nothing but kindness till injustice shows its fangs, and then, lion-like, striking for vengeance....
>
> Graham loved a horse. He had taken a fine gelding with him when he emigrated to the country, and trained him for the turf. Every year he challenged the whole country to the course, and as often won everything wagered against his noble steed. José Castro, a villain with a lean body, dark face, black mustachios, pointed nose, flabby cheeks, uneasy eyes, and hands and heart so foul as instinctively

to require a Spanish cloak in all sorts of weather to cover them, and his Excellentisimo were among Graham's heaviest debtors. Behold the reasons for their enmity.

## Others took a different view of the "old Tennessean":

In '36 he had a distillery and drinking-place at Natividad, and from the loafers about his place, chiefly deserting sailors, raised a comp. of 'riflemen' to support Alvarado in his revolution....At the best, he was a loud-mouthed, unprincipled, profligate, and reckless man, whose only good qualities seem to have been the personal bravery and prodigal hospitality of his class, with undoubted skill as a hunter, and a degree of industry.

Eliza liked him. To her, he was "one of the notabilities of old California...who, with his rifle at his back, and shoes down at heel, presented in his exterior a curious mixture of the hunter and the man of leisure."

As it turned out, not all friends of her husband were friends of hers, most particularly not Joseph S. Ruckel.

## SEVEN

# Trials and Humiliations

NOTICE.—Whereas, my wife Catherine having left my bed and board, without any just cause or provocation, I hereby forewarn all persons from harboring or trusting her on my account, as I will pay no debts of her contracting. My house, at the time of her elopement, was pillaged of money to a large amount and many valuable papers, and I forewarn all persons from trading for any paper or papers made to me or containing my signature. ISAAC GRAHAM, Santa Cruz, April 3rd, 1850.
—*Alta California*, April 20, 1850

DISTRICT COURT.—In this Court, yesterday, in the case of *E. W. Farnham vs Joseph S. Ruckle* [sic], final judgment was rendered in favor of plaintiff, for $3,661.
—*Alta California*, October 15, 1850

To this gentleman I am indebted for what will make his name memorable to me and my children; toils that would have taxed the strength of a man—trials and humiliations which could have been better borne by a saint; anguish of heart, and despair, which, I pray, may never fall to the lot of another. I would not be bitter, but it is not in human nature to have suffered as I have, without sometimes remembering those whose selfishness and dishonesty caused it. A man who could prove recreant to a trust held for the dead and the helpless, must have capacities in his nature that one would rather not prove.

—Eliza Farnham,
*California, In-Doors and Out*

It was Joseph S. Ruckel, administrator of her late husband's estate, who had sent Mrs. Farnham to Santa Cruz with the charming advice to "come empty-handed" to her undertaking, that such dependence would commend her "to the hearts" of her neighbors. William Anderson was one of those neighbors, and Isaac Graham another; and both of them recognized balderdash when they heard it.

Anderson immediately offered to escort Eliza back to San Francisco to see Ruckel.

Graham, as usual, had problems of his own, this time with his wife of five years, twenty-six-year-old Catherine Bennett. Graham was forty-five when they married, in a ceremony that, lacking civil or religious authority, outraged his bride's mother. Mary Bennett finally reconciled herself to the situation following the births of her granddaughters, Matilda Jane in 1846 and Amanda Ann Narcissa in 1849.

But now Jesse, Graham's twenty-four-year-old son by a wife left in Tennessee, had come west, found his father at Rancho Zayante, and reported that his mother was alive and well and living in Texas. Whatever Mary Bennett and her daughter had to say upon receipt of this news is unfortunately lost to history.

In March of 1850, while Eliza fretted over her own money problems, Catherine, assisted by a brother, fled Rancho Zayante with her daughters and an estimated eight thousand dollars in gold. The marital dispute later turned deadly when Jesse Graham killed one Bennett brother, wounded another, and fired buckshot at Catherine's mother. Rumors and accusations flew. Everyone in Santa Cruz had opinions on the matter, including Eliza:

> The little community had been thrown into great excitement, by one of those domestic tragedies that one would never have dreamed of in so quiet and secluded a little world....reports were constantly afloat, that Mrs. Graham was here or there; or that payment by her husband of a thousand or two thousand dollars would restore him his children; or that his son had been arrested; or that people hunting him had got upon his track; or that his children had been heard, on the night of their mother's elopement, crying dismally, along the solitary road that passed some ranch away to the south. One could not but feel that, hard and rough as had been the old man's experience, this was the bitterest cup of all.

Mrs. Farnham's trek to San Francisco to inquire about Ruckel's financial dealings took her across rugged country, then into San Jose. William Anderson, who knew the way, followed the route opened in 1791 when mission Indians cut a direct road from Santa Cruz to the Santa Clara mission and the pueblo at San Jose. The road remained rough, but not without its pleasures:

*Santa Clara, ca. 1856, much as it looked when Mrs. Farnham passed through on her way to San Francisco. Courtesy of The Bancroft Library, University of California, Berkeley (Banc Pic 1963:002:0904-D)*

We set out with formidable preparations of lunch, fire-arms, etc., Mr. A carrying two revolvers, and each of our horses having a satchel of provisions....A habit-skirt, which I was assured I could not wear through the mountains, was packed conveniently, that it might be put on when we reached the inhabited regions on the other side....At this time all the more productive regions were sparkling with the flowers common to the country, chief among them the eshcholtzia, purple and blue lupin, columbine, white and variegated convolvuli, fleur de lis, white lily, and innumerable smaller flowers of exquisite beauty....

From the first summit eastward in this range, you get a magnificent view of the coast-table, the bay of Monterey, and the ocean; from the last you behold a portion of the bay of San Francisco, and the great valley of the Puebla de San Jose, lying spread as it were at your very feet—one of the most beautiful views conceivable.

From San Jose to San Francisco, Mrs. Farnham continued to enjoy her journey, now up the famed El Camino Real, "over a surface so level that you can see the broad bay....An occasional sail seems to be gliding along in the grass over the top of which you look....a ride through the valley is one of the most charming in the country."

She also had the pleasure of "a most agreeable and gentlemanly fellow-traveler, who joined us on the road." He was Dr. William Grove Deal, a Sacramento physician who had emigrated from Baltimore and was now serving in the state's first legislature at San Jose. "We had," wrote Eliza, "most pleasant discourse on various topics, speculative and practical, grave and gay, absurd and rational."

Mrs. Farnham, alas, made the trip for naught. She and Anderson stayed but one day, witness to a city in an uproar of election fervor and festivities. Colonel John C. Hayes, the celebrated Texas Ranger, had been selected by the people as an independent candidate for county sheriff. Bands and processions of carriages filled with musicians jammed the principal streets to the plaza, where a mass meeting of enthusiastic supporters waved flags and cheered spirited speeches. Hayes himself capped the climax, unexpectedly exhibiting his horsemanship by riding bareheaded and unattended into their midst on a black charger. Eliza was not impressed:

> I was obliged to pass through the most excited quarters of the city several times during the day, and my serious belief was that any honors awarded to Mr. Jack Hays [sic] after that day would be posthumous.
>
> No man ever received such treatment at the hands of a friendly mob—now upon their shoulders; now hoisted upon the counter of some public-house; then pulled down, to be borne off somewhere else; now compelled to stop and address a crowd at this corner, and then borne, without ceremony or tenderness, to some other spot; alternately seized by the arm, neck or leg, by men in all stages of drunkenness, and all degrees of popular frenzy—poor Jack Hays seemed to me a man much to be pitied.

The festivities didn't elevate Mrs. Farnham's opinion of the city:

> San Francisco, I believe, has the most disagreeable climate and locality of any city on the globe....the rainy season closes to give place to what is miscalled summer—a season so cold that you require more clothing than you did in January; so damp with fogs and mists, that you are penetrated to the very marrow; so windy, that if you are abroad in the afternoon it is a continual struggle. Your eyes are blinded, your teeth set on edge, and your whole person made so uncomfortable by the sand that has insinuated itself through your clothing that you could not conceive it possible to feel a sensation of comfort short of a warm bath and shower by way of preliminaries.

She returned to Santa Cruz to find the weather good, but not much else:

> When I reached La Libertad, I found a sad state of things. The farmer, who had complained of a sore hand before I left home, had been laid up ever since, and it was now in a dreadful state. Poor Miss Sampson, who had been nurse and housekeeper, was very badly off also, and I, with the fatigue of the journey and the unpleasant anticipations of having to repeat it as soon as possible again, was not in a condition to undertake the cares and labors that required some energetic hand immediately. Of course our farming was suspended —another delay that threatened to be fatal to the business of the year; but there was no remedy.

And there was still the unresolved matter with Ruckel:

> We had already begun to suspect that his motives in withholding our money were less generous than he would have had them seem. In San Francisco, I had been unable to learn anything alarming respecting his solvency, but on the road home, it came to me with such directness that I felt constrained to return at the earliest day possible, and take any steps I might yet be able to take to secure myself and my sons from loss.

A second trip to San Francisco, a week later, proved equally fruitless, and upon returning to Santa Cruz Mrs. Farnham found things worse than before. Tom had his hand in a sling, Miss Sampson was sick in bed—and hordes of grasshoppers were in the fields.

> Not less than half the entire planting was destroyed in the course of sixteen or twenty days. It would be difficult to imagine anything more vexatious or trying than the watching of such a destructive process. After all the labor had been performed, all the care borne, and the prospect of a large and very valuable crop had flattered us in some degree out of our weariness, it was indeed a trial of one's equanimity to see millions of worthless insects consuming the fine growth which had promised so much.

And there were "other enemies to our peace and prosperity":

> These were the immense herds of huge cattle, which, now that the grass had lost its freshness, were intent upon the appropriation of whatever invited their appetites....Charlie and I took the field against the besiegers. How we toiled, raced, watched, and kept up

an active preventive service on the outskirts, not one of which was impregnable....After several days of this sort of skirmishing, I willingly resigned my post, and let it not be reckoned dishonorable that my successor was an Indian. He was a gentleman in his way—after his light and knowledge. I hired him at two dollars per day. He was to catch and saddle his own horse, walk to and fro between the rancheria and the house, and for the consideration of an occasional lunch of *carne y pan*, and sundry supplies of biscuit and gingerbread or other delicacies to his *mujer*, who was *malo*, was to relax his dignity so far as to cut us a few sticks of wood occasionally of a morning. This gentleman occupied a seat distant from the ranch about seventy or eighty rods, and as his house gave him a view of most of the field, he fell, after the first day or two, into the habit of remaining at home until the cattle were fairly into the crop, when he would run lazily up, walk them out, and set out on his return. Once, and only once, was I guilty of the rashness of urging him to quicken his steps, when thirty or forty bullocks were rushing into a distant part of the field. He laid his hand upon his heart, and protested, in the blandest tones, that senora must excuse him; for running made his heart beat *mucho*. In this way he divided the care with Charlie and me for eight days; and, notwithstanding the $16, duly paid, sundry little bags of *arina*, various small stores to the wife, and the disappearance, at the same time, of an entire piece of goods belonging to Miss Sampson, he always casts upon me, when we meet, the kindly patient glance of an abused benefactor.

Plus, there remained the matter of the *casa*, not only insufficient in size and conveniences, but overrun with fleas. "If homœopathic pharmacy had included the use of any property of this insect," Mrs. Farnham wrote, "we could have furnished the North American Continent with mother tincture of it."

Facing failure as a farmer, Eliza rescued her self-esteem with a hammer.

# EIGHT

# Summer 1850

25.—Site of Mrs. E. W. Farnham's Residence, made famous by her book entitled, "California, In Doors and Out." Scarcely a vestige remains of what she had made with so much toil, trouble, and gladness. One mile north from Santa Cruz.

*—Santa Cruz and Monterey Illustrated Handbook,* 1880

**B**y the first of July, lumber for the new house had been sawn. Three days later, Eliza had finished marking the lines of the foundation: thirty-seven feet wide, twenty-seven deep, and a "piazza six feet deep was to cross the entire front." On the evening of the Fourth of July, "after joining in the first celebration of that day ever had in Santa Cruz," she walked the ground that the new house was to occupy:

> It seemed to me a great step taken, actually to see my future house defined on the ground it was to cover....Already, in imagination, I saw its walls lined with the contents of my well-stored boxes, and felt the quiet, happy days stealing by....forgetful, in that first dream, of the days and weeks of toil that must be performed...for—let not ladies lift their hands in horror—I designed supplying the place of journeyman carpenter with my own hands.
> ....My first participation in the labor of its erection was the tenanting of the joists and studding for the lower story, a work in which I succeeded so well that during its progress I laughed, whenever I paused for a few moments to rest, at the idea of promising to pay a man $14 or $16 per day for doing what I found my own hands so dexterous in....I ought not to omit mentioning that I commenced my new business in the ordinary long dress, but its extreme inconvenience in displacing all the smaller tools, effacing lines, and flying in the teeth of the saw induced me, after the second day, to try the suit I had worn at home in gymnastic exercises. It is the same that has since become famous as the Bloomer, though then the name had not been heard of. When I had once put it on, I could never get back into skirts during working hours.

Eliza felt confident of her costume's appropriateness. Once, while she was on the roof, nailing, a visitor succeeded in engaging her interest in a discussion of Swedenborg. After a few minutes, Eliza put down her hammer, took off her nail-pocket, and descended the ladder with the help of her visitor's hand:

> This was early in my experience as a roofer. Afterward I could go up and down alone with perfect freedom and ease. When I reached the ground, I did not apologize for my dress, because, novel as I knew it must look, I felt assured its fitness would be appreciated.

Summer in Santa Cruz promised happier days than those of the problem-riddled spring. Little Eddie's health improved, and he spent much of his time, when the weather was not too hot, watching his mother build the new house:

> It was my greatest pleasure to see him pleased and interested, and to kindle his hopes of happy days in the new house. The agonies he had first suffered on our arrival were, I hoped, forever over; and we all loved him so much that no pleasanter idea could be associated with home than that of his happiness in it.

One evening during that first summer in Santa Cruz, Eliza received an unexpected visitor, a Mr. Allen, who arrived entrusted with a package for her sent from Samuel Wells, husband of her friend Charlotte, the sister of her phrenologist friends Orson and Lorenzo Fowler. It contained "two Daguerreotypes [at] which I rejoiced and almost cried over the dear old friendly faces." In appreciation, she invited Mr. Allen to dine the next day, it being the Sabbath and labor suspended. He accepted.

Sunday, after dinner, Mrs. Farnham and Mr. Allen walked to an adjoining farm on a hill overlooking the ocean, discoursing on various subjects, including marriage:

> Mr. Allen informed me that he had no objection to marriage except to what constituted the principal object of it to most persons! I did not say much in reply for that seemed to be getting pretty well along for the second day.

Monday, Mr. Allen arrived again, just as Eliza was going out to milk. It was, he said, gallantly taking the pail from her, unbecoming for a man to allow a woman to milk in his presence. Eliza unprotestingly leaned against the rails as her visitor milked her cow. He discoursed generally on various topics and then said that he'd been thinking over the conversation of the previous day:

> and had come to the conclusion that I was a person so entirely agreeable, sensible &c that he could spend the rest of his days very happily with me and…he would beg me to accept his hand in the sort of marriage which he had faintly shadowed forth the previous day. My sentiment was very powerfully called into action by the proposal—by the surrounding circumstances…and most of all by the limitations which were to regulate our future lives. It was all so pastoral—so apostolic, in fact!!

Mrs. Farnham declined both the hand and the honor and "laughed at the hills and the tall trees and the bright skies and even the innocent calves who had not proposed—at every thing but Mr. Allen who had strength to finish the milking after I said no and the appetite to take a comfortable luncheon." He never called again.

Alas. She might have been better off, restrictions and all, with Mr. Allen than the man whose proposal she eventually accepted. After her marriage to William Fitzpatrick, laughter disappeared. But until the Irishman sucked the wind from her sails, Eliza had some high times.

There was, for instance, the fine morning, when desperately in need of milk for her children, she disguised herself as a man in order to capture a wild cow.

Miss Sampson had in her trunks a suit intended for a nephew. The outfit, being new, had "an over-smartish look" to Eliza's eye, but she put it on. Next she tugged a too-small hat over her hair, which she had twisted up and secured with a comb. To complete the disguise, she dispensed with her spectacles, though she "could not tell, at twenty rods, whether it was an ox or a man approaching."

Off she rode, half blind and apparently incognito, in company with Tom, her hired man, to capture a calf on the presumption its mother would follow them home to be milked. Almost at once she lost her hat. While Tom retrieved it, Eliza held her hand to her head "to conceal the comb and twist, which is not the usual style of hairdressing among the caballeros I was counterfeiting." Hat restored, she rode the "next quarter of a mile in convulsions of laughter" at the thought of being seen in her masquerade.

This was but the prelude to the roundup. Tom captured the calf and threw it across the saddle of his horse, which then refused to let the rider mount. Tom then hoisted the calf onto Eliza's horse, intending to mount his own and retrieve the calf astride. To this his horse also objected. After numerous attempts the horse finally permitted both calf and rider. Eliza, meanwhile, nervously scanned the distance with her unseeing gaze, unable to "control the beating of my heart when anything moving at a distance suggested the possibility of encountering a stranger at such a critical time." Whether she feared being unmasked as a woman or as a rustler she failed to say.

In any event, Eliza and Tom, with the calf aboard, turned their horses' heads homeward, confident of success. Triumph proved short-lived. The calf's mother, the object of the exercise, wandered off to join the herd, utterly indifferent to her calf's kidnapping. This left two alternatives: either abandon the calf or follow the mother. Eliza elected the latter, allowing her horse, Sheik, full rein to gallop in pursuit of the cow:

> It was an older business to him than to me, and I soon found he understood it much better. I therefore gave him his freedom, and he followed her like her shadow, wheeling when she wheeled, slackening when she slackened, quickening when she quickened her pace; in short, changing his movements so entirely without control or purpose of mine that in the excitement of the chase and of keeping my seat I forgot the annoyances I had suffered—the small hat, want of spectacles, possible neighborhood of strange eyes.

Eventually the cow gave up and walked quietly after her calf. Then came the fun of milking one of the half-wild cows that roamed the vast, unfenced ranchos of California:

> This process is performed by lashing the head of the animal, if she be at all wild, to the fence, or to a post set for that purpose, and her hind feet to each other. If she be quite gentle, and well used to it for years, the rope is only thrown about her legs. Sometimes it is even permitted to drop to the ground; but whatever its use may be, it is never dispensed with. Milking, without it, would be too exciting and perilous a business for people who love labor and adventure so little.

She refers to the Californios, those admirers of horses and fandangos and, in her opinion, indolence. Their bucolic, carefree way of life was just then being erased by the uninvited Americanos who had but recently wrested the country from Mexico and then added insult to injury by promptly discovering gold and over-running it.

Ever observant to the customs of this country, Eliza described how people at that time got their meat:

> Except in the large cities or towns, there are no markets, and the only method of supplying one's-self with fresh meat is by the purchase of an animal on foot. A Spaniard who is in want of a few dollars, gets on a horse, lasso in hand, and goes off in pursuit of a beef, which he will sell, when caught, at almost any price. If he suppose beef may be wanted at some house, he drives the beast thither before him....He proposes to sell it first for twenty-five, then for twenty, then for an ounce [of gold, $16], and, last of all, parts with it for ten or twelve dollars; winds the rope about its feet to throw it, cuts its throat, mounts, and rides away.

Exhausting labor consumed most of Eliza's first summer at Santa Cruz. By day she hammered and sawed, building her house. Evenings she fashioned sacks for the harvest, modest as it promised to be, or read aloud to Miss Sampson and Charlie while they sewed:

> Our choice of books included fiction, poetry, history, philosophy, and religion. Occasionally, we attended the day or evening worship of our Methodist neighbors, or looked in upon the Temperance meeting, where once an indirect invitation to speak so alarmed me that I did not venture back to acquaint myself personally with their proceedings.

On first visiting the Methodists with Charlie, what captured Eliza's attention more than the worship were the worshippers, particularly the young girls:

> Their styles of dress were as varied as their persons, agreeing in only one feature, that of skirts falling to the feet. Hideous bonnets, of all fashions, which their grandmothers might have worn, deformed their heads and concealed their fine faces; gowns pinned at the waist in front; monstrous shoes, or may be none at all, showed the want of supplies in the country.

Eliza was an equal curiosity and her dress likewise noticed:

> When some twenty-five or thirty persons had come together, and one or two hymns had been voluntarily sung, a brother offered prayer,

in which, among other requests, he desired the Lord, if any one had come there to be seen, to put better thoughts into their hearts! What a reproof of meek brown organdy dress and straw cottage!

The rebuke to her fashionable straw bonnet likely annoyed her more than being an object of inspection, a condition to which she was becoming accustomed. That summer, for example, she made another trip to San Francisco, where she purchased a wagon, "to give Miss Sampson and Eddie, neither of whom could ride on horseback, an occasional airing." With a wagon, Mrs. Farnham and her hired man, Tom Russell, could not have taken the mountain trail. Instead, they followed the established road, El Camino Real, toward the mission at San Juan Bautista, and from there traveled west through present-day Watsonville and up the coast to Santa Cruz. Nightfall caught them short of their destination and they stopped at the rancho of one of the countryside's earliest settlers, Isidro Castro, who had come to California as a soldier with the de Anza party in 1776 and eventually acquired extensive landholdings.

Cold and hungry, Mrs. Farnham took refuge in the kitchen, where several young Indian girls were making tortillas and cooking beans:

> A merrier set could nowhere be found; they chatted to me in Spanish, and laughed if I failed to understand them. They laughed when they could not understand my English. They examined my riding-hat, habit, whip, rings, watch, pin—every thing, in short, their eyes could see, and put on whatever they could detach from my person, trying its effect with a critical and generally an approving eye. There was such simplicity and hearty good-nature in all these tricks that I could not feel annoyed, although I was both very tired and very hungry, and could think of nothing so comfortable as getting a good supper and lying down.

Only one serious mishap occurred that summer. At Eliza's request, Tom, who had taken some potatoes to market, sent back to Santa Cruz by sea a number of items needed for the family, supplies for finishing the house, and, in a category all her own, Susannah. Susannah was a pig, a "second Susannah," named for an Illinois predecessor of great charm that Eliza had prized when a bride, a pig fondly admired and fondly recalled:

> Susannah belonged to the Swine family; but it seemed a melancholy perverseness in nature to have placed her there. She was a pattern

of all the virtues that ever dwelt in her race. Comely in person, grave and dignified in manner, she carried in her whole deportment that air of humble merit that quite won the hearts of beholders. Susannah made but little acquaintance with the town swine. Their corrupt morals and lawless habits seemed to disgust her. She never joined their foraging expeditions, never put her nose into a pail, nor looked in at a door as if she thought she had a right to enter. She always advised against the scaling of garden fences and the stealthy visiting of neglected corn-fields. Susannah was therefore not so popular among pigs as many who were less worthy. She was voted an aristocrat, a Tory—a pig of no spirit—a pig whose example, if followed, would reduce the intelligent, enterprising, and highly-favored pig democracy of the town to a spiritless set of man-servers; a set who would eat when food was given them, and mind their own business at other times. What could be more disgraceful or dastardly? ...But exemplary as she was, Susannah had some enemies among the biped citizens...and at last she met her death at the hand of one of these illiberals. She was found one morning to have been assassinated in the vicinity of the sheriff's office, the place having been chosen, doubtless, to give a legal coloring to the act. She was lamented as her worth deserved among those who knew her.

The second Susannah journeyed to Santa Cruz all the way from Australia:

The vessel arrived, and with it a letter, advising that Susannah should receive great care, as, although she was a traveled pig, she was not yet amphibious, and the Santa Cruz surf, if she came to a full experience of it, might prove too much for her. The next day the things were to be landed, and when the young man, whom I sent down to receive them, returned late in the afternoon, he reported the zinc, paint, oil, molasses, and numerous minor articles, lost in the surf. This was certainly provoking enough, but Susannah had not started yet, and there was hope, therefore, that she might be saved when her turn came.

Next morning another boat-load was capsized. She was not in that, but was let fall from the next one, and washed ashore, where a humane carpenter opened her box and resuscitated her; a deed which I would recommend to the notice of the Humane Society, if there were one here....

There had, however, been one loss which was difficult to bear with any degree of equanimity—that of our zinc. We had counted the days of waiting for it, as we had laid the last shingles that could be put upon the window roofs without it; and now it was at the bottom of the bay, and we could get none again within four or six weeks, unless some one should be dispatched expressly for it. It was proposed to cut up the tin pans, pails, etc.; and they were just about to be gathered, as an offering to the god of storms, when it luckily occurred to the carpenter that he might find some large tin canisters at the Mission. He immediately set off on the hunt, and in an hour or so was seen returning through the brown, waste-looking fields with a burden which glittered and shone encouragement to us from beneath the sun.

The season was waning. Late that summer came the anniversary of the founding of the mission, a celebratory event:

We went down with the boys to witness the ceremonies and customary recreations of a bear and bull-fight. What particularly amused Charlie and myself in the festivities of this day was the sight of the church choir turned out, after the rites were over, into a street band. Their instruments consisted of a bass and kettle drum, two violins, a triangle and a banjo. The performers, all Indians, appeared to have suffered in some recent encounter; for every head was more or less damaged, the eyes, foreheads, noses, and cheeks being badly battered, and patched; doubtless a reverent, but certainly not a very reverend choir! We staid to see the combatants pitted and almost refuse to fight, and having examined the bear at our leisure returned to resume our labors.

Despite such occasional diversions, Eliza's life at La Libertad offered more work than play. Her love of nature withered from weary inattention:

Her frowns no longer filled me with ecstatic terror; her smiles no more gave me the delight of the olden time. I lived upon her bosom, and beheld her beneficent operations...all her pomp and glory; all her meekness and patient love, and felt my life little affected by them. A few acres of potatoes, a few thousands of bricks and shingles, and the four walls of a house that should separate us from the winds and clouds...could so weary and subdue my spirit that it settled down in abject bondage to them, and almost forgot that it had ever nobler relations, more freedom, more joyous life.

Exhaustion failed to alleviate her chronic insomnia, and frequently, during wakeful nights, she succumbed to feelings of loneliness and despondency:

Despair of the future plucked from me whatever was consoling in the past. All its toils, trials, and triumphs became valueless, removed so entirely as I was, from everything that could remind me they had had value to any....The isolation of this period was its most disheartening feature....I was, most of all, unhappy in finding myself circumscribed in all action to my small family circle and my private interests. The least endowed and cultivated woman in the community was more valuable to it, if she had health and industry, than I had power to be....that which is most highly prized in advanced conditions of society may, in another, be brought to a market where no demand is.

There was little, she noted, in California society at that time to engage "the higher orders of female intelligence." What she needed most, which her small circle could not provide, was the friction of one good mind against another. She required books, and someone to discuss them with. She required intelligent conversation. She required thought-provoking ideas, and plans for enacting them. She required a friend.

And a friend was coming.

# Geordie

In May of 1850 Georgiana Bruce, restless again, left the comfortable household of Robert Purvis to see what California offered.

Horace Greeley loaned her the money to make the trip, and she chose the fastest way, via the Isthmus of Panama, a route with enough novel experiences for any adventurous woman. At Chagres, the Atlantic-side port, arriving ships unceremoniously cast forth passengers to find their own means to the Pacific. A few travelers booked the limited comforts of a small steamer for the first eight miles upriver to Gorgona or Cruces. Most relied on *bungos,* rough dugout canoes poled by natives.

"Would to God I could describe the scene," wrote Mary Jane Megquier, crossing in 1849. "The birds singing monkeys screeching the Americans laughing and joking the natives grunting as they pushed us along through the rapids was enough to drive one mad with delight."

In 1850, the year Georgiana Bruce crossed, Annie Esther Walton made the trip with three children, including an infant:

> We...reached the rapids at two p.m. Here we ran on a snag, stove a hole in our boat. Of course, I was frightened but the natives carried us all safe to shore. The water was not over three feet deep. Then they hauled our boat up on shore and all the gentlemen put in and mended it. So off we went in a half an hour as good as new. The weather was fine; the scenery beautiful. I never enjoyed anything better in my life.

Villages also offered extraordinary sights. Mrs. Megquier found the church at Gorgona "overrun with domestic animals in time of service, a mule took the liberty to depart this life within its walls while we were there, which was looked upon by the natives [as] of no consequence."

When Jessie Benton Fremont crossed the isthmus, Gorgona's village alcalde invited her to breakfast: "I had a caution given me just in time to prevent my showing my horror at the chief dish, a baked monkey, which looked like a little child that had been burned to death."

From these interior villages, the adventure continued. The road to Panama City, as Emeline Day discovered, all but defied depiction:

> A description...bearing any resemblance to the reality is beyond any feeble powers to give. The road consists of a narrow trace, in many places only wide enough for one packed mule to pass at a time....It has been traveled over by mules until they have worn a track in the earth so deep that the...level was far above our heads, and the track in the earth so narrow we could touch each bank with our hands as we sat on our mules....In places the track down the mountains look like regularly cut stairs and are as perpendicular....For many miles together we traveled where one false step would have precipitated us down over steep and craggy rocks to a distance several hundred feet where no human being could hope to escape alive.

Most travelers rented mules, but the less intrepid dodged this thrill ride by hiring natives to carry them in hammocks. Annie Walton opted for the luxury: "I got along finely until the natives that carried me fell down. That scared me a little."

The road offered multiple excitements, as newspaper journalist Bayard Taylor observed:

> A lady from Maine, who made the journey alone, was obliged to ford a torrent of water above her waist, with a native on each side to prevent her from being carried away. A French lady who crossed was washed from her mule, and only got over by the united exertions of seven men.

Mallie Stafford's attentive husband secured her a "fine large gray mule," and then off they went:

> There was nothing for it but to cling on with all the strength I possessed. As we neared the descent, I noticed the mule pause for a brief second, and to my astonishment, he carefully placed his feet

*"Crossing the Isthmus," a graphic depiction of the trials that awaited travelers through Panama. From Francis Samuel Marryat's* Mountains and Molehills, or Recollections of a Burnt Journal. *Courtesy of The Bancroft Library, University of California, Berkeley (Banc Pic 1963:002:1440:8-A)*

together in a little niche worn in the rock and, giving a spring like a dog, we were down altogether and safe. It gave us a terrible shaking up though....How the fat people on the thin little donkeys, and the timid ladies stood the fearful leap, I leave it for the reader to imagine....Being possessed of the rich heritage of youth, high health, courage and indomitable spirits, I thought little of the inconveniences, annoyances and even dangers to which we were exposed.

The fun never stopped. At Panama City the thrill was in boarding the steamboat in a harbor with no wharf. The procedure caught Sarah Brooks by surprise: "All at once, without a word of warning, I was grabbed from behind. One black arm was around my waist, another under my knees, and I was lifted up and carried straight out into the water. I wanted to scream."

Georgiana Bruce, when her steamship arrived in San Francisco, immediately wrote Eliza. She hoped to see her, she said, before engaging in any occupation. The letter languished at the post office for two months before an acquaintance of Eliza's discovered it and carried it to Santa Cruz. In the meantime, Georgiana accepted a position providing "short meals with a long grace" at a "deplorable washing establishment" where she "ironed shirts, cooked & slept on the kitchen floor for $75 per month."

The eventual receipt of Georgiana's letter at La Libertad created a pandemonium of jubilation. Such joyous tidings! Eliza instantly replied that Georgiana must come to Santa Cruz at once, that by good fortune Tom Russell was then in the city and would bring her down.

The momentous issue of the day, however, for which neither Eliza nor Georgiana left any surviving comment, was California's impending statehood. The fact that California would be admitted to the Union as a free state was, of course, no small matter to these committed abolitionists. But, perhaps like pioneer Walter Colton, they recognized that California's opposition to slavery arose from motives more practical than political. As Colton observed, "All here are diggers, and free white diggers won't dig with slaves....They have nothing to do with slavery in the abstract...not one in ten cares a button for abolition...all they look at is their own position; they must swing the pick, and they won't swing it by the side of negro slaves." In ten years, California's status as a free state would indeed be political, even pivotal. But in 1850, civil war still seemed unthinkable.

Meanwhile, California's admission to the Union, on September 9, 1850, remained unknown to its residents until October 18, when the steamer *Oregon* arrived. The news instantly threw San Francisco into a convulsion of celebration. The rejoicing populace swarmed thoroughfares, crowded saloons, hung bunting from buildings, ran flags of all nations up masts in the harbor, and dragged two large guns into the plaza and discharged them in salute. Throughout the night lights blazed, bands played, fireworks flared.

In Santa Cruz, however, the event of far more immediate consequence at Rancho La Libertad was the imminent arrival of Geordie: "The appellation by which we called her was Georgie; but dear Eddie, whose joy was greatest of all, because Georgie could tell stories and sing, unable to give our sound of it, adopted one of his own, Geordie, which found greater favor."

Once the little household at Santa Cruz knew for certain that Geordie was coming, that Tom was in the very act of bringing her from San Francisco, every day of delay threw Eliza into a fret:

> The arrival of her Majesty at any town in the Irish corner of the realm could not produce greater agitation than our little rancho was thrown into....It would have been an event to know that any good woman was coming into the neighborhood, how much greater, then, to receive a friend into my own house to be of us and not belong anywhere else?...
>
> Every evening, from the roof we cast weary glances in the direction of the mountains, and every night left us to wonder and inquire more impatiently, Why don't they come?

And at last they did, in a pouring rain, the guest wet, chilled, hungry, and laughing. Such a bustle, to provide breakfast and dry clothes. While Eliza and Charlie and Eddie delighted in the arrival, Lucy Sampson, seemingly everywhere at once, hung wet clothes on hooks, fetched dry ones from trunks, poured hot chocolate, sliced bread, kept up the fire in the stove. Of course, there was Georgiana's tale of travel to hear, the long night of troubles with the horses, the darkness of mountain ravines, how she shivered in the wet and trembled in fear all night in expectation of bears, and how very hungry and tired she was.

After breakfast, a short nap was all Eliza allowed Georgiana before sitting on the cot beside her and beseeching her for news:

> There were endless tidings to be heard—as Geordie had left home a year after my departure—of coteries; of societies; of individuals; of late books; of reform movements; of successes and failures; of marriages, births, deaths; of Eastern friends...—in short, of the thousand persons, events, and subjects in whom and which my interest was painfully revived....we ran confusedly over authors, editors, washerwomen, reformers, prisoners, doctors, clergymen, judges, artists, poets, shoemakers, female medical colleges and practitioners...water-cure, spiritual knockings, Swedenborg revelations...the World's Fair...and whatever else we could remember at so short notice, that was new to either—and there had been enough in the five years' experience we had had apart to occupy a good portion of the happy day.

Now the new house must be finished with all possible dispatch, for the household was large and winter coming. And there was the matter of the flour mill to attend to as well. Tom, who claimed himself a millwright, a mechanic, and a farmer—"a 'Jack at all trades' and good at none," in Eliza's unhappy estimation—rented an old mill below the rancho and declared that with some slight repairs and a new dam the poor place could be set to making flour for them all, a laudable improvement over the sour stuff they bought in San Francisco at forty to sixty dollars the barrel.

The renovations proved slow and then questionable and then distressing for, during their hopeful and supposed progression, Miss Sampson and Eliza permitted their small provisions of flour to fall perilously low, then lower. And then, alarmingly, they had none at all:

> The flour-barrel was empty, and Miss Sampson and I in a state of despair. This, however, was nothing novel in our experience; for we were always destitute of something essential to comfortable house-keeping. Either the beef, or the tea, or the sugar, or salt, or molasses, or flour, or butter was out, or the cows staid away, or something we had sent for in time to save ourselves from want was lost in the surf or stolen from the beach.

With all their hopes for bread pinned to the mill, when word arrived that the wheel was in fact finally turning, "the entire population of the rancho rushed with acclamation to behold it," and little Eddie clapped and clapped.

On November 15, Eliza, with spirits lifted by Georgiana's arrival, wrote her friends Orson and Lorenzo Fowler. She apologized for not writing sooner, laying her long silence off to her many vexations and the lawsuits against the *Angelique*'s captain and Ruckel. Now, with despondency behind her, she praised Santa Cruz:

> Already the beautiful green of your June is on our hills and plains. In two months the sunward slopes and sheltered places will be sparkling with gayest flowers and the redundant clover will be piled piled [sic] beneath our feet as cushions of softest verdure. It is a faultless country except that it lacks the delicious influences of showers in Summer.

She even extended a guarded approbation to the local Methodists:

> Their Minister is a self-educated and tolerably intelligent man who studied Phrenology & taught it before he went to College to prepare

for the ministry. His early studies have somewhat counteracted the virulence of theology but he rants occasionally of fire and brimstone.

Mostly she gloried in Georgiana's presence:

> She fills up a great place in my dark world and comes to me like a pleasant breeze or a bright sun after one of our long rains. We are going to be very independent and free here wearing the Albanian Costume and dashing about at our discretion.

And of course, they wanted books, lots of books. Eliza asked the Fowlers to send her their *Water Cure Journal* and their *Phrenological Journal,* several volumes of poetry—Tennyson, Burns, Emerson, Browning—Henry James' *Moralism and Christianity,* Emerson's essays, Carlyle's *Miscellanies,* pamphlets on Swedenborg, "and any works on Psychology you know of that have been lately published. Especially any thing touching the Knocking Spirits which I am exceedingly anxious to hear of."

In December, Eliza and Georgiana focused their combined attention on the new house, where two rooms—partitioned, floored, carpeted, and the walls lined with a calico that Eddie called "a nice rag"—were pronounced, if not finished, at least habitable. Moving commenced that month, and at any hour of any day passersby might have seen Eliza or Georgiana or Charlie struggling up the hill with a basket or a trunk, a few books or dishes, a solitary chair or picture:

> And so we gathered gradually our "plunder" into the "mansion," and the household followed slowly—first Charlie, then Geordie, Eddie, and myself; and last of all, Miss Sampson, who had swept and dusted the old place so many, many times that she felt a real affection for every inch of the black boards, and could, I think, with very little persuasion, have been brought to think it quite comfortable, with a window, a tight floor and roof, and new, fresh walls, which would not have been making, as she insisted, a new house of it; for the same rafters might remain.

So closed 1850, and thus began 1851.

# TEN

# Agricultural Operations

To the struggling advocates of Woman's Rights, it may seem a hopeful sign of the times that one of their own sex should put forth a book claiming to be in any degree descriptive of farming, especially when they make the delightful discovery that the writer speaks in a great measure from personal experience in the business. But it must not be forgotten that life in California is altogether anomalous, and that it is no more extraordinary for a woman to plough, dig, and hoe with her own hands...than for men to do all their household labor for months.

—Eliza Farnham, *California, In-Doors and Out*, 1856

In Santa Cruz the winter of 1850–51 hardly seemed winter at all. There would be a day or two of rain and then weeks of bright, sunny weather, so conducive to making plans. "As the winter wore on, and the season of planting approached," wrote Eliza, "Geordie and I having concluded to enter upon 'agricultural operations' for the year, began to consider what were the first steps to be taken."

A neighbor had planted potatoes the previous season on three acres he leased from the landowner in return for 25 percent of the proceeds. In the fall he had paid out a thousand dollars and pocketed three thousand.

Persuaded that potatoes offered the best chance for a good return, Eliza decided to put in ten acres of them. Using the abandoned shanty for a staging area, she and Geordie cut the seed:

> Day after day we sat in the dark, dirty place, over this disagreeable pile, with hands muffled in old gloves or new gloves, white rags or colored ones, just as chance permitted, but always the same hands....When a day came for planting, we rejoiced to rush out into the open fields, and, with basket on arm, or sack suspended by a strap over the shoulder, march up and down the furrows, laborious though it was.

Geordie and I always made a procession in getting off to any distance—she invariably falling some six or eight steps behind with her spade, hoe, or whatever it might be, swinging as a walking stick; and there was always about her, in these walks, a plodding, matter-of-fact air that irresistibly amused me, when, as it often happened, I was compelled to turn back to address her. In her air, look, and manner, there was something that seemed to suggest that it was a very old business with her, and that she was mentally comparing the prospects of this year with those of some cold, or hot, or wet, or dry season, of years ago.

Another promising crop was wheat, and the winter being so mild that year, Tom completed the sowing of more than twelve acres before the first of February. Georgiana and Eliza repaired fences, dug irrigation ditches, superintended the flour mill, and occasionally took a turn at the plow. They planted, besides the potatoes, various vegetable seeds—many of them twice:

> most of the seed having either failed altogether, or been so very slow in coming that one or two subsequent crops were put in the same beds, so that when they did appear, we had parsnips, carrots, and onions growing on the same ground, and not enough of all to make one crop. But this sort of discouragement did not fully overtake us till we had somewhat exhausted the novelty of our new calling, which was not nearly so soon as would have been supposed.

They set grapevines with the help of "gentlemen of leisure in the neighborhood." Eliza sent to New York for fruit trees, trusting, unwisely, the promises of the express company for their prompt transit across the isthmus. A neighbor advised that his orchard of pears and olives had prolifically produced, in addition to fruit, young trees the women could have free for the digging. Enthusiastically, Eliza and Georgiana set out after a spring rain, attired in the bloomer-like outfits so appropriate for such work:

> We had never before left the farm in costume and red top boots, but it was so wet now that it was idle to think of going, and on such an errand, in any other garb. We had but two houses to pass, and could enter the orchard from the rear, so if a few persons did see the elephant out of his cage, we did not care.

Tom accompanied them, carrying spade and ropes, and while he was digging up the trees destined for transplanting, the women discovered some prickly pear cactus they thought would be good to take as well. Accordingly, Tom, appointed to carry the cactus, consigned to Eliza and Georgiana the burden of the young pear and olive trees, which he tied to a pole the two women could carry, one of them fore, one aft, the trees slung between them. Eliza found the outing marvelously amusing:

> Tom staggered off under a mountain of the thorny cactus, to which his frieze coat proved but an indifferent armor. Many a hearty, but, I fear, heartless, laugh had I, toiling along, with Geordie plodding gravely at the other end of the pole, at sight of the wriggling and shifting by which I knew he was seeking to displace one thorn at the hazard of inserting half a dozen others in fresh places....We passed a young lady from Missouri on the road...who was struck into a state of such profound astonishment at sight of the procession....The intenseness, the utter abandon of her stare, I never saw equaled.

Eliza wanted the cactus for a living fence, an idea better in the imagined stage:

> Geordie and I set the trees and cactus, the thorns of which, perforating our boots and gloves, so annoyed us that before they were half planted, we abandoned the half mile of hedge we were at first resolved upon setting along the stream, and voted them ugly and undesirable.

A larger disappointment was the fruit trees so confidently and expensively ordered from New York. They arrived, to Eliza's great distress, dead as "Mr. Scrooge's partner":

> Geordie and I lamented and groaned over them, knife in hand, cutting carefully here and there, to see if, by chance, any lingering sign of life might be discovered, and denouncing the Express people, whose extraordinary pretensions to punctuality had beguiled me to entrust so perishable and invaluable a charge to their care.

The women planted the trees anyway, in a choice spot near the grapevines. For three months of declining hope they watched the dead trees for signs of resurrection, after which they spoke of them only "in some despairing moment."

And then there was the "insufferable nuisance" of wild mustard:

> It began to appear among our wheat when it was from six to fourteen inches high, and gave us incredible toil in the removing.

Geordie and I first attacked it in the strong confidence of inexperi-ence....This was very severe labor—more so than digging, if that were possible. I failed at it first, and was obliged to leave the field to Geordie and the Indian—a soft-spoken, persuasive old fellow, who, if left alone, would stand erect by the half hour watching the black-birds, the clouds, the plows, the Mission—anything that he could make himself believe was worth his attention, and he would bestow it very cheaply.

When the mustard defeated both the Indian and Geordie, the women surrendered their independence to feminine wiles. They would host a mustard-eradication bee:

So notes were sent out to some eight or ten gentlemen, informing them of our forlorn condition, and appealing to their humanity to aid us. They all presented themselves on the appointed day, and, notwithstanding that a smart shower drove us in some half hour too early, we overturned a great many sturdy enemies during the after-noon. And yet, a great deal was left for us to do, and we had many a weary day in the great field before we gave up hope of exterminat-ing the hateful weed.

But the exhaustion that nature exacted, it also repaid:

When weariness overtook us, the earth was beneath for a bed, and the warm, bright sky above for a canopy. Life looked a curious spec-tacle from those quiet points of view. One or two plows moving slowly in the distance, followed by scores of white sea-gulls, gathering the worms it unhoused; hundreds of blackbirds wheeling and chatter-ing just above us; and, higher up in the still and sanctified blue, a buzzard, lying lazily upon his outspread wings; [these] were objects that rather aided than interrupted the wondering retrospect one could not but fall into at such times.

How far away, even unreal, seemed the life they had led, and left behind, in New York:

Were cities, with their din and clamor, a dream; or had we, indeed, been at some time atoms in the great mass we now dimly remem-bered as heaving and surging in its eternal restlessness? Were there really such things as railroad cars and steamboats, whirling men and women along their accustomed ways, as the wind does the dry leaves of autumn? Could it be possible that hurry and confusion were still anywhere on the earth that was so full of repose about us; possible that people were anywhere swallowing hurried, leaden meals, and rushing off to narrow counting-rooms or noisy manufactories, with no blessed earth to stretch their weary limbs upon, nor blue heaven to pour serenity into their souls, nor birds, nor sighing winds, nor chime of sea to drive the din of the stirring world from their ears? One could easily forget that one had ever been an undistinguished grain on that great shifting sand-mountain....World's fairs and conventions, reform meetings, political agitations, even Hungarian revolutions, seen at this distance through so quiet a medium, seemed too exciting to be conducive to life. We grew large in that calm state, and seemed able to look back upon those yet remaining out of it with a sort of "poor-things" sentiment.

Occasionally, for a respite, Georgiana and Eliza rode unescorted into the countryside, exploring the valleys and hillsides—and their respective views of things:

> The rights and position of woman were a theme of endless talk—Geordie standing upon the platform of the Worcester Convention, and I upon one of my own, the limits of which, at some points, lay considerably within hers. She always insisted that my theory and practice were at war on this question, as I actually did many of the things which her party demanded freedom to do, and yet would not subscribe to their demands. It was in vain I protested that necessity prescribed my practice, and only reason, taste, and conscience my theory. I was scarcely credited with honesty in this matter, there was so formidable [an] array of suspicious circumstances against me.

Unlike the meeting at Seneca Falls in 1848, the Worcester Convention of 1850 passed resolutions linking the struggle for women's rights with the struggle for racial justice, and thus embraced Georgiana's beliefs completely. Eliza fully supported abolitionism but not the women's plea for the very rights she so impressively personified: economic independence, property ownership, governance over one's children.

Eliza Farnham's views were well known. In 1843 she had debated one of the great supporters of women's rights, John Neal, editor of the *Brother Jonathan*, in the pages of his magazine. At that time she argued that woman's position was different, neither inferior nor equal, just different. Eventually she would declare herself opposed to the fight for equality because she believed profoundly that woman was not man's equal, but his superior.

Meanwhile, Eliza continued the debate with Georgiana, in conversations prized for their "natural frankness."

> In our lives there had been sadness and struggle enough—as in what earnest life is there not?—to give us a keen and abiding interest in human happiness, events enough to give character to our experience, and enough of triumph and failure to make the basis of our respective theories, which in many points differed so essentially as to give rise to prolonged and animated discussion.

They discussed Spiritualism at length, and that spring Georgiana wrote Charlotte Wells, the Fowlers' sister, to again invite news of the latest Spiritualist intelligence.

> Many times the conversation I had with you...the hour before I sailed for Cal. has recurred to me & I have wished that *we here* might be partakers in the experience that is arousing faith in the most stubborn materialists. If you have communication with those who have put off the natural body will you not enquire if the same be not possible to us at Santa Cruz & if you have not will you express our earnest wishes to this effect to some one who has. Our motives are good & reasonable in desiring this as the spirits will attest. It grows out of no idle curiosity for both Mrs. F & myself are firm believers & do not stand in need of evidence but we want religious teaching advice & consolation in our exile.

It was a long, chatty letter:

> As for me I am in excellent health & spirits &, notwithstanding that I do not think transplanting onions to be fancy work I intend to brave it out & shall remain in Santa Cruz for some years certainly. I have never regretted coming...& now that I luxuriate in the unparalled [sic] freedom of turkish pants & tunic with frequent rides on horseback—not forgetting the onions, regret would be equivalent to apostasy. By the way it is my belief that this modification of the Turkish & Albanian dress which Mrs. F & I find so convenient will eventually become the fashion here for you see we are amenable to no vulgar public opinion &—I say it with all due modesty—we are *the* people of the place—live more like civilized beings than any one else & if any thing worthy does come to S.C. it comes to our house. There is one other woman & only one who is not a wooden spoon...& she has engaged me to fix her some dresses & her husband has always wished her to dress so. After six months freedom from petticoats you will permit me to say that you dont know what you suffer.

Late in May, Georgiana and Eliza, sans petticoats, planned to ride up the coast on horseback to dig wild strawberries for transplanting into the garden, an expedition long anticipated. During the wearying months of exhausting labor, cutting and planting potatoes, and weeding mustard, they would "borrow encouragement" by imagining the excursion. They intended a three-day outing, camping two nights.

And with so many gentlemen of leisure in Santa Cruz, why make such a journey alone?

# ELEVEN

# A Last Holiday

Mr. R. C. Kirby, who, since 1850, has been extensively engaged in the manufacture of leather in Santa Cruz, was born in 1817, in Staffordshire, England. Having served a seven years' apprenticeship to the business in Dudley, he left England in 1842 to try his fortunes in the United States.
—W. W. Elliott, *Santa Cruz County, Calif., with Historical Sketch,* 1879

**G**eorgiana, while crossing the isthmus, had slept outside on the ground, so camping was no novelty for her. Eliza never had and consequently anticipated the holiday all the more. She must, of course, take books for campfire reading. She packed a book satchel with both informative and entertaining selections, including an essay on the church by Unitarian minister William Ellery Channing, well known to Georgiana from their mutual association at Brook Farm; and for lighter fare, Douglas Jerrold's *The Chronicles of Clovernook; with some account of The Hermit of Bellyfulle.* Lucy Sampson packed food for the women to take: ham, bread, butter, cakes, nuts, raisins, brandy-peaches, and last but not least, Dombey and Toots, formerly feathered friends, but now roasted and carved and put into jars.

For escorts the women had the assistance and attention of the local tanner, Richard Kirby, and his friend, identified only as "Mr. G" by Eliza, who observed him to be "in very delicate health, and wholly unused to sleeping on the ground." The four adventurers set off in good order, provisions and camp furniture on an extra horse, and everyone well mounted—except Eliza. Having lost her own saddle sometime previously on a runaway horse that returned without it, she was compelled by necessity to borrow one for the outing. And the loaned saddle simply wouldn't do:

> I was not at all suited with it. It was a Spanish, or California side-saddle, made for the rider to sit facing the right hand—the fashion of all the native women....and I was told that it could be ridden nearly as well on one side as the other.

But the experience of the first fifty rods contradicted this assurance. It was impossible for me to ride off a walk with any dignity; and as I considered myself responsible for a certain style, I protested the sacrifice of my pretensions to any such mean necessity, and insisted upon being properly equipped before we left "the settlements."

So, about four miles from their start, they stopped and borrowed an American saddle for her. Then the gait of her horse was a problem, so Richard Kirby exchanged her horse for his:

He was a frisky, dashing-looking fellow, with easy gaits and a kindly spirit; but before we had gone far, after remounting, it was perceptible that the saddle did not fit his back. Thus there was another (a third) dismounting and remounting, at which Geordie, looking comfortably on from her reliable old roan, laughed triumphantly.

At last, with Eliza's horse properly saddled and she satisfied, they were off in earnest. Some ten miles up the coast they came upon the last habitation for the next forty miles. The owner treated them all to a pitcher of milk and gave them radishes and turnips to take, along with the disheartening advice that strawberries were scarce that year. But the foursome remained undeterred, "fully resolved upon taking our full holiday, whether we found any or not."

The sightseeing was worth it. On their left lay the vast Pacific, a "bold coast," in Eliza's estimation:

The great variety of forms made in its outline by the gaps, fissures, arches, and broad gateways, through which the rocks admit the surf, and about which, on the detached fragments and great bases that project from them, the tremendous seals congregate for their sports and social shore-parties, make the seaward view sufficiently diversified and interesting.

And on their right, the hillsides literally bloomed with color:

The hills that swell into very considerable heights offer you smooth curves and slopes of exquisite beauty, sometimes covered, and again richly flecked with golden, purple, scarlet, and pink flowers; among which the yellow lupin—a very beautiful shrub of large size—the low purple and white lupin, the mallows of bright pink and rose color, and a flaunting euchroma, twin brother to my old friend of the prairies, abound. Innumerable smaller flowers, of almost every imaginable color, lie below these showy dwellers of the plain, and shade the bright hues more softly.

*Coast view from the Cliff Drive, Santa Cruz, by Carleton E. Watkins.
During a rare holiday outing, Eliza and Georgiana visited this "bold coast,"
as Eliza described it, with its "great variety of forms made in its outline by
the gaps, fissures, arches, and broad gateways through which the rocks admit
the surf." Courtesy of the Phoebe Apperson Hearst Museum of Anthropology
and the Regents of the University of California (13-1306m)*

They rode north with the wind in their faces, to the sound of
the sea beating against the rocky shore. It was glorious. But the
delayed start, the visit for milk and advice, and the occasional
stops to watch the seals soon wore away the day. At four o'clock
they came upon a tiny valley facing the sea, luxuriantly carpeted
in wild oats, dramatically sheltered by eighty-foot cliffs—a perfect
place to camp. They christened it Oatnook.

In half an hour the men had the horses staked, a fire blazing,
and blankets spread. Eliza and Georgiana decided on chicken
for supper:

Mr. Toots was accordingly produced, and portions of him served
on the small tin plates, which constituted the chief part of our

dinner-service; but he had fared so hardly in life—having been the fag of the entire poultry-yard, and the unhappy recipient of so much (fowl) treatment—that, after the first few morsels, the flavor was voted bilious, and the ham taken in his stead.

This was really nice; and as we sat about the warm, bright fire, and saw the chill mist driving over the hills before us, and heard the surf madly chafing at the foot of the rocks, we felt much of the cosy comfort of home.

After supper, to shield the women from the night chill, wind, and fog, the men built a makeshift protection from tree boughs and blankets. There, sheltered and warm, the four of them gathered, and Eliza read from *The Chronicles of Clovernook*:

The hills resounded to the shouts of laughter, and the seals on the rocks responded in an occasional bellow, as if the Land of Turveytop were a familiar country to them....We read till a late hour; then we talked till a later one, inspired by the incomparable book—by the novelty of our situation—by the stern majesty of the darkness which brooded over us, and let loose the wings of thought, and unsealed the fountains of memory—so that the life of the past seemed to have compressed itself into those hours.

After the men retired from the shelter, Geordie slept soundly through the night while Eliza endured her chronic insomnia. During the long night, doubtless due to the conversation, her thoughts flew to her early years:

My whole past life surrounded me. The earliest recollections of those years...rose as vividly before me as if they were not memories but passing realities.

The hopes, the triumphs, the disappointments of each successive period arranged themselves there....I have heard many persons... express the painful want of satisfaction with which they reviewed their early successes. To me, such expression seems tantamount to a confession that their early ambition was false, their pursuits unworthy, and their triumphs, therefore, vain, ephemeral, and unproductive of good to their after lives.

Childhood is so inestimably blest, where nature is its nursing mother. My early hopes had been inspired by her; my victories gained at her bidding; and I thanked the great Father devoutly, as I lay there in the silence, that I scarcely could recall one which had not made me a happier child, a better girl, a more earnest woman.

It's a generous appraisal of a childhood tormented by a step-mother who cruelly abused her, a childhood surrendered to servitude on a remote dairy farm. Yet life there had not been without its pleasures, possessed as it was of secret places for a lonely, unloved child, trees to hide in and bowers tucked away near streams, and all the wonders of changing seasons to awe and delight. Little Eliza, charged with care of the poultry, and with no person to love, loved the tiny chicks and ducklings, but she loved nature best of all.

It was recollection of nature that stirred her thoughts that night, in the place she and her friends named Oatnook, to pleasant remembrances of a childhood otherwise barren of happiness. Perhaps it was that night, awake in the dark, listening to the surf, remembering hidden copses and maple trees, that Eliza decided to write her childhood autobiography, a book she would dedicate, in 1859, with heartfelt devotion to "G.B.K."—despite, or perhaps because of, their painful estrangement of 1853.

But for now, on a holiday excursion in search of wild strawberries, on a June morning in 1851, when Eliza rose from her sleepless bed and Georgiana woke refreshed, each was still the other's best friend.

The morning remained foggy while the travelers washed at the spring, ate breakfast, converted the sleeping arrangements to sitting ones, cleaned and stowed away the dishes, and packed their provisions. To while away another hour as the mist slowly cleared, Eliza read again from the book that had amused them so much the night before. Then, at last, blue sky and fleecy clouds, and "an irrepressible desire for movement" saw them "unanimously and swiftly" off from Oatnook:

> The horses were as impatient as ourselves, and when we had reached the sandy tract over the hills and descended to the beach about a mile from our camp, they literally flew along the hard sand. The delicious breeze, the great surf rolling in and dashing its spray among their feet seemed to inspire them, as it did us, with overflowing life. We scarcely broke a gallop for five miles.

After riding along the beach, they ascended into the hills and eventually came upon a knoll covered with wild strawberries:

> We all alighted, and several handsful were gathered, some of which were ripe, and large enough to give us a correct notion of their

quality...very like the garden strawberry of Chile. The fruit is firmer, and more deliciously flavored than those we have in the old states; and, when full grown, three or four times larger than the largest there.

And then it was time to set up camp again. In looking for a sheltered site, they came upon the remains of freshly slaughtered beef left behind by Californios headed home from the large grazing ranchos of these hillsides. Richard Kirby sliced their dinner from a fine quarter and that evening roasted it upon a stick over the fire. Eliza thought the meat delicious and the simple preparation admirable: "How it shamed the elaborate arts of French cookery! It is the trapper dish. I recommend it to the attention of epicures."

Richard Kirby could have known how trappers cooked only by a passing association; he never claimed such an occupation as his own. After he arrived in America from his native England at the age of twenty-four, his chief employment was whaling, a business not particularly to his liking. When opportunity presented itself off the coast of Oregon, he and five others abandoned the enterprise in a stolen whaling boat. A storm caught them unprepared and three men drowned. Kirby and two others, only by good fortune, reached shore and helpful Indians.

For a time he tanned leather in Astoria, and then, in the spring of 1846, he traveled south to California. It was a five weeks' trip partly in company with a number of French Canadians, quite likely trappers, and it was probably then that he learned to cook over a fire. In California, Kirby briefly worked for Captain Sutter at his fort on the Sacramento river, dressing out leather for saddles from hides the Indians had tanned.

Afterwards, Kirby had his own tannery in San Francisco, a primitive affair he relinquished when invited to Santa Cruz to tan leather on Joseph Majors' ranch. And that was where he was when news of the gold discovery reached the coast. His was a story not much different from other men's, and he was willing to tell it:

> I at once prepared to leave for the mines...by way of the San Joaquin to Mormon Island, at which place I found many acquaintances. In three weeks I made $3,000; then I returned to Sutter's Fort, the great trading point, and laid in a stock of dry goods for trade with the Indians in the diggings.

Having quadrupled my means, I returned with it to San Francisco for the winter, enjoying whatever there was there of enjoyment for money to purchase.

In the spring of 1849, I started with a few others on a trading expedition to the Southern "diggings." On arriving with our boat at Stockton, we were persuaded to sell out our stock on favorable terms to a company.

We now went...to Mormon Gulch, near Wood's Diggings. On Monday morning, my partner and myself went to work and on Wednesday evening had 11 1/2 lbs. of gold for our pains.

We left this place for the Merced diggings, where we...remained ...till fall, when we again returned to San Francisco. There I was persuaded to invest my easily earned thousands in a most uncertain and hazardous undertaking.

And so it was that, in the fall of 1850, poorer but wiser in consequence of this risky investment not further elaborated upon, Richard Kirby determined to set up as a tanner in Santa Cruz and now found himself on a strawberry-hunting excursion, roasting beef over an open fire for the two remarkable women of Rancho La Libertad.

From the little cove by the beach where they had elected to pass the night, the adventurers collected driftwood and from it built another blanket shelter, which they christened "Strawberry cottage" on the strength of "expectations." After dinner they gathered around a fire while Eliza again read to them, this time from Channing's essay on the church:

> The reading, and running comments, occupied us until ten o'clock, when we retired, agreeing upon an early stroll in the morning, on the beach. There were no seals that night, or if there were, my sleep was too deep to be interrupted by them.

They rose late, replenished the fire, breakfasted, strolled on the beach, read some more, and laughed some more:

> And then we betook ourselves to the strawberry beds, with a deep, precious sense of the rare freedom of coming and going at will, of lounging, sitting, reading, eating, riding or walking, at the bidding purely of our pleasure, for another whole day.

They collected strawberries and seashells, read poetry, and passed another day enjoying the pleasures of their special excursion.

That evening, however, they sat somberly about the campfire:

> We were not gay; for the happiness we had anticipated was now a memory, and we discoursed as people always do who are secretly unwilling to confess that there is less to be expected than has already been enjoyed.

For Eliza, the feeling applied not just to the day, or even the excursion. The sentiment, as she may have suspected when she expressed it, seemed to encompass her life. Less happiness and fewer expectations lay ahead, in the years left to her—much less than what she had already enjoyed.

The next morning, at about ten o'clock, with strawberries and seashells safely packed, and the startling discovery made that they had only radishes and butter to eat on the road home, the excursionists mounted their horses and set off in higher spirits than the night before. They stopped first to collect more of the beef the Californios had left behind, and then at Oatnook, their first campsite, to look for a brooch Georgiana thought she had left there—"in the scattering frame of mind common to her," observed Eliza. They stopped again at two o'clock, for a last dinner of roasted beef, and a little past sunset, arrived back at Eliza's unfinished house.

In their absence, the shanty where Eliza and her boys and Lucy Sampson had first made a home in Santa Cruz had caught fire and burned to the ground.

The holiday marked the end of an era—in more ways than one.

# TWELVE

# Observations

In the accessions the state is constantly receiving to its female population, and better classes of its male inhabitants, in the multiplication of its homes, its churches, its schools, its temperance and other benevolent organizations; in its more settled basis of trade; in its institutions...for the cultivation of science and literature; in its more respectable judicature; in its less shameful legislation, may be seen the dawn of hope over its hitherto darkened history.

—Eliza Farnham, *California, In-Doors and Out*

In the summer of 1851, Eliza Farnham started writing a book about her California experiences from the journal she kept. Whether she had always planned to write such a book, or whether she did so from need of the money it would bring, *California, In-Doors and Out,* published in 1856, distinguished itself as the first book about California written by a woman.

As Eliza began writing, she filled chapter after chapter with vivid depictions of her daily life in California—the surf-tossed arrival at Santa Cruz in February 1850; assembling the recalcitrant stove; the first planting on her farm, with borrowed stock pulling her plow; chasing cattle from the fields; the trips to San Francisco; dressing as a boy to capture a wild cow; building a house in her gymnastics costume; Georgiana's arrival; battling mustard; transplanting cactus; gathering wild strawberries.

After the account of the strawberry excursion, lively descriptions of personal experience cease. Readers do not hear again about the pig christened Susannah the Second or chickens named for Dickens characters. There is nothing more about planting potatoes or attending anniversary celebrations at the mission. Or building houses. Not even Lucy Sampson and the boys. Nor Geordie.

Mrs. Farnham's abrupt abandonment of her entertaining recitations of private experience occurs just over halfway in her book. The remainder of her volume she filled with observations on life in California—not her life, but California life in general. She discusses the climate; she describes the travails of emigration to California by sea and by land; she laments the country's demoralizing influences on women and children; she proclaims the superiority of women; she opines on the characteristics of emigrants, particularly their shortcomings:

> There appears to have been a prominent class of emigrants, from a region that has become famous throughout our country—Pike county, to wit. It would seem that the people of this celebrated region could not...have mixed very largely with the world; for they were so little smoothed down in the great human mangle, and shortly became so marked, that Pike county superseded the name of its state, and soon of the whole West. To be catalogued as from Pike county seems to express to all that large class of Americans who are neither Yankees nor Missourians; a little more churlishness, a little more rudeness, a greater reserve when courtesy or hospitality are called for....Pike County, in short, is not likely to derive from the settlement of California a reputation as the cradle of the graces, the amenities, or the liberalities of life. Nor, indeed, considering the degeneracy of more cultivated people, could it be expected.

In the second half of her book about California, Mrs. Farnham extols, at length, the virtues of women, their value to a California society so needful of kindly female influence. She laments the vices of gaming and drinking and swearing, and general social and public immorality. She applauds the formation, in 1851, of San Francisco's Vigilance Committee. And perhaps from having enjoyed the justly famous hospitality of Californios, she waxes poetic over the life they led before the gold discovery:

> Where was ever a people so steeped in contentment, as that which was found here?...How they luxuriated in the ease of their abundance! How they reposed on the generous soil whose redundant energies sprang to their coarse husbandry with a profusion scarcely equaled in any other clime....With what a pleasing, but unlaborious joy we may imagine them hailing the rare arrivals of the trading-vessels that visited their coast! Their herds multiplied without care....Their horses were fleet, and so numerous....Their quarrels were not mercenary, for they were surrounded by plenty, and a hospitable table awaited them in every house....But now, how are all these aspects of their lives changed!

She cites statistics on San Francisco: population figures; the costs to merchants from recurring fires; the numbers of churches and schools and theaters; and school enrollments. She lists the names of newspapers.

Some of her observations are not without interest. For the unacquainted, she describes the city's gambling establishments:

Every variety of face, clothed with every possible expression, from the most stolid indifference to the keenest excitement, surrounded one in those glaring rooms. Every garb, from fine broadcloth and showy linen, to the dirtiest and coarsest habiliments worn by miners and wagoners, was there intermixed.

In one corner, a coarse-looking female might preside over a roulette-table, and, perhaps, in the central and crowded part of the room a Spanish or Mexican woman would be sitting at monte, with a cigarita in her lips, which she replaced every few moments by a fresh one. In a very few fortunate houses, neat, delicate, and sometimes beautiful French women were every evening to be seen in the orchestra. These houses, to the honor of the coarse crowd be it said, were always filled!

Curious and striking scenes were at times enacted in these places. A rough-looking, bearded man, with slouched hat, from the mines, might enter with one, or may be two, considerable leathern sacks filled with gold. He would walk up to the heaviest laden table, and throwing down his burden, boldly say, "I'll tap your bank." This was explained to be equivalent to saying, "I will stake the whole of my treasure against your money." And in five minutes thousands of dollars changed hands. I am told that California gaming is distinguished from the same vice in any other part of the world by the...perfect coolness with which both the winning and the losing party took his fate. Certainly I never saw cooler faces than were many of those who, at the instant I was studying their features, were receiving or paying over hundreds or thousands of dollars, lost or won in as little time as it would take to count it; and this is very quickly done by measuring the piles of coin instead of counting each one.

As travel guide, Mrs. Farnham offers information on what to do and what to see: "The chief recreation of our state is the equestrian exercise which we take from our Spanish predecessors. It is much practiced by the citizens of San Francisco."

Interested readers are advised that near Mission Dolores, on Sundays, bull-and-bear fights may be witnessed, and refreshment taken close by:

*"Every variety of face, clothed with every possible expression," Mrs. Farnham wrote of California gambling halls, "from the most stolid indifference to the keenest excitement, surrounded one in those glaring rooms. Every garb, from fine broadcloth and showy linen to the dirtiest and coarsest habiliments worn by miners and wagoners, was there intermixed." "Interior of the El Dorado" from* Annals of San Francisco *by Frank Soulé et al.,* 1855

Drinking shops present a lively appearance of business which ought to be very gratifying to their proprietors, since it is painfully the reverse of this to sober travelers and persons who love to see industry, order, and thrift characterize a community.

For those with more refined tastes, she recommends the theater:

The population of San Francisco has been more liberally provided with dramatic and musical entertainments than that of any other city of its size in America. Notwithstanding its remoteness from the old states, and its isolation from any thickly-peopled country, it has had, since the city was a year old, from one to three theatres open continually, and however their performances may be marred by the occasional appearance of a stick where a living man or woman should be, there are generally clever persons enough on the boards to keep the entertainments, at the worst, up to decent mediocrity.

Of course, no visit to California was complete without a tour of the mines. For the armchair traveler, Mrs. Farnham obliges by describing the terrain of the gold-digging regions as well as mining methods and implements, and she tours the reader through a typical mining camp, with a warning about the steep descent of the hills:

> You scramble down them, in the best way you can. Sometimes you feel as if your horse were about to turn a summerset, but you push back as forcibly as possible, by way of helping him to preserve the centre of gravity, and, with an occasional halt and then a rush—a detour to the right and another to the left—a fearful looking forward, and an anxious glance backward, you finally reach the bottom...and ascertain that, deep down as you are, there have been plenty before you; that Mary Avery keeps a boarding-house for miners on your right, and that Patrick Doyle has the best of wines and liquors for your refreshment in his shanty or tent, on your left; that John Smith, honest man, is a carpenter and no swindler, as he has so often been represented to be in the wicked world you have left up yonder...that the National, or the United States, or the American hotel is kept in that rough one-story hut, which, as you pass, discloses dismal rents in its cotton walls and ceilings, and allures the thirsty wayfarer by a display of a bar, bristling with bottles—and that at the El Dorado or Pavilion are billiards and bowling.

It is in this detached second-person voice that Eliza relates her trip to the mines. There is in the telling none of the exuberance and vibrancy that characterize previous depictions of her adventures. In adopting the second-person point of view, by writing "you" and not "I," she might be telling secondhand someone else's trip, so disconnected is she from the events she describes. She permits, in recounting her trip to the mines, only a rare lapse into the first person, the briefest reference to her own experiences and perceptions:

> In entering the mining country, one of the first features of it that arrested my attention was that there appeared to have been a vast deal of labor wasted in turning over ground that had yielded nothing.

I was often, for the first several miles, as we rode along beneath the summer sun, saying mentally, poor fellows, how many a weary day has been spent here, without reward, and I enjoyed afterwards not a little amusement (which was also mental) at my own simplicity, when I was reminded that these very diggings had, perhaps, abounded in gold, which might at that moment be circulating in Wall street....I did not remember that the earth would not resume her original aspect, after the loss of her treasure, and that my grandchildren might walk over the ground I was then upon, before it should cease to be vexed with the gold-hunters' implements.

...I washed one panful of earth, under a burning noon-day sun, in a cloth riding-habit, and must frankly confess that the small particle of gold, which lies this day safely folded in a bit of tissue paper, though it is visible to the naked eye, did not in the least excite the desire to continue the search.

There is in this account a suspicious lack of affect from a woman previously given to such spirited reports. Where once her laughter rang against the hills, now there is only a silent, mental amusement at her own naiveté. Where once she described her companions, now she doesn't even mention whether she has one. The color has gone out of her descriptions, the life out of her writing, and clearly, the light out of her eye.

Obviously, something happened to her. Something in 1852, the year Eliza never mentions, changed everything. Eliza never provides a clue to what it was, never tells.

But her son Charles does. And so does Georgiana.

# THIRTEEN

# March 23, 1852

There is much belonging to the relation of marriage beside the love which should precede its existence; but when that is confessed, both parties are too apt, I think, to hurry over all other considerations, and assume positions, which, neither of them having fully weighed and estimated, may, for that reason, become sources of pain and disappointment, instead of happiness and fruition.

—Eliza Farnham

[My mother] married as her second husband, William Fitzpatrick...an Irish engineer, who was one of the four men who rescued Louis Napoleon, afterwards Napoleon III, from the fortress at Ham. He was cultivated and gentle and delightful, when sober. But...a fiend when drunk.

—Charles Haight Farnham

**G**eorgiana had troubles of her own. She possessed expectations. When she had first come to live with Eliza at Santa Cruz, she had intended to open a school for girls, to do what she loved best to do and was best qualified to do: teach. And there were girls there to be taught. Santa Cruz had been settled by families, not by gold hunters—families that emigrated west before the gold discovery, seeking not wealth but opportunity. They had established homes and made a community. They were the Hecoxes, Imuses, Bennetts, Hollenbecks, Anthonys, Moores, Sawins, Meaders, and Cases. Georgiana came to know them all:

There were many girls belonging to these western families of sufficient promise to interest me in them. I could and desired to not only instruct them in books but in their personal habits of cleanliness, neatness, order, courtesy, how to make and mend clothes and so forth.

But she was a latecomer to the scene, and a mixed school was already in progress, taught by a Methodist, a Mr. H. S. Loveland— in Georgiana's opinion, a "pious young villain" who eventually "seduced some of the young girls and had to leave in the night."

And there were other obstacles to Georgiana's hope to teach at Santa Cruz:

> The regular local minister, Mr. Brier, a self-conceited, brawling brute, without a spark of tenderness, used all his influence against me in this, and, added to the unpopularity of Mrs. Farnham, at whose house I was staying, rendered the entire plan abortive.

Possibly Georgiana earned her own unpopularity with the Methodists. Her opinions about God and religion lay far afield from their camp:

> I have the most intimate sympathy with the views advanced by Henry James....How heartily I agree with him in his contempt for the teachings of the modern church, mean, cringing, self-blaspheming. I am happy in remembering that notwithstanding the soul-searching religious experience I went through in my youth—lasting indeed through years, I never for one moment believed God regarded me in any other light than a friendly one. I never knew what remorse meant. I never believed that God would bless me for Christ's sake....
> I was interested always in theological questions and yet theology would by no means cling to me, God be thanked, for it was all false and would have made me less loving and less intelligent than I am.

So, with the Methodists running the school, Georgiana Bruce settled for "agricultural operations" with Eliza; instead of planting ideas in young girls' heads, she had planted onions and potatoes in the fields of La Libertad. And that hadn't worked out either:

> The soil proved too sandy for onions. Russell, Mrs. F's farmer, who had induced me to leave San F. by a series of lies about Mrs. Farnham's wealth and what she would give me, failed afterward to help me in any gardening as he promised. He managed so badly that after dropping 10 acres of potatoes the estate was so much in debt....For more than a year I did not make one cent.

That was 1851. When prospects for 1852 appeared no better, Georgiana left Rancho La Libertad:

> I had grown old in fretting about Mrs. Farnham's troubles and per-plexities. She was so ignorant of business, so careless, so easily imposed on, and at the same time so determined to get so much under weigh at once that she was constantly in debt or in hot water somehow....she took Russell, an Irishman without self-respect, without system, without knowledge of how to treat or deal with men and

with no idea of straight-forwardness, of speaking the truth—simply a skillful and industrious worker, and trusted to him management of her farm.

In hope of a better opportunity, Georgiana went down to the Pajaro Valley, a promising agricultural area located between Monterey Bay and the coastal range. James Bryant Hill, an old acquaintance from Brook Farm, had just leased two thousand acres of this prime property, and he needed a housekeeper:

> He was the first American that settled there and I remained there six months in a house without a chair or bedstead or table (with the exception of the boards on tressels that we and the men ate off). For three months we had no windows, the light came through the door which was left open, no looking glass, no flat irons. I ironed the bosoms and collars of two white shirts with a half-pint, tin tumbler kept constantly full of boiling water. I worked very hard indeed. My only comfort was a game of whist after eight o'clock with Mrs. Thrift, a young New England woman who had married an illiterate young Southerner....She was avowedly an abolitionist and I respected her for this and hoped to find in her a companion and friend, but I found her selfish in the extreme, without a shadow of aspiration, self-willed and wholly wanting in the common traits of New England women— judgement, skill in the various domestic departments, economy and so forth. I was very sorry to give her up but she obliged me to.

A farmhand echoed Georgiana's assertion of isolation, with one important Saturday exception:

> From November 1851, until the harvest of 1852, we lived on the ranch in perfect seclusion. Once in a while a solitary horseman might be seen wending his way, seeking shelter for the night at our camp, and now and then the *natives* would pay us a visit, and manifest their surprise at (to them) the new fangled plows, and other agricultural implements of "los Americanos." For our supply of letters and newspapers we were indebted for some time to the courtesy of a gentleman of Santa Cruz...engaged in the manufacture of leather. His visits were made regularly every Saturday, for some time, with pertinacity truly astonishing; but they were suddenly brought to a close, by his leaving us and going into another *state*.

The state of matrimony undoubtedly appealed to Georgiana, too, after six months in the Pajaro Valley without a female friend, a bedstead, or even a chair. Plus, she was tired of fending off the unwelcome marriage proposals that every single woman, and not a few married ones, received in a society as predominantly male as California's at that time. So, as Georgiana was fond of saying in later years, she "took the little tanner."

It was March 23, 1852, when she and Richard Kirby rode up to the home of a Santa Cruz County justice of the peace, George Parsons. Not one to stand on ceremony—literally, on this occasion—Georgiana didn't even dismount her horse to get married. Excepting the horses, the casual civil ceremony went unwitnessed and, for reasons known only to the participants, unrecorded until June 22.

What did get properly recorded for March 23, 1852, however, was an exchange of deeds and promissory notes between Eliza Farnham and Richard Kirby. On this busy day, Eliza granted to Richard Kirby, for two thousand dollars, "All those pieces of land...known as the one-half part of the former farm of the freed Indian Jose Anesia, situated near the Mission of San Jose in said County of Santa Clara." And in a second transaction, involving two promissory notes in the like sum of two thousand dollars, "all that certain tract of land...near the mission of St. Joseph and adjoining the land owned and occupied by I. C. Horace...formerly belonging to the estate of Thomas Jefferson Farnham deceased, the same being two hundred acres."

Also notarized and filed for the record on March 23, 1852, was Eliza Farnham's grant deed to Thomas Russell, in exchange for seven thousand dollars in promissory notes, conveying a portion of her property near the Santa Cruz mission, including a tract she had purchased the previous September from Jose Ramon Buelna for $149. And on that same date Thomas Russell, also for seven thousand dollars, deeded to Eliza all his "right title and interest" in property near the mission, surveyed and duly described.

Eliza needed cash, but the transactions may also have been an attempt to validate title. California's Land Act of 1851 established a board of land commissioners to investigate and confirm titles of property acquired prior to statehood. For several years Land Commission cases, a tangled review of records and clouded titles and adjudicated claims, occupied California's courts and supported lawyers handsomely. As it happened, a year later, in Mach 1853,

*Marriage license, Georgiana Bruce and Richard Kirby. Georgiana Bruce married Richard Kirby on March 23, 1852, but the marriage was not recorded until June 22. Courtesy of the Santa Cruz County Recorder's Office.*

Eliza Farnham and Tom Russell filed joint claims before the Land Commission in a contested title over the Buelna property.

There was yet another agreement signed on March 23, 1852:

> This is to certify that on the 23rd day of March A.D. 1852 before me Lambert B. Clements, one of the Justices of the Peace in and for the County of Santa Cruz, William Alexander Fitzpatrick and Eliza W. Farnham, both of Santa Cruz County State of California were legally joined in Marriage each of them being of full age and declaring themselves free respectively from prior engagements or other lawful impediments.
>
> In witness whereof as well they the said William Alexander Fitzpatrick and Eliza W. Farnham, She assuming the name of her husband as I the said Justice and others the said witnesses present have Hereunto Subscribed our names the day and year before said.

The two witnesses' names subscribed did not include Eliza's dearest and closest friend. Given Georgiana's disapproval of

Fitzpatrick and her exasperation with Eliza over the failure of their agricultural partnership, possibly she wasn't even there.

One witness was Jean Baptiste Arcan, who arrived in Santa Cruz in 1850 with his wife Abigail and their infant son. The Arcans had traveled from Salt Lake City to California with the James Briers, the very Methodist minister Georgiana described as a "self-conceited, brawling brute, without a spark of tenderness."

In November of 1849, the Arcans and Briers had been among more than three hundred people following a guide familiar with the Old Spanish Trail to Los Angeles. When a pack train overtook them and a man with a map touted a shortcut, it was the Reverend Mr. Brier who fired others with his zeal for the cutoff. Against the guide's advice, twenty-seven wagons, among them four families, including the Briers and the Arcans, turned off from the trail and into a vast and desolate desert, a hellhole they would name Death Valley.

The Reverend Mr. Brier, his wife Juliet, and their three sons reached safety in February, after much suffering. The Arcan family, heroically rescued by two selfless young men, escaped the valley of death on March 7—four months and three days after their fateful decision to take the cutoff.

Nearly everyone in California had a story to tell in those days. Almost everybody was from somewhere else and had come to California the hard way, there being no easy one. How Thomas Russell, the other witness to Eliza's wedding, came to California, supposedly from Ireland, is unknown. But he was destined for a terrible story, just the same. Almost ten years to the day of witnessing Eliza Farnham's marriage to William Fitzpatrick, Tom Russell's body would be discovered in a small ravine above Richard Kirby's tannery, with one shot to the head and his murderer never apprehended.

How William Alexander Fitzpatrick met Eliza Farnham is another mystery. Perhaps Tom Russell, on one of his trips to San Francisco, stopped at a tavern for a little something to wet his whistle, met a fellow Irishman, and exaggerated over a beer or two his employer's wealth and property, as Georgiana claimed he had to her.

Whatever the story of how William Fitzpatrick persuaded Eliza Farnham to marry him, Eliza never told. In none of her writings does she even mention his name.

*Rancho La Salud, the Kirby homestead. "Our rancho with its hollows
and gulches and noble sweep of hills exactly suits me," wrote Georgiana Kirby.
Courtesy of the Society of California Pioneers (C022515)*

To the extent Eliza chose poorly, Georgiana chose well. Several months after her marriage, she confided to her journal, "My husband has so many excellent qualities that I am deficient in, and also so excellent a temperament." She loved the home Richard Kirby made for her near Santa Cruz, at Rancho La Salud. "Our rancho with its hollows and gulches and noble sweep of hills exactly suits me," she wrote:

> The other day Mr. K. brought home a balm of Gilead tree about 4 1/2 feet high and planted it just opposite the kitchen window. It really gladdened my heart as I watched it constantly during the day as I would a child. It was the first step in the way of *refined* cultivation and gives me faith in the future roses, lilies, dahlias, and so forth, gives me faith that I shall one day gather glorious red currants and Antwerp raspberries and luscious English gooseberries in our own garden.

It was the evening of a cold and rainy day in December when she imagined this future garden of fruits and flowers. That morning, after breakfast, she had gone for a ride:

It always puts me in good spirits to gallop up the hills and view the wild mountain scenery, so on my return, after taking in the clothes and all the wood that was chopped, as the clouds seemed ominous, I concluded that today for the first time in my life I would commence a journal.

On this first day of what would prove to be sporadic journal keeping, Georgiana lamented the absence of female friendship. Her husband had taken her to visit neighbors, Mr. and Mrs. Sawin, two days before, but "for more than three months previous to this I had not been off the rancho or seen a woman":

Those women who have side saddles and horses at command are yet so occupied by their housekeeping cares that they are unable, excepting at distant intervals, to leave home for a day. There are no sisters or aunts or grown-up daughters to take their places while absent and if it should happen...that any such sisters, aunts, or grown-up daughters did exist, then before you could turn around they would be certainly snatched up and themselves immediately in the same plight as the rest of the women and quite as badly off as before.

Although Georgiana had not seen Eliza for several months, she heard talk about the Fitzpatricks:

She married the greatest blackguard in the country who strikes and otherwise ill treats her. At the time I write she has returned to him for the second time. Her children are tossed about here and there and her property wholly unattended to and unproductive.

How fortunate then was Georgiana, by comparison, to have chosen the devoted "little tanner":

Mr. K, kind, active, and ever cheerful, gets up and prepares breakfast, brings me chocolate and toast or whatnot to bed—kills and dresses a chicken for my dinner or saddles the horse for me to take a short ride—then hurries off to the tan yard (two miles or so). At night he often goes to the mission after closing work and is then sure to bring home a variety of articles with which to tempt my appetite or in some way contribute to my comfort.

Richard Kirby's tender attentions were no doubt inspired by the fact that his wife was suffering from what she called "the ordinary ailments of such a condition." She was pregnant.

So was Eliza.

# FOURTEEN

# Babies

I am persuaded that it is better a woman should love, even though it prove to be unworthily, and marry, even if her hopes be disappointed, than ignore so much of her best life as she must in living singly. And if to the marriage be added the glory of motherhood, she is thereby victor over much pain and wretchedness. God is her ally in that, against the world. Ask any wife who has had the prayer of her heart answered by the birth of a child to the man she loves, even though he be an oppressor and tyrant, and she will tell you that all her past wounds found healing there, and that she felt the universe had declared for her in the strife.

—Eliza Farnham

Since the age of eighteen, Georgiana had been "ever conscious of the most intense desire to become a mother." In youthful imaginings the anticipation of pregnancy would fill her "whole being with joy." This despite the fact, as she admitted, that she was "not especially fond of little babies." She trusted the instinct to develop. What she wanted was to "watch the unfolding of character and intellect...to arouse moral ambition, to instill by precept and example a thorough respect for labor."

These were the thoughts that occupied her as December became January, as rains came and went. The wet winter and her discomfort kept her from walking, which she now found fatiguing. She read until she exhausted what there was to read, the mail coming only every two weeks with the publications she favored: the *New York Tribune*, the *Anti-Slavery Standard*, the *Pennsylvania Freeman*. She read them hurriedly, and then carefully, and then she would be back in the same deprived state as before. She suffered from dyspepsia and had no energy for study, which she regretted. In January she filled two weeks, during the hours she felt well enough, with writing long letters to friends in the East. She was spurred to thoughts of old friends by the arrival in Santa Cruz of John Bowman, a Quaker farmer from Byberry, Pennsylvania, who had spent a recent month at the home of her friend and former employer, Robert Purvis:

> I was glad to hear all the news, though I thought it an uncommonly stupid place the 10 months I spent there. R. Purvis is the beautiful star that gives the place any character at all and there are a few pretty fair women, but all hampered by their miserly dolts of fathers or their poverty.

Critical of a great many who came within her view, Georgiana confided to her journal an opinion of Mr. Bowman she probably didn't share with him:

> His nasal tones and too great enthusiasm at first made me very nervous and irritable....I wish he were more quiet and had some sufficient satisfaction with his own labors, great and small, so as to avoid the necessity of telling of every little thing he does and every movement he makes. It detracts so much from a man's manliness, the constantly asking suffrages of his fellows. He talks and explains in one endless, nasal monotone and with the most tedious prolixity about all sorts of unimportant and commonplace things, never seeming to think that the people he is talking to be as well informed on the subject as himself, or that the trifling incidents he so minutely describes may be thoroughly uninteresting to his auditors, who for civility sake are obliged to listen against their will and respond occasionally. It is a thousand pities that no one warned him of the disagreeable habit when he was a young man; it serves to alienate many who would otherwise be his warm friends, I doubt not.

A hired hand's manner of speaking bothered her, too:

> He is very ignorant and has a blustering way of delivering himself, always laughing with a coarse common laugh and emphasis on every sentence with "I'm bothered," "The beggar of a horse," or "beggar of a thing." It is no matter who is talking—how calmly or sensibly and not, of course, directing their conversation to him, he must always join in with his giggle and common-places and vulgarisms as if he were as well informed as anyone. It annoys me more than I could wish.

Georgiana, even when not easily irritated because of her pregnant state, held firm opinions about voice:

> The human voice is the truest index to the interior qualities of the soul. The manly, frank, clear-headed person has a voice pleasant to

listen to; the timid one, the time server, and scatter brains, quite another. Owing to Lucretia Mott's sweet and gracious social affections her voice is music itself, rich and never failing. A person with merely her intellect, or with less affection, could by no possibility have such delicious intonations. Mr. Bowman's nasal, monotonous, blarneying voice so disgusted me.

Pregnancy disagreed with Georgiana. She was uncomfortable, depressed, and lonely. She needed a friend—"a congenial female companion with whom I could chat and be merry—sympathize and advise." She missed Eliza:

> Every good woman needs a companion of her own sex, no matter how numerous or valuable her male acquaintances, no matter how close the union between herself and husband; if she have a genial, loving nature, the want of a female friend is felt as a sad void....If I had a nice friend with me it would recall me from my vague dreaming to the worth of the actual present. It is folly in moral philosophers to talk absolutely about persons making their own circumstances. It is utterly impossible for me to cause a state of mind in myself which would naturally result from the conflict in other minds. I never *think*. All the nobler intellectual faculties lie dormant.

Eliza agreed—and was eloquent on the subject:

> It is the great wealth of our mortal life—this of companionship—yet how few possess it, in husband or wife, in parent or child, in brother or sister or friend. We all sustain these relations, but who of those that fill them is the companion of our soul? How many can measure its rejoicings and mournings—share its enthusiasms—its unuttered hopes—its secret life? One who is my companion must know me by the language of the eye—the cheek—the tone, which is not framed into words—by the clasp of my hand—by the raised or drooping head—by the swift or slow step—by the whole dynamic utterance. When I have thrown down the walls of my being to such a person— man or woman—the interior kingdom is as much theirs as mine. One who will lovingly and clearly read me, is a part of myself; and such a soul, when I have found it, is never more lost to me.

Though lonely this January of 1853, Eliza was not bereft of family. Luther Farnham, her late husband's brother, had come to Santa Cruz to help administer his nephews' estate by selling 248 acres Charlie and Eddie had inherited. The property was "so situated," testified Farnham in his petition to the Santa Cruz County probate court, "that it produces no income sufficient to support them or to furnish them with the necessaries of life...."

Georgiana, meanwhile, was feeling better, and the February weather permitted an overnight visit with the new Methodist minister's wife, Sarah Dryden. Then Mrs. Whiting called on Georgiana, a visit "which has quite made me forget myself and my ailments." Mrs. Whiting was expecting, too:

> The place has become proverbial for its fruitfulness. We are all in a state of partial anxiety about doctors and nurses, those here of the former class being bunglers, giving calomel to a confined woman and losing healthy patients frequently, and most of the latter being filled more or less with old women's superstitions as regards the treatment of new-born babies.

Early in March, five months pregnant, Georgiana, for the first time, felt her baby move. Believing devoutly in the baby's susceptibility to her own moods and activities, she confided to her journal, "My life has been and is likely to be so free from excitement of every sort during this experience that the child if not stupid, should, at least, be equable in disposition."

In mid-March, she lamented again: "I am not at all well, think a journal a stupid and heartless affair and have come to the conclusion that the peculiar characteristics of a child are the result of inmost indescribable and perhaps unrecognizable states of mind."

In April she visited the Whitings—and returned in a worse mood:

> Whiting is a shallow, conceited, dogmatic, insolent, pro-slavery braggart and I came home quite sad and hopeless about the progress of truth and justice in this country, where it is the universal custom to call sin virtue—to boast of oppression and brag of the freedom of this great country, all in a breath—to hate with a wolfish hatred those who dare to advocate the most obvious right, what reason have we for hope? I despair....
>
> I should live where I can have the sympathy of abolitionists. It makes me bitter and cold and contemptuous, the mixing only with the shallow tyrant or timid apologist.

In May, Georgiana felt better physically, enjoying the candy treats her husband brought, of which she was "extravagantly fond," and otherwise subsisting mainly on bread, milk, cream, and blackberries. Most of June came and went without complaint. And then, near midnight on May 29, she brought a daughter into the world. In fondness for a Brook Farm friend, Deborah Gannett, Georgiana named her baby Ora.

Four days later, Eliza also brought a daughter into the world. She named her Mary, in remembrance of the beloved sister she had buried in Illinois. Whatever Eliza's confused feelings about the child's father might be, she adored her daughter. Eliza loved being a mother. It was, to her, a woman's highest calling:

> It is a Godlike joy to know that the being derived from our own is not vitiated or enfeebled by any act of ours; that the health and power which we have inherited, fortunate if they were in generous measure, we have transmitted to them, enlarged and strengthened by worthy use. Oh, not for worlds would I have it now to remember that I had ever deliberately, or consciously, or ignorantly, if the ignorance were not unavoidable, done an act that could diminish my power and value to my children as their mother.

Ten years previously, in 1843, in her great debate with John Neal on the rights of women, Eliza had argued that woman "is the first to greet man when he enters upon his earthly life, the last to leave him when that pilgrimage closes for ever. Her declaration of Rights is, 'I am a wife and mother. To be these is my freedom—to be other would be slavery.'"

But in 1853 her thoughts more likely turned not to idealistic pronouncements but to experience. Did she fear that this child, like Eddie, might suffer a defect at birth? Or, worse, that this child might be fated an early demise, like her firstborn, a beloved little boy buried in Illinois? Did she revisit the terrible time of loss from which she had not recovered when her husband took to westering and left her alone with her grief? If so, it would prove a bad omen.

For Georgiana, the first month of motherhood was a confrontation with the realities of babies. Little Ora cried a great deal. She had a rash on her face that Georgiana fretted over. And she appeared to have a cast to her left eye that Georgiana thought might have been caused by "bringing her suddenly into too strong light." There was so much to do and no time to do it.

By September Georgiana felt lonely again. She lamented the absence of letters from Robert Purvis. And the Kirbys had financial problems. They had planted potatoes, and the price had dropped. They lost money on two shipments, and worms had got into the late crop. They had no ready funds with which to pay "various bills for labor." And there were the promissory notes owed Eliza on the property near the San Jose mission, which galled Georgiana: "These considerations, with Mrs. F's dishonorable conduct making Mr. K. liable for $2,000 next spring and summer, keep me in a state of unrest."

In November, things looked rosier. Ora rarely cried now, and Georgiana adored her—and wanted more children:

> Baby is well...remarkably strong...and is so very happy in her existence that I quite envy her, wishing I myself were a child again and so cared for....She observes much for her age, loves to be out of doors early in the morning when the deer and other animals are about. I am wholly satisfied in the child....She is, indeed, the light of the household. Her father takes great pride and pleasure in her. I have forgotten my great suffering and wish for two more children— one girl and one boy—the latter to please my husband only, for I love girls best.

Georgiana was reading again. She reread Bulwer-Lytton's *The Caxtons* and was struck anew by "the true wisdom embodied in it." Thackeray's books she thought "aimless, superficial, and unimproving." Harriet Beecher Stowe's *Uncle Tom's Cabin* was of "quite another stamp." Georgiana needed books, needed to read to think:

> Without this connecting link I could not live so far from any centre of thought. My mind would shrink to the modicum of those with whom I associate and growth be a mere word in the dictionary. The Tribune and A. S. Standard do indeed supply me with the bread of life.

And she needed Eliza: "I love Mrs. F in spite of the anxiety and trouble she has caused us and may yet, by her past culpable action."

In December the two women, finally, after nearly two years, repaired their ruptured friendship. Georgiana took Ora to Eliza's home to visit for a few days. There was so much to join them, these two old friends and new mothers with baby daughters to praise and appraise. Georgiana thought little Mary beautiful and admired the baby's "splendid head and a joyous generous face." With their shared belief in phrenological dispositions, it was impossible for the two women not to examine the little heads and deduce inclinations. Compared to Mary, little Ora's head was thought to be "lacking in breadth—imagination and cautiousness."

But Ora was "wide between the eyes," and Eliza quoted an authority who said that meant "music." This of course pleased Georgiana, who had hoped for "some monumental noble trait—some beautiful spiritual gift, like music."

And so ended 1853, which, despite the joys of new motherhood, had been a difficult year for both women.

For Eliza, the months ahead would be even harder.

# FIFTEEN

# Heartache

Died. In Santa Cruz, of spinal disease, on Wednesday, the 9th of August, Edward Hallock, youngest son of the late Thomas J. Farnham, aged 9 years and 6 months. A sweet character and noble mind have been withdrawn, in the death of this beautiful boy from the love of those who have watched his long suffering, and also from the world, whose true wealth is such spirits as his.

New York and Illinois papers please copy.

*—Alta California*, August 23, 1854

In 1849, when the *Angelique*'s captain abandoned Eliza in Valparaiso, she was not distressed for herself but for her young sons, and most particularly Eddie, the little boy crippled from birth and so dear to her heart:

> I knew there were feeling hearts on board that vessel in the bosoms of both men and women, and I knew that, above all, my excellent friend, Miss Sampson, would devote to them the whole of her little strength; but…how could I suppose that a tender and feeble child, who had, most of his life, had one person devoted to him, and often two, could receive from her the attention necessary to his health and comfort? It was this anxiety that chiefly pained me.…None can sympathize with this anxiety but mothers whose lot it has been to rear such a child, inestimably dearer for his infirmities, and compensating all by rare gifts of heart and mind.

Upon arriving in San Francisco, when Eliza found her sons still aboard the *Angelique*, it was Eddie's declined health that narrowed her happiness at reunion: "I cannot forget the paroxysms which brought great drops of sweat upon the brow, and blanched the thin cheeks, and whitened the quivering lips so often, during our first wretched summer in the country."

In Santa Cruz she delighted in her son's regained strength, his anticipation of Geordie's arrival, his joyful presence as she shingled the roof of the new house.

Eddie died four years after the traumatic separation at Valparaiso. Although Fitzpatrick had entered Eliza's life, it was the *Angelique*'s Captain Windsor she implicated when the child died. Or so the reader, who is never told Fitzpatrick exists, might presume from Eliza's mention of her son's death in her California book: "His brief life of physical pain and spiritual beauty and sweetness has closed, and, though I cannot forgive, I can almost pity, the wretch who has to recollect that he ever willingly added one pang to it."

Did she allude to Captain Windsor? William Fitzpatrick? Both? Regardless, Eddie's death affected her deeply:

> If so terrible an experience should ever again be mine, I should open a view of the future to the child, and endeavor to prepare him for the changes by familiarizing his mind with the beauty of that world—the pure joys—the love—the tenderness that await him there. I should give him the thought that to die was only to go to a pleasanter home in a world as real as this. I should feel less pain now if I had treated [Eddie] so.
>
> I go alone and look at the sunset over the ocean....I see and feel him in a world of light and growth, where all is *living* power, beauty, expansion, and progress; where low conditions do not imprison, and darkness does not hinder or becloud his radiant soul. I feel that my child is there. I think of him in these relations, and am conscious that he is not lost to me in that grave; and yet I cling to the memory of it, because it is the one spot on earth that is identified with that beloved form...whom my soul loves, and will rejoice in when we meet face to face again...whom these arms have cherished, whom these lips have kissed, and this heart of flesh delighted itself in...so I yearn toward it painfully, as I should irresistibly toward the dear form, were it now here before me.

Did the domestic discord of the Fitzpatrick household diminish the frail child? Fitzpatrick was a dread. Young Charlie, during one of Fitzpatrick's violent, drunken rages, grabbed baby Mary, ran out of the house, and hid with her in the cornfield. Did Eliza blame herself, suspect that her ill-considered marriage to William Fitzpatrick contributed to Eddie's failing health?

There were so many failures for Eliza in 1853, 1854, 1855—strained relations with Georgiana, Fitzpatrick's abuse, Eddie's decline and death, finances.

Farming proved hopeless. Financial problems plagued everyone in 1854, including the Kirbys, as Georgiana confided to her journal after a sixteen-month lapse:

> Rather a wearisome, hopeless time—pecuniary difficulties make such hard work for the honest minded. Last December we moved to the mission leaving...the farm which we had been unable to sell. Since January the new tan yard has been in successful operation and we are living in a droll little white-washed house not five minutes walk from it.

Ora was nearly two years old. Georgiana had lost a second pregnancy, miscarried, as she thought, "from over-exertion." Now she was pregnant again, and consequently "desirous of recording my circumstances and states of mind in order the better to learn the effect of these on the character of the child." Her mood was not light as she once again took up her pen:

> I have no leisure for the quiet dreaming that occupied me so much before Ora's birth and yet my mind is no more clear or orderly. For a long time the music seems to have died out of me—no melody, no sense of rhythm. Mr. K. is also quite exhausted with the close application of four years. He looks older by ten years and is easily attacked by sickness now.

The only bright note in Georgiana's journal entry was that "Mrs. Farnham has taught our common school for the last five months and if she continues we may hope something for the place."

Eliza, in addition to teaching the school, grieving for Eddie, worrying about Charlie, and caring for baby Mary, had finished her book about California. Early in 1855 she sent the completed manuscript to a New York publisher, and then wrote to an acquaintance there, Parke Godwin. Godwin's father-in-law, William Cullen Bryant, had supported Eliza's California Association of American Women and endorsed her circular with his signature. Godwin worked for the *New York Evening Post.* Eliza asked him to act for her in her book's sale:

> By the last mail I wrote you a note accompanying the ms. of a vol. on California which I sent to Appleton directing him to deal with you in ref. to terms of publication etc.
>
> I took the liberty of referring to you (and I know it was one) because I trusted your...recollection of me would be kindly enough

to save me the pain of being reckoned altogether troublesome or obtrusive.

Let me pray your patience and good nature and your kind offices in making the best bargain for me that is practicable....

There is one passage I wish altered or struck out. I cannot name the page in the copy you will receive. The passage discusses my first going to Church in Santa Cruz, say somewhere about pp. 200 All that I wish omitted is the passage descriptive of the sermon. I have, since writing, become acquainted with the family of the preacher and rec'd kindnesses from them. I w'd not wound them. You will understand. If you think it best to retain the description which is literally true give it some other locality...where it will not be misplaced in the connexion. Such preaching! abounds in the country.

I hope to hear from you soon. Please address under cover to Col. Edward Briant [sic] San Francisco. Letters bearing my name on the envelope are not always sure to reach me. Make my kindest regards to Mrs. G. and believe me

> Yours very truly
> E W Farnham

As requested, Parke Godwin apparently took his pencil to the passage describing Adna Hecox. The published version lacks the offense Mrs. Farnham implied for the original:

His sermon, though pronounced in the language of an illiterate man, did not lack good common-sense or moral tone. "Is our souls sot heavenward?" he exclaimed; "if they be, we shall move on the road to it; but some folks, talking of going to heaven and hoping to get there, is like a man at home in the old states saying he hoped to get to *Kellyferny,* while all the time he sot still."

At the time of writing, Eliza had given up on Fitzpatrick and the farm. More loss awaited. When next she wrote Parke Godwin she poured out her heart:

Since writing my last to you, I have met with a loss which life can never repair. My little daughter the hope and light of my future here died on the 18th July of acute hydrocephalus. She was two years old and already gave evidence of such wonderful mental powers and such exceeding loveliness of person and spirit as made her an idol to us all. Her death leaves my life so void that but for a great work to which I feel myself specially called in consequence, it would be almost insupportable. You have never lost a child I believe, at least you have never lost the last one so that your house had no more baby glee, no more loving welcome for you—you can not therefore feel my grief. I have now but one child left—my son Charles, a fine youth of 14. Alas he is not a daughter nor a miracle of promise. I hope to send him to New York this fall by the first of Sept to be placed in school and to follow him myself in March or April next.

I could enjoy writing more freely to you in my present state of mind had I heard from you. I am so cut off from communication with the Eastern world and so frozen up in this Polar Sea of humanity that I am very wretched most of the time, sometimes almost desperate. I do not know if I shall ever find my full measure of life again in the mortal state. My only rejoicing is in the thot of that which awaits us beyond.

The diagnosis of acute hydrocephalus suggests a sudden onset, meningitis, perhaps, or a blow to the head. Yet, Georgiana's observation is recalled, that Ora had not Mary's "breadth of the head." Was the unfortunate little Mary born with the fatal condition, her death foreshadowed? Did Eliza suspect or ignore the anguish she must endure again in a third burial of a child she had borne and loved? Her thoughts must have gone back to 1838, to the terrible loss, in Illinois, of her firstborn:

Our boy never grew better; he sunk from the time of my sister's death, and spite of all that skill and tenderness could do, just two weeks from the day on which her life closed, he yielded his, and we were wholly bereft. Even to the day of his death, I did not anticipate the event. It is true, I had fears, anxieties, sympathy, which only a mother can feel, but preeminent over all these, there was *hope*.... When, therefore, the kind doctor, who had stolen an hour from his arduous duties to spend it with us, said to one of those present that "the little sufferer would soon be released," his words seemed to dry the very springs of life within me. I had no word to say, no tear to shed, but I gazed upon the little panting form, and glassy eye, with every faculty suspended by that dreadful sentence....

There he lay, in his little crib, where I had so often frolicked with him, the lips now all cold and leaden, which, in his last agony, had called imploringly on me, by the dearest name to which the heart of woman ever responds; the eyes, which had so often looked into mine, overflowing with merriment, with silent wonder, of appealing tears, closed forever. What could I do? How impotent is every form of expression, which grief can take, to relieve the heart oppressed with such a burthen.

Again the spot where we had stood so few brief days before was visited. The little coffin which seemed to carry my very heart into the earth with it was lowered close beside my sister's grave....

Oh...who shall ever tell what a mother feels when she returns to her silent house from the new-made grave of her only child?...I shall never forget the pang that wrung my bosom when one morning, two or three weeks after we were alone, I found a toy of pine wood indented all over with the print of small teeth. The last hand that had touched it was my babe's, its familiar form and bruised surface brought the happy little owner so strongly before me that I seemed to live the terrible parting over again.

For a woman who had lost so many—mother, father, sister, first-born, husband, and two more children—Spiritualism, the belief that we do not die, offered solace. No wonder she embraced it. Her writing sustained her, too. She wrote Parke Godwin of practical matters:

I am hoping very earnestly to hear from you by the next steamer. But in the meantime trusting that the ms. sent on by express on the 15th of June has arrived safely, and that the arrangements for its publication will not be long delayed. I now write to say that as soon as it is published I should wish if the Messrs Appleton agree, to have 300 copies sent on to me by express. Persons acquainted with the book market here recommend about this no. by first express and 100 to 150 by each succeeding one till we can receive some by shipment around, which could not probably be within four mos of the time of publication.

I am urged to order some copies of Prairie Land...but I do not know if the book is in print. Would you find it troublesome to call on the Harpers and ascertain and if it be, get them to put up 100 or 200. You would greatly oblige me by doing so.

I am advised that about 200 copies a month ought to be shipped from the time of publication until our market is supplied. But when I receive your letter and learn its contents I shall be able to address myself to the publishers direct in what it may be necessary to say hereafter. If you will be kind enough to arrange for the first shipment both by express and Clipper you will do me a great service. Make very kindest regards to Mrs. G—and her father and mother.

Weighed down by emotional despair, domestic disappointment, and financial troubles, Eliza moved in with the Kirbys and sent Charles to New York. After Mary's loss, Eliza had no heart for teaching, and she resigned from the Santa Cruz school. Georgiana sympathized:

> All hope of growth in Santa Cruz through Mrs. Farnham's influence in the public school is at an end....bereft of her only consolation [she] was unequal to the task of drudging through the few remaining months of her school year—the rowdies again have matters in their own hands and a low-bred ignoramus teaches a private school. In October, doubtless, the narrow-minded, sanctimonious Frick will again vent his spite on the children of the district....I long to be teaching somebody myself, but there is not sufficient appreciation of the higher sort of culture to make any parent anxious to part with even one out of six girls. The question still, could I be of service to my kind elsewhere? I am of none here.
>
> ...During the four most important months of this pregnancy I had a class of girls for three hours each day. Those that really interested me were Maria and Ellen Hecox and Katherine Imus. They went through "Combe's Constitution of Man," and we used to have all sorts of discussions with it. The Methodist minister tells the parents that none but infidels believe in phrenology and that this is an infidel book. It is quite common here for girls to be engaged at twelve and marry at fourteen, so I and Mrs. Farnham...endeavor to impress upon them the great truths of marriage, maternity—the moral and physical laws affecting children and so forth....
>
> I met with great opposition from Mr. Kirby about these girls coming to me, but I like to teach and knew that it would be beneficial to the child, keeping my mind clear and practical and active instead of dreary. Mrs. Farnham's presence, too, is the greatest blessing. We are so suggestive to each other....
>
> ...I trembled every time K saw the girls. He threatened to order them out of the house—said their parents would abuse me as they had Mrs. F. and tell lies about me—that people would say he could not support me and so forth. It was only by the greatest calmness and firmness that I avoided trouble and all for the sake of the result.

Georgiana turned her attention to her unborn baby. For several months she studied geometry for an hour each evening, in hope of giving "more intellect and more character to the child."

Eliza turned her attention to earning a living.

# SIXTEEN

# Tickets at the Door

MRS. ELIZA FARNHAM. This gifted and successful authoress will soon, it is said, give a course of lectures in this city. The first will be upon the application of the organic laws on the conditions of life, the second on the value of a true system of Mental Philosophy, and the third on the characteristics of the present civilization.

—*San Francisco Daily Evening Bulletin*, January 21, 1856

At half past seven on the evening of January 25, 1856, at San Francisco's Musical Hall, located on Bush street between Sansome and Montgomery, Mrs. Eliza Farnham approached the lectern. She saw before her an audience that expressed their doubt by receiving her silently, without applause. They saw before them a woman of forty, "somewhat tall, of good form, but rather spare than stout, with dark hair, dark complexion, black eyes, and intelligent face." She wore a simple dress of black silk, elegant in style, "tastefully relieved by a moderate amount of white lace."

Mrs. Farnham, in the face of this unwelcoming silence, prepared to read from her written lecture. The *Daily California Chronicle*'s reporter, who had so carefully described her dress, further noted that "a new actress, with a tithe of her ability or reputation, would have been 'rapturously received.'" Mrs. Farnham began, her voice well modulated, her enunciation distinct, even "clear and musical," though not strong:

> Her style of reading was grave throughout, unimpassioned and unsympathizing, even after the audience had been forced to relent, to be pleased, and to applaud by the flowing style, the felicitous description, and the epigrammatic, and not entirely orthodox sarcasm of the lecture. As running comment to her ideas of physical education, she described in general terms the lives of the "respectable," do-nothing criminal, and of the outcast criminal. Her ideas were appropriate, forcible and sometimes bold, although clothed in a chaste language which commanded respect. She was repeatedly interrupted by hearty applause, and every one present could not but consider her lecture as entirely successful.

The response would not have surprised Mrs. Farnham. She was, after all, not a greenhorn lecturer. She was a veteran.

Eliza Farnham had been only twenty-four years old when she placed her first lecture notice in a newspaper. In June 1840, while visiting in St. Louis, Missouri, she announced a "free Lecture on Phrenology, as illustrating the practical duties of females, (to Ladies exclusively)" that afternoon, in the "School Room opposite the Court House." She added that "Mothers are particularly invited to attend."

By 1840, phrenology was all the rage. As early as 1834, the *Boston Christian Examiner* had declared:

> It is well known to most of our readers, how suddenly the doctrine established itself, and how rapidly it gained ground in this region. No sooner had its late distinguished apostle [Johann Gaspar Spurzheim] appeared in our city, than a *Pentecost* was witnessed, such as philosophy had not known before....Heads of chalk, inscribed with mystic numbers, disfigured every mantelpiece. Converts multiplied on all sides....A general inspection and registry of heads took place....In short, this theory of man obtained a speedy and signal triumph.

Spurzheim, popularizer of the phrenological theory originated by Franz Joseph Gall, had come from Europe to spread the news in America. He arrived in New York in August 1832 and brought dramatic attention to his cause four months later by collapsing and dying in Boston.

Among the first Americans to jump on the phrenological bandwagon was Orson S. Fowler. In 1834, newly graduated from Amherst with "nothing special to do," he became fired "with an ambition to try my hand at lecturing on Phrenology." Resolve served as sufficient qualification to launch this line of business, the only other necessity for young Orson being "studying up my form of notice for my proposed handbill and advertisements; and finally studying our improvements in my chart, in giving the definitions of the Faculties." He then "bought paper, hired printer, and got out a thousand copies, along with my handbill; ordered a bust, and thirty-two dollars' worth of works on Phrenology, opened my lectures, threw out my card, charged men twelve and a half cents for a phrenological chart, marked, and ladies and children six and a quarter cents; cleared forty dollars in the place, and started for Saratoga."

Another entrepreneurial head-reader was none other than Eliza Farnham's brother, Kelly Burhans. Kelly heard his first lecture on phrenology from Dr. Amos Dean, professor of medical jurisprudence at Albany Medical College. Kelly, not incidentally, met a young lawyer there, Thomas Jefferson Farnham, whom he introduced to his studious young sister, then enrolled at the Albany Female Academy.

Kelly Burhans, like Orson Fowler, was youthful, ambitious, and looking for something to do. Like Fowler, he required nothing more than intention to become a lecturer on phrenology. And he was good at it:

> I am the greatest Phrenologist ever lived I expect, that's the talk anyhow, that is examiner, my analytical knowledge is far inferior to many others, but to read of character by the head I presume to say & report says the same I have no equal. The principle reason of my analytical deficiency is that to tell the truth, although my examinations are far more successful than my partners yet I never gave the subject a candid thought or perusal knowing that I should not follow it long, I never have been able to fix my mind upon it people generally think that I am a regular graduate etc. etc. You know there is a great deal in looking wise, that's about half the job.

The bandwagon Kelly Burhans jumped on was hauled by a cash cow. A year later he wrote his sister Mary from Indianapolis:

> I am going the whole hog bristles & all, my name has spread on the wings of fame throughout this state like a whirlwind, I have succeeded beyond all possible anticipations, why I am toasted & extolled, conducted by honorable senators to the speakers chair, & spout to them like a young whale, only think of it here *little I,* am teaching philosophy & wisdom to all the talent of Ia. a poor empiric holding forth to men of classical education, & listened to with the profoundest respect & attention & applauded beyond measure; I say sis I think it's a new era in the annals of science, God grant that it may hold out....I have been here 18 days & yesterday...took $45.00 have now $700. clear, shall overrun a thousand before this month expires. Don't let Farnham know of this. My course is eastward to Columbus O. shall reach there about the Middle of Feby. Buchanan has left me, we can do much better alone I can make more money than any six Phre[nologis]ts in the states, & make more friends to the science, there was scarcely a believer in this place when I arrived & now there is but few who doubt its truth....The state house was

never so full on any former occasion as at my lectures[,] from 800
to 1000 Ladies & Gentlemen.

By 1840, Eliza's brother was "Dr. K. E. Burhans." That year
Eliza—her husband having contracted the westering fever and
gone to Oregon—joined Kelly on his lecture tour to Missouri. And
dipped her own toe in the lecture-circuit waters.

She was a natural, and soon a professional, as the *New York
Tribune* affirmed:

> MRS. FARNHAM, a Western lady, proposes to give a Course of Eight
> Lectures to Ladies (only) at the Society Library, Broadway, com-
> mencing on Wednesday, at 11 A.M. Mrs. F. has lectured in Baltimore,
> Troy and other Cities to large classes of her own sex, with decided
> approbation, and has the strongest testimonials to her ability and
> worth. The subject of which she treats, terms, &c will be seen by ref-
> erence to her card.

So, in 1856, it was no novice who booked San Francisco's
Musical Hall. The *Daily California Chronicle*'s laudatory review of
her presentation was no surprise to Eliza. What may have surprised her, though, was a letter to the editor of the *San Francisco
Daily Evening Bulletin*:

> Mr. Editor:—I have been so much pained and surprised by the
> result of our interview this morning in regard to Mrs. Farnham's
> proposed course of lectures in this city that I cannot resist the temp-
> tation to say to you on paper what I think of your position.
>
> You decline to *recommend* her course of lectures to public atten-
> tion and patronage, although willing *to notice* them, because, how-
> ever able she may be, and capable of giving public instruction, she
> is a *woman* and in lecturing is acting out of *woman's sphere*," &c.
>
> With you it matters not that she is possessed of moral and intel-
> lectual faculties of a high order, and lectures with a view to educate
> and support herself and child, who have lost their natural protector.
> She must not be allowed the legitimate exercise of her higher fac-
> ulties because she is a *woman*. If she were a man in like condition,
> the effort which she proposed would not only be right, but highly
> commendable. It is not "woman's sphere," forsooth! What is that
> sphere? Nursing babies, cooking, or making shirts at ten cents a
> piece, I suppose—on one level of society?—or lounging in carriages
> making fashionable calls, and attending balls and parties, in another?
> What a sublime philosophy must dictate such noble sentiments!

How much flattered women should be at such a lofty conception of their dignity and destiny!

Hitherto, I had always supposed that the possession of any useful faculty was a *divine warrant* for its exercise, when exercised with a proper regard for the rights of others. How stupid, how irrational, how utterly absurd (you will pardon me for saying) the *idea* that *sex* is the criterion to determine the propriety or impropriety of the exercise of moral and intellectual power, in any legitimate sphere.

The *Daily Evening Bulletin* continued to "notice" Mrs. Farnham's lectures:

The second free lecture by Mrs. Farnham was delivered last night at Musical Hall.—The audience was very large—nearly half being ladies. The address was fully equal in point of interest to that of the first, and all who listened to it were highly gratified. At the conclusion a collection was taken up to defray the expense of the Hall.

Mrs. Farnham's third and last lecture, on the characteristics of our present civilization, will be delivered at Musical Hall tomorrow (Tuesday) evening, Jan. 29, at 8 o'clock. Tickets 50 cents at the door.

The *Evening Bulletin*'s editor, James King of William, seemed unable to please his readers, but he gamely published their letters:

Mr. King.—…Say to Mrs. Farnham that if she will collect all the information she can relative to good bread making, and embody it into a lecture to the ladies and housekeepers in general of this State, she will accomplish more immediate good than if she were to lecture a year on other subjects.

The *Daily California Chronicle,* however, remained strongly in Mrs. Farnham's camp:

MRS. FARNHAM'S LECTURE LAST EVENING. Musical Hall was crowded last evening by a respectable and intelligent audience, to hear Mrs. Farnham's lecture on "Mental Philosophy." A portion of her remarks were directed to a just and able tribute to the genius and labors of Gall and Spurzheim; men who, in the true spirit of philosophy, had given their lives and fortunes to science. She expanded upon the science, as taught by them; deprecated the prejudice and folly with which some of the vulgar treat it, and showed that statesmen, poets and in fact the greatest minds in all the various professions treated it with marked respect. In the course of her remarks she spoke of fashion and the ladies of San Francisco, and her brilliant and pointed

sarcasms called forth repeated bursts of applause, particularly from
the gentlemen, of course. The lecture was entirely successful.

The *Daily California Chronicle* positively gushed in its review of
Mrs. Farnham's closing lecture:

The third lecture of Mrs. Farnham was listened to at Music[al] Hall
last evening by the most attentive, quiet, engrossed audience we
have ever sat among. The entire people present seemed determined
not to lose a sentence. They were right. There was not one word but
deserved attention; not a weak, worthless paragraph in the whole of
it. The impression left predominant was that the entire lecture was
all of thought. There was no maudlin sentimentality in it. It was the
production of an earnest, philosophical, enlightened mind, cog-
nizant of the great facts of political, religious and scientific history,
imbued with clear perceptions and pure aspirations.

The lecture was a complete whole. Had we the manuscript before
us, it would be difficult to select particular parts for publication;
unless such as her beautiful and just analysis of the pure hearted,
whole souled poet, philosopher and man, Wordsworth, to whose
head, heart and genius she paid a tribute which the admirers of the
man of Rydal Mount could best appreciate. The three epochs of civilization—that of muscle, bone and war; that of invention and discovery; and the last one, of science, literature and arts—were artis-
tically delineated. The latter, which most concerns us, was depicted
with the pen of a master. The application of the different sciences
to the amelioration and progress of the human race was dwelt upon
with an earnestness and truthfulness quite refreshing. The immense
changes which the last fifty years have wrought in literature, science
and religious tenets were graphically depicted. And if the forbid-
ding dogmas and teachings of the church, as it was half a century
ago, were severely handled, the religion and morality were sustained
in their high and holier aspects and influences, with an earnestness
and truthful explication exceedingly gratifying to the hearty seeker
after what is worthy of approbation. The lecture was one of the most
perfect it has been our pleasure to listen to, and would have convinced us—had we been doubting—that God has not recognized
any such thing as sex in mental structure.

There is not a man among us, whatever his pretensions or attain-
ments, who might not have been proud to be the author of the lecture. And its closing pages were the most perfect representation of
the obligations and duties which each intelligent progressive creature
owes to himself, to humanity, and to God, that we have yet heard.
We wish every one of the community might hear and appreciate this

expression of a high souled existence, whose aspirations are for that pure and ennobling condition to which all who truly appreciate man's capacity and destiny anticipate with abiding faith. Mrs. Farnham visits Sacramento to repeat her lectures.

But before visiting Sacramento, Mrs. Farnham would take a look at the state prison at San Quentin. Mrs. Farnham knew a thing or two, and held an opinion or three, about prisons.

# SEVENTEEN

# Prison Report

STATE PRISON.—A report from the State Prison Committee is looked for daily. Some rich developments relating to the manner in which the affairs of that famous institution have been managed since June last may be looked for. It is rumored outside that the State has been involved for building a wall, &c., in the sum of three hundred and eighty odd thousand dollars. At this rate a couple of years will suffice to completely bankrupt the State. If ex-Gov. Bigler saved the State a hundred thousand dollars by retaining the State Prison Bill, probably some of his friends can tell by cyphering how much he and his friends saved the State by taking possession of the prisoners and involving the people in a debt of nearly four hundred thousand dollars for taking care of them six months and building a wall to hedge them in. This is economy, with a witness.

*—Sacramento Daily Union*, February 12, 1856

With her lectures a success in San Francisco, and her only surviving child, Charles, in school in the East, Mrs. Farnham duly and truly resumed the world. And did not look back.

Immediately ahead, north across San Francisco Bay, on Point San Quentin, lay California's state prison. Prisons interested Eliza Farnham. She was, of course, intimately acquainted with Sing Sing; further, she had toured state, county, and city prisons in the eastern and midwestern states, as well as Canada. She wanted to see San Quentin.

California's first legislative acts as a new state in 1850 included the creation of enforceable laws, which in turn required facilities for incarceration, as well as overseers for the incarcerated. County jails soon proved inadequate for the State's large number of disappointed fortune-seekers resorting to criminal activity. The State established a prison system the following year, temporarily solving facility and administration needs by converting abandoned sailing ships into prisons and, to supervise the prisoners, letting contracts to private citizens. They in turn hired out the prisoners for labor, to pay expenses and, it was hoped, provide a profit. One of the first ships to serve as a prison was the *Waban,* and one of the first leases under the prison franchise system went, in 1851, to General Mariano Vallejo and James Estell, to supervise it.

The proceeds derived from convict labor paid the salaries of keepers, as guards were then called. Obviously the fewer the keepers, the greater the profit to the franchisees. Also, the fewer the keepers, the greater the number of escapes, which, aboard the overcrowded and isolated *Waban,* quickly became a problem. General Vallejo soon sold out his portion of the contract to Estell, who, responsible for feeding and caring for the prisoners as well as guarding them, found the enterprise less profitable than anticipated.

In 1852 the *Waban* was towed to Point San Quentin, a location the state, resuming its responsibility, soon deemed suitable for a permanent structure. There the convicts commenced building their own prison, in the course of which escapes remained frequent, and frequently violent. In September 1854, eight prisoners killed a keeper while making their escape; the following month saw more escapes; and December saw more again as the two-story edifice neared completion. In November 1855 a surrounding wall intended to prevent escapes was finished, just two months before the arrival of the first female visitors, Eliza Farnham and her traveling companion, a Mrs. Hall.

San Quentin did not impress Mrs. Farnham. And she was not reticent in saying so:

> There are nearly 400 men confined there, under conditions which, in many respects, a humane and enlightened farmer would object to for his swine or his horned cattle. In saying this, I wish to be understood as conveying no reproach to the officers now in charge of them....
>
> There is no branch of the public service in which an enlightened humanity is more imperatively needed than in the construction of prisons and the management of their inmates. In the first of these particulars the State has indeed been deeply disgraced. After all the light that has been shed on this question by the earnest labors of so many noble and wise men both in Europe and America, it is grievous to see that California, boasting its wealth and intelligence, though perhaps something shamed in its morality, should have erected for itself a prison that would have disgraced the least enlightened of the old States twenty years ago.

*"A Correct View of the State Prison, at Point San Quentin." San Quentin elicited severe criticism from Mrs. Farnham when she toured it in 1856: "The State has suffered deep wrong and disgrace in the erection of that building at such a cost.... When another prison is to be erected, as there must soon be, let intelligent and humane men—not pirates—have control of it." From the* California Police Gazette, *April 10, 1859. Courtesy of the California History Section, California State Library (4672)*

Among her several objections was the construction, which she faulted particularly for its failure to provide light and air:

> The architect at Corte Madera has proceeded in sublime indifference to what other States and men search the world over to find the best means of accomplishing. He has put a door of solid iron to each cell having a small slip in it by which a little light and air may enter. The cells are about ten feet by six and a half feet, and between eight and nine feet in the middle of the arch. At the sides they are about five feet in height. Into this dark den are thrust four individuals. Around and above them are the stone walls and iron door. Only one at a time can suck in a breath of pure air at the aperture, and see a glimpse of the out-door world. When a face is at the door, the others are in darkness.
>
> Can any one imagine themselves sharing such a room for two or ten years with three other persons, if they would understand why men become desperate and would rather be flogged to death or

shot in a vain attempt to escape, than remain there? But bad as this is, there are only cells enough to receive, even in this infernal association, a little more than half the prisoners. The remainder are shut up in one room, white, yellow, and black, old and young, feeble and strong, depraved and innocent together....a man cannot be reformed, or made in any sensible degree better who is condemned to breathe in darkness for 10 hours out of every 24, so foul an atmosphere that it will barely sustain his life. His whole system becomes disordered and unstable under it—mentally and morally dead, but in all animal senses painfully and morbidly alive. He behaves ill; is punished, and every punishment makes him worse—more desperate and ready to transgress again.

She particularly found offensive the intermixing of "depraved and innocent," and called it a "monstrous abuse":

I never anywhere saw so revolting and disgraceful a spectacle as this at our state prison. Imagine for one single moment the variety of character, condition, and nature there thrown together. No restraint upon any man's words or deeds—no escape from the tumult of depraved tongues—no momentary respite from the corrupt life raging around. That there are not frequent suicides there augurs either inability to accomplish the suicidal purpose, or a terrible and swift destruction of all sense of degradation, which is almost more deplorable than suicide.

Also exasperating were the huge expenditures of public funds lavished on the new prison:

The State has suffered deep wrong and disgrace in the erection of that building at such a cost. It is unfit for any use consistent with humanity and good discipline. The central columns of the long room unfit it for a workshop, and the cells above are something larger than will probably be ever afforded to one prisoner. If grated doors were substituted for those brutal iron plates, they would serve by and by, when a high and wise discipline shall have become practicable, for solitary cells.

Architecture and expense aside, there remained the matter of discipline to which she might also object, and she did:

But leaving the cells and the long room, let us take one more glance at their wretched inmates. Listen to them at night when they are locked up. What a tumult! In every other prison silence is the inexorable law, which all discipline and power are exercised to preserve.

And then, as always in her hierarchy of "kindness to prisoners," not to mention necessity to the soul and mind, there was the matter of books:

> In the long room, there are faint lights here and there, around each of which eight, ten and fifteen men assemble to hear another one read from a bit of newspaper or some stray printed page; for there are no books here—nothing to banish the evil thoughts of the past or the horrors of the future and the rebellion they excite. In all other prisons books are allowed and sought, and every Government in Christendom, except California, provides its State prisoners with Bibles and generally prayer books. Here is none of either. There is no Chaplain, nor have there ever been meetings of the prisoners held for religious or instructive purposes.
>
> Now I appeal directly to the religious and humane portion of the community, the women especially, to do something to better the condition of these wretched people. Books might, with a very little industry, be gathered for them. There are many ladies who are weary of every day idleness, and they might benefit themselves and the people I speak of, by collecting and sending up to the Warden or Physician a library for the prisoners. I speak at random, but are there not idle women enough in the Oriental and Rassette houses alone to get together in the next fortnight or month, 500 volumes? All sorts of books that are good in their character, from children's to the best that are brought to the country, could be profitably used.
>
> And until a chaplain is engaged, will not some of the divines of San Francisco leave occasionally, for one Sabbath, their fine churches and fashionable audiences, and go, as Christ said he came to those that are in prison?

Mrs. Farnham's "at random" reference to women residing at the Oriental and Rassette hotels was not lost on them—and their spokeswoman responded in kind:

> I too might speak "at random" and say if Mrs. Farnham instead of perambulating the State and making pathetic appeals to the blue-shirted and wifeless miners upon the "sufferings of woman," she should employ her time in the discharge of the household duties—in acts of unobtrusive charity and kindness, she would in so doing better perform her obligations to society, reflect more credit upon her sex, and lay up greater rewards hereafter. But I will not enlarge on the topic.
>
> The convicts at the State Prison may be fit subjects for sympathy and charity, and Mrs. Farnham, actuated by worthy motives in her

efforts to better their conditions however ill advised her attack on the ladies of San Francisco, who forsooth, because their sympathy and benevolence find in the helpless orphan, the sick and distressed females who crowd our city, more worthy recipients than the lusty murderer or house-thief, must be excoriated in the public Press! The ladies of San Francisco appeal to the records of the Orphan Asylum; to the books of the "Ladies Relief Society," and the hundreds of recipients of their generosity and kindness, to refute this charge of "idleness." They need none other.

Ignoring her critics, Mrs. Farnham, with characteristic acerbity, delivered her final volley of righteous objection to the state prison: "When another prison is to be erected, as there must soon be, let intelligent and humane men—not pirates—have control of it."

Being neither shy of opinions nor disinclined to express them, Mrs. Farnham probably shared her fresh indignation with the pirates—or powers—then sitting in Sacramento. Leaving San Quentin, she headed inland to the state's capital. Her next lecture would be there, in the assembly chamber, to the legislature.

## EIGHTEEN

# Sacramento and Beyond

SECOND LECTURE BY MRS. FARNHAM.—This lady, whose mind of masculine mould has enabled her to overcome, triumphantly, obstacles which would have proved insuperable to others of her sex, has, we are informed, succeeded at last in obtaining an eligible and spacious room in which to deliver another lecture. The subject which this learned has selected is "The Cultivation of Character;" and the place of delivery, the Fourth St. Baptist Church, and the hour for the commencement of the exercises, 7 1/2 o'clock.

*—Sacramento Daily Union,* February 8, 1856

LECTURE ON SPIRITUALISM.—Mrs. Farnham will deliver a Lecture on the above subject at Musical Hall, on Sunday Evening next, the 20th inst. Lecture to commence at quarter before eight o'clock. Admission 25 cents. Subject—"Spiritualism Illustrated by Facts and Experiences." Tickets for sale at Valentine & Co.'s Bookstore, 178 Jackson street; E. G. Hall's, 168 Montgomery street; and at the door on the evening of the Lecture.

*—San Francisco Daily California Chronicle,* April 19, 1856

During California's formative years as a state, its government was as famously footloose as its population. In 1849, Monterey hosted the constitutional convention, but delegates designated San Jose the capital. In 1850, the first state legislature convened in San Jose while other cities, both established and imaginary, vied for the capital prize. Mariano Vallejo bid a gift of land plus money for the erection of buildings, and the legislature voted it an offer they couldn't refuse. In January 1852, when the lawmakers arrived at the new city of Vallejo, however, it was evident that General Vallejo had failed to keep his various promises, including a proper place to hold legislative sessions. The state government packed its bags, boarded the steamer *Empire,* and departed for the city of Sacramento, which had waved the invitation of its grand new two-story courthouse.

*Benicia briefly hosted California's government before Sacramento offered the free use of its courthouse. Courtesy of The Bancroft Library, University of California, Berkeley* (California Mission Sketches *by Henry Miller, 1856*)

As the official capital remained the city of Vallejo, however, in 1853 the state government once again attempted to meet there. And once again accommodations failed to pass muster. And once again everyone decamped, this time to an eager little town called Benicia.

Consensus on Benicia: Nice building. Too small.

Sacramento, meanwhile, found it had a taste for status, and determined to have it back. Voting yea in 1854 to an offer of free use of Sacramento's handsome courthouse, plus a deed to a block of land on which the government could build to suit itself, the legislators returned to Sacramento and started building.

It was a fine structure, properly imposing, 80 by 120 feet, more than 60 feet tall. Ten massive pillars supported the front portico of the Ionic structure of two floors, with chambers for both the senate and the assembly. And in the spirit of those go-ahead times, it went ahead so quickly that on January 1, 1855, the government moved in.

It was at that impressive edifice that Eliza Farnham arrived on the first Sunday evening in February 1856. She was scheduled to speak there, in the assembly chamber, and such satisfactory publicity attended her visit that the spacious hall was "densely crowded with a very intelligent audience, among whom were many ladies." Also in attendance was the legislature, "including attaches," with the "galleries and lobbies completely filled by citizens and strangers."

The local newspaper obligingly described the speaker for those unable to attend:

> The personal appearance of Mrs. Farnham is just what one might be led to expect from those positive traits of character which have been so frequently and conspicuously exhibited. She has a decidedly intellectual cast of countenance, dark, thoughtful eyes, with decided but not displeasing expression. In figure she is tall, but spare, and of years scarcely sufficient to be classed among those who have reached the half-way house on the human highway.

Despite the writer's misgivings about women speakers in general, he declared Mrs. Farnham's presentation quite acceptable:

> The subject selected for her address was that of "Organic Laws Applied to Human Conditions," and although the views which we entertain and have heretofore expressed, as to the propriety of woman appearing "in public on the stage," have been unshaken by this feminine effort, we nevertheless cheerfully accord to the lecturer of Sunday evening our hearty assent to every sentiment uttered. The treatise was elaborate, exceedingly clear, the thoughts methodically arranged, and expressed in chaste and elegant language..... The enunciation of the lecturer is unobjectionable, but her voice is by no means strong. The audience, however, preserved throughout such quiet that we are confident her address was lost upon none present.

Her address, however, he declined to summarize:

> It were doing the lecturer unfairness, and her discourse injustice, to attempt even a synopsis of her remarks, but we cannot refrain from alluding to the graphic and life-like picture drawn between the moral and physical condition of the high born and low born....
>
> Some well-timed suggestions were made in regard to the necessity of personal good habits, and particularly that of daily ablutions, and of the intimate relationship existing between cleanliness of body and purity of thought and action.

After the lecture, a collection was taken up, which benefited Mrs. Farnham's purse by fifty dollars.

She was scheduled to deliver two more lectures in Sacramento, in the assembly chamber. Perhaps, having the ears of the legislature that first Sunday evening, she shared her low opinion of their expensive state prison and thus disgruntled the legislators, specifically Mr. Oxley. Or perhaps Mr. Oxley took personally her "well-timed suggestions" regarding "daily ablutions." Whatever his originating impulse, he opposed Mrs. Farnham's further use of the assembly chamber.

On Monday morning following her lecture, Mr. Oxley introduced a resolution stipulating that "during the present session, the Legislative chamber shall be used for no other than for Legislative business." Mr. Taliaferro objected by moving to lay the resolution on the table. Mr. Hawes said he would support the resolution, as "it was not known where the practice of appropriating the Assembly chamber might stop." Mr. Taliaferro then suggested amending the resolution by inserting, "unless with consent of two-thirds of the whole House." Mr. Bell offered a substitute resolution that thereafter when a "female woman is granted the privilege of lecturing in the hall, that the honorables who vote for it 'pan out' more extensively than on the two last occasions." To this puzzling metaphor, the Speaker responded by declaring the substitute resolution "not in order." Mr. Oxley then said he was willing to amend the resolution by inserting, "unless with the consent of two-thirds of the House."

The resolution, as amended, passed. Mrs. Farnham, the "female woman," would have to find another venue for the second lecture in her series.

The Baptist church on Fourth street promptly obliged. The *Sacramento Daily Union* noted that a large audience listened "with marked attention, pleasure, and we hope profit" to Mrs. Farnham's discourse on the "cultivation of human character." The reporter was definitely impressed: "Mrs. Farnham is unquestionably a woman of true genius, and none who have a just appreciation of literary statements will deny that she possesses them in a degree seldom seen in any representative of her sex."

The *Sacramento Democratic State Journal* also approved: "Her manner was mild and expressive, and her voice clear and of sufficient scope to fill the house. The most fastidious could scarcely find fault. She is the only female lecturer we now have in California, and the most pleasing, by far, we ever heard."

After delivering her third lecture in Sacramento, on "the characteristics of our present civilization," Mrs. Farnham moved on to Oroville, where an observer noted:

> I had the opportunity of listening...to...Mrs. Farnham, at Oroville....Her subject was, the improvement of man by the observance of the organic laws. The lecture was highly interesting, and largely attended. She informed me that it was her intention to visit all the principal towns of California, for the purpose of lecturing upon the above and similar topics. Mrs. Farnham is a lady of superior talent, and very correct literary taste.

The next principal town on her itinerary was Auburn, where the *Placer Herald* concisely summarized her visit: "MRS. FARNHAM.— This lady lectured in Auburn on Thursday and Friday evenings of last week. Her lecture was carefully written, well delivered, and favorably received."

Next stop: Nevada City.

Eliza followed in the footsteps of another female lecturer, the peripatetic temperance speaker Sarah Pellet. The *Nevada Journal* had opinions about them:

> FEMALE LECTURERS.—Lately was chronicled by the press with more or less unction, according to the gallantry of editors, or their want of the same courteous quality, the exodus of a strong minded woman from our shores.
>
> It is whispered, she was more provident in her apostolic peregrinations, than the twelve of old. Rumor has it that she provided her purse with the necessary against a rainy day, to the tune of $25,000. This can hardly be true, yet such has been the scarcity of women in certain parts of the mining region that Miss Pellet could not fail to accumulate something of a pile by merely exhibiting herself in woman's array at two bits a sight. Simple curiosity to see a woman would have emptied hundreds of gulches of their crop of old bachelors. But when it was announced that she would spout cold water to the miners, there was a charm of novelty about the thing that could not be resisted. Open mouthed listeners faced a column of oracular Merrimack, heard their much loved beverage unmercifully berated and paid for the abuse with the same liberal spirit, and from the same motive that they would pay to witness the antics of a wooden-headed punch.

Miss Pellet suffered more wear and tear of body than of mind, in her ejaculating circuits among the hills. No one who ever heard her went away with a feeling of sorrow that an over-taxed intellect was wearing itself out. Water was her element, but she dabbled in it where it was shallow. The stream that flowed from her lips was "one weak, washy, everlasting flood"; muddy and tasteless. In a word, Miss Pellet was a humbug. Whatever praise may have been courteously bestowed upon her we challenge pretended admirers to produce a single sentence of hers that exhibits a mark of individuality, or proves talent in the least above mediocrity. But she has gone, and in her stead has come another lecturer of her sex, and of a different order. The one was a type of the age of bronze, the other of the age of gold.

Mrs. Farnham is a woman of mind, of culture, and of large observation and experience. Men will listen to her lectures for the wealth of thought and beauty of language which characterize them. She fills a house, and keeps the audience interested in her subject which she handles in masterly style. Every sentence that drops from her lips, bears with it a burthen of thought. There is nothing trivial or common-place in her discourses, no blue stocking affectation, or ranting of a moral reform exhorter. Her address is made to the understanding, the taste, the intellect.

We understand Mrs. Farnham will visit this city next week, when our citizens will have an opportunity of hearing subjects well treated in the strongest, yet finest language by a woman.

We are not particularly well disposed towards female lecturers, but as even cold water papers say, "if you will drink go to friend Teal's and get the genuine article," so we say, if you will hear female lecturers, go and get the worth of your time and money, in listening to Mrs. Farnham.

Eliza did not disappoint her admirer: "Mrs. Farnham delivered two lectures in this city this week. The matter and manner were worthy the reputation enjoyed by the lecturer."

After Nevada City, Mrs. Farnham delivered two lectures at Marysville, where she received what must have been a most gratifying letter signed by fourteen gentlemen in San Francisco:

Dear Madam:—As very many persons were prevented hearing your third lecture "On the Characteristics of our present Civilization," in consequence of the inclemency of the weather at the time, we should feel gratified if you would favor us with its repetition on your return to this city.

We remain, Dear Madam, yours very respectfully,...

Mrs. Farnham promptly replied:

Gentlemen: I have the pleasure to acknowledge the receipt, on my arrival at this place last evening, of your kind and complimentary note of the 21st ult. requesting the repetition, on my return to San Francisco, of my Lecture "On the Characteristics of our Present Civilization." It is my intention to be in this city on Friday next, and if the time be agreeable to yourselves it will afford me pleasure to comply with your request on Sunday evening, 9th inst.

While Eliza was traveling in the interior, she may have read the *Sacramento Daily Union*'s reprinted article from the *San Francisco Herald*:

THE SPIRITUAL MANIA IN SAN FRANCISCO.—It is a startling assertion, but one that can be well substantiated, that there are in this city hundreds of victims of the spiritual delusion. But even more startling is the fact that many who profess to believe in spiritual manifestations are also professed believers in the doctrine of Divine truth. In many respectable families the subject of spiritualism forms a topic of interesting conversation, and in several of the large hotels "spiritual circles," so called, meet regularly to waste the precious hours in silly (if not blasphemous) invocation, of "the spirits."...The miserable fanatics who accept the theory of spiritual manifestations as truth are deserving of commiseration; while those who, although unbelievers, yet permit the practice of spiritual tricks within their own house, thus exerting a pernicious influence upon weaker minds, are deserving of more than condemnation.

Eliza Farnham believed unquestionably and unquestioningly that the dead communicated with the living. And she wasn't shy about saying so:

I accept the alleged phenomena, so far as I am acquainted with them, as altogether in harmony with what I believe of human capacity and spiritual power. But if I rightly apprehend their bearing, the most they can do for me, is to confirm and clear foregone conclusions.

...Here is no dogma which conflicts with one you have before received. Here is no arbitrary assertion, contradicting another arbitrary assertion which you have before trusted. It is philosophy and religion wedded, which have before been blindly and bitterly divorced. It is love translated by wisdom—light falling from higher and purer eyes than ours, upon the clouded fields of life—bloom and radiance descending into dark and rugged vales of fruitless belief, faith stealing noiselessly into the infidel soul.

*"Sacramento City: Waterfront with Contemplated Improvements," by J. B. M.*
*Crooks & Co. Among Sacramento's earliest "contemplated improvements" was*
*an imposing building for the state legislature. After Eliza Farnham spoke there,*
*the state assembly passed a resolution against further lectures by "female women."*
*Courtesy of The Bancroft Library, University of California Berkeley*
*(Banc Pic 1963:002:1535-E)*

When Mrs. Farnham returned to San Francisco to repeat her
original lecture series, as promised, as well as to speak on
Spiritualism, the daily papers took note:

*Alta California,* April 21, 1856: MRS. FARNHAM'S LECTURE.—The
lecture of Mrs. Farnham at Musical Hall last evening, on
Spiritualism, was quite largely and respectably attended. The
address was characterized by the same intellectual merit which all
her previous lectures are entitled to, and evinced a well-read and
cultivated mind; but there was very little in her remarks calculated
to advance the science or doctrine of modern table-tipping, or spiritual rapping. The lecture embraced copious extracts from able writers, interspersed with the sentiments and opinions of the speaker;
and, aside from its spiritual feature, may be considered a very able
and interesting address.

It was rendered apparently with a greater volume of voice and
with greater distinctness than her lectures on former occasions.

*San Francisco Daily Evening Bulletin,* April 28, 1856: MRS. FARNHAM'S LECTURE.—This lady's lecture at Musical Hall last night we are told was very successful. She proposes to lecture again on Friday night when she will speak on the subject of "The Women of the Pacific States."

*San Francisco Daily California Chronicle,* April 30, 1856: MRS. FARNHAM'S NEXT LECTURE.—A lady of taste desires us to call attention to the fact that Mrs. Farnham will lecture at Music[al] Hall, on Friday evening. Her subject, we understand, is "Heroism of Women"; our California women being to a considerable extent the theme of the lecture. Our informant assures us that the lecture, which she has heard or read, is the best ever written by the able author. Very high praise, and worthy the attention and approbation of the ladies particularly.

In her "Women of the Pacific States" lecture, Mrs. Farnham claimed that "the true rights and duties of men and women could never conflict with each other, that they might play their complete parts in their respective spheres harmoniously." In so doing, she reaffirmed her long-held position against such women's rights objectives as "political privileges" for women. While the movement campaigned for suffrage and access to the professions, Mrs. Farnham averred that woman's sphere was essentially maternal and "consisted in doing the uncorrupted, unrestrained promptings of her nature."

In reviewing the lecture, the *Daily California Chronicle* noted:

Her concluding remarks were directed to the social condition of the California community, and contained many good suggestions, which if carried into practice would make a happy people of us. As usual in this lady's lecture, there were a number of very powerful and scathing sentences. One of the anecdotes, for instance, was of a man, whom we supposed from the story to have been a preacher, with his wife and children coming across the plains to California. They met with difficulties, and for a long time travelled at the point of starvation. The *lord* gave completely out, and being, as it seems of a cowardly and contemptible spirit, left all the responsibility and labor of reaching a settlement to the wife, himself, a hectoring master before, lying in the most comfortable part of the wagon while she yoked the cattle and pushed forward. Mrs. Farnham afterwards met this specimen of a man and asked him what he thought of the efforts of his wife. He answered, "She has been an instrument in the hands of the Lord to preserve my life." "Impossible!" Mrs. Farnham replied, "the Lord could never have prostituted so noble an instrument to so mean a use." She was frequently applauded during the course of her remarks.

During all her travels about the state, lecturing nearly nonstop, Mrs. Farnham apparently found time to attend to some vexing personal business. The *Sacramento Daily Union,* on June 30, 1856, noted: "Divorces in San Francisco.—On Friday...Eliza Fitzpatrick (Mrs. Farnham) from William Fitzpatrick."

Meanwhile, back in Santa Cruz, Georgiana Kirby remained immersed in baby care, having welcomed into the world another daughter. She named her Georgiana, and called her Georgie:

> She was born on the 12th of December, 1855 and was the quietest and best of babies, apparently perfectly well, only the left eye was weak which I attribute to my having done so much sewing, especially as my eyes are quite weak when enceinte.

Despite this new baby being so quiet, her mother apparently was too busy to keep up her journal. This was always a task attended to in fits and starts, and this time Georgiana abandoned her journal keeping in August of 1855 and would not take it up again for three years. In consequence, it contains no entry for July 5, 1856. But on that date she surely must have had mixed thoughts and feelings, upon reading in the *Santa Cruz Pacific Sentinel:*

> Elisa [sic] W. Farnham.—This highly intelligent and well-known lady, who has been for seven years a resident of this county, and who has lately been engaged in lecturing through this State, took her departure on Monday morning last for her former home in the State of New York, we have not the pleasure of an acquaintance with Mrs. F, but we are assured by persons of her acquaintance that she is a lady of extraordinary intelligence; too masculine in mind to enjoy happiness in the condition of feminine domestic life; her situation since her residence in this State has been unhappy and most unfortunate; she obtained a divorce from her husband for cruel treatment but a few days before she left. She will find circumstances and society in the east more congenial to her feelings, and we hope she may spend the remainder of her days in enjoyment, she is yet in the vigor of life.

*Vallejo street wharf, ca. 1866, photographed by Lawrence & Houseworth.
The Pacific Mail Steamship Company's* John L. Stephens *departed
San Francisco's Vallejo street wharf in 1856 with Mrs. Farnham and her son
Charles aboard. The line advertised a "safe, pleasant and expeditious transit
from ocean to ocean." As no complaint survives from Mrs. Farnham, who was
not shy about voicing one, the company apparently kept its promise. On her
return trip aboard the same ship, she complained only about the weather.
Courtesy of The Bancroft Library, University of California, Berkeley
(Stereographs 3, 1994:032:5)*

# NINETEEN

# The First by a Lady

MRS. FARNHAM'S NEW WORK.—A work on California, with a concluding chapter on the *morale* of the action of the Vigilance Committee during the last summer, by Mrs. E. W. Farnham, is about being issued from the New York press, and will be forwarded to this city per steamer of the 20th October. Mrs. Farnham ranks with the most finished and popular writers in the United States, and our reading public may anticipate an intellectual entertainment of no ordinary character.

—*Daily California Chronicle,* October 2, 1856

The volume before us we repeat, is descriptive of adventure, climate, scenery, soil, population and production.—Of mining, farming, grape-growing, gardening, milling, ranching, and dreaming.—Of men and women, their education, pursuits, social habits, and condition; of what they have been, are, and can be. In fact, of almost everything that is interesting in and to Californians, from digging gold to raising calves; not omitting some suggestions of improvement to men and women.

It is an interesting book, fluently and pleasingly written, and we commend it to our readers. It is, moreover, the first book that has been written in, or concerning California, by a lady. Buy it.

—*Hutchings California Magazine,* January 1857

O n Saturday, July 5, 1856, the very day the *Santa Cruz Pacific Sentinel* announced Eliza's departure from California, she boarded the Pacific Mail Steamship *John L. Stephens* at San Francisco's Vallejo street wharf. Advertisements for the line advised her that "mails, passengers and treasure" would be landed at Panama's railroad terminus and "proceed immediately by railroad across the Isthmus" to Aspinwall. The steamship line further promised travelers that:

> According to arrangements now completed, Passengers
> Arriving at Panama in the morning, invariably leave Aspinwall
> For New York and New Orleans, in the afternoon of the
> Same day, thus affording regularity in the through trip;
> a safe, pleasant and expeditious transit from ocean to ocean.

For Eliza Farnham, this "safe, pleasant and expeditious" journey must have seemed the height of luxury. In 1849, her voyage from New York to San Francisco—not including her unscheduled stay in Valparaiso—consumed nearly six months. Now, with the Panama railroad complete, she departed California in July and in August she was in New York.

Soon after visiting her son, Charles, at school in Milton, Eliza was in New York City, impatiently writing letters. She needed money. On stationery borrowed from Fowler and Wells, she wrote to Dix, Edwards & Co., the publisher of her new book, hoping to publish more of her writings:

> I have waited as long as it seems possible for me to wait in this Babel in the daily hope of seeing you....Will you be kind enough to write me during the coming week if you have any news for me, as to Mss or Story. I brought another down and will have it left here for you to dispose of if it is convenient. What of Emerson & Putnam as a market? Do you know Mrs. Okes Smith? She is the editor I believe and I think this story would suit her taste in regard to women.

Anticipating a market for her book in the West, Eliza wrote the editor of the *Daily California Chronicle* in San Francisco that Dix, Edwards & Co. would ship copies of *California, In-Doors and Out* on October 20.

On October 21 the *New York Tribune* advertised her new book:

> Mrs. Farnham's philanthropic project for colonizing California with virtuous and self-sustaining women in 1849 will be recalled with interest by thousands in this community and in San Francisco, including many of the most influential citizens in both places. That noble effort did not utterly fail, since it has brought forth this most instructive and entertaining account of California development. We have here the true panorama of life in the El Dorado, from the first scrambling for gold at Sutter's Mill to the high-handed but wholesome supremacy of the Vigilance Committee.
>
> The chapters devoted to the Committee are of surpassing interest, and the whole is what we might expect from so brave and clear-minded a woman.

Reviews, good ones, started rolling in:

*Frank Leslie's Illustrated Newspaper:* "This is a personal narrative...written with considerable liveliness and graphic power of description."

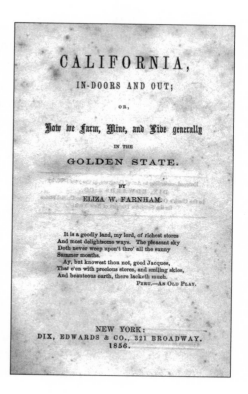

*Excerpt from a letter from Eliza Farnham to Joshua Dix. Hoping not only to earn money by writing but to instruct her readers, Mrs. Farnham wrote, "I could write many tales, bearing in some kindred manner upon the follies or vices of society, and teaching perhaps, some valuable truths to those who are not overapt at learning them. Do you think such could be disposed of?"*

*Title page,* California, In-doors and Out. *In praising this, the first book about California by a woman,* the Philadelphia American Courier *claimed, "The wildest romance could scarcely excel in strangeness and interest the simple incidents of fact there set down in the experience of an energetic and self-protected woman."*

CALIFORNIA,

IN-DOORS AND OUT;

OR,

How we Farm, Mine, and Live generally

IN THE

GOLDEN STATE.

BY

ELIZA W. FARNHAM.

It is a goodly land, my lord, of richest stores
And most delightsome ways. The pleasant sky
Doth never weep upon't thro' all the sunny
Summer months.
Ay, but knowest thou not, good Jacques,
That e'en with precious stores, and smiling skies,
And beauteous earth, there lacketh much.
PERU.—AN OLD PLAY.

NEW YORK:
DIX, EDWARDS & CO., 321 BROADWAY.
1856.

*Boston Transcript:* "Mrs. Farnham has now written a book about California which we take to be the most authentic and graphic picture of life there, as exhibited to female eyes, which has yet appeared. She sees things as they are, and reports the trials, pleasures and experiences of the emigrant with honest emphasis."

*Boston Advertiser:* "Mrs. Farnham relates many interesting stories of the energy displayed by women with whom she came in contact, and her book will be read with interest, containing as it does a great deal that is new and remarkable of the peculiarities of life and manner in California."

*Philadelphia American Courier:* "'California In-Doors and Out' is easily and naturally written, and the wildest romance could scarcely excel in strangeness and interest the simple incidents of fact there set down in the experience of an energetic and self-protected woman."

*Portland Transcript:* "Mrs. Farnham has done well to give us her Story of California Life; and so far as we have read it, it is at once life-like and woman-like."

*Philadelphia Merchant:* "If you wish to become acquainted with some of the strangest developments of this fast age, look upon the picture of California as presented in the pages of this volume."

*Putnam's Magazine:* "Mrs. Farnham is a person of such keen observation, and such originality of judgment, to say nothing of her unusual opportunities, that whatever she writes has an attraction and value."

As gratifying as reading her reviews must have been, Mrs. Farnham was not one to sit still. New York was alive with compelling activities. In November, the Seventh Annual National Woman's Rights Convention met at the Broadway Tabernacle, and her old friend, Mrs. Francis Wright, now Paulina Wright Davis, was president.

Despite Eliza's stance on the women's rights controversy—that she held woman's natural position as not equal to man's, but superior—the roster of speakers must have commanded her attention, including as it did Lucretia Mott, Wendell Phillips, Elizabeth Jones, the Reverend T. W. Higginson, Frances D. Gage, Ernestine L. Rose, Susan B. Anthony, and Lucy Stone.

New York's newspapers reported many matters of interest to her from the West, certainly a "Meeting of Californians":

A general discussion of the wants of California was entered into, and the opinion of the meeting seemed to resolve itself into a determination to secure land in that State, of which there is abundance to be had, for settlers, at as cheap a rate as practicable; to diminish the cost of transportation; provide agents in San Francisco to receive, lodge and forward emigrants at fair rates, and to establish an organization which shall loan to settlers such means as they may require until their first crops are gathered, payable at some future period. They also intend to urge upon Congress the immediate importance of a good wagon road across the Plains, well guarded by United States troops from the predatory attacks of hostile Indians. By these means it is believed that a wholesome and much-needed emigration from the Eastern and Western States and from Europe may be induced to flow to and settle in the Golden State.

She must have read with interest the *Tribune's* long article on "Life in Sing Sing Prison" and discovered, if she did not already know, that her old adversary John Luckey had recently regained the position of chaplain lost in 1846 when he had so publicly opposed her reading to the female prisoners. Now he had not only returned to the prison to provide religious instruction but—in a turn of events undoubtedly gratifying to Mrs. Farnham—to supervise teachers hired to instruct the prisoners to read and write.

Newspaper advertisements and notices also likely caught her eye. The *Spiritual Telegraph,* "The organ of communication from Spirits," announced weekly publication at a subscription of seven dollars per year. Always interested in books issued by Fowler and Wells, she must have taken note of their publication of Dr. R. T. Trall's *Illustrated Hydropathic Encyclopedia,* "The most comprehensive and popular work yet published on Water-Cure."

With her son Charles's musical talent and inclination in mind, she may have attended the lecture at Clinton Hall by Professor Andrade, who offered singing classes in "the new, simple, and wonder-working French Method."

Lecturing remained a popular interest in New York, and Eliza duly re-entered the speaking arena. In November, when the *Tribune* published a roll of speakers engaged for the "lecturing season," giving "the names of those avouched to us as having been hitherto engaged in that capacity, and having so acquitted themselves as to induce further invitations," Eliza Farnham made the list, one of only three women. The list was further distinguished by the names of Henry Ward Beecher, A. Bronson Alcott, Ralph Waldo Emerson, and Henry Thoreau.

That winter Mrs. Farnham visited family in Illinois and Iowa. While in Iowa, she met Colonel Vaughan, Indian Agent for Nebraska. He had spent seventeen years among the Indians and told her he believed that among the tribes with which he was familiar, "there was as much mechanical talent as among an equal number of Whites who were as little instructed." He had a carving, he told her, the work of one of "his Indians," that was "matchless in beauty and perfection of finish, and...by no means so uncommon among them as we are apt to suppose it." But, he added, "We lack all means of educating [them]...for want of some right help, they waste themselves and their poor resources." He believed that within fifteen years, without some new provision for the Indians, "they must be destitute and starving."

In consequence of this meeting, Mrs. Farnham felt particularly sympathetic to a letter she received the following spring:

> The many excellent thoughts to which your tongue and pen have given utterance, together with the experience you have had in Frontier Life, prompt me to ask your views in regard to the most appropriate means for the prevention of Indian hostilities, and of elevating both Races above the love, or occasion of war.

She replied at once to the writer, John Beeson, expressing at length her sympathy with his cause:

> I have always felt a deep interest in the Indian Race, and as an American woman have lamented the wrongs my country has inflicted on those people....
>
> That the Indians are capable of being raised from the Savage state, and developed to a condition which would place them within the pale of Civilization, and give them the blessing of mental and spiritual growth, I have not, for many years, doubted. They are a people of strong character, and, in their natural conditions, possessed of noble physical endowments. There is not a better nature on the globe, in many respects, than our Red Man possesses. How rarely, until mean and selfish Whites compel him, does he debase himself by the indulgence of low appetites!

Mrs. Farnham's position was advanced for the times, when even the well-meaning and well-educated considered Indians "only grown up children." Nonetheless, in keeping with general public opinion, she opposed the Indians' claim to independence:

> We are better tenants of the earth than he was; and our titles ought to be paramount to his, because the great purposes of God are better served by us than by him. But the right to dispossess him is ours by virtue of our superiority; and this ought to be his perfect guaranty against wrong from us. Has it been so? Has the one Democratic Government on the globe—the example to all nations—cared for, or oppressed and destroyed its independent tribes? Alas! History answers this question too mournfully to every human soul!
>
> Our Indians are now dwindled down to mere handfuls of scattered men, and women, and children, who have neither the grandeur of the Savage, nor a semblance of the power of the civilized human being. The labor that has been done among them, for the most part confined to religious teaching of opinions and Faith, has been very nearly, if not quite, counterbalanced by the evils which have followed close upon the advent of the Missionary.

Her answer to the "Indian question" may have surprised her correspondent:

> The women of America could put their hands to a very humane task in reforming the treatment of the Indian, and thereby redeeming the Nation from the shame and disgrace of a wrong pursued to the extermination of its victims. If some widely concerted plan of action could be adopted throughout our country, and means be raised, whereby humane and intelligent persons could be secured to cooperate with a National Association for the purpose of improving and elevating the Indian, what a noble work might thus be done! I speak of my own sex particularly, because it is taking its position in organized philanthropies more broadly and generally in this day than ever before, and because I fully believe that the world is to receive its highest and purest service of this sort from us. The heart of woman is the purest fountain of human love and charity on earth, and could we but rightly appeal to the American Women in behalf of the Indian—could we bring before them the wretchedness and degradation of these unfortunates, whom their charities could relieve—could we make them see the Indian mother and her children in their houses of poverty and misery, robbed of the joys and satisfactions of savage life, with nothing in their place but sin and desolation—I am sure their hearts would not be cold to the appeal so made. There is benevolence enough among us to answer these calls, could it but be moved to an appreciation of their reality and its own power of relief.

Mrs. Farnham's personal problem remained money. She spent the summer in Milton, at the home of friends, visiting with Charles and writing—often to her publisher, Joshua Dix:

> Enclosed with this, is a story, which somehow or other has written itself by my hand, within the last three or four days.
>
> It embodies a truth which I think of the highest importance, and I hope in an unexceptionable form. I thot it might suit Harpers Monthly. Will you offer it to them? Read it first yourself, if you have the time & inclination—I think the writing tolerably legible—and do with it what you think best. I am much in need of whatever it will bring, and shall therefore be doubly thankful to hear of its acceptance in some good paying journal.
>
> I could write many tales, bearing in some kindred manner upon the follies or vices of society, and teaching perhaps some valuable truths to those who are not overapt at learning them. Do you think such could be disposed of?
>
> I send also the Mss of the novel, to which I have done all but the chaptering. I thought my nerves would feel less under that labor, some weeks hence, after I know somebody would publish it, and it does not hurt it for reading, that it is not divided.

A week later she wrote him again:

> As I have not heard of your receiving the parcel I sent you a week ago tonight, I have asked my friend Mr. Hallock to call and inquire for me. I have remembered since sending it that you told me you might be absent from the city for awhile; and my anxiety to hear the fate of the Mss prompts me to send this messenger & note.
>
> I hope to hear some good news before long. If you can get the favor of an early decision on the last one, "Experience" and it should be a rejection, what do you think of sending it to Philips and Sampson? They are not bound by church associations nor the opinions of any set, as I think both Harpers & Appletons are. I should be so very glad to get them both in hands very soon.

Eliza had sent Joshua Dix the manuscript of her third book, an autobiographical narrative of her youth up to the age of nineteen, which she thinly disguised as a novel by changing the names of the people involved, including her own. Although it would be published under a different title, Eliza's choice was *Lucia Woodson*. Dix's reply questioned whether the book ought to end where it did. Eliza responded:

The alleged fault of Lucia Woodson is very probably the one it has. But...as the book is complete in itself, and I have a right to choose whether I will ever add another vol. or not, what do you think of the wisdom of leaving the title page silent on that question? I think the criticism of my reader would be more upon the merits of the book so presented to him. If you agree in this opinion, will you be kind enough to copy the title page, omitting the words Part First and those in brackets? If then you think well of offering it to Appletons, or... any one else in New York, I shall be thankful if you will do so. I do not know but that the book ought to be abridged and shall very cheerfully yield to such a decision when I think it is made upon the merits of this written part and not with reference to what may follow it.

Eliza Farnham, in need of money, possessed but one sure avenue to attaining it: her pen. After writing Joshua Dix, she wrote Colonel James Warren, editor of the *California Farmer,* in San Francisco, and he agreed to pay her to write for his newspaper. Eliza's first effort as a newspaper correspondent was a piece on— the weather. When there was nothing else to write about, there was always the weather:

LETTER FROM MRS. FARNHAM

New York, Sept. 3d, 1857

EDITORS, FARMER: I have heard myself, and others in like unfortunate exile here, designated as Californians *lost* in the East. The phrase is a happy one, that is, if a phrase describing unhappiness can ever properly be pronounced happy. To be in the East after having spent years on the Pacific coast, especially in that garden of it, California, is to be indeed lost. The winds are indeed fitful, as if a many-phased demon breathed them over you. To-day he prostrates you with insupportable languor. A fortnight or a month ago, he pierced your very marrow with a foul eastern blast. Three months hence he will convert you into a solid icicle.

If you reached these shores in summer, you probably found the heat more insupportable in New York than at Panama. Your thinnest garments were not half thin enough....But two or three weeks after... you are confounded by a sunless morning, dark and ominous, and before night you are distractedly shivering over the tumbled remains of merinos and cashmeres, and warm satins, which have the hateful odor of the vile steamships (on this side) yet left in them. Your friends are quarreling over their priority of right to certain favorite dressmakers, and you find the world all around you in a confusion

of preparation for the coming winter. Not one sweet-tempered, delicious rainy season, but winter, which the mercury tries in vain to
escape by running down; which sends needles through your blood,
and thickens your ears, and stiffens your lips, and purples your
fingers, and pinches your toes till you are unconscious whether they
are on your own feet or perambulating the snows of Lapland, with
that human locomotive Bayard Taylor.

We were used, all of us, to talk of coming East as "going home,"
when we were in California. Now, our complaint *here* is, that we can't
go *home there*. In Chicago, last winter, I received a California mail,
one day, containing letters from several dear friends, among others
one, who, writing from San Francisco, complained of the unusual
severity of the weather. "Think of our weather," she said; "I am writing this at 10 o'clock a.m., and the white frost is actually lying in the
street yet!" At the moment that I read those words, the mercury
stood at 21 degrees below zero. A fellow sufferer from San Francisco
was present, and we laughed bitterly, indulging ourselves, meanwhile, in heartfelt abuse of the country where we were.

"Why do you stay?" I asked.

"Stay!" was the reply, "if I were not restrained by the choice of others, whom I feel bound to consult, I would as soon as cut off my left
hand as remain here."

This is the mind of all Californians, almost without exception.
Their testimony to the *charm* of the country is unanimous. I wish all
Californians who think of the East *as home* could come here. It would
be a service to the State, for it would insure their permanent settlement on their return thither, and then they would feel they had a
stake in the State, and its character and institutions, which now they
are willing to neglect, and leave to be tarnished and defiled by
unworthy hands.

We are anxiously hoping for the opening of some additional
route to San Francisco, this fall or winter. At the present rates of fare
it is impossible for men with families, unless they are also men of
fortune, to get there. The Pacific Company appears to be the most
efficient enemy the State has, beyond her geographical limits. All
the worse, too, for possessing so indubitably as it does that advantage
which corporate bodies are generally supposed to enjoy—a flatulent
vacuum where should be a soul.

The *San Francisco Evening Bulletin* helped itself to Mrs. Farnham's
weather letter and reprinted it under the heading "THE CHARM OF
CALIFORNIA CLIMATE—LONGING OF ABSENT CALIFORNIANS TO
RETURN."

Complacent San Franciscans read it in the *Bulletin* on October 20. The coming winter for them would mean a little rain, a little fog, a little inconvenience.

In the East, the coming winter for many New Yorkers would mean starvation. In New York, the stock market had crashed in the aftermath of a stunning loss of California gold.

In New York, the financial panic of '57 had commenced.

And Eliza Farnham had a new mission.

*"The Central America engulphed in the ocean, about eight the ship began to settle rapidly, when she momentarily righted and went down stern foremost."* Hand-printed lithograph by J. Childs, courtesy of The Bancroft Library, University of California, Berkeley (Banc Pic 1963:002:0331-B)

# TWENTY

# Women's Protective Emigration Society

AID TO SUFFERING WOMEN.—The following circular came to us by last mail, with a note from that noble hearted woman, Mrs. E. W. Farnham, who, it is well-known, is laboring to elevate the character of her sex, and awaken them to a more just conception of their ability and influence, and to arouse them to a higher and holier ambition for their own sex. Mrs. Farnham's letter in this number of the Farmer will be read with deep interest by all who have a taste for the "good, true, and beautiful." We sincerely hope the circular, which we here append, will awaken our people to devise some way by which Californians can either bring the most deserving of those who need our help here, or send aid to them.

—*California Farmer*, San Francisco, January 8, 1858

O n June 27, 1857, the *New York Herald* predicted a stock market collapse as a consequence of speculative western land and railroad securities. Political uncertainty over whether Kansas and Nebraska would become slave states further weakened the market, as did the unexpected shutting down, on August 24, of the New York branch of the Ohio Life Insurance and Trust Company.

All of this was but the calm before the storm, a literal storm, as it happened, that took a fortune in California gold to the bottom of the ocean and sunk the nation into three years of economic depression.

On August 20, 1857, in the regularly scheduled service that had taken Eliza Farnham from San Francisco to New York the year before, the Pacific Mail Steamship Company's SS *Sonora* departed San Francisco for Panama City. There, passengers and cargo duly transferred to the Panama Railroad and crossed the isthmus to Aspinwall. Awaiting them was the side-wheel steamship SS *Central America*.

On September 4, the day after Mrs. Farnham lamented New York's weather for the entertainment of the *California Farmer*'s readers, the *Central America* was one day at sea. Nearly three hundred feet long, the ship carried 477 passengers, 101 crew members, and a staggeringly valuable cargo of California gold, much of it destined for expectant, and over-extended, New York banking firms. The *Central America* was some two hundred miles off the Carolina coast when tragedy struck. Weather had gone from bad to worse, swelling a fierce storm into a hurricane. High seas and furious winds united to send huge waves crashing onto the ship. An uncontainable leak admitted sea water that rose higher and higher and, despite heroic bailing by hundreds of men, eventually extinguished the boiler that provided steam for both the paddle wheels and the pumps, leaving the ship to the storm's mercy. When crew desperately raised sails, shrilling winds shredded the canvas to tatters. There was one saving grace, literally: a chance encounter with a sailing ship, the *Marine,* temporarily crippled by the storm. Three lifeboats succeeded in transferring the *Central America*'s thirty female passengers and twenty-six children to the *Marine* while the *Central America*'s crew and male passengers frantically continued to bail in hopes of keeping the foundering vessel afloat.

To no avail.

The SS *Central America* went down on the evening of Saturday, September 12, its stoic captain at the wheel in full dress uniform. Several hours later, past midnight, the helmsman on a passing ship, the bark *Ellen,* heard cries in the dark. The *Ellen*'s crew plucked forty-nine half-crazed survivors from the water. In all, 428 lives were lost in one of the greatest maritime disasters in American history.

Financial disaster followed. On September 25, the Bank of Pennsylvania failed, the first of many. On September 30, the *New York Tribune* predicted there was worse to come:

> There is manifestly a hard Winter in prospect for our laboring class—for those who are usually workers for wages. Tens of thousands of them will not be able to find employment, while others will be forced to work at some vocation in which they can earn very little, and will probably receive even less. We estimate the National loss from inability to find employment during the next half year at not less than One Hundred Millions of dollars. Of course, this involves a very large aggregate of individual privation and suffering.

On November 25, Mrs. Farnham probably read in the *Tribune,* with particular interest, a letter from Illinois, promising employment opportunities in that state:

> The farmers are nearly all short of help, and although they would not be willing to pay high wages in the Winter season, still they would be willing to give more than enough to board and clothe the persons employed, and as soon as Spring opens there will be plenty to do at good wages. There are thousands of acres of corn that I have passed since I left home that are not yet harvested for the want of any help to do it. And as for girls to do housework, any number of them can find employment. Mr. Watkins of the Dement House, Fulton City, whose card I inclose, says he has no doubt but that he can find employment for 100 girls at $1.50 per week and board.

On November 28, Mrs. Farnham wrote James L. Warren of the *California Farmer:*

> Sir: The extreme suffering and destitution of working women in our city call for some immediate measures of relief at the hands of those who may be able to devise and carry them forward....An investigation into their numbers and condition has convinced those who have made it that there never was a time in the history of this city when her welfare was more deeply imperiled by crime and depravity than it will be this winter, if charitable and thoughtful persons do not interpose to rescue the destitute from their extremity of exposure; and also, that never before, in any period of distress, were there such ample means at hand for averting its most deplorable results. Thousands of our homeless, starving females are wanted all over the vast West, only thirty-six or forty-eight hours' travel from us; and could we but bring them there we should have done a lasting service to the place they leave, as well as to that whither they go.

On December 4, the *Tribune* exhorted women to the aid of their sisters:

> There are women who will hear and read of the "Hard Times" who will feel nothing of their withering grasp. To you the fates are kind....But, alas! for the great company who toil, suffer and die alone....Already thousands are without the means of subsistence. And the fact of the young girl, who, when she found that she could have no more work, went to her lodgings and cut her throat, proves how appalling is the present state of affairs to those whose life has a single choice, work or shame.

Eliza Farnham needed no urging to act on behalf of women. She was already in action, organizing the Women's Protective Emigration Society. At a public meeting held in New York City's Mercantile Library on December 4, she reported what the society had already achieved and what it proposed to do. The Common Council, she said, had been "memorialized" for a donation of three thousand dollars, the claim urged "upon moral and economical grounds." There were thousands of women in the city, she added, "good, honest, industrious folks—and duly deprived of their means of subsistence, who for months had been living as best they could by pawning their furniture and clothing." Those with whom she and others had conversed "were on the brink of starvation, and every day sent scores of them upon the streets." She closed by saying that "whatever was done, must be done at once."

In California, Eliza's dear friend Georgiana might have wished she could assist such a worthy cause, but her time and energy necessarily were committed elsewhere. On December 29, 1857, Georgiana presented Richard Kirby with his third daughter and named her Cornelia. The next day, in New York, Eliza Farnham saw forty women sponsored by the Women's Protective Emigration Society leave for domestic positions in Indiana. Eliza and Georgiana now lived a continent apart in geography and a world apart in their daily activities. While children consumed Georgiana's energy, Eliza devoted hers to philanthropy and writing.

Eliza Farnham, as a newspaper correspondent residing in New York City and writing for San Franciscans, knew her audience. Californians liked to hear they'd made the better choice in coasts. She wrote to the *California Farmer's* subscribers that the "lost Californians," those who had returned to the East, avidly read the *Farmer* for its "delicious fruit items." They read and remembered, "with sparkling eyes and proud hearts," and said to themselves, "Ah that is the country":

> We dilate, mentally, if there be no audience present, on the grain crops; and potato crops; and big trees; and grand Fairs; and gold products; and if there be a man or men, woman or women at hand, we relieve the pent up enthusiasm by a few words which astonish or provoke their unblessed apathy into expression. "Oh, you are insane with regard to California," say they; "clean daft, we never expect to hear a reasonable word from you about it."

That, retorts the exile, is because of your benighted ignorance. When you have never grown a California crop, how can you know its wealth; when you have never trodden California soil how can you know its richness; when you have never felt a California breeze, how can you know the freight of life it bears; when you have never seen a California sky, how can you know the glory of its deep clear, tranquil blue!

The bad times then being endured in New York, she attested, the financial collapse and bitter weather, stirred easterners to dreams of California:

In this crisis, had there been any reasonable means of getting to San Francisco, you would have received great numbers of good citizens from the East; people who were broken up and had to look for new homes somewhere. It is cheering in the midst of all the discouragement that has beat every body to the earth here, to get good tidings from anywhere, and yours come with especial welcome to our pride as well as our affection for the land they speak of.

But of course there were other topics, such as artistic endeavors, engaging Mrs. Farnham's attention. And when such events could further her celebration of women, so much the better:

The lovers of Art are now enjoying a rare treat for America at this time. There is on exhibition in this city a collection of French pictures, a gallery of British paintings, and separately, the great work of Rosa Bonheur, the Horse Fair. Indisputably this is *the* picture of the day...Never was such a *mass* of rollicking, snorting, rearing, plunging, willful and vicious life put upon canvas by a masculine hand, as this lady hath portrayed....It is a picture to rejoice in, to draw inspiration from, to make the basis of grand and glowing hopes for our own sex, in the divine world of Art. Rosa Bonheur is only a representative woman. She speaks to-day for the future of womanhood, which has not in all the ages, ever had such a promise as is now made for it.

Like women's possibilities, politics was a subject never far from Mrs. Farnham's pen. And a chance for expressing her personal opinions was an opportunity not to be missed:

You have yet some bad men in office in California. When death comes to relieve you of them, as he good naturedly does, once in a while, don't let him transform them from living ruffians and debauchees into *gentlemen*—from ignoramuses into scholars, and from corrupt placemen into patriots and noblemen. It is astonishing how instantly and greatly death magnifies the infinitesimal virtues of public men. I have known him make heroes of arrant cowards in a single day, and honest men of the veriest rascals, in the twinkling of an eye. We exhaust ourselves in praising men dead, whom, alive, we warned our sons and brothers against. I do not see any great merit in a bad man dying in office. It may be very convenient and suitable that he should do so; the most suitable thing perhaps possible to him, except leaving his place to a better, without awaiting that dismissal. But we are guilty of something worse than folly, I think, when we pour out eulogy upon a man whose vices we abhorred in life and whose memory in death has only their bad odor clinging to it.

On February 5, 1858, the *Farmer* published a letter from Mrs. Farnham written on the third of January, demonstrating the increasingly speedy transit between East and West—and Eliza's droll humor:

> In my last I said a word about pictures; at present I would speak of books, if there were any worthy of mention; but that you will readily understand, cannot be the case, when neither I nor my friends are in the field. The holy days have brought to the gift-bestowing and gift-receiving public much less than the usual amount of elegant muslin and gilt trash, along with several magnificently made books, the outward promise of which is not a lie. There is an edition of our beloved Bryant, more costly and splendid than any preceding one; but the publishers, in sending out their gift copies, have forgotten your correspondent, and therefore her memory is not at this present enriched by their names. Perhaps Santa Claus, who enjoys a monopoly of this branch of the press business, could tell you if it was the Appletons. It is like some of their old tricks.

Such playfulness was the exception in Eliza Farnham's letters to California, consumed as she was by the plight of New York's working-class women in need of employment:

> The number of women who have been driven from honest industry, since the present financial troubles commenced, to swell the outcasts of the street, is at least *fifteen hundred!* How far this appalling statement is likely soon to be surpassed in fact, may be inferred from what follows: Very recently nearly one thousand applicants gave in their names, within a few days, to some benevolent ladies who had desired to test the extent of destitution amongst skilled and unskilled workwomen, with a view to devise and apply the necessary relief. Some

The Horse Fair *by Rosa Bonheur, ca. 1853. Of Rosa Bonheur's* Horse Fair, *Eliza wrote: "the picture of the day...Never was such a mass of rollicking, snorting, rearing, plunging, willfull and vicious life put upon canvas by a masculine hand, as this lady hath portrayed....It is a picture to rejoice in, to draw inspiration from, to make the basis of grand and glowing hopes for our own sex, in the divine world of art." Bonheur, to avoid attention while sketching at the Paris horse market, dressed as a man. Courtesy of The Metropolitan Museum of Art, Gift of Cornelius Vanderbilt, 1887 (87.25)*

few of these applicants possessed one or two dollars each, but the majority were wholly destitute and some had not tasted food for twenty-four hours. And these, be it well noted, were of the industrious and respectable working young women of New York, shrinking from the dole of charity, and asking only leave to live by their labor. A sight full of pity to see; or horror to reflect upon, when all the possibilities of their future rise up before the mind.

Mrs. Farnham's plea for donations succeeded, by February, in sending several hundred women to Illinois and Indiana, their transportation contributed by the railroads.

In March, Eliza escorted fifty women to Decatur, Illinois, and on her return to New York shared rail passage with a fellow passenger whose large size was exceeded only by the extent of his rudeness. She bitingly immortalized him as "Mr. Hog" for the *California Farmer's* readers:

It was my inestimable privilege to share Mr. Hog's progress from the West....He left Dunkirk [Indiana] with us at 3 a.m. of the coldest morning we have had this winter; mercury 18° to 24° below zero....

When we entered the car that was to convey us, there was visible at the aperture of the stove door a little flickering blaze, which waned by slow degrees into absolute blackness. The room was as if we had entered a dark cavern in the bowels of an iceberg. There were at first eight of us, shivering with high shoulders, our lips and feet as insensible as those which rest in the stirrups of the bronze statue at Union Square. Presently Mr. Hog bustled in, doubling our number at least, if not trebling it. He grunted, snorted, blew, stamped, routed a poor little four-months infant from a seat near the fire, thereby cutting the mother off from any approach to the warmth which we trusted would come by and by, and so installed himself.

Mrs. Farnham had been on the road seven days and six nights, with but a single day's rest. She was cold and she was tired. Under the best of circumstances, she was not disposed to timidity, and Mr. Hog's rude presence did not incline her to adopt it now. When he went to get a drink, he left the door open and the cold rushed in. Mrs. Farnham closed the door.

When he returned with his drink, he left the door open again:

"Did you intend to leave that door open, sir?" I croaked.

A noise between a growl and a snort was the only reply deigned to my inquiry. The goblet was carefully replaced, and then the porky biped walked aft and closed the door.

The cars were now in full motion, and we rolled on an hour or more, when, on opening my eyes, I saw Mr. Hog, spread to his utmost capacities on the seat adjacent to the stove. His carpet-bag occupied the one next to it, and the poor freezing mother and baby were dozing and shivering on the third one. This also seemed a state of things to be corrected if possible, and your correspondent rose and addressed herself to the work.

Despite Mrs. Farnham's objection, Mr. Hog decided, and so informed her, that he would stay where he was. And his offenses had but begun:

He had not long remained there...when it seemed suddenly to occur to him that a cigar would enhance his comfort, and he proceeded to light one, deferring to our presence only so far as to walk to the back end of the car....

"Is that man to smoke here?" said I to the brakeman who passed at the time.

"Pray, stop him," chimed in the mother, on the other side; and so Mr. Hog was compelled very reluctantly to give up his cigar.

He resumed his seat, bringing an extra cushion forward wherewith to support and comfort his body, and proceeded with indescribable contortions of its porkerous bulk to endeavor to dispose it for sleep. Success or failure in this undertaking seemed to me to be of little moment, and I dozed again, leaving him in the full tide of experiment....

But sleep he did. And not quietly:

His vocal gifts...had a sort of double-toned performance, as if a pair of huge underground giants were at a duet. Mr. Hog was not a winning man awake and fully conscious of himself and his doings, but at the end of a half hour's nap I think we all felt disposed to admire him awake as compared with the other condition.

Awake, and eating, Mr. Hog did not present a pretty sight:

Breakfast came, and here Mr. Hog was doubly himself. He ate and drank with something above a zest rather more than a gusto; in fact, one might have said with an eagerness rarely seen but at the trough....What a paradise, we thought, Mrs. Hog must pass existence it! What a privilege to live and share life with such a soul, in such a body!

Mrs. Farnham continued to write for the *California Farmer*, describing a subsequent journey on behalf of her Women's Protective Emigration Society, aboard Canada's Great Western Railway: "Capital road is the Great Western; broad-gauge cars, made for comfort; gentlemanly managers and conductors; time good, and everything most satisfactory to the traveler throughout." She wrote about politics, and the Kansas border war, about the British art exhibition, the weather, the generosity of a New Yorker, a plumber "who by industry has accumulated a small fortune":

He opened a dining room, where people of all colors and conditions have free admission for one substantial meal each day. The fare consists of meat, bread, and vegetables; is very neatly served on clean tables, with clean dishes for every succession of partakers. There is plenty for all who come...on some days, a thousand persons—seldom less than six hundred; and he magnanimously refuses to be helped in his undertaking, bidding those who offer him assistance go and use their means elsewhere, to relieve the want which he cannot reach. Seeing such work, one feels that times of trial are not altogether unprofitable to the character of the people to whom they come. I believe that many men and women have found impulses of compassion and tenderness in themselves this winter, which years of prosperity would never have convinced them of.

Religionists regarded hard times as evidence of transgression and the need for repentance. Mrs. Farnham philosophized:

You have heard of our great Revival. Has it reached your shores, or is it yet due there?...The ministers tell us that we are living in solemn and fearful days....But days of promise too let us hope. Wise is the bee who extracts the honey only from the flower, leaving the bitterness....So I would do with human life, and with the "times" which it exhibits to us, whether they seem evil or good, solemn or gay, dark or bright. I suppose time is the only inalienable heritage of every soul. It is like a casket given to us at the beginning of a journey, which we must needs fill during its progress. It may be with gems, it may be with rubbish, but whatever we put into it will be our possession and our only possession at the end. When the goal is reached, how many of us will be doomed to painful disappointment, on finding that what we have so carefully gathered, and treasured, and toiled to keep, is without value! Alas, for the weary and heavy-laden who come up with these burdens instead of the imperishable treasure of good works; of growth helped on; of truth succored in its time of need; of suffering mitigated; courage renewed at the point of fainting; or despair turned into hope.

From such musings one might suspect Mrs. Farnham felt midlife's intimations of mortality, of thinking she had but a short time left in which to succor truth, mitigate suffering, do good works. Indeed, if she did expect her time was short, she was right. Only a few years remained to her—and she used them remarkably.

## TWENTY-ONE

# Woman's Appropriate Sphere

We are...encouraged to know that the course we have taken to open our columns to the *cause* of Woman, the education and elevation of Woman to her *appropriate* sphere as the educator of the child-man, is receiving a just approval from the best minds in our country. We are not forgetful, however, of the fact that there are those in our community that *misrepresent* our efforts in their behalf, and assert that the FARMER is an advocate of *all the doctrines of woman's rights;* such is not the case. We defy the most fastidious critic to find that we approve any other doctrine than that of educating woman for the sphere of *Home,* her only and appropriate sphere; there, angel like, she can guide, guard and educate the Sons and Daughters of our land, and fit and prepare them to become the guardians of our noble institutions, and thus secure and perpetuate the freedom of the world.

—*California Farmer*, October 1, 1858

But I seek to establish a higher claim for woman than man asserts or aspires to for himself.

—Eliza Farnham

O n May 13, 1858, in New York City, women's rights advocates convened their eighth national convention. They met at Mozart Hall, corner of Beaver and Broad streets. Susan B. Anthony presided, devoting the morning session to preliminary business matters, the choosing of new officers, and the presentation of resolutions.

At the afternoon session, Thomas Wentworth Higginson and Eliza Farnham offered additional resolutions. One of Eliza's resolutions was to compliment the "Hygeic-Therapeutic College of this city, which, from the first, had been open to women." Miss Sarah Grimke "read an essay which was not heard"; the Reverend Antoinette Brown Blackwell urged unemployed women to become farmers, citing several instances of success, as did Lucy Stone, who knew of "a woman whose two-months' labor in gardening netted her $1,600."

Mary Davis said she thought "emigration to the West impracticable for the working women of New York. They might as well be moved into the Pacific Ocean, if we wanted to get rid of them."

That night, for the evening session, organizers charged twenty-five cents for admission to the hall. An eager crowd readily paid it, filling every chair and every space for standing, including the platform and steps, in anticipation of a remarkable roster of speakers: Lucretia Mott, Lucy Stone, William Lloyd Garrison, Antoinette Brown Blackwell, and Eliza Farnham.

Lucretia Mott, dedicated abolitionist and midwife to the birth of the women's rights movement, had presided over the historic Seneca Falls Convention. She had been the first to sign the Declaration of Sentiments—the call for equal treatment of women.

William Lloyd Garrison, the leading figure in the antislavery movement, ardently supported the cause of women's rights. On the evening of May 13, he rose, surveyed the audience thronging Mozart Hall, and said, "Those who have inaugurated this movement are worthy to be ranked with the army of martyrs...in the days of old. Blessings on them! They should triumph, and every opposition be removed, that peace and love, justice and liberty, might prevail throughout the world."

Lucy Stone had organized, in 1850, the first national women's rights convention, held in Worcester, Massachusetts, where she had converted Susan Anthony to the cause of woman's suffrage. It was Lucy Stone who had refused, upon marrying Henry Blackwell, to change her name to her husband's, and had distinguished herself as the first woman in Massachusetts to earn a college degree. And when antislavery advocates objected that her speeches on women's rights diminished their cause, she doubled her efforts by speaking weekends for abolition and weekdays for women.

Antoinette Brown Blackwell, an energetic speaker and writer for women's rights, temperance, and abolitionism, was the first ordained woman minister in the United States.

Frederick Douglass was present, too. Prevailed upon by calls from the audience, he added his famous oratorical talent to the evening. World-renowned for the autobiography of his life as a slave, Douglass campaigned tirelessly for the cause of abolition and also believed in women's equality.

Eliza Farnham didn't.

When Mrs. Farnham rose to address the audience in Mozart Hall, she told them she recognized "man...to be the conqueror, the mechanic, the inventor, the clearer of forests, the pioneer of civilization." But woman, in the "dawning of a higher era," would assume her "true position in harmony with her superior organism."

It was a long speech Eliza made that night, arguing that woman's "delicacy of structure, her beauty of person, her great powers of endurance" made her "not only man's equal in influence and power, but his superior in many of the noblest virtues."

Due to the female's "creative power during maternity," Mrs. Farnham believed woman to be "second only to God himself." Woman should, Eliza argued, "recognize man as John the Baptist, going before to prepare the world for her coming."

In short, Mrs. Farnham sought recognition not for woman's equality but her superiority.

Mrs. Farnham's "theory of woman's superiority...was received with apparent satisfaction by the audience," conceded a convention organizer, "though several on the platform dissented from the claim of superiority, thinking it would be a sufficient triumph over the tyrannies of the past, if popular thought could be educated to the idea of the equality of the sexes."

Lucy Stone objected to Mrs. Farnham's focus on maternity as too provocative and likely to undermine their attempts to gain public support for suffrage.

Eliza remained unswayed, committed to her conviction that motherhood was the noblest service any earthly being could render humanity—and committed as well to telling people so. Two weeks after the convention she wrote her friend and publisher, Joshua Dix:

> I propose if nothing happens to hinder me, going out to Elizabethtown on Tuesday eve of next week. If I do not hear from you I shall assume that Mrs. Dix and the little ones are at home and well. I shall only be able to stay the night but if I may suggest—as our object is to see the good, live women of your circle there—I would ask that a few of them be requested to visit me there.

After Elizabethtown, Mrs. Farnham visited Perth Amboy, New Jersey. She had enrolled Charles in the Eagleswood Academy there, at the failing utopian community of Raritan Bay Union. The school was headed by noted abolitionist Theodore Weld, who had married one of the famed Grimke sisters, Angelina, and brought both her and her sister Sarah there to teach (and to serve the Underground Railroad). Eagleswood, in the opinion of Henry Thoreau, invited to lecture there, was a "queer place":

> "The City of Perth Amboy" is about as big as Concord and Eagleswood is 1 1/2 miles S W of it, on the bay side. The central fact here is evidently Mr. [Theodore] Weld's school—recently established—around which various other things revolve. Saturday evening I went to the school room, hall, or what not, to see the children & their teachers & patrons dance. Mr Weld, a kind looking man with a long white beard, danced with them. . . This Sat. eve-dance is a regular thing, & it is thought something strange if you don't attend. They take it for granted that you want *society!*
>
> Sunday forenoon, I attended a sort of Quaker meeting at the same place—(The Quaker aspect & spirit prevails here—Mrs. Spring says "does thee not?") where it was expected that the spirit would move me (I having been previously spoken to about it) & it, or something else, did, an inch or so. I said just enough to set them a little by the ears & make it lively...all the speaking & lecturing here has reference to the children, who are far the greater part of the audience....Imagine them sitting close to the wall around a hall—with old Quaker looking men & women here & there. There sat Mrs. Weld (Grimke) & her sister, two elderly grayheaded ladies, the former in extreme Bloomer costume, which was what you may call remarkable; Mr. [Arnold] Buffum with broad face & a great white beard, looking like a pier head made of the cork tree with the bark on, as if he could buffet a considerable wave;—James G. Birney, formerly candidate for the Presidency, with another particularly white head & beard.

A member of the Eagleswood community offered a less critical view:

> This is a lovely spot of retirement, beauty, and great capabilities of being made to promote human wants and happiness. The society includes a school of the first order conducted by Mr. T. D. Weld, consists of more than 150 persons and the most part of very intelligent and congenial minds, kind and Christian with a variety of religious theories tho for the most part Spiritualists. The families here live apart and can cook for themselves or take their meals at the public table. There is a large handsome palace-like-looking unitary dwelling and the old Mansion. In the latter we live which commands most beautiful country....We have a meeting here every first day

morning pretty much like friends' meeting except that sometimes we read scripture or other works and generally sing once or twice.

Mrs. Farnham anticipated a receptive audience at Perth Amboy—and found it:

> We have been having a visit from Mrs. Farnham...She is lecturing here to the women, on "Woman," and I have been to two of these meetings....It is all new to me,—not the views, all of them,—but I never heard the subject discussed before. She does not assume the equality of the sexes, but considers woman both physically and spiritually to have a higher being than man, etc....She has spoken remarkably well, and has said many excellent things...All that she said on the subject of Gestation, Pregnancy, Chastity, etc., was more beautifully, simply and purely expressed than I ever heard any one do it. I am convinced that the whole subject, treated in that way, would be elevated to the serious and religious ground it ought to occupy.

Mrs. Farnham's next stop: Rutland, Vermont.

A circular addressed "To the Friends of Human Progress" invited "all Philanthropists and Reformers in and out of the State to meet in Free Convention at Rutland, Vermont, on the 25th, 26th, and 27th of June" to discuss "the various topics of Reform that are now engaging the attention and effort of Progressive minds." The invitation to "friends of Free Thought" urged, "Come one, come all. Men of all religious creeds, and men of no creed, shall find equal welcome":

> And woman, too, let her come; both to adorn by her presence, and strengthen by her thought, and give depth and earnestness to the action of this gathering in behalf of Humanity. Let her vindicate, by her own eloquence and zeal, the social position she is so nobly and rapidly winning for herself.

Three days of discussion and debate! What an enticing proposal! Eliza couldn't resist it.

And neither could, to the great dismay of Rutland's citizens, the nearly three thousand other reformers who converged to camp, while local conservative religious groups held prayer meetings against the invasion. Organizers had intended a platform for antislavery sentiments, but the invitation attracted a "medley of people...of heterodox notions...come up to have sweet counsel together...to discuss abolitionism, spiritualism, free-love, free-trade, and all other queer things."

Other "queer things" included temperance, abolition of capital punishment, medical reform, women's rights, and land reform. Spiritualists dominated the convention, resolving that "the phenomena of what is called modern spiritualism have abundantly demonstrated the fact that an intercourse between embodied and disembodied spirits is both possible and actual." In debates on other issues the Spiritualists declared, "We must first ascertain the truth concerning the immortality of man, before we can know any thing, to any good purpose, of the nature of man, of the responsibilities of man, and of the rights of man....No man, no community, can really understand their rights, or be in a position to maintain them, unless they have a deep and abiding sense of their future endless existence."

Dissenters objected that this otherworldly focus depleted energies needed for the business of reform. Ernestine Rose, women's rights activist and atheist, argued, "If the Convention was not called for the benefit of man, it is useless; if it is...the time is not ours to discuss the life hereafter and neglect the life here."

Debate raged on. Methodist minister and Spiritualist James Steven Loveland retorted:

> My friend, Mrs. Rose, thinks that the question of the life to come should be held in abeyance until we first attend to the life that is. This, perhaps, would be well, if we knew what the life that is really is. That is, if we were perfectly sure that the life that now is was measured by the bounds of what we term time and space, it would be so; but if the life that now is is but the embryonic manifestation of a life that is to run through the eternal ages, then...that question should be settled.

Meanwhile, radical women's activists addressed the issue of reproductive rights:

> The most sacred and important right of woman is her right to decide for herself how often and under what circumstances she shall assume the responsibilities and be subject to the cares and sufferings of Maternity; and man can commit no greater crime against woman as a wife and mother, against his child, against society and against Humanity, than to impose on her a maternity whose responsibilities and sufferings she is not willing to accept and endure.

Eliza spoke on Saturday afternoon, the second session of the second day. Ernestine Rose introduced her. Although scheduled to speak on woman's rights, Mrs. Farnham "took considerable latitude," in the opinion of a newspaper correspondent who tersely summed her contribution:

> She began with the announcement that her views "struck into the metaphysical," and her leading proposition was that "woman is made organically superior to man, as she is confessedly his superior spiritually." Woman must be educated and developed equal to man, for an imperfect woman must bring forth imperfect children. What she said beside this she has said a hundred times before, and her views on the subject are perfectly familiar to all those who have read the various reports on the subject.

The reporter did Mrs. Farnham a disservice in ignoring one rather surprising assertion. Eliza declared:

> I believe that to-day, with the force of the truths I have, I could go into the Five Points in New York, and take a class of women,—the lowest I could find,—capable of being mothers, and so educate them that they should never, after the day they had seen me, bring such children into the world as they had before. I know this, not because I am eloquent or gifted, but because truth is all-powerful, and this truth appeals to the innermost, dearest life of every woman. The soul of every woman answers to that appeal—I know it!

Newspapers generally had a field day with the event. The editor of the *Brooklyn Daily Times,* none other than the poet Walt Whitman, wrote:

> One of the queerest conventions on record even in this land where all extremes of belief meet upon a common ground and all sorts of odd-fishes do most congregate has been in session during the last few days, in Rutland, Vermont, much to the astonishment, no doubt, and not much to the edification of that quiet country village.
> Here all the uneasy spirits of the day seem to have met to enter a protest against conventionalisms and to find a safety-valve for the erratic ideas with which they are boiling over....During the days that the convention continued in session, more ideas and sentiments were gotten off that were utterly repugnant to all preconceived ideas than at any other previous gathering of which we have any knowledge....everything new was declared to be right, and everything old was pronounced to be wrong.

After Vermont, Mrs. Farnham returned to New York City, where she failed to collect the money due for her *California Farmer* articles. In need of the money, she wrote the paper's editor, Colonel Warren, to say that she had twice called upon the person whom she was told would pay her, "but he informs me that he has no arrangement that would justify him in paying your draft in my favor. I will be obliged to you therefore if you will take the necessary care to enable me to draw the money, at your earliest convenience."

In September Mrs. Farnham was scheduled to opinionate in Utica, at yet another reformers' convention. The *New York Times* had opinions, too:

> THE CAUSE AND CURE OF EVIL.—Such is the comprehensive topic to be discussed…by a Convention of self-styled Reformers.…[T]he "cures" in vogue among the quack medicine tribe of moralists have been widely advertised for years. Their nostrums have not eradicated the disease in any case whatever, although fairly tried upon themselves.…
>
> The creed of these people assumes that there is no such thing as justice; no such thing as crime…Evil they regard as the creature of unfavorable circumstances.…To realize this theory they have invented new forms of society, organized communities, and established socialistic farms, most of which have ended in utter failure. They have not reached the root of evil.
>
> But this is a country where talking, and meeting to talk, are free. The only restraints come from the collisions of these people, who usually quarrel with and gag each other. There is no one so intolerant as a stickler for free speech, and none so ferociously malevolent as your professional philanthropist. Judging from the list of orators, male and female, announced for the Utica gathering, we conclude that whatever may be done, evil speaking will be reported incurable.

Even the usually supportive *New York Tribune* began to weary of "free conventions." A correspondent reporting on the Utica gathering of the "Friends of Human Progress" summed the event briefly:

> About 1,500 persons were present on the last day. The resolves adopted are strongly Anti-Slavery, slightly Disunion, broadly affirm the Equal Rights of Woman, assert that human intercourse with disembodied spirits is a demonstrated and imported fact, and favor Liberty of Divorce between persons unfitly married. Such is the

substance of the doings of this Convention, and is quite as much as the majority of our readers will desire.

Throughout 1858 Eliza had devoted herself to spreading the gospel of the greater glory of motherhood. Back in Santa Cruz, Georgiana contended with maternity's more practical aspects—and they made her a little irritable.

# TWENTY-TWO

# Seldom the Best Intellects

Ora was a most troublesome child....No one could imagine the mischief such a really good child could accomplish. Then to cook, wash, iron, house-clean, bake, mend, nurse, write letters, receive and pay visits, read, etc., all of which was necessary if I would really live like a civilized being, was too much for one person.

—Georgiana Bruce Kirby

In 1858 Georgiana Kirby was the tired mother of three little daughters—Ora, five; Georgie, two and a half; and Cornelia, just six months. Resuming her journal after a three-year lapse, Georgiana recalled those years as "a constant strain on my powers, bodily and mental. I used to wash at the tub when I trembled all over from weakness constantly, and it was so discouraging to go to bed at night feeling that notwithstanding such exertions the work was all behindhand."

And more:

> I hope I shall not have another child, for I am sensible that my con-stitution is not what it was. From the time Ora was born I did not work until Georgie was six months old, not being at all equal to it, it seemed to drag me down so as I can never recover from it. I keep pretty well as long as I keep quiet, but directly I exert myself I get ill....I feel that at forty my constitution is gone and even if I had a boy he would not be what we should expect.

Despite the demands of caring for her children and house-hold, Mrs. Kirby retained a keen interest in her community. For one thing she wanted a Unitarian minister. She had spoken to the Reverend Rufus Cutler, who had presided over a Unitarian con-gregation in San Francisco since 1854, and he had promised to write East to see what could be done, but Georgiana never heard further from him. She was displeased that in Santa Cruz "the

Congregationalists and Presbyterians have united and have quite a thriving church, but I do not believe the cause of true religion is helped by the ministrations of Mr. Zelie."

John Sheridan Zelie, the Congregationalist pastor, had erected a church in 1857, at a cost of three thousand dollars, of sufficient size to accommodate two hundred and fifty worshipers. In July of 1858, members held a "festival" to raise money for furnishing the church. Santa Cruz was not so lively that the Kirbys were inclined to miss such an event. Georgiana was suitably impressed: "There was a supper, a post-office, and a 'grab-bag' for entertainment and it all went off extremely well. They cleared above expenses $330. All the town was there."

Still, Mrs. Kirby did not much like John Zelie, and she was no more inclined to mince words than her friend Eliza Farnham:

> He is by nature a hard, vindictive, tyrannical, mechanical sort of person without the principle of growth in him at all. He talks about grace and change of heart, but I don't know any one who needs those things more than he does, or one whom the change is less possible to.

She thought his voice was too loud, and she didn't like his sermons anyway—"none of them are on Christian virtues but all on the dogmas of the church":

> Last Sunday he proved to his own satisfaction that morality, love, charity, benevolence, etc., were not of the slightest use to save a man from Hell, only belief that you deserved to be damned and then accepted Christ as a saviour somehow. It must be very much easier and so require less ability to dish up doctrines in this way than to enlarge for an hour on brotherly love, peace-making, patience, teachableness, humility, or such subjects, making them pointed and interesting. For my part, believing that this is to be my home I shall not cease to work in every possible way to procure liberal teaching for those that will accept it.

Mrs. Kirby did indeed do everything possible to spread her liberal convictions. She wrote the Reverend Mr. Gannett, the Unitarian preacher who had first employed her in Boston, and he sent her tracts addressing the issues between liberal and orthodox Christians. She "circulated all of Parker's sermons" available to her—the writings of a theologian who had grown so skeptical of orthodoxy that he established a new free church in Boston, where he typically addressed such social issues as abolitionism. She distributed tracts "tending to a reasonable and affectionate and intelligent state of mind" and "especially the noble anti-slavery literature of the day."

Mrs. Kirby also remained dedicated to teaching: "I long to teach and so improve other children." A "fuss in the common school at Watsonville" outraged her:

> ...two colored children, nice, intelligent, well-behaved children all say, but disgraced by their skin. I understand that the children are admitted but put off by themselves, poor things, and not allowed to take places no matter how much they out-spelled those above them. The more violently pro-slavery do not permit their children to go to school at all. The ignorant, white people from the slave states are the curse of California, they are so stupid and so conceited they think one man (to-wit, themselves) just as good as another, providing there be not the least drop of African blood in them.

For a time, Mrs. Kirby took several local girls under her instructive wing. Maria and Ellen, the Hecox daughters whose instruction had so troubled Richard Kirby three years previously, continued to be of special interest:

> Maria I had much to do with—taught her for a time French and German especially, generally instructed her in morals, manners, and so forth. She was neat, bright, affectionate, brave, impulsive. As she outgrew the narrow Methodist set, her mother became disturbed and ended by hating and insulting me.

Maria, as it happened, "took her destiny into her own hands," left Santa Cruz, and at seventeen married a Dr. Tilden—an association that ultimately provided Eliza Farnham a new calling in California. Meanwhile, Georgiana remained committed to trying to educate girls in Santa Cruz, despite difficult and disappointing pupils like fourteen-year-old Mary Jane Morgan:

> She cannot even read intelligently, and of books of any sort is quite ignorant....She talks a lot of rambling nonsense, calls my friends by their Christian names, and pronounces her wretched English in such a shocking manner that sometimes I give up and think I will try not to be interested in her, but that is nonsense, for I cannot help myself.

Mary Jane proved a failure and, to Georgiana's exasperation, so did her sister Salome:

> She staid away on the least excuse and no one at home paid any attention to her coming over at the right hour....They represent pretty well the "poor white trash" of the slave states where the parents were born and married. Get up late, dawdle about and do forever a long string of nothings. Let the children drink tea and coffee and up as late as the parents. Live principally on buckwheat cakes, send the children to school a week and keep them out two months, borrow incessantly everything from indigo to a pair of stockings to go to a party in. I believe I've given up trying to do anything for them.

But Georgiana's greatest regret was the isolation of Santa Cruz from people of ideas. "There is not one person of cultivated, enlarged mind in the place. Sometimes I seem quite collapsed for the want of spiritual food."

She had friends, particularly Margaret Voorhees, a New Yorker who, like Georgiana, had emigrated from England and had lived in the United States about the same length of time. Mrs. Voorhees, an artist and the mother of two young boys, visited Santa Cruz for two months in the spring of 1858. The two women shared a similar anxiety for their children: "We see the evils of a new country with no old institutions, no grand old buildings, and seldom the best intellects and characters to call out reverence."

Still, Georgiana missed Eliza: "No one, tho, begins to fill Mrs. Farnham's place."

The feeling was mutual—as everyone learned from the dedication in Eliza Farnham's latest book.

# TWENTY-THREE

# To G. B. K.

MRS. ELIZA W. FARNHAM is sufficiently distinct in her style and exceedingly graphic in her descriptions of men, women and scenery, but in her new volume, entitled *My Early Days,* she is so ambiguous in narrating the events of the history that we cannot positively determine whether the story be an autobiographical sketch, or a work of fiction....In the introductory essay, in the form of a dedication to "G.B.K.," it is true that the author intimates that *My Early Days* is a genuine autobiography, and she says that it is the interest in human experience which is at once the cause and the evidence of that sublimest of all phenomena, human growth, which calls for and justifies that life-analysis by which our literature is beginning to be very noticeably marked, "and of which courageous autobiography is, perhaps, the best form."

—*New York Times,* May 21, 1859

N ew York publishers Thatcher and Hutchinson had accepted Eliza's autobiographical manuscript, *Lucia Woodson,* and retitled it, more aptly and descriptively, *My Early Days.*

The story opens in the year 1825 at a remote farm near Lake Erie. In one of the first scenes, set on a warm summer morning, an unkempt nine-year-old girl, small for her age, darkened by the sun, and wearing a ragged dress, toils up a hill toward the farmhouse, carrying a heavy pail of water from the spring, the hardest of her many chores. The family's hired man, knowing her to be unwell, has come down the hill to take the pail. No one else, in the nearly four years she has labored here, has shown her such kindness or sympathy. She is moved nearly to tears. She knows she ought not to let him take the pail; fetching the water is her chore and the woman she calls "aunt" will be angry if she escapes it. But she is very small and her burden is very heavy. And so she surrenders it into the hand of the man she calls Mr. Radford.

It is on this memorable day that the child who will grow up to be Eliza Wood Burhans Farnham discovers in herself the resoluteness of courage—a most valuable trait for the woman whose remarkable life will demand it of her time and time again.

"Aunt," enraged to see Mr. Radford place the pail upon the stoop, cuffs the girl and upbraids her hired man. If she wants him to bring water, she scolds, she'll tell him. When she sends the girl, she adds, she doesn't want anybody to help her. She turns her fury on Eliza and tells her to pour the water into the gutter and go fill the pail again:

> I was not astonished at the order, yet some spirit, good or evil, prompted me to ask, "Shan't I put it in the kettle?" In fact, I felt so extremely weakened by that time that it seemed impossible to bring more water. It was always one of my very hardest tasks—the hill was so long and steep, and I was so very small. The little remonstrance I uttered kindled broad the slumbering flame of passion. She left her seat, seized me by the shoulder, and whirled me through the passage and out of the door, which was a step from the ground, so furiously that when I reached it I could scarcely stand on my feet, and then, lifting the full pail that stood near, she dashed its contents over me. She had often done this; and though it was intended as a high expression of her anger, it was one that gave me the least pain or sense of outrage. At this time it braced me wonderfully. The water was very cold, and...the shock brought an instantaneous reaction. My courage rose with my bodily warmth and energy; and when I came up dripping with the second pailful, and she dashed that over me, and sent me for a third, I felt I did not care at all how long she went on doing so.

How came this stalwart little girl to a childhood of such servitude and abuse?

Eliza Burhans was born November 17, 1815, in the little village Potter Hollow, near Rensellaerville, New York, surrounded by the Helderberg mountains of Albany County. Her father was Cornelius Burhans II and her mother Mary Wood Burhans, both Quakers. Three siblings had preceded Eliza's entrance into the family: the oldest sister, Phoebe, was seven at the time of Eliza's birth; brother Kelly was four; and sister Mary, two. Three years after Eliza's birth, Mary Wood Burhans delivered a fifth child, Henry, a birth from which she steadily weakened.

When Eliza was just four and baby Henry only two, Mary Wood Burhans died, and her two youngest children went to live with their grandfather and his second wife, Anna Legg Burhans, in New York's Catskill country. At six, Eliza was sent off with a childless, middle-aged couple who owned a farm in western New York. She thought she was being adopted, that "Uncle John" and "Aunt Phebe" were her new parents. But, upon reaching the farm, the woman's geniality deteriorated into ill temper, which she turned upon Eliza:

> I had ever a dread of a violent temper. Nothing in my own nature warmed to meet it. I could defy it, but it was an internal, calm defiance, breathed from conscious superiority to such rage. I could not quarrel, but I could be always cool and strong. Hence, when her fury was turned upon me, my small self-possession and indifference to her cruelties seemed only to increase her rage. She called me fool, witch, devil. She was baffled, defeated, dissatisfied, and never victor; for when she had threatened and beat me, she felt I was not yet subdued.

The hired man's concern propped her up, and she relied on his kindness. But he often teased her and laughed at her childish observations. He called her Dolly, which she didn't like. And although she could tell him "external" things, the essence of herself was internal, mental, a silent refuge of thinking and questioning and observing. In the face of constant abuse, the relentless servitude, the housework, the milking of eight cows every day and sometimes twelve—"I could have wept with the pain in my hands and arms almost every night and morning, but that I had so much else to do and think of"—Eliza retreated to her imagination. She envisioned herself gone from the farm and its incessant labors, pictured herself grown up and independent and rich. She fantasized that with those riches she would lift up the needy, rescue the helpless, return the unjustly imprisoned to hearth and home and loving families: "Had I loved, and been loved by any tender, intuitive person, I should have speculated less...and so I was called old-fashioned, queer, foolish, and, in the passionate language I heard every day, a fool."

Her hungry mind devoured whatever came before it, and for want of children's books, she read what was at hand, primarily political newspapers. By age ten she was conversant on congressional debates, cabinet reports, and governors' messages. She formed opinions upon tariffs, federal sovereignty, and states' rights. Eliza so craved books and learning, she even prayed to the "Something

Invisible that I believed in" to go to school. The prayer went unanswered. Eliza learned early not to rely on heavenly intervention. She learned to rely on herself.

*My Early Days* is particularly revealing of how the adult Eliza perceived the child, what she recalled as having occupied her mind as a youth. Besides abuse, the major chords are a constant reiteration of her yearning for books and school, a love of nature, and a desire to do something worthwhile in the world—a life of service. A curious but minor note is her frequent reference to herself as homely, her conviction of personal ugliness.

A child's pain over her appearance and her yearning for beauty, and even the adult's recollection of it, hold much pathos. One concludes a lifelong ache in so public a revelation. Here, she is saying, this is my constant hurt, the companion of my youth, the familiar of my maturity, my curse and regret: ugliness.

It's a small concession in an account of aspirations otherwise so exemplary. More than anything, even more than beauty, the child Eliza craved books and learning and, most of all, to go to school. The craving was denied until she escaped her involuntary servitude at fifteen, and her brother Kelly paid her tuition for a year at a Quaker boarding school and then, when she was eighteen, a year at the Albany Female Academy. And those two years comprised the sum total of her formal education.

Eliza Farnham was forty-four years old at the time of the book's publication, over forty when she wrote it. She had fed her hunger for knowledge for nearly thirty years. She had been "one of the workers of the world," as she pledged, having lectured widely and served as prison matron and teacher in an effort to do good. She already had published two books. Why did she write this one?

Eliza Farnham wrote her childhood autobiography for two reasons, and for two audiences. The first reason, and not least, was money, the audience being the book-buying public that knew her through her accomplishments and her previous two books. As these had been well received, she had every expectation of making money from *My Early Days*. The second reason for writing a memoir of her childhood, and perhaps the motivation for the book, was to tell her life not only to the public but to one special person, identified only by the initials in the book's heartfelt dedication:

To G. B. K.—Not by way of introduction or explanation to you, dear friend, who know me so well, do I write this exordium. Neither that I may put you forward as the apology for the book which now lies before me. If I felt that it needed any, (as to its motive) I should return it to the shelf whence I have just taken the manuscript. If I believed that, (as to its execution) it was inferior to my best power, I would not ungraciously charge you with the responsibility of its production. Then why do I place your sign upon this page? Because, in view of what is done, there are a few words to be said which can be more freely and vitally said to you than to any other individual, or to that vague personage, the public.

We have each trodden the steep round of the globe of life by difficult, though different paths. And the toil has brought to each a kindred result. You know it is one article of my Faith that like natures have like experiences, however the outward phases of them may vary....

...you and I, sisters on the way to the vast Beyond, have a common joy in....the life embodied in the soul—the life which possesses the great future....

You will say perhaps that I have begun too abruptly, but if I had dated two years back of the time I have chosen, I should only so far, and as I think fruitlessly, have extended the painful relation of my early sufferings. And I like directness. With a life history to tell it seems to me as well to begin at once, as to hover in preparation, wearying both auditor and narrator. And that we may be spared that too common experience, I will say no more, except that I rejoice in you, as it is rarely given to one woman to rejoice in another.—E. W. F.

When Eliza's book came out in May 1859, she was still in New York City, writing and lecturing. The Cooper Institute hosted "Mrs. Farnham's Conversations," the first lecture titled "The Organic Traits and Rank of Woman." The announcement promised that "Mrs. F's views on the question of woman are peculiar." After the first lecture, the *New York Tribune* reported in its May 25 edition that:

Her remarks referred to woman and her organic traits and destiny, and were intended to arouse the sex to a proper appreciation of their own dignity of character, that woman's influence might be more felt in shaping the institutions of society. The discourse was highly entertaining and instructive, and was listened to with marked attention. The second of the series, on the uses of food and their relation to human development, will be given at the same place on Thursday, at 3 p.m.

Mrs. Farnham probably attended the lectures of her friends, too—like Judge Edmonds, her old supporter from her Sing Sing days, who presented discourses on his embrace of Spiritualism. She read the newspapers regularly and must have taken especial pleasure in reading in the *Liberator* of May 27 that the American Anti-Slavery Society had appointed Georgiana Kirby its vice president for California.

Georgiana, meanwhile, had confided to her journal:

> I hear that Mrs. F will not return to Cal, although I have all along believed that her proper place was among more advanced minds and characters than those here. I am at once led to ask, "What then am I to do? How can I live?"

These poignant questions would keep. Georgiana was about to be surprised.

# TWENTY-FOUR

# A Spiritualist Season

Here I am at last after three years absence returned to the country and the place where so much of the thrilling experience of life came to me and where if nature had not done her kindest for me I should either have died literally or have suffered the insuperable loss of all hope....I ought to love a country in which I was able to bear so much and even to grow in the bearing. That after all must be the true test of all uses and experiences that life is capable of taking on itself. If we grow *with* them it proves their value and the happy relation between them and our strength. If we grow *in spite* of them it proves a grandeur in the interior life which fills one with self trust on looking back to the times of their endurance. And if we are crushed and robbed by them of our consciousness of power or sufficiency it sh'd be evidence to us that the wisest care we could bestow on ourselves would be that which would keep us in moderate seas and before friendly winds.

—Eliza Farnham

Mrs. Farnham has returned to Cal. and to us. I was in San F. early in July and felt myself alive once more on meeting her. She has greatly improved in the three years (tho I was quite satisfied with her before), being more patient of the low condition of what is called civilization, with a quieter spirit, greater intellectual ability, and unabated zeal in the cause of larger truths. Her manner of advocating spiritualism is very effective.

—Georgiana Bruce Kirby

The Pacific Mail Steamship *John L. Stephens,* which had taken Eliza Farnham from San Francisco's Vallejo street wharf in 1856, fetched her and Charlie from Panama on the evening of June 17, 1859. The ship reached Acapulco on June 24, where it encountered heavy weather, and from there it made slow headway up the coast. "It was also very uncomfortable," reported Mrs. Farnham, with "rain, fog, heat, and chilliness alternating all the way." On the morning of July 2, they arrived at last in San Francisco, where Eliza and her son stayed briefly before proceeding to Santa Cruz.

The immediate concern was the property. The news was not good. On July 24, Eliza wrote Colonel Warren, editor of the *California Farmer,* who still had not paid her:

I find myself so straitened since my arrival here by the condition of my son's property (which has not produced a dollar for him in the last five years) that I am constrained to try to make productive resources which I hoped I should have no more need to consider, when I saw you. Therefore I have to ask that if convenient you will hand the bearer (who is Mr. L. Farnham, my brother-in-law) whatever sums you find to be due me according to the understanding between us, for my late letters....I shall feel greatly obliged if you can comply with my request.

In need of money, Eliza immediately turned to lecturing. On July 30 the *Santa Cruz Sentinel* announced that Mrs. Farnham would speak the next evening at the Santa Cruz courthouse on "The Present State of the Religious World." She also undertook less formal engagements. Georgiana was a great booster:

She had a class of women, the most respectable in the place, to whom she gave "conversations" on her view of woman. It being that woman is superior, spiritually, to man. This she proves by the added organs and functions, the greater delicacy of organization, greater beauty and the fact that she holds a large—immense—balance of power over the character of her offspring....Dr. Rawson, for some unknown reason, has given himself up to circulating the vilest reports of her teachings.

The controversy had barely begun.

Nonetheless, lecturing and writing provided Eliza's only livelihood, and she committed herself to both. On August 9, she wrote Joshua Dix, in New York:

I send you a slip with some corrections to be marked in the printer's copy for the next edition of Early Days—supposing it shall ever be needful to print another....Please tell me what you know of its prospects and if any speck appears on the horizon yet with promise for the other book....[These seem] to me to be the best months for issuing a book, Oct, Nov, Jan, Feb, and March. But I shall leave the matter to you and fate....I have a class of ladies here and have spoken in public twice at the urgent solicitation of the people who are literally starving on the mouldy crusts of Methodism and Presbyterianism doled out to them by fishy-eyed ministers who are sure that the very essence of piety is a long face, a horror of dancing, a hatred of infidels to their respective creeds....

On August 24, journalist William N. Slocum, in launching the first edition of the *Santa Cruz News,* reported Mrs. Farnham's second and third Santa Cruz courthouse lectures in detail, doing himself no small harm by printing what to many readers amounted to blasphemy:

> The Church teaches us to pray and agonize for the forgiveness of our sins, in the belief that when it pleases God's grace and mercy to hear our prayers, He can wipe out the most terrible records that sin has made upon the soul, and make the penitent as happy and good as if his life had been unstained by them....The Church teaches faith first—works next—and faith last; but the works so thoroughly subordinated to faith throughout that a vigilant professor may commit every known sin without losing his chance at salvation. Even he himself, knowing the foulness of his own life, believes or half believes he shall escape its consequences...for the Church teaches that salvation is effected if you can keep the devil's clutches off by any means.

In her second lecture, Mrs. Farnham concluded, "The difference between the...theological and the spiritual view may finally be briefly stated in some such formula as this: The former is the product of an undeveloped, low, gross condition, which while it was well enough suited to the period of its promulgation, is unfit for our time and aims."

In her third lecture she combined her two chief interests: Spiritualism and motherhood:

> It is objected to by some that the spirit cannot have the power to return to earth after death has loosed it from the body; but does not the power to go imply the power to come, and all believe that it *does* go. And if it have the power to come, and death does not so transform it as to cast out all the affections, interests, hopes and purposes which have made up the body of life, then ought it not to desire to come? Ought the mother, separated by death from her children, never to desire to place herself near them again when she has reached the life beyond this? If not, we cannot count her existence immortality, for she must have lost the ruling motives, the strongest loves and deepest yearnings that made her the individual that she was here.

Churchmen went wild. Georgiana confided to her journal that they wanted to roast Eliza at the stake:

> Deacon Wm. Anthony says she is a "She Devil"; Mrs. Ruffner that "she is worse than the keeper of a brothel." Dr. Rawson circulates the most scandalous lies purporting to come from her. These are all

leaders in the Congregational Church. But she has steadily good audiences and makes as earnest friends as enemies by her most valuable services. She extemporizes always, commands her hearers unbroken attention from the first moment to the last. Her large philosophical brain, her tender, religious, womanly nature carry conviction to all capable of progress.

Those in high dudgeon possessed sufficient ire for Mrs. Farnham's ideas to have some left over for Slocum, the young editor with the temerity to publish them. Georgiana sympathized: "such a storm as poured on his head. The pious complained, threatened, abused, as usual...He suffers terribly from want of sympathy, want of means...to cope with...this violent, coarse tirade....We cheer him all we can....He has gone down to the Pajaro [Valley] for subscribers."

Mrs. Farnham went to Watsonville, invited to deliver her lecture series to the women there. Georgiana sniffed:

> The women in Watsonville are an uncultivated, undeveloped set. It is bad enough here but it is fifty times worse there. However, I consider it a gain that no orthodox church is yet permanently established there. There are (nominally) two Methodist churches, the M.E.C. North and the M.E.C. South. The latter permitted Mrs. F. to lecture in their house (not on religion). She described the room as being lined with smooth blacked cloth. There were no tin reflectors or other arrangements for candles. These they melted a little, dropping the grease on the desk or bench back and quickly clapping the candle down on it to stick. This fact indicates the sort of civilization that [is] there.

A man at Eliza's Watsonville lecture was "much pleased with the enthusiasm manifested" by one of his "bachelor friends" for the lecture and the lecturer:

> I began to fear he had a "pop the question" feeling; but I think he will forget it when the memory of that persuasive eloquence dies away. All willingly admit that we listened to a lecturer who is endowed with talent, improved by study and research, and thoroughly capable of presenting a subject scientifically and plainly. We like to hear her handle a subject in which there is no need of sophistry. She says the human mind wants something new. That is true. It is characteristic of children to be always wanting something new, and "men are but children of a larger growth;" and many times they want that which is not good for them....The majority of young

men in California want billiards and whiskey, but they might have something better if they would. Men and women (more especially the latter) have been wanting what they ought not to have ever since Eve had a hankering after the apple.

In her third lecture at Watsonville, Mrs. Farnham was asked to speak on politics. She replied that:

> If they desired her to speak of the integrity of party politics, she should find herself in the same difficulty with the celebrated Mr. Spurgeon, who, when he was requested to preach against the absurd fashion of the small bonnets, arose, and looking critically over his vast audience, said,—"I have been requested to speak against the fashionable bonnet, but upon my word, I don't see any."

By the end of the month, even the San Francisco papers had heard that Mrs. Farnham was creating "a great sensation." And then she went to San Francisco, at the request of the Society of Spiritualists, to create it there. At the same time she received a request to visit Sarah Moore Clarke at her luxurious home in San Leandro. Mrs. Clarke had, in 1854, commenced publication of the *Contra Costa*, a newspaper addressing, in large part, women's issues. Ill health and limited subscriptions forced her retirement a year later. Still ailing, she sought Eliza's advice.

On September 6, while at San Leandro, Eliza received a letter from Joshua Dix with bad news about Burt & Abbey, publishers of *My Early Days*. Eliza replied at once:

> It was the first news I had of B & A's failure but I might have known it would be so before I left New York....For myself I can only say that if the effects of the firm are sold I sh'd be glad to become the owner of the plates myself....if upon receipt of this the $60 which was forwarded for books is not so appropriated and the sale is likely to take place before we can have further correspondence please reserve half of it for the purchase and send only $30 worth of books. This of course in case that circumstances of which I am ignorant do not suggest a better or other way to you.
>
> I am very sorry to hear of the failure and beg that the other book may go into sound hands whether late or early.

By mid-September, Eliza was back in Santa Cruz, staying with the Kirbys and writing, as Georgiana noted, "a book on woman, her uses, position, destiny." She also wrote opinion pieces for

Slocum's *Santa Cruz News*. Inspired by the headline-grabbing duel in which California Senator David Broderick had lost his life to proslavery leader David Terry, she wrote a lengthy article on "Dueling and Duels"—in her own inimitable style:

> The settlement of personal difficulties by the duel is a method which belongs to those times and phases of development which are by common consent termed barbarous or semi-barbarous. And we might leave barbarians and semi-barbarians to adjust their personal relations in this way, admitting that they are the best judges of the value of their own lives, and that in heroically surrendering them "at the pistol's mouth" they will seldom deprive the world of much worth, but may on the contrary often rid it of persons most "stale flat and unprofitable" for all noble and good uses. Therefore, in its own place, and amongst the people who can see no better remedy for personal wrong than polite murder, I have no quarrel with the duel. It is the cheapest, most expeditious and *decent* method of dispatching worthless and troublesome men on that journey which they cannot take too soon for their country's good—of whose career it might indeed be said that nothing in their lives so much became them as their leaving it.

Publishing Mrs. Farnham's opinions didn't help the beleaguered editor of the *News*. Eliza's first article on duels appeared on September 21. On September 28, Georgiana noted:

> Deacon Wm. Anthony wrote to Mr. Slocum to stop his paper, "he did not wish it to be read by his family." They are real puritans and have the spirit that a century or so ago would have roasted people. S. meets with so little encouragement here that he thinks of moving to the Pajaro where as yet there is no paper. They offer to raise $500 by subscription if he will go there.

Meanwhile, Mrs. Farnham was back in San Leandro. "Mrs. S. M. Clarke, an intellectual, useful woman," wrote Georgiana, "will die of prostration caused by the Uterine disease if nothing can be done in the use of electricity for her. She believes Mrs. F. can do this and so the latter reluctantly leaves for a while her writer's work."

From San Francisco, Eliza wrote William Lloyd Garrison, archabolitionist and editor of the *Liberator,* enclosing her article on dueling, offering her opinion on California men, and hoping for a review of her autobiography:

I send you herewith a paper (the Santa Cruz News) not for your edification but as a testimony that we are not altogether dead or idle out here. The article on Dueling & Duels is an attempt, by myself, to show the real character of the relations between north & south in those aspects whereof it treats. I will send you the remainder of the series as they appear....This last terrible tragedy in our State will prove I think the most fruitful lesson our people have ever had. The sense of actual loss in Mr. Broderick is very deep and I hear...such expressions as "Well we had better let the South go than be treated in this way; they are bound to kill all good men who stand up, in any strength, for the North. They killed Gilbert, and King, and Ferguson, and now they have taken the last man we had."

There is hope in such talk; the first I have ever distinctly seen in this country. Of course, however, one has to write & speak far behind the tone of your Eastern work but our folks are brimful of life & power and come rapidly along when once they set out in any particular way. You would not have to prove or assert that dueling was a relic of barbarism, because eastern people are prepared to assume it at the outset of any treatment of the question of personal relations which among us might lead to it. There are in this state a few able earnest women to whom I look for true thought & work much more than to any man; the standards are so low, selfish or politic among men.

I never see the Liberator since I left New York and so have not seen your verdict on "My Early Days." If you have read it, and made any, will you be kind eno to send me the paper to Santa Cruz Cal, where my house is and whither I shall return in three or four weeks. I ask for this because I believe that whatever you should take the pains to say would be both critical and just and therefore profitable to me. In hearty sympathy with your work and your thought...

Mrs. Farnham's second installment on duels and dueling appeared in the *News* on October 12, and two more followed, as well as a series on the history of African slavery, which she signed "Historicus." Meanwhile, she was lecturing in San Francisco to more appreciative audiences.

Last evening the Hall of the Sons of Temperance was densely packed with an attentive audience, who listened with intense interest from the commencement to the close of a most intellectual and philosophical discourse, which would bear comparison with the performances of many of the most eloquent speakers of our day. The Spiritual Philosophy was presented in contrast to the old and effete theological systems with a clearness and force seldom equalled by any public speaker. A committee was appointed to solicit a copy of the lecture for publication: Arrangements were made for another lecture by Mrs. Farnham on Sunday evening next....

Her discourse was listened to with wrapt [sic] attention. At times, when the talented lecturer got off something good in her own peculiarly dry way, (and that was quite frequently,) the audience would go off into hysterics of laughter, while Mrs. Farnham showed no visible symptoms of hilarity, although the really witty remarks had but just fluttered from her lips. Her style is so singular we hardly know how to describe it. The fact of the matter is that all those who desire to hear something rich and sparkling gotten off in good style should take the trouble to visit the lecture hall when Mrs. Farnham speaks.

In December Mrs. Farnham brought her talents back to Santa Cruz. The editor of the *News* happily anticipated the event, even if all his readers didn't:

LECTURE.—All of our readers will be interested, and most of them much gratified, to learn that Mrs. E. W. Farnham will address the citizens of this place, on Sunday evening next, on a subject which, in San Francisco, was treated by Mrs. F in a manner so instructive and entertaining as to call forth the warm encomiums of every Daily paper in the city. Musical Hall was crowded on the occasion, and many persons went away, unable to get into the building. We trust there are a sufficient number of liberal minded, intelligent men and women in this community to fill Exchange Hall. See advertisement in Special Notice column.

So ended 1859, a year Mrs. Farnham crammed full of instruction for the improvement of humankind.

Only five more remained to her in which to complete the work.

# TWENTY-FIVE

# Exalted Possibilities

Never were such exalted possibilities set up before men and women, as we are growing familiar with in our time....But let us remember that the possibilities of defeat bear their proportion to those of success. If you would cross the Alps and fail, it is something more than if you had proposed the passage of the hill in your homestead orchard. Only this again is always true for our comfort, that every faithful, worthy endeavor to ascend the mountains of difficulty, is sure to be rewarded by increased power and resolution, though itself, as a single act, may be a failure. Therefore, for our final profit, the goal cannot be set too high; the loftiest summit is better chosen than the lower one, though it cost some humiliating temporary defeats and seasons of heavy discouragement to reach it.

—Eliza Farnham

The year 1860 opened with Georgiana Kirby feeling pensive. On January 26 she took up her journal for the first time in several months, jotting a brief note of sympathy for Mr. Slocum's newspaper, one for herself, and one for women everywhere:

> "The News" still continues its starved existence. People are so slow to exert themselves—even those whose sympathies are right. A few say it, the paper must not stop, as it could never be resuscitated when needed for the next Presidential election. I found myself enceinte in September, '59 and went to the city to refresh myself for the effort. The mountain road was in shocking condition which, coming on my already irritated and weak state, caused a severe miscarriage in the city, from which I but slowly recovered....
>
> My thoughts in those days ran on the freedom of women—on what slaves we are and have been to the decisions of men. A hundred years hence it will be looked on with astonishment that a woman is prevented by public opinion from having a child unless she finds someone whom she wishes to accept as master for life.

And with that prescient observation, Georgiana closed her journal and never took it up again. Later that year she found herself again "enceinte," and in April of 1861 presented her husband with his first son, Richard Bruce. Providentially, the Kirbys' fortunes outpaced their increasing household. In 1860, the Kirby tannery numbered among the largest and most successful in the state, employing fifteen men and capable of processing, by steam power, more than a thousand hides a month.

For Georgiana Kirby, the 1860s would be devoted to family and community, but like Eliza, she was never too busy to advise on correct behavior:

> Women who give undue attention to dress are lacking in radical self-respect; they are conscious of their own emptiness, and seek to atone for it, to themselves and others, by outside finery. I must, however, do them the justice to say that men, as shallow as themselves, have done, and still do their full share towards impressing them with this false idea....I maintain that it is principally a want of self-respect that makes otherwise sensible and worthy women so extravagant in their clothing. They do not estimate themselves as they ought. They think more of making a good personal appearance than of becoming intelligent, affectionate, capable human beings....One of the greatest evils attending too great variety and extravagance in dress is the time it consumes. How can the mind be improved, if there is such constant straining in order to preserve a certain style in dress? Many a young woman—yes, I am sorry to say, many a mother of children—thinks it most praiseworthy in her to spend all her spare time in embroidering her clothes, or those of her children, when the same time spent in walking and reading would improve both body and mind, one or both of which is often sacrificed to this ill-balanced love of the beautiful. What is more beautiful than health?

And further:

> Let the ladies of San Francisco come and take a lesson from those of Santa Cruz, who, I am proud to say, belong to the genus *woman*, and not to that of "fine lady." I don't believe there is a community in Christendom where as much good taste and simplicity is manifested, in this respect, as here. When I think of how universal, in this vicinity, is the absence of devotion to the "frill-frals and tificks," I am astonished as well as gratified. When people *begin* right, they generally go on in the same way; and, for this reason, I do not fear to prophecy that, in refinement and intelligence, the women of Santa Cruz will, in the not distant future, rank among the first in the State. I do not know *one* woman in town who would be a bit disturbed if seen washing dishes or blacking her little boy's shoes. The reason is, they have *some* furniture inside their heads, and therefore lay less stress on the outside.

At this time in the nation's history, citizens everywhere, including far-off California, followed the news of an imperiled Union. Even the remote community of Santa Cruz heard of the events at Harper's Ferry, Virginia; the *Pacific Sentinel* picked up the story from St. Louis newspapers:

> A train had been stopped by the insurrectionists, and the telegraph wires cut. The first reports were telegraphed from a station east of Harper's Ferry, and consisted of mere rumors. It was stated that a band of abolitionists and negroes had seized the U.S. Arsenal and fired into the train, killing a negro boy. They had stopped the train, had stopped a wagon loaded with wheat, and had filled it with rifles, which they sent into Maryland. They were said to consist of 250 whites and a gang of negroes.

But for editors, local news remained paramount, particularly if it provided an opportunity to vent indignation. In February, John McElroy, editor of the *Santa Cruz Pacific Sentinel,* offered his view on a favored subject of the day: "We prate loudly about the debasing effects of superstition during the middle ages, and laugh at the witch-burners of New England, but…we are evidently about to relapse into a degree of stupidity more pitiable than that of our predecessors."

Spiritualism apparently was making Californians crazy, literally:

> The evil effects resulting from the propagation of this monstrous delusion in this State is becoming painfully apparent.—There are over forty persons in the Asylum at Stockton, rendered insane by mental excitement growing out of this subject. The San Francisco papers chronicle two new cases during the past week, and also the fact that three jurors in one of the Courts in that city permitted their judgments to be governed, in agreeing to a verdict, by the supposed opinions of the spirits of Franklin and Webster, whom they invoked on the occasion.

As the editor well knew, one of the chief proponents of Spiritualist beliefs resided in Santa Cruz. Had McElroy known that within little more than a year Mrs. Farnham herself would take up residence at the Stockton institution, he likely would have mentioned it. Meanwhile, she fearlessly advised the citizens of Santa Cruz, in lecture after lecture, that Spiritualism had bested the church, had found it to be, indeed, "vulnerable and superannuated":

No wonder that while they look each other in the face, one smiles good naturedly, while the other is grim and ungracious. It makes a vast difference, in the attempt to hold your temper under difficulties, whether you find yourself identified with a perishing or an augmenting power....And...what thrilling peace and rest come...at the thought, "I live for all time...." Then the splendors of material nature are accepted as prophecies of the greater ones which await us when we shall have risen to fitness for them....We pronounce life a boon, and feel that, in regard to its goings and comings, a thousand years are indeed as a day, and a day as a thousand years.

In this year of 1860, while residing with the Kirbys, Eliza further devoted herself to writing her "great work" and to lecturing, chiefly at the Santa Cruz courthouse. Still, her name remained newsworthy in San Francisco newspapers:

A notice of Santa Cruz would scarcely be complete without mention of Mrs. Eliza W. Farnham, its greatest nobility. Other residents are not generally known beyond the State, but her books (*California In-Doors and Out, My Early Days,* and *Prison Discipline*) are read throughout the Union. She is engaged in her occupation of authorship, and occasionally she delivers lectures or sermons on spiritualism, religion, and the duties and position of women. Her congregations are usually large. As a consequence of the active part which she has taken in the social life of Santa Cruz, she has made some enemies, but she is respected and admired by many.

That summer, at the Santa Cruz courthouse, Mrs. Farnham offered her opinions to the populace on the various "grades of character, in society," the editor of the *Santa Cruz News,* Mr. Slocum, advising that "No one need be deterred from attending under the impression that the discourse will be of a nature so profound as to give them the headache to comprehend it."

Mr. Slocum was not deterred, and despite complaints that the overcrowded room became too warm for comfort, reported Mrs. Farnham's ideas at length, particularly noting her description of an inferior grade of character in society—the gossip:

Mental and moral idleness is the cause of gossip; and women, being less engrossed with the cares of money-getting—not one of the highest occupations of life, by the way—are more given to idle conversation than those of the other sex; but the term, gossip, is not, by any means, limited, in its application, to females. The male gossip of the

*The Santa Cruz courthouse as it looked on the several occasions that Eliza Farnham lectured there. The editor of the* Santa Cruz News, *an admirer of Mrs. Farnham's speaking talents, advised that "No one need be deterred from attending under the impression that the discourse will be of a nature so profound as to give them the headache to comprehend it." Courtesy of Covello & Covello*

lowest grade is far more gross and more numerous than the female. The women generally belong to a higher and less offensive order of the *genus*. The coarsest gossips are those who attribute to others their own gross and base motives, in order to drag them down to their level....

The self-defensive gossip lacks vigorous life—lacks tone of character—and hence seeks eagerly to learn all that is said of himself and others. He has no faith that his own life will justify itself—that he will finally live down the lie. Another class delight in obtaining the most minute details respecting the evil doings and sayings of their neighbors, affecting, meanwhile, great merit as defenders of those against whom the reports are made. [They never fail to convey to the vilified [sic] party an exaggerated report of the slanders against which they were so magnanimous as to defend him.]

...This sketch, of course, is a very imperfect report of the lecture, which, although spoken extemporaneously, or with little preparation, was replete with excellent thoughts, and fine illustrations, all of which it is not possible to give from memory, even had we the space.

Unfortunately for the spirited young editor, the citizens of Santa Cruz failed to provide sufficient support for him to give space to anyone. In July, the paper ceased publication, providing the rival *Sentinel* an opportunity to gloat: "Died of starvation at Santa Cruz, the *Santa Cruz News,* aged eleven months...though stuffed to repletion with unsubstantial pablum. Peace be to its ashes."

Slocum's departure left John McElroy, editor of the *Pacific Sentinel,* the only local avenue for news on the controversial Mrs. Farnham. Although McElroy rarely agreed with her views, he knew good writing when he read it—and he daringly printed one of her letters, written with pen dipped deeply in the sarcasm she kept in ready supply. That she attacked local authority was, perhaps, no matter. Provocative copy was sure to be read:

> Mr. Editor:—Will you give the following statement of facts a place in your journal, for the public good?
>
> The public school in the Soquel district is taught by a Mr. Bailey—....a noble spirited man...inclined to a severe, ascetic, disciplinary course of self-treatment, which he manages, no doubt with difficulty, to overcome so far as to spend his evenings and hours out of school, in the saloons of Soquel and Santa Cruz, at the card and billiard tables. I mention these unobtrusive sacrifices of his in order to do him justice....
>
> On Thursday night of last week, the Professor...took a larger than his stated dose of discipline at the card table, remaining there in pure excess of noble determination to conquer himself, until the small hours of Friday overtook him....
>
> He was then in his very best estate when, during the forenoon exercises of Friday, a boy of about thirteen failing to answer the questions put to him...was sent to his seat. The boy...sat down, unconscious, as boys of thirteen are apt to be, of the eye that followed him and presently detected him,...the degenerate boy of thirteen years, wrapping a little roll of paper inside the shirt band of his next fellow pupil. [The Professor] called the boy of thirteen to stand up before him and put to him the very natural inquiry, after witnessing such an act in him, if he came to that school to run over him (the Professor)? To which the boy of thirteen replied that he did not. Whether this was felt to be an improper answer, or whether the Professor thought the boy of thirteen failed to apprehend the real object for which he was there, and hence needed to have his perceptions brightened, does not fully appear, but upon this answer he produced his raw-hide from within his desk, where he kept it (with

his Plato and Bacon doubtless), and directed the removal of the top garments from the boy of thirteen, that the virtues of the instrument might more directly be observed, and immediately and straitly proceed through the skin to the benefit of his imperiled soul. The boy of thirteen refused to have the benefit so administered, alleging that his mother, blind unreasonable woman, had directed him not to take his jacket off to be raw-hided....

But of course the Professor was not angry. How could such a man raise his hand in anger to punish a child of 13? The bare suggestion is abusive, and shows how great and good men may be misunderstood—how he might be if I were not here to do him justice. After a good number of strokes, some of the witnesses say sixteen, some twenty, the boy of 13, foolishly supposing, as boys of 13 are apt to, that he had received the benefit that would accrue from that application, darted away from the hand that grasped his collar, and out at the door. The Professor thinking the movement premature, followed, overtook, and overthrew, the boy of 13; brought him (carefully) back in his hand, had his top garments off, this time, and continued the ministration, thus leaving purple whelks of four, then to six inches long, up and down the entire back, and a wound on the side of the throat as large as half a dollar.

In due time the child of 13, (what was his judgment?) and the Professor differed again as to the profit of continuing the application, and the boy, darting out of an open window, ran, and reached home without being overtaken.

Now, it is a little remarkable...that the mother and sisters of the bleeding, lacerated child actually felt indignant at his benefactor, when they looked at his wounds and heard his cries of pain. Indeed, they were so incapable of appreciating such a great and manly effort...as to feel that the noble Professor deserved punishment instead of thanks. One sees how unworthy they were to be the recipients of such service when they did not wash the wounded skin with brine and send the atrocious culprit back...to the Professor—that instead they....actually went the length of having him arrested for assault and battery. But the good and noble are rarely unfriended when suffering for the performance of duty....And therefore we are not to wonder that the District Attorney, who is also a trustee of the school, and a patron, friend and admirer of the Professor, should have seen to it that he was acquitted....

Now, are we to wonder that the Jury, as enlightened, high-minded, thoughtful, humane a dozen of men...as could be picked from among the frequenters of the Soquel saloon and gaming tables, promptly and indignantly returned a verdict of "not guilty"—nor that the partisans of this abused citizen...should assure the mothers of the neighborhood, that if they took their children out of school because they were cut up with the raw-hide, the school would be broken up, and they—the trustees—would not try to find another teacher? (Why should they, indeed, when such a man could not please them?)...Doubtless all these, I say, feel how noble it is to have such a man grace their town and their rooms with his fine, pure presence, his improving manners, his refined tastes, his exalted aims....Doubtless these men reckon the $80 or $100 per month which the Prof. receives and disburses among them a paltry consideration compared with the duty and privilege of sustaining the principle which he represents—namely, the principle of regulating boys and girls by the raw-hide. But notwithstanding that these enlightened views and liberal feelings *prevail* around him, there are people ignorant and narrow enough to misjudge such a man, and even to doubt that he is the very best that could be found for his place. Fortunately for him and the Att'y-Trustee, you and I, Mr. Editor, are not of this narrow sort. We realize with the Prof. and Att'y-Trustee how much better off the Soquel youth are than if they had fallen into the hands of some milksop who consider[ed] it his or her duty to win their trust and affection, to interest them in their studies, made them *desire* to go to school, inspire[d] them with a spirit of study and a love of knowledge, and with reverence for high standards of man and womanhood....

Now I know the ingratitude of human nature so well, and its inability to appreciate when it is well served, that it would not surprise me at all if some of the narrow people I have spoken of; fathers and mothers who presume to judge for themselves...should attempt to get rid of the Prof. and look for some inferior person to take the instruction of their children. Well, if they do, it cannot be said that I have not done my duty. I have warned them, and set his merits forth. If now they will not be reasonable and support such a man, and the other nice one, the Trustee who supports *him;* if they will be blind to the beauty of raw-hides...I cannot help it, or them, I fear.

Mr. Editor, you see my cause. I hope you sympathize both with me and my clients, the Prof. *and* the Att'y-Trustee, and will not be found wanting when you can speak a word for us....

P.S. I was near forgetting the extraordinary sacrifice which my Prof. makes for the public good. He actually spends many of his Sundays and Sunday evenings at card and billiard tables, that he may enter upon his Monday duties with the moral, intellectual and passional equilibrium so necessary to their successful conduct. Wonderful man! But I believe our State contains many such, and that there are many districts in it where Trustees, whether District Attorneys or not, appreciate and prefer them. Fortunate State!

Like Mr. Slocum before him, Mr. McElroy had Mrs. Farnham to thank for lost subscriptions.

> Thanks to our neighbor for his offer of condolence on the loss of a few thin-skinned subscribers, of Soquel, who took offence at Mrs. Farnham's communication, in last week's paper. Inasmuch as they have made an issue with us, holding us responsible for the opinions of others, we have no apologies to offer. It is too late a day to attempt to intimidate us, either by a withdrawal of patronage, or in any other mode. We venture that those discontinuing will borrow their neighbor's paper before it is dry from the press.

In any event, Mrs. Farnham ceased being a problem for the newspaper. She was about to depart Santa Cruz again, and two years would pass before she returned, to attempt to improve its citizens for the last time.

# TWENTY-SIX

# Stockton

THE HOME OF THE AFFLICTED. The history of any insane asylum can never be read with pleasure, for it is the history of wrecked minds. The history of the California insane asylum is of more painful interest than common, because of the circumstances surrounding each case and the shattered intellects that lie within its walls. The slow, sluggish mind seldom rises to any prominence in society or becomes insane. It is the quick, active-impulse brain that makes its mark, or becomes diseased....The life into which every pioneer was ushered when he entered this State was one of excitement and trouble, and many of them, through disappointment, loss of fortune and relatives, gambling, disease and exposure, became insane and were confined.

—George H. Tinkham, *A History of Stockton*, 1880

In May of 1851 the California legislature provided for the establishment of a State General Hospital and appointed a board of trustees to find suitable accommodations in various locations and doctors to staff them. In Stockton, a Dr. Reid assumed the care of thirteen patients housed in a converted saloon and ten-pin alley.

As the state's population increased, so did those adjudged insane, and in 1852 the legislature ordered them all sent to Stockton. By May of 1853, Dr. Reid had 272 patients in his care. A Stockton resident described the scene:

> Every building from Center to El Dorado Street was filled with patients. Sometimes the mentally ill were chained to the oaks in the yard as there was no room indoors for them. It was a typical mad house with a few padded cells and some of the patients were in straitjackets.

That year the legislature passed a law establishing an Asylum for the Insane, specifying that they, the legislature, would elect the physician in charge by joint ballot every two years and pay him a salary of five thousand dollars per annum. Both the asylum's location and the position of physician to oversee it were considered plums for the successful applicants.

Eager little Benicia having won, albeit temporarily, its campaign for state capital, it now sought the asylum. But there was no trumping Stockton's offer of a hundred acres for the purpose. Sacramento wouldn't do because, as a Doctor Ryer had pointed out to the legislature, the insane were believed to be especially susceptible to "miasmatic and congestive diseases," which were more common in Sacramento than in Stockton, and it was "plain as good sense and justice that the asylum should be in the neighborhood of Stockton."

The clinching argument came from the New York City Health Department's statistics for death rates in various American cities: "It appears from the tables that the city of Burlington, Iowa... enjoys the pre-eminence for health, its annual death rate being only 4.84 deaths per 1,000 souls. Stockton, California, stands next—7.47...."

A contract was let for construction, buildings were erected, and by the close of 1853, Dr. Reid had in his care 284 patients suffering various forms of dementia from a myriad of supposed causes. Forty-two patients, for example, had been diagnosed as "insane from intemperance, 24 from disappointment, 20 from masturbation."

The resident physician's position being an appointed one, Dr. Reid, a Democrat, was thanked for his services in 1856 by newly elected Governor Johnson of the Know-Nothing Party, who intended the appointment for a physician of his own political persuasion. The legislature, however, was satisfied to have Dr. Reid continue and demurred, refusing to appoint a replacement. The governor officially declared the office vacant and appointed Dr. Samuel Langdon to fill it. Then everyone went to court, which found, upon appeal, for the governor. The resident physician position remained a political dispensation, and in 1861, with the election of Republicans, the prize went to Dr. W. P. Tilden.

And Dr. Tilden was married to Maria Hecox, who had come to Santa Cruz as a child, had grown up there and known, and approved, and been approved by Mrs. Farnham and Mrs. Kirby. Someone had the good idea that Mrs. Farnham was the ideal candidate for the matron's position at Stockton, possibly Maria Hecox Tilden herself. In any event, she urged her husband to make the appointment, Mrs. Farnham accepted, and in April 1861, Eliza left Georgiana to the demands of three young daughters and a newborn son, Santa Cruz to its own fate, and went to Stockton. The *San Francisco Daily Times*, in its April 18 edition, applauded:

A GOOD APPOINTMENT.—It is announced that Dr. Tilden, recently elected Resident Physician of the Insane Asylum, has appointed Mrs. Eliza W. Farnham Matron for that Institution. She is a woman of mind, of thought, of human sympathies, one of the ablest of the women who are too often, by the weak minded, or weak-moraled men, designated "strong-minded." She has experience as Matron of Sing Sing, and from her experiences and observation, wrote and published an interesting book on the subject. We would give great odds in a bet, if making one, that she will do more, if allowed to exercise her knowledge and experience, towards curing the insane, than all the doctors and political attaches that have ever belonged to the Hospital.

The state's asylum had steadily enlarged from its initial humble accommodation in the saloon/ten-pin alley. From necessity and a generous legislature, a new building or a new wing on an existing one arose nearly every year on the donated hundred acres. Staff increased proportionately to the number of patients. In the year 1858, for example, 244 patients were admitted, 43 of them women. "Supposed Cause" for confinement for men ranged from "disappointed avarice" to that consistently problematic affliction, masturbation. Women found themselves diagnosed as demented due to "disappointed ambition" or suffering from idiocy caused by religion. The staff required to attend these unfortunates included, besides the resident physician, assorted keepers and assistant keepers, housemaids and gardeners, an apothecary, carpenters, cooks and waiters, washerwomen, messengers and, of course, a matron for the female patients.

As usual, Mrs. Farnham's reputation preceded her. Stockton's newspaper noted her appointment by reporting that "this lady fills quite a space in California history....In 1850 Mrs. Farnham conceived the idea of bringing out a large number of young women from New York, as wives and 'help' were in great demand then, but the scheme rather fell through." The editor had the date off by a year, but the end result, Mrs. Farnham would have agreed, was essentially as described.

The editor of the *Santa Cruz Pacific Sentinel* observed, "The appointment is one well deserved by the talents and acquirements of this lady. We do not know the pecuniary value of the position, but hope it may be such as to properly reward the exertions of our talented neighbor."

When Dr. Tilden, with his family, and Mrs. Farnham, with her son, Charles, arrived at Stockton, they found themselves in charge of a population numbering nearly twice the facility's designated capacity of 250 inmates. They also found themselves in the midst of controversy. A senate investigating committee had visited recently and praised the asylum's cleanliness, but faulted the staff for lack of cure. Newspaper editorials based on the committee's report decried the expense of the hospital as well as its apparent ineffectiveness. The *San Francisco Daily Times* declared the asylum an "expensive failure":

> For the current year, ending June 30th, 1861, the total amount of appropriations, including salaries, amount to...over two hundred and eleven dollars per head for the inmates. We believe an individual could give better treatment, better accommodations, cure more patients than is done under the State organization, and clear fifty thousand dollars by the operation....In 1858, out of 248 cases treated, only twelve were cured, less than five per cent. This is a sad showing for the medical treatment followed.

Of one department, the committee reported:

> The mad house—its construction—the confinement and treatment of its inmates, cannot be too highly deprecated. Such an appendage to an asylum is at least fifteen years behind the age, and should be superceded by well-ventilated rooms, kind care and humane treatment of its inmates, which means are successful substitutes for controlling, in a majority of cases, even the raving maniac.

The committee conceded that "insanity is more prolific in California than almost any other state in the Union...and what peculiar causes are operating to render it less curable your Committee is not prepared to say."

The recommendation made to the legislature was that an investigation be conducted during the next recess to "examine thoroughly the institution in all its departments."

Meanwhile, Dr. Tilden and Mrs. Farnham had in their care more than four hundred patients who had journeyed to far-off California either in doubtful mental health or had been reduced

*State Insane Asylum,
Stockton, 1855. Courtesy
of The Bancroft Library,
University of California,
Berkeley (Banc Pic
1963:002:1305-E-ALB)*

*State Insane Asylum,
Female Department,
photographed by J. Pitcher
Spooner. Courtesy of
The Bancroft Library,
University of California,
Berkeley (Camp Collection
10, 16362)*

to it by the experience. Inmates represented twenty-two states and twenty-three foreign countries, including England, Ireland, France, Spain, Germany, Bavaria, Denmark, Italy, Mexico, Australia, Chile, and China. Nearly a quarter of these unfortunates were women.

Mrs. Farnham's duties were clearly spelled out:

> The Matron...will be with the female patients...as much as possible; see that they are kindly treated; that their food is properly cooked...that their apartments are kept clean and in good order, and properly warmed and ventilated....The bedding, table linen... furniture, carpets...as well as the clothing of the female patients, shall be under her general care and supervision. She shall direct the employment and amusements of all the inmates of the female wards; in short, it will be expected of her to look frequently and carefully into every interest connected with her department; and thus, by devoting her whole time to the Institution, aid, in every way in her power, in securing the comfort and recovery of the patients.

It was a tall order in every regard, particularly for a population of women diagnosed as suffering from melancholia, dementia, mania, and idiocy, these unhappy diagnoses stemming from such diverse "supposed causes" as dissipation, religion, domestic troubles, destitution, fright, misfortune, desertion, seduction, childbirth, and gestation. One female patient had been committed on account of insanity induced by "dissatisfaction with her boarding house." Upon inquiry, the woman's former abode was revealed to be the county jail, where she had been a frequent inmate at the county's expense.

The new administration discovered that criticisms reported by the press were accurate. Dr. Tilden confirmed that, in his opinion, the asylum was "a most signal failure":

> The more carefully I inquire into the condition of the Asylum, the more thoroughly am I convinced that we have in it a prison, and nothing more—that if there is any marked difference between it and a well conducted State Prison, it is in favor of the latter, from the fact that means of employment are provided for its inmates, while the inmates of the Asylum spend their days in idleness....The cleanly and orderly state in which the Institution is kept cannot compensate for its crowded condition and for its utter want of curative agencies.

Overcrowding, with some patients forced to sleep on the floor, resulted in conditions offensive to the "olfactories," "sickening exhalations proceeding from rooms filled to their utmost with men." One of the good doctor's first expenditures was for latticework doors to replace solid ones, to improve ventilation. He also began construction of a badly needed sewage system. When he and Mrs. Farnham arrived, they had discovered that previous administrations had directed the burial of offal and refuse matter in wells or simple holes in the ground, the levelness of the country offering no natural sewage disposition:

> These cesspools had become rather numerous, and, during the hot weather, the stench from them was intolerable, while, during the winter, when the water was near the surface of the ground, the cesspools would overflow, and, around their surfaces, create an intolerable nastiness.

As for "curative agencies," there were none. The new administration immediately installed a small gymnasium and a library, and hoped for funds to do more, for "it could scarcely be expected that even insane men would be disposed to spend all their time in reading newspapers and in gymnastic exercises":

> The evils of idleness are as great…in an Asylum as elsewhere, and the importance of employment is nowhere shown to greater advantage. The attention it gives to the otherwise wandering mind, and the contentment it affords, cannot be too highly estimated in the treatment of insanity.

Mrs. Farnham knew how to build a library: appeal to the public. An advertisement in the *Stockton Independent* for contributions resulted in the donation of sixty-seven books. It was a beginning. And she knew the importance of keeping idle hands occupied, as well as idle minds. She obtained for the female ward a Wheeler & Wilson sewing machine and put the women to work making dresses, skirts, drawers, chemises, curtains, table covers, sheets, towels, aprons—and flags.

The idea for making flags likely arose from a series of flag "incidents" in Stockton in consequence of the election, in November 1860, of Abraham Lincoln. The prospect of civil war loomed ever closer, and rumor had it that southern sympathizers in California, Oregon, and Nevada intended forming a Pacific Republic. The notion was not so far-fetched, given the number of state officers sympathetic to the South. In January and February of 1861, more than one flag design, proposed to represent a seceded California, appeared in Stockton. On February 22 Stockton's Unionists, in response to these emblems of disunion, not only paraded the Stars and Stripes through town, they hung the flag on staffs, buildings, trees, and fences. A cannon salute capped the event as the Stockton Cornet Band played "The Star-Spangled Banner" and "Yankee Doodle" from the roof of the Corinthian Building.

In March, Lincoln's inaugural address appeared in the local papers, but not until April 23 did residents read that, on April 12, Confederates had fired on the flag at Fort Sumter.

In the East, civil war had begun in earnest. In the West, loyalties to North and South commenced a wave of partisanship. The notion of a Pacific Republic evaporated as the populace took sides by forming "Union" clubs or advocating the southern cause in public displays.

The *Stockton Daily Republican*, in anticipation of July's Independence Day observance, urged "every Union man, and there are few or no others in our city, however much we may differ upon the means of preserving the Union" to "heartily contribute in making the celebration one of the most imposing ever witnessed in Stockton." The editor wanted to see flags, lots of them. "We wish to see our little city buried up in them. Every horse, wagon, dray, buggy or other carriage, should travel with them on that day."

And to the great surprise of the city's residents, on the fourth of July they awoke to a celebratory display of flags at the asylum. A flagpole that had recently been erected atop the steeple was gaily arrayed with flags, four long lines of them, reaching from the top of the staff to the ground. Fluttering in commemorative salute were flags representing every country on the globe, with the Stars and Stripes waving proudly above them all. And every one of them had been sewn by the inmates.

Satisfaction with this splendid accomplishment, however, failed to repay Mrs. Farnham for the difficult and unrewarding task of working with society's cast-offs. And here she faced, as she had at New York's Sing Sing, another committee of investigation. In August, a special senate committee investigated conditions at the hospital. They praised recent improvements, the cleanliness and order, but the great problems remained: overcrowding, a general absence of curative measures, and insufficient outdoor exercise for the inmates.

One flourishing form of outdoor exercise, praised by the local press, was gardening:

*"Inundation of the State Capitol, city of Sacramento, 1862," a view
of J Street, from the levee. The winter rains of 1861–1862 created an immense
inland lake nearly three hundred miles long and twenty wide. Like Sacramento,
low-lying Stockton flooded, with the State Asylum under two feet of water at
the shallow depths. Mrs. Farnham saw fences float off, and patients from
the 'Mad Houses' had to be moved to the main building. Courtesy of the
California History Section, California State Library (5495)*

ASYLUM FARM.—Among the most thrifty and thoroughly cultivated
farms in the immediate vicinity of the city, is that of the State Insane
Asylum, most of the labor upon which is voluntarily performed by
patients. Since the institution came under its present charge, the
area of ground under cultivation has been very materially improved
and enlarged, and will this year [1862] supply an ample quantity of
produce for the use of the patients....A few years hence, and this
farm will become a resort for visitors to our city, and a model which
practical gardeners with sound minds will do well to imitate.

The garden's productivity may have been due in part to the
remarkable watering it had received during the winter of 1861–62.
The rains had commenced in November, and before long,

Stockton's Camp McDougall, which had been established for Union volunteers, had deteriorated into a fever-plagued quagmire. By month's end, the last six companies had abandoned the camp in favor of winter quarters at, perhaps not surprisingly, Benicia.

By December 9, the *Sacramento Daily Bee* was editorializing the "Great Flood of '61." And the deluge had but begun. On Christmas Eve, the rains intensified, and they kept falling—for another month. During this relentless downpour, the rivers comprising the vast watershed of the western Sierra—the Bear, the American, the Yuba, the King, the Mokelumne, and all their various and generous tributaries—plunged down the mountains and emptied themselves into the great Central Valley. And the valley began to fill. And when at last the rains had ceased, California possessed an immense inland lake, extending north to south nearly three hundred miles, averaging, in breadth, twenty miles. And in the center, under two feet of water at the shallow depths, had sat Stockton.

On the first of March, the Committee on State Hospitals arrived for another investigation. They discovered little serious damage. True, most of the fences had "floated off," and there had been a "temporary removal of the patients from the 'Mad Houses' to the main building," but the hospital's ordinary daily routine suffered no interruptions.

But they found, as had the special committee visiting the previous November, an "intolerable overcrowding":

> In the portion of the Asylum occupied by the female patients there are but three wards, including the mad-house for females.... There are two yards connected with the female department, for outdoor exercise, but neither of them is in a wholesome or cheerful condition. The mad-house for females is in one of the yards, and...is used to confine many patients who are not mad, but for whom there is no room in the main building. These so-called wards, and especially the sleeping apartments connected with the same, are not of sufficient capacity to properly accommodate more than one half the number they now contain.

By April Mrs. Farnham had made her decision. There were more interesting things to do than cope with mud and the mentally muddled or tour fault-finding committees critical of conditions they failed to ameliorate. Or perhaps she agreed with the findings of the special committee that the state hospital's "senseless and

*Platt's Hall, northeast corner of Bush and Montgomery streets.
Mrs. Farnham lectured on Spiritualism here in May 1862, denouncing the
Church for its "stale dogmas and dreary platitudes." Courtesy of The Bancroft
Library, University of California, Berkeley (SF Views 4, Cityscapes 10, 72)*

unreasoning babble would drive a sane man crazy." In any event, when her year's contract expired, she and Charles gathered up their things and her manuscripts and, with new intentions, left Stockton.

In May, Mrs. Farnham was in San Francisco again, lecturing at Platt's Hall, corner of Montgomery and Bush streets. Her subject was Spiritualism. Which meant her subject was also "the Church"—on which her opinions had not reformed:

> People have a position if they belong to a Church. It throws around them certain lines, within which they find social advantages, recognitions and relations, which it would take more time to establish outside. And there are not wanting those who intimate that it would take more of some things else beside time to gain these points in good communities, outside the Church—more character, they say, more integrity, more activity in useful works than a man or woman

need to employ in it. The certificate of membership goes, doubtless, for a good deal. When that is accepted, you are entitled to presume that the good works will appear, and sometimes you are left to indulge the pleasant presumption a long time before they do appear. Neighbors like to meet in the Church, when the sermon is not too afflictively dull, also there is a thin, gray shadow, fading now, of respectability attached to pew-holding. Good women, who are the most active ministers to the material needs of the Church, delight in sewing circles for her support, and in fairs, and festivals, and collections; husbands indulge their wives in making them because they like them. It is popular, and the minister is such a nice man—more agreeable out of the pulpit than in it, generally; because out of it he may talk like other men if he has the ability, while in it he is condemned to wander amid stale dogmas and dreary platitudes, (ghosts of truths long since departed from those forms), and tiresome repetitions of doctrinal statements, which can have no interest to his hearers, because they have outgrown them, and because, however they may will to respect him in the utterance, they cannot take his words for truths.

In June she lectured in Santa Cruz. Her subject was the war.

In July she rejoiced with the citizens of California: President Lincoln had signed the railroad bill. Back in 1856 she had presciently written:

But let the "talking-wires" span free soil from the Atlantic to the Pacific, and let free labor, with its enterprise, progress, and intelligence, possess and build up Kansas and Nebraska, through which California will ultimately be connected, by railroad, with the East, and, in a few years, she will be garden of the Union.

As history would have it, neither Eliza nor Charles would see the railroad's arrival, or the prediction confirmed. In San Francisco, taking her final leave of the state where "so much of the thrilling experience of life" had come to her, Eliza Farnham boarded the steamer *Sonora* for Panama, with connection to New York: Mrs. Farnham had another book to publish.

But before her "great work" would see print, she would see firsthand, as few Californians would, civil war.

# TWENTY-SEVEN

# Gettysburg

UNKNOWN HEROINES.—The war has developed a national character that was not suspected....Angels of mercy, and peace, and enlightenment, they follow the advancing lines of bayonets. Their work is little heeded; their names are unrecorded; but...these women early heard and obeyed the divine whisper.

—*Harper's Weekly,* July 2, 1864

In transit between the coasts for nearly a month, Eliza arrived in New York City late in September of 1862 to find the country truly at war. Late August had seen a second battle at Bull Run. Mid-September witnessed Antietam.

Mrs. Farnham's Quaker heritage likely disinclined her for war. Even more likely would have been her aversion to seeing Charles, the one child left to her and now a young man of twenty-one years, subscripted. Eliza's old friend and benefactor from her Sing Sing days, John Bigelow, was now the American consul in Paris, and possibly that connection prompted her decision to send Charles to France to study drawing and music.

Her personal preoccupations were literary. She needed to finish the new book and, due to the failure of the publishers of her autobiography, *My Early Days,* and its small printing, she wanted to reissue it under her original title, *Lucia Woodson.*

And beyond her private concerns loomed larger issues, for her and many women, in this time of war. In wartime, it was the women who rolled the bandages, collected contributions, and formed relief societies. The women of New York had been at it since April 1861, when ninety-one of them decided to supply "extra medical aid to our Army" and announced the intention in the city's newspapers. "Should our unhappy war be continued, the Army is certain to want the services of extra nurses," the undersigners advised, and called upon the populace to find, prepare, and send "bands of women, of suitable age, constitution, training

*"The Influence of Woman," from* Harper's Weekly, *Sept. 6, 1862.*
*Courtesy of the Library of Congress (LC-USZ62-102383 and 102384)*

and temperament, to the Army at such points and at such times"
as they might be needed.

This effort planted the seed that grew into the United States
Sanitary Commission. That men took charge of the women's
intentions was a slight not lost on Elizabeth Cady Stanton, Susan B.
Anthony, and Matilda Joslyn Gage:

> Dr. Bellows enjoyed the distinction as President of the Sanitary
> Bureau, which originated in the mind of a woman, who, when the
> machinery was perfected and in good working order, was forced
> to resign her position as official head through the bigotry of the
> medical profession.

The Sanitary Commission provided medical aid, services, and
supplies that the War Department could not. Contributions
poured in to fund the undertaking, far-off California generously
sending more than $400,000 by the end of 1862, twice the
amount contributed by easterners.

In the spring of 1863, the women organized again. In March they published in the *New York Daily Tribune* a call for a "meeting of the Loyal Women of the Nation" to convene in New York. And women responded in "immense numbers," crowding into a church on May 14, to be greeted by those whose names had become synonymous with the great issues of the mid–nineteenth century: Susan B. Anthony, Elizabeth Cady Stanton, Lucy Stone, Angelina Grimke Weld, Ernestine L. Rose, the Reverend Antoinette Brown Blackwell, Eliza W. Farnham.

On that day they organized the Women's National Loyal League for the purpose of abolishing slavery through an amendment to the U.S. Constitution. This they proposed to do by collecting signatures, hundreds of thousands of them, on petitions they planned to present to Congress. Susan Anthony nominated Lucy Stone for president. Eliza Farnham was named vice president for California.

If Mrs. Farnham spoke at this meeting, history did not record it. Perhaps she felt no need to, not after hearing Mrs. Chalkstone of California address the assembly with opinions so representative of her own:

> I consider women a great deal superior to men. Men are physically strong, but women are morally better. I speak of pure women, good women. It is woman who keeps the world in the balance.
>
> I am from Germany, where my brothers all fought against the Government and tried to make us free, but were unsuccessful. My only son, seventeen years old, is in our great and noble army of the Union. He has fought in many of the battles here, and I only came from California to see him once more. I have not seen him yet; though I was down in the camp, I could not get any pass. But I am willing to lay down all this sacrifice for the cause of liberty. We foreigners know the preciousness of that great, noble gift a great deal better than you, because you never were in slavery, but we are born in it.

The next month, Mrs. Farnham was in Philadelphia, addressing a circle of Spiritualists there. First organized as the Harmonial Benevolent Society, and then as the First Spiritualist Association, they had been meeting regularly for nearly fifteen years. Among the speakers engaged to address them was Judge Edmonds, Mrs. Farnham's earliest supporter at Sing Sing, and he may have recommended her to them. The group's most prominent leader was Dr. Henry T. Child, a physician trained at Philadelphia's Jefferson Medical College.

To be in Pennsylvania in June of 1863 was to be in the path of history. In that month, the Confederate army invaded the Keystone State. On July 1 the opposing forces engaged, fearfully, historically, at Gettysburg.

When the fighting ceased, word of the terrible aftermath traveled quickly to Philadelphia. Here, now, at once, was desperate need for the doctors and volunteer nurses of the U.S. Sanitary Commission. Dr. Henry Child was one of them. And his youthful sister-in-law, Cornelia Hancock, wished to be included:

> After my only brother and every male relative and friend that we possessed had gone to the War, I deliberately came to the conclusion that I, too, would go and serve my country. I confided this resolution to my sister's husband, Dr. Henry T. Child, who lived in Philadelphia where he was well known in philanthropic and antislavery circles. He promised to let me know of the first available opportunity to be of use.

The call came on the morning of July 5. Cornelia, over her mother's objection, joined her brother-in-law in Philadelphia that afternoon:

> Every hour was bringing tidings of the awful loss of life on both sides. Dr. Child, with a number of other physicians, had determined to leave that night by the eleven o'clock train for Gettysburg. I was to accompany him.
>
> He and the Hon. Judge Kelly had aided Miss Eliza Farnham, a well-known public-spirited woman, with a number of others of "suitable age," to get passes as volunteer nurses. The ladies in the party were many years older than myself, and I was under the especial care of Miss Farnham. At eleven p.m. we were wending our way out...to...the depot....The morning found us in Baltimore....Here Dorothea Dix appeared on the scene. She looked the nurses over and pronounced them all suitable except me....Miss Farnham explained that she was under obligation to my friends who had helped her get proper credentials. The discussion waxed warm and I have no idea what conclusion they came to, for I settled the question myself by getting on the car and staying in my seat until the train pulled out of...Baltimore....I got into Gettysburg the night of July sixth—where the need was so great that there was no further cavil about age.

In Gettysburg, they were met by Dr. Horner, a resident, and spent the night at his house. The next day Cornelia saw the consequence of battle:

> Every barn, church, and building of any size in Gettysburg had been converted into a temporary hospital. We went the same evening to one of the churches, where I saw for the first time what war meant. Hundreds of desperately wounded men were stretched out on boards laid across the high-backed pews as closely as could be packed together. The boards were covered with straw. Thus elevated, these poor sufferers' faces, white and drawn with pain, were almost on a level with my own. I seemed to stand breast-high in a sea of anguish.

Cornelia wrote her cousin a letter that evening:

> I am very tired tonight; have been on the field all day—went to the 3rd Division 2nd Army Corps. I suppose there are about five hundred wounded belonging to it. They have one patch of woods devoted to each army corps for a hospital....There are no words in the English language to express the sufferings I witnessed today. The men lie on the ground; their clothes have been cut off them to dress their wounds; they are half naked, having nothing but hard-tack to eat....I was the first woman who reached the 2nd Corps after the three days fight at Gettysburg. I was in that Corps all day, not another woman within a half mile....To give you some idea of the extent and numbers of the wounds, four surgeons, none of whom were idle fifteen minutes at a time, were busy amputating legs and arms. I gave to every man that had a leg or arm off a gill of wine, to every wounded in Third Division one glass of lemonade, some bread and preserves and tobacco—as much as I am opposed to the latter....
>
> It is a very beautiful country. Women are needed here very badly, anyone who is willing to go to field hospitals, but nothing short of an order from Secretary Stanton or General Halleck will let you through the lines. Major General Schenk's order for us was not regarded as anything; if we had not met Miss Dix at Baltimore Depot, we should not have gotten through.

And Eliza wrote Georgiana that same evening:

> Let me tell you, dear, how I have spent this day. It will be, most probably, a fair history of what will follow for three weeks, or a month, if I can stand it so long. In the first place, let me say that on Saturday last (being in Philadelphia) when the news of the great battle arrived, I determined to come down and do what I could. I got a

cheap calico and made it up in a few hous....Lectured on Sunday evening for the Spiritualist society, and at midnight started with three other women who had joined me for this place, via. Baltimore; had a battle there with the red-tape department, but finally got through, and arrived at six last evening. This a.m., at six, breakfasted and then went out into the hospital across the street, (the Lutheran church). Spent 2 1/2 hours in service there. Such sights and conditions! All states from health to death before us. The whole town, about 3000 inhabitants, is one vast hospital; all public and a great many private buildings full of sufferers. At a little past nine we set out in a field-ambulance for the field-hospitals, on and near the battle ground, which extended from the streets of the village to five miles away on the south and east. It is impossible, in a letter, to give you any idea of what awaited us at the end of that drive. The road, for long distances, was in many places strewn with dead horses; the human dead having been all removed by this time. The earth in the roads and fields is ploughed to a mire by the army wheels and horses. Houses are occasionally riddled with bullets, cannon or shell, and the straggling wounded line the roads, and rest against the fences, (where the latter is not torn down, or burnt up). Breastworks, and the places where batteries were planted, loom up here and there in the desolated fields. The putrid remains of slaughtered bullocks, the cast-off clothing of the dead, and wounded, lie scattered around.

Well, at length we left the road and returned into a trampled meadow toward a wooded height. On all hands, as we went, cities of tents (detached from each other) were seen, the field-hospitals of the different corps that were engaged in this fearful battle. When we reached the place we were bound to, there appeared before us avenues of white tents under the green boughs, and many men moving about. But good God! what those quiet looking tents contained! What spectacles awaited us on the slopes of the rolling hills around us! It is absolutely inconceivable, unless you see it. There are miles of tents and acres of men lying on the open earth beneath the trees. I never could have imagined anything to compare with it. Dead and dying, and wounded, in every condition you can conceive after two days in such a rain of missiles. Old veterans who have seen all our battles say that there never has been such firing anywhere for more than half an hour or so as there was here for the greater part of nine hours. No wonder that men who were rushing upon and through and upon it should be torn to pieces in every way. I worked from ten till half past four, without five minutes cessation, in spreading, cutting and distributing bread and butter. Such thankful eyes and stifled voices, and quivering lips, from poor fellows without legs, or arms, or hands, or terribly wounded otherwise, who had seen nothing but hardtack since they were hurt!

At last I came to a group of confederate prisoners. Such destitute, abject looking creatures as the privates were! Enough of them to cover four such lots as your house is in [1 1/4 acre lot].

If Mrs. C. is in Santa Cruz tell her I had the pleasure of giving a piece of bread and butter to a friend of hers—Colonel Fry, of Sacramento. He is shot through the ankle, but seems well and very resolute. There was a man and his son lying beside him, each having lost a leg; other men with both legs gone. But the most horrible thing was to see these limbs lying, piled up like offal at the foot of a tree in front of the surgeon's tent. Adieu. I do the same work tomorrow, and shall be too exhausted to write soon again.

The next day, July 8, 1863, even young Cornelia had barely energy to write her sister:

We have been two days on the field; go out about eight and come in about six—go in ambulances or army buggies....I feel assured I shall never feel horrified at anything that may happen to me hereafter. There is a great want of surgeons here; there are hundreds of brave fellows, who have not had their wounds dressed since the battle.... I hope you will write. It would be very pleasant to have letters to read in the evening, for I am so tired I cannot write them. Get the Penn Relief to send clothing here; there are many men without anything but a shirt lying in poor shelter tents, calling on God to take them from this world of suffering; in fact the air is rent with petitions to deliver them from their sufferings.

By the end of three weeks, all the supplies the women had received had been given out. And the conditions under which they labored had declined as well. Cornelia wrote her mother that "when we get up early in the morning, our clothes are so wet that we could wring them out. On they go, and by noon they are dry."

A healthy young girl tolerated the damp better than a woman nearing fifty, a woman whose mother may have died of consumption, a woman whose sister almost certainly had. Cornelia transferred from the 2nd Army Corps Hospital to the General Hospital at Gettysburg. Eliza could stay no longer.

Eliza had developed a cough, a bad cough. She returned to New York. Had she the strength and health for it, there was much in the city that summer of 1863 that in other times would have urged her to action. Girls who sewed umbrellas at six to eight cents each, yielding wages of three or four dollars a week, went on strike, asking first for a two-cent raise, then for a penny, and got nothing. Poverty crippled much of New York City's population, with Horace Greeley estimating that twenty-five thousand of them lived in cellar tenements. The lives of women residing in the Five Points quarter, the women Eliza Farnham had bravely declared in 1858 that she could change, had not improved with the fortunes of war. Describing the area in 1862, a visiting Englishman called it "as miserable a haunt of vice and misery as it was ever my lot to witness in Europe," adding:

> The Broadway saloons with their so-called "pretty waiter-girls," and Lager Bier haunts in the low quarters of the town, whose windows are crowded with wretched half-dressed, or undressed women, formed, indeed, about the most shameless exhibition of public vice I have ever come across, even in England or Holland.

The city was rife with poverty and discontent. Opponents of Lincoln's leadership organized. Samuel F. B. Morse led the Society for the Diffusion of Political Knowledge, dedicated to telling the public the government's actions were illegal or, at least, improper. The Conscription Act of March 3, 1863, intensified the gulf dividing rich and poor, allowing any draftee with three hundred dollars to buy his way out of the war. The consequent and violent "draft riots" of July 1863 cost many lives and more than a million dollars in destroyed property.

When Mrs. Farnham returned to this city of turmoil, she did not stay. She was ill, and she had her own work to do. She retired to the care of friends on Staten Island—to write.

# TWENTY-EIGHT

# The Great Work

In the afternoon I devoted myself to reading Mrs. Farnum [sic], the whole glorious chapter on "Woman in the Kingdom of Uses." There is nothing finer in the English language, nothing more prophetic, I am sure, in the whole realm of spiritual foresight. I long to have you read it. One-sided as she certainly is, and leaving out of her argument a body of facts that are against her theories, she still opens such a possible, such a truthful and holy career for women, and such a lifting of Humanity through the feminine element, that one cannot but feel conviction on every page. The book never went through but one edition; it is out of print, but I predict that fifty years hence it will be a great book, read and appreciated by millions.

—Susan Lesley, July 25, 1870

For years Eliza Farnham had been formulating her idea, weighing and sifting its supporting evidence, organizing her argument, getting it onto paper, page after page after page. While in California, she had permitted Mrs. Day, editor of the *Hesperian*, a monthly literary periodical in San Francisco, to publish excerpts. The first passage appeared in the December 1860 *Hesperian* as "Some Extracts from Mrs. E. W. Farnham's Forthcoming Volume on the Subject of Woman." The selection matches almost identically pages 279 through 293 of the book published four years later, and indeed, Mrs. Farnham had all but completed her "great work" while in California.

But it was in January 1864, at Staten Island, that she wrote the preface that declared not only her belief in Woman, but her unapologetic position on the issue of women's rights:

> Nearly twenty-two years have elapsed since the Truth which is the burthen of the following pages first took possession of my mind. It has ever since held its place unwaveringly, there. No conflict of theory or purpose, with regard to Woman's nature, the greatness of her responsibility, or the moral magnificence of her destiny, has ever been possible to me since that day. Hence, I have never been able to co-operate with any party on the Woman Question, and have

## DEDICATION.

TO THE FEW BELOVED FRIENDS,

### WOMEN,

ON BOTH SHORES OF THE CONTINENT, WHOSE FIRESIDES HAVE AFFORDED ME THE
REST AND PEACE OF HOME, FOR THE EXECUTION OF THIS WORK; WHOSE
APPRECIATIVE SYMPATHY HAS GIVEN ME BOTH LIGHT AND
COURAGE FOR ITS DIFFICULTIES: AND TO

### WOMAN,

WHOSE GIFTS AND RESPONSIBILITIES IT SEEKS TO SET FORTH; WHOSE EARNESTNESS
IT AIMS TO KINDLE INTO DIVINE, UNITARY CO-WORKING FOR THE
BLESSING OF HUMANITY; WHOSE CONSCIOUSNESS IT ASPIRES
TO INFORM OF TRUTHS HERETOFORE HIDDEN,

THIS BOOK IS

*AFFECTIONATELY DEDICATED*

BY THE AUTHOR.

*Dedication,* Woman and Her Era

constantly, therefore, been exposed, by its stringency among us, to the disadvantages one always suffers who is a sympathetic, yet dissenting spectator of any earnest movement. It is impossible to escape the reproaches either of its opponents or its advocates. None more than I has respected the effort for Woman, wherever made, and on whatever theoretical basis. That it has seemed to me, as conveyed in its most current nomenclature, of Woman's Rights, erroneous in philosophy, and in many practical matters, partially mistaken in direction, has not prevented my just appreciation of its value to society, or of the courage and faithfulness of those conducting it. I will yield to none in grateful admiration of those pioneer struggles whose fruits we are now enjoying, in the partial emancipation of Women from the legal and social disabilities under which the sex has labored from the beginning.

Eliza dedicated her book to "WOMAN, whose gifts and responsibilities it seeks to set forth; whose earnestness it aims to kindle into divine, unitary co-working for the blessing of humanity; whose consciousness it aspires to inform of truths heretofore hidden," and found a publisher for it.

A. J. Davis & Co., of New York, also agreed to reissue her autobiography, retitled once again. In February 1864, Davis & Co. announced the availability of *Eliza Woodson; Or, The Early Days of One of the World's Workers, A Story of American Life* at $1.25, with the promise that it could not fail to "elevate and instruct." Further:

> The most highly wrought tales of fiction fade into insignificance beside this vivid drama of real life....The book will be found not only entirely unexceptionable in style, plot, and incident, but a work which, while it attracts by its graphic interest, cannot fail to elevate and instruct, inaugurating, in an eminent degree, a *New Era in Fiction*....The book is one which no person can read without profound interest, and neither old nor young can rise from its perusal without feeling helped to nobler purposes and truer action.

Publishers, of course, are expected to say nice things about the books they offer for sale. But what would reviewers say? Happily for publisher and author, an early review from the *Chicago New Covenant* compared *Eliza Woodson* to none other than *Jane Eyre:*

> We took up this book just as the lamps were lighted, and the children were dropping off to sleep in their little beds, and when we laid the volume down, the dawn of another day was looking in at the windows. It had cost us the loss of a night's sleep.
>
> Since reading 'Jane Eyre' we have read nothing in the way of autobiography half so interesting—nothing in the way of fiction half so thrilling.

The *New York Tribune* also reviewed it favorably:

No one can take the volume in hand without being impressed by the deep experience in which it must have had its origin...and the minuteness and fidelity of touch with which the secrets of a remarkable interior life are brought to the surface.

The *New York Atlas* liked it too:

If this story be true, the author has contrived to render a narrative of actual life as entertaining as any work of fiction; if fictitious, she has learned the greatest secret of all art—to conceal art and imitate nature most closely and successfully.

A review in *Life Illustrated* glowed with praise:

Mrs. Farnham has long been known and respected by us, and we have always been of the opinion that she had not many equals, and but very few superiors, of either sex. Yet of her child-life we were ignorant; but now that we know so well her strong heart, and her warm, tender sympathies, we are exceedingly interested in reading the incidents of her early days, which exhibited the germ of what has since been developed....We cannot describe the book, but wish it could be read by everybody, for it is pure fact; *not* a fictitious story, written merely to *entertain* the reader for a time.

The *San Francisco Daily Times* added its compliments:

Mrs. Farnham is one of the ablest and clearest thinkers of the day, and the book is written in her best style. She instructs in the principles of a profound philosophy and pure morality while writing the every-day experiences of a young but oppressed spirit, struggling with high aspirations against vulgar surroundings and brutal taskmasters. It is a very superior book.

But for Eliza Farnham, the reissue of *My Early Days* was plowed ground. It was her "great work" that mattered, and finally, on April 5, the publishers announced:

READY TO-DAY: A BOOK FOR THE CENTURY!
WOMAN AND HER ERA.
BY MRS. ELIZA W. FARNHAM.

Mrs. Farnham is well known as a philanthropist, and widely acknowledged as "one of the ablest and clearest thinkers of the day"...The Publishers do not hesitate to pronounce this crowning piece of a score of years' faithful labor one of the ablest works on the subject ever written—if not, indeed, *the greatest book on Woman extant*. Never before has there appeared a work so entirely original, so ample, exhaustive and fundamental, upon this important question.

So confident was the publisher of the book's importance and the prospects of its sale, it offered the two-volume work in a choice of formats: white paper with a muslin binding for $3; tinted paper for $3.50 and, for a dollar more, "extra gilt"; or both volumes in one, on library sheepskin, for $3.50.

The publisher was not disappointed. A second printing went to press only one week after the book's initial offering.

Meanwhile, laudatory reviews continued to roll in for *Eliza Woodson*. The *New Nation* called it a "work superior to most of its kind." The *American Literary Gazette* declared it would "have an elevating and stimulating influence," while the *Lyons Republican* confessed, "We have been deeply interested in this book."

But the book Mrs. Farnham cared about was *Woman and Her Era*—the distillation of her conviction, the marshalling of her evidence, the presentation of her *proof* of woman's superiority.

In the style of scientific deduction, she opened her book with a syllogism:

> Life is exalted in proportion to its Organic and Functional Complexity; Woman's Organism is more Complex and her totality of Function larger than those of any other being inhabiting our earth; Therefore her position in the scale of Life is the most exalted—the Sovereign one.

Any resemblance to Darwinian argument was purely intentional. Her "organic argument" consisted of "nature's testimony" that the most complex organisms represented the highest development of the species. She offered scientific pronouncements on plants and mollusks, followed by the unassailable assertion that "the human type crowns the living creation on our globe." And any comparison of the masculine and feminine representatives clearly revealed the feminine as more complex, as it possessed not only the physiological capacity to produce another being but, unlike the rudimentary and nonfunctional mammary gland of the male anatomy, "the capacity of lactation, a power to which there is no equivalent among the normal masculine capacities."

Her "religious argument" advanced the "moral superiority of Woman"; her "esthetic argument" the testimony of woman as inspiration. For "historic argument" she listed the names of women of brilliant accomplishment:

Many of these women have proved the noblest possibilities for themselves, and helped others to realize theirs, as not many of the men of even more brilliant intellect have aimed to do....We all know....at least one good woman, pure in heart, *loving progress for herself and others,* willing to work for it....

History is not often happy in its treatment of females.... Because history is made up of external details...Life must give Woman a theater, and history must rise above wars and diplomacy, and concern itself with human progress...must ascend, in short, to the plane of psychical motives and forces, where she has her stage of influences, before it can furnish testimony at once copious and just of her life and powers.

Mrs. Farnham was not blind to the failure of women to attain the exalted domain of Woman-with-a-capital-W, however inherent their capacities. Society distracted with fashion and expectations, enslaved their labors, subverted their natures, enticed them to "a life of degrading, because dwarfing and stultifying, ease...empty stagnation which they miscall peace":

> Or, if very amiable and gentle, they may give up the highest and best they are capable of to the exactions of hospitality, becoming entertainers of bodies merely, and losing, while they are devising and ministering palate-pleasures to successive rounds of visitors, all capacity to receive or give mind- and soul-entertainment.... Thousands of...wives live only or chiefly to spread laden tables before swift succeeding platoons of guests—the times between their going and coming being chiefly occupied in setting the house in order, and filling the empty pantries for the next arrival. Nothing that we call social pleasure could be more misnamed than this senseless round of feasting....It swallows up years of the best part of her life, that would have been inestimable for the self-improvement of the mother, and the culture of her growing children.

Mrs. Farnham's "arguments" united in a clarion call, a judgment, a promise, and an assurance of women's superiority. Women could rise to any heights they imagined, become whatever they wished: "For, after all discussion of spheres and places, in the long run, *success in any position is warrant for taking it,* and *compels* respect to its occupant, whether woman or man." And more:

> Wherever Woman as Thinker, Worker, Artist, Reformer, Philanthropist, presses her way individually to honorable recognition, she leaves a broad, inviting path behind her, in which others of her sex

will infallibly follow her leading, and gain assurance and renewed determination at every sight of her advancing footprints. And in this day, the most needed service to humankind is that which will commend Women to confidence in themselves and their sex, as the leading force of the Coming Era—the Era of spiritual rule and movement; in which, through them, the race is destined to a more exalted position than ever before it has held, and for the first time to form its dominant ties of relationship to that world of purer action and diviner motion, which lies above the material one of intellectual struggle and selfish purpose wherein man has held and exercised his long sovereignty.

No one could fault the earnestness of Mrs. Farnham's arguments, the passion of her plea, the fervor of her conviction. But she was, after all, propounding the thesis that women were inherently superior to *men*—in a book whose prominent reviewers would be men. Or perhaps she anticipated their criticism when she wrote:

> I write in the hope of being read by Women—by some who have little time for labored or abstruse reading, and little need of it....If I were seeking primarily to reach the slower and more doubting understanding of men, elaboration would be necessary.

Or perhaps she was merely naive.

When the first review for *Woman and Her Era* arrived, the publisher appeared delighted to announce:

> The Publishers take pleasure in informing the reading public that the ROUND TABLE has at last found a work to criticize! They have the authority of that paper for the statement that "Mrs. Farnham totally repudiates what is known as the Woman's Rights Theory."
>
> Also that the Author,
>
> "Marshall's [sic] Metaphysics, Esthetics, Physiology, Theology, History, and current opinions in her train, and marches forward with a determination akin to heroism."
>
> Read the criticism—or if you have not time to read THE ROUND TABLE read the Book itself.

But the *New York Tribune* criticized it, too, in a lengthy review that concluded:

> We wish to do justice to the nobleness of its aims, the value of its suggestions, and the reflective power which it indicates. The authoress has calmly struck out a new path, and entered upon it

with admirable freedom and boldness, almost indeed with a certain grandeur of movement that must command respect. She is far enough, however, from being an agreeable, or even an interesting writer. Her style is heavy, diffuse, overloaded with epithets, and of course languid; often evincing great rhetorical pretension, with but little rhetorical skill; nor are her logical powers, which she parades with rather too elaborate ceremony, of a high order; her apparently nice distinctions often cover but a slight show of meaning; and her habitual accumulation of synonyms exhibits a want of mastery of language rather than precision of thought.

A review in the *Continental Monthly* conceded Mrs. Farnham's ability, on one hand, while delivering a blow with the other:

> She traces the proofs of her assertions to the most profound sources, presents them in her acute analyses and philosophical arguments, and draws applications from them. She is sincere in her convictions, and able in her arguments....Will our women read it? We think not.

The *San Francisco Evening Bulletin* quoted passages from the work, including Mrs. Farnham's idea and purpose, as she wrote them:

> This Idea is THE SUPERIORITY OF WOMAN. The purpose of this volume is to bring to this Intuition of the early ages, of the most emotional, devout lives, and of all souls in their best and clearest moments, the support of such Truths, both of Form and Phenomena, as are at present known to us.

And then the *Bulletin* delivered its blow: "This affectation of a learned and logical method pervades the entire work; and if it does not exhaust the subject, it assuredly exhausts the reader." The editor tossed the author a sop: "Notwithstanding, however, the dry, didactic style of the writer, the work contains many philosophical and beautiful illustrations of the diverse character of the sexes." This grudging respect likely cheered the author but little.

A devastating review in *Harper's New Monthly Magazine* followed:

> We say in the outset that in our judgment the book is every way a bad one: bad in purpose, bad in tendency, bad in execution....the argument of the book...is spread over two volumes of cloudy phrases. ...The final conclusion is reached near the close of the second volume. Here it is: "The question of Rights settles itself in the true statement of Capacities. Rights are narrowest where Capacities are fewest—broadest where they are the most numerous....It is plain,

then, as between masculine and feminine, where the most expanded circle of Rights will be found; and equally plain the absurdity of man, the narrower in capacities, assuming to define the sphere of Rights for Woman, the broader." Such is Mrs. Farnham's idea of "Woman and Her Era." We trust that it will be long before Woman adopts it.

In September the *Atlantic Monthly* took a turn, highly praising Mrs. Farnham's effort but condemning the performance:

In the three and a half centuries since Cornelius Agrippa, no one has attempted with so much ability as Mrs. Farnham to transfer the theory of woman's superiority from the domain of poetry to that of science. Second to no American woman save Miss Dix in her experience as a practical philanthropist, she has studied human nature in the sternest practical schools, from Sing-Sing to California....The chapter called "The Organic Argument"...is really the pith of the book, and would, perhaps, stand stronger without the other six hundred pages. In this chapter she shows the strength of a system-maker, in the rest the weaknesses of one; she feels obliged to apply her creed to everything, to illustrate everything by its light, to find unexpected confirmations everywhere, and to manipulate all the history of art, literature, and society, till she conforms them to her standard. She recites, with no new power, historical facts that are already familiar....

....These are merely literary defects; but Mrs. Farnham really suffers in thought by the same unflinching fidelity to her creed. It makes her clear and resolute in her statement; but it often makes her as one-sided as the advocates of male supremacy whom she impugns. To be sure, her theory enables her to extenuate some points of admitted injustice to woman,—finding, for instance, in her educational and professional exclusions a crude effort, on the part of society, to treat her as a sort of bird-of-paradise, born only to fly, and therefore not needing feet. Yet this authoress is obliged to assume a tone of habitual antagonism towards men, from which the advocates of mere equality are excused....Mrs. Farnham is noble enough, and her book is brave and wise enough, to bear criticisms which grow only from her attempting too much.

This concession the reviewer enlarged by at least saying something nice about *Eliza Woodson*:

The autobiography of her childish years, when she only aspired after such toils, has an interest wholly apart from that of her larger work, and scarcely its inferior....one can hardly recall in literature a delineation so marvellous of a childish mind so extraordinary as "Eliza Woodson." The few characters appear with an individuality worthy of a great novelist; every lover of children must find it altogether fascinating, and to the most experienced student of human nature it opens a new chapter of startling interest.

Twenty-two years of devotion to the "great work" had come to a crushing close. Ill since Gettysburg, Eliza Farnham had one last effort to make on behalf of her fervent belief in woman's purpose, potential, and place in the universe.

# TWENTY-NINE

# Unfaltering
# and Fearless

NEW BOOKS RECEIVED. H. H. Bancroft & Co., booksellers, Montgomery street...*The Ideal Attained: Being the Story of Two Steadfast Souls, and How they Won Their Happiness; and Lost it Not*...A novel, the scene of which is laid partly in San Francisco, in the early days of the gold-hunters to California. The author, Mrs. Farnham, was very well known on this coast, and some of her most recent works, such as *Woman and Her Era*, and *Eliza Woodson*, have obtained considerable reputation. She died about a twelvemonth ago at the East.

—*San Francisco Evening Bulletin*, July 1, 1865

About a year since Eliza W. Farnham laid down her weary head. I did not know her, nor did I sympathize with her theories. They were sustained by her imagination rather than her reason; by her impulses rather than any practical judgment. No moral superiority can justly be conferred on either sex of a being possessed of intellect and conscience. God has conferred no such superiority; yet I gladly name Mrs. Farnham here as a woman whose life—a bitter disappointment to herself—was useful to all women, and whose books, published since her death, show a marvelous mental range. I name her with sympathy and admiration.

—Caroline H. Dall, *Report made to the Eleventh National Woman's Rights Convention*

**E**liza Farnham had written a novel, a romance. It was, indeed, a thinly veiled fiction in which Eliza herself found happiness and love—if not in life, then in fancy. In *The Ideal Attained*, the perfectible man of her imagination recognizes her worth, and she is exalted into the sphere of womanhood she has championed. The tale provided the cloth upon which Mrs. Farnham embroidered her beliefs and observations regarding Spiritualism, the relations of men and women, motherhood, and the potential of human-kind. The novel came fast on the heels of her monumental *Woman and Her Era*, in which she had so carefully delineated her philosophy and arguments for women's superiority. But in this book, the ideas were applied and the "ideal attained."

The work also provided another canvas for her convictions about the future of Woman-with-a-capital-W: "Whoever lives to see the twentieth century ushered in, will, I believe, find our sex on a vantage-ground of true freedom and self-sustaining development, which will prove the first step in such a social revolution as time has never yet seen."

She had no expectation of seeing such prophecy fulfilled, but she might have hoped to at least see her visionary words in print.

Alas, she was denied even that small consolation.

In 1858, Georgiana Kirby had noted, in the journal she still occasionally kept, the welcome two-month visit to Santa Cruz of her good friend Maggie—Margaret Voorhees—with her two sons, Hermann and Theodore, from New York. As with so much else, Georgiana and Eliza shared good friends. It may have been some comfort to Georgiana to learn that Eliza was not alone when death came for her. Maggie Voorhees had been with her:

> MRS. ELIZA W. FARNHAM, well-known throughout the nation as a philanthropist, and an author, died on Thursday morning, at the residence of Mr. B. F. Voorhees, in this city. Mrs. FARNHAM was in the 49th year of her age, having been born at Rensselaerville, Albany County, New-York, in November of 1815. Her maiden name was BURHANS, and she was married in Illinois to Mr. T. J. FARNHAM, the traveler and writer, in 1836. Mrs. FARNHAM took a deep interest in every variety of philanthropy, particularly in prison reform....She was also the author of a number of books devoted to the amelioration of the condition of the female sex, and a vindication of their rights. Her writings were vigorous and forcible.

Her body was taken to Dodworth's Hall, 806 Broadway, for funeral services. "Anyone in attendance," wrote one who was, "could not but feel that the occasion was no ordinary one. The Hall, although very large, proved much too small to accommodate the crowd; hundreds going away unable to obtain standing room":

> The exercises were opened by singing, and were followed by a short address from the Rev. Mr. Frothingham, upon the character of the deceased, whom he had known only for two years, but whom he considered to be one of the leading women of the age, and whose intellect he considered to be of an order quite beyond the appreci-

ation of mediocre minds. Judge Edmonds followed, speaking at great length. His remarks were quite at variance with the usual tenor of discourses of this kind. He spoke mostly of her deeds while living, and these, as he remarked, speak for themselves with the eloquence of virtue and worth. Dr. Hallock concluded the exercises, by a brief, but eloquent eulogy upon her noble and exalted character, and great intellect.

The *New York Daily Tribune* further reported:

Before the exercises began, the coffin, containing the body, was brought into the room, and placed before the pulpit. It was decked with chaplets of pure white flowers, and the features of the lifeless occupant were uncovered....The audience in attendance was very large, the aisles as well as the seats of the hall being filled, and there was a large throng about the door.

Mrs. Farnham's coffin was taken upstate to Milton, a small village on the west bank of the Hudson. There, in the Friends Cemetery established in 1830, she was buried in the Hallock family plot.

Eliza Burhans Farnham had traveled far in her nearly fifty years upon the earth, and she had indeed been "one of the workers of the world," as she had wished. And now she had come full circle: this daughter of Quakers was laid to rest in a Quaker churchyard barely fifty miles from the tiny village of Potter Hollow that saw her birth. As to death, she had on that subject, as she had on nearly everything, an opinion:

I believe not only that death is no termination to us, but that it ush-ers us into a future which is strictly and inevitably consequent upon our present life. There the sensualist, cut off from his accustomed and cherished pleasures, will find, in the wretchedness of his lot, a necessity to seek other enjoyments; there the malignant and hating will be deprived of much of the power they have possessed here to gratify their exaggerated passions; there the selfish and mean will find no possessions to covet, and no advantage to be gained by base-ness; there the ignorant and darkened souls will see a little more clearly than through the curtain of the flesh; and there the merci-ful, the wise, the pure and the loving, will find abundant occupation for the powers they have developed here. That is a rude, poor sketch of my heaven, dear friends, and it will not much matter what articles of faith we adopt, if only we *adopt* them, and do Godlike work from Godlike motives and aspirations; we shall reach it some day.

*Eliza Farnham is buried here, in an unmarked grave in the Hallock family plot, Milton-on-Hudson, New York. Author's photo*

*Title page,*
The Ideal Attained

THE

## IDEAL ATTAINED;

BEING

The Story of Two Steadfast Souls, and how they
Won their Happiness and Lost it not.

BY

ELIZA W. FARNHAM,

AUTHOR OF "WOMAN AND HER ERA," "ELIZA WOODSON," ETC.

"We had experience of a blissful state,
In which our powers of thought stood separate,
Each in its own high freedom held apart,
Yet both close folded in one loving heart;
So that we seemed, without conceit, to be
Both one, and two, in our identity."—MILNES.

NEW YORK:
C. M. PLUMB & CO.,
274 CANAL STREET.
1865.

Charles Farnham returned from France, and it was he who entered into copyright *The Ideal Attained,* his mother's final literary offering to the world she believed perfectible. The publisher, C. M. Plumb & Co., provided the preface:

> One who gave her entire life so sacredly to philanthropic labor of hands or brain, as did Mrs. Farnham, would be likely to regard the production of a work of fiction as incidental and subordinate. The manuscript of the volume here presented to the public was prepared some years since, in a surprisingly brief time, and under peculiar circumstances. It was then, evidently, laid aside for other, and, as the author believed, more important work, and only during her final illness was it confided to the care of the Publishers.
>
> The pictures of natural scenery upon the Pacific shore, and of social life during the early years of California, will be recognized as eminently faithful. The chief interest of the work, however, lies in the characters given to the two leading personages, whose vivid portraitures constitute noble embodiments of an exalted ideal, conveying a fresh and striking reflection of the author's own rare and peculiar genius.

The *Tribune* advertised the book's imminent availability on April 15, 1865—a date made memorable by the assassination of President Lincoln: "Mrs. Farnham's great fiction"…"No common novel"!

The story is both autobiographical and wishful. The protagonist, Eleanore Bromfield, is a young widow with two sons who journeys to California aboard the ship *Tempest* in company with a spinster friend, Anna Warren. Miss Warren is the narrator, obviously based on Lucy Sampson. Mrs. Bromfield is none other than Eliza herself:

> [Eleanore Bromfield] was frank to a daring degree; habitually and constantly so, except in the great inmost experiences of joy and suffering; and these, when she willed it, could be buried so deep within that those of her household would never conceive their presence….She was courageous….as unflinching in thought and nerve as the hardiest man. Unfaltering and fearless, she pressed impetuously forward to her object; yet laid her hand as gently upon it, when she reached it, as the most delicate and sensitive girl. Her heart was a full fountain of tenderness and most ecstatic love, yet with the firmness and apparent coldness of the least womanly woman, she pressed down and sealed it within her bosom. Shallow people thought her hard and cold, when the inward fire of that life, smothered and checked by the strong will, would have blinded and scorched their weak souls, had it been permitted to blaze forth.

Anna, forty-two, hopes to earn sufficient income in California to support her retirement. Mrs. Bromfield has been invited by her uncle to join him in California. Also aboard the *Tempest* is an Englishman, Colonel Leonard Anderson, whose admiration for the widow exceeds propriety when he unexpectedly, and without invitation, kisses her. She is affronted, he apologetic. The attraction, however, is mutual. The ship has been ninety days at sea when the adventure Mrs. Farnham was spared in reality occurs in fantasy: the *Tempest* is struck at sea by another vessel and the passengers are forced to abandon their ship in favor of an open boat. After eight days adrift on the open sea, they make land, an obscure island, where Mrs. Bromfield's youngest son, Harry (based on Eliza's son Eddie), dies from sunstroke. The survivors are rescued by the *Garonne,* a ship out of Hong Kong and bound for Callao, whose sympathetic captain delivers them—for $250—to San Francisco. There Mrs. Bromfield discovers that her uncle has died in a recent fire, and she is cast upon her own resources.

Not only does the story reflect Mrs. Farnham's situation upon arriving in California, it portrays the plight of women whose dependence on men reduced them to destitution or their own resources, much as she had been when Farnham left her in Illinois and ventured West, and again when he died.

Mrs. Bromfield and Miss Warren accept the joint position of managers of a San Francisco hotel, while Anderson goes off to the mines. Eventually, the hotel job becomes onerous for various reasons, not least the disrespect offered women in such exposed circumstances. Miss Warren accepts a teaching position in Stockton, and Mrs. Bromfield abandons California in favor of Valparaiso, where she is hired as governess to a Spanish family of means. Anderson soon follows when a mining position is offered him there, and he marries Mrs. Bromfield. Anna Warren joins them and she likewise marries. And they all live happily ever after.

Mrs. Farnham employed her story not only to portray the strengths and vulnerabilities of women, but as a platform for her views on the inequality of the sexes:

> Does not the world, because you are a man, give you full freedom to use all your powers in the largest and most agreeable and lucrative field where you can find place? Does it not, because I am a woman, do exactly the reverse by me, though my necessities may be even

more imperative than yours? The world *employs* you, and undertakes, by its theory, to *provide* for me. You, by the development of your power and skill, become its master—I, through dependence and inaction of my best capacities, its slave.

Of California's future, Mrs. Bromfield opines on behalf of Eliza:

Depend upon it…there will one day throng these plains and hills and valleys the noblest people on the globe. Art will flourish, because the love of the Beautiful will grow into all souls, and wealth will nourish it with culture and refinement…The Yankee sharpness and assiduity were a valuable root on which to engraft the heedless largeness of the Western soul; the two may be several generations in blending into a harmonious and beautiful one, but they will ultimately.

Mrs. Farnham, through her character, also offers this poignant, poetic judgment on growing old:

I have mourned through endless summer days and long twilights, and counted the hours which removed me further from the hope, the strength, and the joy of youth.…It is not so now. I have found such wealth allotted to womanhood—such relations, such uses, such power!

…It moves me to pity to see a woman shrink from the touch of the unrelenting years.…To dread to grow old, to shrink from the sum of the years already past and to look on each coming one as an enemy, to seek by poor falsity to make their number seem less—oh! it is very pitiful, is it not?

Better pity than contempt for such weakness, which we ought to grieve at rather than despise, since the whole of human history has educated us to feel that our power is in our personal charms. Take youth and beauty from a woman, and you disarm her.

…but her lack of power in middle and advanced life comes less from her having lost those than from her want of development—of unselfish loves—of pure and rich interior life. Her career has been a prolonged struggle to keep what God has desired that she should give up.…She loses what she cannot retain, and in the strife, becomes that dreaded thing, an 'old woman.' Oh, my heart burns with rebellion and shame at what that epithet expresses! As if God created us to decline from admiration to contempt—from power to puerility—from love to loathing. I honor a man whose hoary head and benignant furrows record the numerous years of a well-spent life; but I am impelled to worship a woman whom I see grow old and wrinkled, with the radiance of a warm, sweet, tender soul shining out of the ruins of that beauty in which she delighted years ago. I rejoice in growing old. The hopes of youth may fade like the gorgeous colors of that evening sky. Let them.

A few months after the publication of Eliza's last book, Susan Anthony went to Milton, where she spoke to an "excellent audience in the Friends' meetinghouse" and visited Eliza Farnham's grave.

Eliza and Georgiana had always shared friends. Possibly Miss Anthony described the lovely setting of the Friends Cemetery—the sheltering woods, the peaceful pond, the mournful call of loons—when, a few years later, she and Elizabeth Cady Stanton went to Santa Cruz at Georgiana Kirby's invitation, to make history. Or perhaps Georgiana saw Milton herself on a visit she would make to the East in a few years.

Eliza's work was done, but Georgiana's was not—not nearly.

# THIRTY

# Sweet Recollection

This is one of the most beautiful places I ever saw in my life, and as secluded as if it were a hundred miles from any city or village. There are woods, in which we ramble all day without meeting anybody or scarcely seeing a house. Our house stands apart from the main road, so that we are not troubled with passengers looking at us. Once in a while we have a transcendental visitor, such as Mr. Alcott; but generally we pass whole days without seeing a single face, save those of the brethren. The whole fraternity eat together; and such a delectable way of life has never been seen on the earth since the days of the early Christians.

—Nathaniel Hawthorne, Brook Farm, May 3, 1841

Whatever might be said of...Brook Farm, the social structure was of the richest. Those who ever lived there usually count it to this day as the happiest period of their lives.

—Thomas Wentworth Higginson

**B**arely two weeks after Eliza Farnham took her last breath, Phillip Bruce Kirby took his first.

On January 2, 1865, Georgiana, at age forty-six, became a mother for the fifth time. Three weeks later, the *Santa Cruz Sentinel* reprinted from the *New York Tribune* the report of her dearest friend's funeral. Whatever Georgiana may have felt upon reading of Eliza's death, she left no record of it. Five years before, she had closed the journal in which she had confided her feelings from time to time. And so it remained.

Mrs. Kirby's children undoubtedly occupied nearly all of her time and energies. Her firstborn, Ora, was almost twelve; little Georgiana was ten; Cornelia, eight; Richard Bruce Kirby just four years, and now a newborn's demands were added.

Meanwhile, national affairs were not without interest to Georgiana Kirby. Early in April of 1865, Richmond fell. Two weeks later President Lincoln was assassinated. In May, Confederate troops surrendered and ended the Civil War that preserved the Union and freed the slaves.

*Interior of the Kirby Home. Courtesy of the Society of California Pioneers (C022518)*

*The Kirby Home. Courtesy of the Society of California Pioneers (C022516)*

In Santa Cruz, life went on for the Kirbys much as it had for more than a decade, with the charming coastal community gradually increasing in population and prosperity. The eye was on the future. The pioneer past was gradually receding into memory, and ties to it were severed.

In 1868 the Kirbys read in their local newspaper, undoubtedly with some nostalgia:

AN OLD LANDMARK GONE.—The old and singularly shaped house, above and fronting on the potrero, built many years ago (but never finished) by Mrs. Farnham, has been torn down to be replaced by a new farm house. The former building had five gables and was a wild looking edifice. Its dormer windows strangely contrasted with the beautiful fields and romantic scenery surrounding it.

For Georgiana, regardless of the increasing comforts of her own home, California still failed to provide the richness of culture and intellect she continued to crave:

In spite of our much vaunted climate, the wheat crops, and even the *Overland Monthly*, it takes a long, long time for an adopted Californian to become acclimated. We suffer—not like the Englishman in New York, from "same sickness" produced by the monotony of the always repeated blocks of houses, but from what may be called non-cohesion. We are from the extreme West, the south-west—England, Ireland, France, Australia. We have torn up the roots that fastened us to the old homes, the old associates, and cautiously, slowly, put down slender fibres into the new soil. Hence, in full possession of the wheat, grapes and *Overland* we are conscious of faintness, almost starvation at times. Only the children are in a healthy condition, and happy, those who have lived in one place long enough to call it "home." This want of union is deplored.... Cliques are numerous, and friendships few. No one is to blame, but the situation. Time will surely by attrition and accumulation mould us into a homogenous whole at last. Our one prayer just now is for the first class lecturers. Will the railroad bring them? Sitting by my own hearth, with the reliable oak wood blazing (not snapping) at my feet, I read the beloved STANDARD, companion of twenty-five years; read therein accounts of Radical Clubs in Boston, and Women's Parliaments in New York; of Social Science Conventions, and Freedmen's schools and sigh to think that our isolated position and our unassimilated population forbid our participating in similar activities.

As Mrs. Kirby's thoughts turned to the past, to the East, to friends not seen for twenty years, she decided to make a visit. While there, she discovered that the history of the long-disbanded Brook Farm association, which had informed her youth so richly, had not been written. She determined to correct the oversight:

I should not have ventured to try my weak, unpractised hand thus, had I not found...that no one of those concerned, better qualified for the task, was likely to assume it. Twenty years had elapsed since the association had dispersed, and the more salient features of our experience were fading from the remembrance of even the youngest and brightest of our number. This decided me.

Interestingly, Mrs. Kirby's article did not argue the merit, or recite the history, of associationism. She did not even allude to the reform spirit initiating George Ripley's social experiment to establish a "more pure, more lovely, more divine state of society than was ever realized on earth." She but sparely touched upon transcendentalism at all, providing only a re-created conversation among fellow associates:

"What do you mean by the word transcendentalism?" I inquired.

"It's well you asked me. I am the only one who has given the word sufficient attention," he said, quickly. "It means, my dear, obscure, vague, ambiguous, hidden, nebulous, enigmatical, sealed, mystical, impenetrable, incomprehensible, mysterious, inscrutable, inconceivable, etc. It's really dangerous to live in such a place as this, you will find."

"Don't mind his nonsense," said Margaret, rather gravely, and aside. "This rattle-brain way he has is all that is left of his former unruly character. He's at heart a noble fellow. Transcendental we interpret as above mere reason, freely, religiously, intuitive, spiritual; at one with Nature."

"Why need you explain to her?" joined in Sybil, who, with empty pail beside her, had for some time been leaning on her mop. "She is one of the elect, herself; she must respect her own thought more, and take the pains to examine it more closely, and she will *see she* is a transcendentalist."

What Georgiana recalled of Brook Farm, more than almost anything else, was how "worthwhile" the talk was:

You never heard the words "fashion," or "beau;" no shallow, purposeless words, such as you were often bored to death with elsewhere....And I will here acknowledge that I was struck, from the first—and not disagreeably—with a novel phraseology common at the Community. The word "somewhat," for instance, pleased me as delightfully indefinite, and I adopted it at once into my vocabulary. The words "consciousness" and "unconsciousness," "intuitive," "analogous," I got along with pretty well; but I was floored by "subjective" and "objective," and it is doubtful if I am to-day on my feet regarding them.

Mrs. Kirby recalled the "lively conversation" at Brook Farm, the lectures and discussions, meetings and recitations, entertainments and singing, the pleasure of work shared, quiet walks in the woods, the "perfect freedom." These recollections she wove into a story of two of the company, and the love of a young man she called "Leander" for a woman she named "Hero." Georgiana quizzes her:

> "Will you marry him, then?" I continued.
>
> "My dear child, you do not understand. I could not install myself teacher for life! He is not twenty; I am twenty-six....Do not fear. He will overlive it. Everyone of any account, you know, has such an experience."

Georgiana took liberties in substituting the names of mythical and literary figures for those of actual residents, and in turning her recollection of Brook Farm into a tale of unrequited love. She was criticized. She was unapologetic:

> It was objected to by some of the old friends that I had stepped outside the facts to create a fragment of romance. The truth was, I could not in any literal statement give an idea of the spirit that actuated us, and the manner in which this was expressed. I was obliged to disguise the real personages under fictitious names, and in one or two instances combine one character with another, in order to give any thing like a true description of that romantic episode in sober New England life, and at the same time save myself from the charge of being grossly personal.
>
> Sincerity and devotion were the warp, and cultivation the woof, of the fabric of our lives. The love affairs, which I sought to veil while disclosing, were, like the conversations, incidents, and situations, genuine.

Brook Farm had "promised just the spiritual hospitality" young Georgiana Bruce had longed for, and she had found her days "full of affection and sunshine." Now, more than twenty-five years later, Georgiana Kirby happily recalled them. She wrote four more articles of Brook Farm reminiscences, reliving once again those happy times. Of Hawthorne's departure after spending a year at the community, she wrote:

> No one could have been more out-of-place than he, in a mixed company, no matter how cultivated, worthy and individualized each member of it might be. He was morbidly shy and reserved, needing

to be shielded from his fellows, and obtaining the fruits of observation at second-hand. He was therefore not amenable to the democratic influences at the community, which enriched the others and made them declare in after years that the years or months spent there had been the most valuable ones of their whole lives.

Not a few members were out of place. As Mrs. Kirby recalled, "There was not one man at Brook Farm who would kill any animal larger than a chicken." A neighboring farmer did the butchering necessary to put joints of beef and ham on the community table.

But what the Brook Farmers lacked in practical skills, they more than compensated for with ideals. Among those ideals was equality. For women. At Brook Farm, women had been equal with men as members. Women had held office at Brook Farm. Women had voted at Brook Farm business meetings. Georgiana had voted.

If then, why not now? Georgiana had been a supporter of women's rights for years. Although the Fourteenth Amendment, ratified in 1868, defined "citizens" and "voters" as male, she had seen Wyoming Territory organize the following year with a woman suffrage provision. If women could vote in Wyoming, why not in California?

Why not, indeed?

# THIRTY-ONE

# Fighting for Suffrage

CALIFORNIA.—The advocacy of woman's rights began in Santa Cruz county, with the advent of that grand champion of her sex, the immortal Eliza Farnham, who braved public scorn and contumely because of her advanced views, for many years before the suffrage movement assumed organized form. Mrs. Farnham's work rendered it possible for those advocating woman suffrage years later, to do so with comparative immunity from public ridicule.

*—History of Woman Suffrage*

For nearly a score of years after the great incursion of the gold seekers into this newly-acquired State no word was uttered by tongue or pen demanding political equality for women—none at least which reached the public ear…and even that mental amazon, Eliza W. Farnham…thought and wrote for the whole world of women without once sounding the tocsin for woman's political emancipation.

—Elizabeth T. Schenck

SUSAN B. ANTHONY'S LECTURE.—The great and justly popular lecturer, Susan B. Anthony, will deliver her famous lecture on "The Power of the Ballot" at Unity Church, in this place, on Saturday evening, Aug. 5th. At this time when the question "shall woman possess the right to vote in common with the negro" is so widely agitated, it would be well to hear the subject ably discussed by one who represents a large majority of her sex who have no male relatives to represent their views on political matters.

*—Santa Cruz Sentinel*, August 5, 1871

It was January 26, 1870, a Wednesday afternoon, when Georgiana Kirby joined the other women filling San Francisco's Dashaway Hall. Elizabeth T. Schenck, California vice president of the National Woman's Suffrage Association and organizer of California's first local suffrage society just six months before, called the meeting to order. Their purpose was to form the first statewide California woman's suffrage organization.

Mrs. Kirby, representing Santa Cruz, one of nine existing county societies, was appointed to the committee on credentials. Laura de Force Gordon, who had lectured on woman's suffrage in San Francisco two years previously and was recognized as California's leading light in the cause, urged liberality in the admission of delegates, arguing that everyone in sympathy with the movement who signed the roll and paid the fee should be admitted. A total of one hundred and twenty women, and men, qualified themselves.

An entertaining discussion followed on whether to address the president as Mrs. Chairman or Mrs. Chairwoman, the decision finally going to "Mrs. President." The timidity with which most of the women responded with "aye" or "no" to questions from the rostrum prompted Mrs. Gordon to scold, "The ladies must not sit like mummies, but open their mouths and vote audibly. This disinclination to do business in a business-like way is discreditable." The reprimand received cheers.

Sarah Wallis, a woman of some fame and long residence in the state, upon being named president for the convention, thanked the audience for their "high esteem and confidence," adding, "I regard this as a severe ordeal, but, having already been tested in this respect, I do not fear the trials to come. I shall persevere until the emancipation of women is effected."

For four days the women met and talked and argued and strategized, and by the close of business on Saturday, January 29, 1870, they had organized a state society. Mrs. A. A. Haskell of Petaluma agreed to serve as president. Georgiana Kirby was named one of ten vice presidents. The plan was to keep up a general agitation, with speakers addressing audiences throughout the state. The burden of this responsibility went to Laura de Force Gordon, who delivered more than one hundred lectures that year.

Georgiana Kirby returned to Santa Cruz with an opinion, or two, about Laura de Force Gordon:

> Mrs. Laura de Force Gordon...is a young person of pleasing appearance and abundance of curls. She has considerable talents as a lecturer, but owing to an unfortunate vanity and a habit of pushing herself forward unwisely, losing ground after gaining it. Unfortunately also for the lady's reputation, she has unscrupulous and coarse advisers, and she allows them...to drag her fair banner through the mud.

She even had opinions on opinions:

It is the opinion of very many of the best men that it is inadvisable for women in the present stage of the movement to admit men...as members. The good men are slow to use any influence, being anxious that the women should move freely in arranging their own affairs, whereas the agile politician, who thinks he sees the day not far distant when women will have the vote, is always on the alert with his harangues and resolutions. In the language of sympathy, but the spirit of tyranny. Now, women have been accustomed to defer to men, and when this politician makes motions and counter-motions, pushing his plans, we are not as able to meet him as we could a woman of the same stamp, because we have never learned the trick of deferring to the opinions of our own sex, being equally slaves with them before the law, and blandishments would count for nothing. We are then advised as I said by many of the best men to have open meetings for discussion of the question at issue, but to take time by ourselves in arranging our own business matters.

People had opinions about her, too:

Mrs. Kirby lives in Santa Cruz. Progressive woman; writes for local papers; criticizes lecture of Catholic priest; clergy indignant; call on Mrs. Kirby; want her to take it all back. Mrs. K. rears; priest rears; all Santa Cruz rears; Rome howls; Mrs. K rushes for pen; denounces the inquisition; branch of the Ecumenical Council sits at Santa Cruz; decides that the Father was a trifle over-zealous. Mrs. K. snaps her finger at the Pope.

Mrs. Kirby had, characteristically, criticized a lecture by a clergyman, which prompted a visit from the Reverend Father Call. He "ordered me to make a written apology," Mrs. Kirby indignantly reported. The cleric did not know with whom he was dealing. Mrs. Kirby set him straight:

He must have been laboring under the delusion that he was in Spain with the Inquisition at his back, or, at least, in Rome, where (with the help of French bayonets,) the Church has for the present the luxury of silencing heterodoxy....

"Leave my house, instantly," I commanded, and at once preceded him to the door, out of which he went, muttering savagely, "I will take up a collection this very evening to put you in an iron jacket!"

....At the church, in the evening, the threat ended in smoke. Father Call made an apology to his brother priests, and to the church, for getting in a passion; he told them of "the mighty purpose he had had, to get up a mighty subscription to purchase an iron jacket for the writer of that article." He also told them that I had "blackguarded the Catholic Church by circulating among them a petition for Woman Suffrage; but he had concluded to let the matter pass as insignificant." He left me "in the hands of Almighty God, who will"—so Father Call declared, (and of course he ought to know)—"one day put me in an iron jacket." I am quite content to be left in the care of the Infinite Father, who is moved as little by puerile selfish prayers, as curses.

As 1870 drew to a close, Mrs. Kirby lost none of her feistiness, despite a bad fall. While visiting a friend in Santa Clara she mistook a cellar door for her bedroom door, fell down the stairs and struck her head on the cement floor, where she lay, unconscious, for half an hour before recovering. She fortunately broke no bones, but returned home badly bruised.

The year 1871 was an election year in California. Throughout the spring and summer of 1871, Georgiana Kirby and the residents of Santa Cruz found the *Sentinel* filled with news of political conventions, party platforms, speeches and meetings, rallies and fundraisers and nominations and the names of men. But not until August 5 did the paper take notice that a longtime and respected Santa Cruz resident, Ellen Van Valkenburg, a citizen, a widow, a taxpayer, and sole support of her family, had demanded that Santa Cruz County Clerk Albert Brown permit her to sign the voting register. Or that he had refused. Or that, in consequence, Mrs. Van Valkenburg had initiated legal proceedings.

Susan Anthony, who would employ the same gambit in Rochester, New York, the following year, undoubtedly knew about Mrs. Van Valkenburg's attempt, although she apparently didn't mention it the night she spoke at Santa Cruz's Unity Church. But Miss Anthony did impress her listeners:

> The general sentiment of the large audience who had the pleasure of listening to her was that she handled her subject in a masterly manner. Her statements were so clearly and forcibly made as to surprise many who are strongly prejudiced against the cause which she is advocating, and her warmest friends must have received new inspirations and taken fresh courage in their labors to secure Woman Suffrage. Miss Anthony's power, as a lecturer, consists in the plain straight-forward manner with which she presents her subject. She

does not deal in glittering generalities as has been too often the case, with those who advocate Universal Suffrage, but she takes a practical view of the question. In speaking of the "wrongs of woman," she told many truths, which could not be contradicted, and which should be remedied at once by those who have the power.

Miss Anthony was less successful in nearby Watsonville, where only thirty or forty turned out to hear her, possibly owing to limited notice. But "her speech was listened to with great attention, and all were highly pleased." The local newspaper expressed regret that "a good house did not greet this eminent woman."

Elizabeth Cady Stanton also journeyed to distant California in 1871 to lend her distinguished voice to the "agitation." She spoke first in San Francisco and then in Santa Cruz, where she delivered three lectures. The *Sentinel* urged its readers, "The popularity of this estimable lady is too widespread to need any comment, and all should avail themselves of this, their only opportunity of seeing and hearing her before she leaves the State":

> For more than a quarter of a century she has been an earnest advocate of the cause of which she is the acknowledged leader. She is a lady of fine presence, and her voice is both rich and musical. She does not deal in harsh embittering words, but treats all who differ with her on the great cause of the enfranchisement of women in a generous, kindly spirit. She seems to understand and appreciate the fact that the prejudices of the men cannot be overcome by applying abusive epithets to them.

Mrs. Stanton did not, however, mince words as she rose to address the audience gathered at Unity Church on Saturday evening, August 19:

> I feel somewhat depressed in appearing before you this evening. One of your Judges in his decision this week has denied women the right to vote. He stated that in the eye of the civil law we are persons, but in representation we are not persons, and women have no political rights which men are bound to respect. The women must now take a new departure, the same as the Democrats took in Ohio. Now, the Fourteenth and Fifteenth Amendments decide the question as to who are citizens. The Fifteenth Amendment says that any person &c, yet your Judge said that women are not persons, and that he could decide in no other way. Does such language show him to be a man of sense? It is debasing in a man of his elevated position

to use it. Ben Butler in his minority report says that under the Fifteenth Amendment women are citizens, and have the right to vote. Mr. Bingham argued that women were not. Of course he had to take that ground, because when he allowed that they were persons they were citizens and had the right to vote.

Santa Cruz's Judge McKee had heard the argument in the Van Valkenburg case, and in rendering his decision, he said:

Under the civil law women had certain rights and were entitled to and received the protection of the law; but this conferred upon them no political rights....In the state of California the right of suffrage was confined to white male, native born and naturalized citizens who have reached political age....Under the Fourteenth Amendment women had their civil rights guaranteed to them, so had the Indians and male infants, who had not reached political age, but it conferred on them no political rights. Physically they are persons, politically they are not. The Fifteenth Amendment was a special act, intended to confer political rights upon male Africans, who had been slaves, and was confined strictly to that class of persons. The word sex is not used in the Fifteenth Amendment, but it is in the Fourteenth Amendment, which prohibits any State from denying political rights to any male inhabitant qualified to exercise such rights. But this did not include women, and she did not come within the meaning and intention of the law. Women have never been permitted to take part in the affairs of government and in framing the laws their case was not probably thought of. It was not considered necessary to do so. The counsel would hardly contend that infants had political rights, yet they are persons, and if by the operation of the word person females may claim the right of suffrage, why not infants also? In order to confer political rights upon women, special legislation will be necessary, in the same manner as has been done in the case of male Africans. I do not think the Fourteenth and Fifteenth Amendments confer any political rights upon women. I deny the application.

Local advocates for suffrage gathered at Unity Church to share their indignation against Judge McKee's decision. Richard Kirby chaired the meeting, addressing the large audience with remarks explaining Mrs. Van Valkenburg's circumstances. "In 1862, she had become, under the most painful circumstances, a widow...and for ten years she had been obliged to manage her own affairs, pay her own taxes, and struggle along alone to bring up her family."

## And now she was leaving Santa Cruz:

Convinced that what she had done was proper, legitimate, womanly, and she should leave the town where she had suffered and enjoyed so much, in a very hopeful state of mind; believing that the work which was now definitely commenced would, in a short time, be crowned with success.

Georgiana Kirby, gaining confidence in her ability to write, summarized the speeches made that night in a long article for the local newspaper. The Van Valkenburg case went to the California Supreme Court. Meanwhile, the great agitation for woman's suffrage in California in 1871 achieved one surprise: in San Joaquin County the Independent Party nominated Laura de Force Gordon to the office of state senator. Although Mrs. Gordon's eligibility was contested, and the idea ridiculed, she received, in the November election, about two hundred votes—all of them, of course, from men.

Mrs. Kirby summed the otherwise disappointing fight for woman suffrage:

If any doubt existed as to the really low opinion men entertain for women in their present abject political condition it would be wholly dispelled by a glance at the columns of facetiae that grace our daily journals, since at least two-thirds of these remarkably brilliant little paragraphs are made up of sneers at the grandmothers, mothers, sisters, and daughters of the land. According to these multiplied and reiterated slanders, woman is vain, frivolous, idle, vacillating, jealous, extravagant, cowardly, false, selfish, garrulous, unable to keep a secret, and generally idiotic; while the masculine critic is, by inference, the permanent possessor of all the opposite virtues. As proof that this spirit of detraction is dependent on our powerless political estate we call attention to the fact that since the enfranchisement of the colored man all those charming items about the negro (with the very humorous two "g's") in which he was made to enjoy slavery, to reverence the white man, to misquote Scripture, and to demonstrate generally his relation to the baboon, have totally disappeared from the public press. He is "our colored fellow-citizen," and with the consummation of this tardy justice disappear the coarse jokes and the vulgar flings at his imaginary characteristics, as well as all reference to his real peculiarities, and it requires no special prophetic power to predict that one month after woman is made an equal before the law, we shall search in vain among the funnyisms of the *Alta* and *Bulletin* for one slight reflection on her intellectual or moral qualities. Men feel respect for acknowledged power.

Two weeks later the *Sentinel* published, without apology, an article that must have spiraled Mrs. Kirby's indignation. Titled "Will a Lady Ever be President?," it concluded:

> We hope so if she is pretty. What fun to be under petticoat government, without any immediate danger of a broomstick or a scolding! Every good looking chap would have a chance for office then. How glorious to be closeted alone with the fair Executive of the nation, on business of a private and confidential nature!...the Presidentess must be either a widow or a maiden lady so as to give an ambitious fellow a chance.

In February 1872 the *Sentinel* published a lively debate on social change, in which a local resident, John Dimon, tangled with the no-holds-barred Mrs. Kirby, who concluded her first response archly:

> I must close by saying that if John Dimon has...learned his lesson no better than his communication in the Sentinel would indicate, he ought to begin at the primer, and review a little. He might then perhaps discover that he had held the book upside down, or that it was a spurious edition, and he might possibly acknowledge that any earnest and honest attempt to organize society on the principle of the golden rule was worthy of respect.

Dimon handily held his own in verbally jousting with the redoubtable Mrs. Kirby:

> I was much disappointed after reading the article of Mrs. Kirby in last week's Sentinel. I expected, with the boasted talent of the lady, and the knowledge she pretends to possess of Internationalism, to become enlightened; and that if I had interpreted any portion of the nine articles of the creed wrong, she could set me right by presenting the facts.
>
> The article has no more reference to the subject than to the first chapter of the book of Genesis. I have not brains sufficient to understand what she intends to convey; there is neither logic, wit, sarcasm or talent displayed. It appears more like a production of a dyspeptic brain than a healthy one.

More interesting to Mrs. Kirby early that year, however, was the disappointing news that the Supreme Court had upheld Judge McKee's decision in the Van Valkenburg case. The *Sentinel* clearly approved: "This settles the question of the right of suffrage being extended to the women, in the State of California, for the present. As they cannot vote directly themselves, let all single ones exercise their privileges this year, get married and vote by proxy."

After that defeat, life for the Kirbys in 1872 resumed its accustomed rounds. Georgiana continued to host regular meetings of the local woman's suffrage association. Richard Kirby, perhaps inspired by Georgiana's trip to the East, visited England. He returned home, "looking finely," according to the *Sentinel*'s editor, B. P. Kooser, who added that Kirby:

> speaks in glowing terms of the pleasures experienced during the trip, and the wonderful scenes and improvements in London—the metropolis of the world. In common with hosts of friends—Kirby is truly the poor man's friend, and without a why or wherefore—we welcome him back to Santa Cruz. In our experience we have never met a better or greater man to help the struggling poor along the rugged path of life than R. C. Kirby.

The following year, at the county's third annual farmers' club fair, the Kirbys' daughter Cornelia displayed a "pair of candlesticks 117 years old" in the category of "Fancy Products," and R. C. Kirby entered "pewter plates over 100 years old" and "a pair of China images."

With abolition accomplished and suffrage, for the moment, defeated, Mrs. Kirby, a longtime believer in the curative powers of water, turned her improving attention elsewhere. In March of 1874, she chaired the inaugural meeting of women organizing the Santa Cruz Temperance Union. The *Sentinel* duly reported the occasion:

> Mrs. Kirby briefly described the object of the call. She referred to the moral, intellectual, and pecuniary loss to the town, the number of places where liquor is sold to be drunk on the spot and where the fathers of families set the example to their son of spending the evening in…playing cards for whiskey. Mrs. Kirby closed by averring that the evil called for some decisive action on the part of women who were the greatest sufferers.

The women made a surprising success of their anti-liquor crusade, with temperance a brief victory in Santa Cruz until the county's saloon keepers took the issue to court. On October 3, 1874,

*"Woman's Holy War: Grand Charge on the Enemy's Works," Currier & Ives, 1874.*
*Mrs. Kirby chaired the inaugural meeting of the Santa Cruz Temperance Union*
*in March 1874. Courtesy of the Library of Congress (LC-USZ62-683)*

California's Supreme Court reversed the "cold water decision" as unconstitutional.

Despite continued rebuffs, Mrs. Kirby remained faithful to reform, in whatever guise it might lift its worthy head. Any opportunity to edify the *Sentinel*'s readers was worthwhile, even another woman's presentation. Mrs. Kirby summarized visiting lecturer Addie Ballou's address as:

> mainly an eloquent and forcible plea for mental and moral courage. The American people have a fatal habit of shirking responsibility; the responsibility of examining the latest truth, social or political; the responsibility of opposing the deadly assault now being made on our public schools by the church which has always kept the intellect of the people in leading strings, and paralyzed. We stand by inertly while place and preferment are bought with dollars. By our indifference we are hastening another crisis more bloody and disastrous than our late civil war, a war between all priestly tyranny and its opposite enlightened individualism. The lecturer was listened to with the closest attention. It is seldom that such warm logical argument is heard in Santa Cruz. We bespeak a full house (Unity Church) on Sunday evening next, May 2, when the admission will be free and a collection taken.

Mrs. Kirby had become, in the words of a visitor to Santa Cruz in the summer of 1877, "an institution—you felt she might put you on a list."

The visitor was Mary Hallock Foote, niece of Sarah Hallock, who had buried Eliza Farnham in the family plot at Milton. And Mary Hallock Foote was a writer with the gift of observation:

> The Kirbys were called rich; Mr. Kirby...was not at all a bookish man nor intellectual in his wife's sense of the word. They lived in a large house in a garden that filled a whole block. There was neither symmetry nor arrangement but much that was beautiful and botanical, and it gave you a sense of largesse, of crowding, of casting and giving away, in keeping with the climate. It had a grape arbor like a long green-lighted alley where I used to draw the Kirby girls, especially Georgie, who was the prettiest and the gentlest.
>
> Mrs. Kirby's life, as she depicted it with her extraordinary gift of language, struck me as being somewhat like her garden, heterogeneous and crowded, yet there was room in it for great loneliness, one surmised. She was a difficult woman to be quite just to; she made a great appeal to me. Intellectually she was far in advance of

the town, of any town of those days no older than Santa Cruz. Some of her theories that were new at that time and risky, to say the least (like birth control), she drove so hard that whoever did not agree with her was quite likely to hate her. Reformers are seldom tactful and she...made me at times excessively uncomfortable, not to say "mad," talking to me about my most private affairs with a view to a sort of enlightenment I should not have dreamed of asking from her....

She took me for many drives (I can't think of any kindness she did not try to show) along roads she had galloped over when they were cattle trails, telling me in her fashion of the monologue the early history of each home as we passed it. It was the truth as nearly as one with such a fatal facility in words could be expected to tell it, and she was bitter-shrewd! The life of the place had been rather cruel to her....

Mrs. Kirby...never could forget that once she had wiped dishes with Margaret Fuller and sat on doorsteps on spring nights and talked philosophy with George William Curtis—young, then, and quite godlike in appearance as she described him. The Brook Farm chapter must have been a short one, but it seemed to have altered the values of her whole subsequent existence and given her a slight sickness of the soul. What could come after the intensity of companionships like those!

What indeed? Actually, quite a lot, if one counted teaching, and working at Sing Sing, and crossing the isthmus during the California gold rush, and supporting abolition, and woman's suffrage, and temperance, and planting potatoes with Eliza Farnham, and raising five children, and never giving up hope for improving the world around her. And Mrs. Kirby's race was not yet run. She was also a writer—and about to publish a book.

# THIRTY-TWO

# A Mother's Influence

It is my wish to impress on women the grave truth, than which none can have more importance, that with them, with the mother, rests the greater power to mould for good or ill, for power or weakness, for beauty or deformity, the characters of her unborn children, and that with power comes the responsibility for its use....To the sensitiveness conferred by nature on the child-bearing woman is due her superior capacity to improve or degrade the race. To her varied mental, emotional, and physical conditions during her periods of gestation are due the wildly different characters of the children born of the same parents....The compass and tone of each individual is absolutely decided before birth.

—Georgiana Kirby

We would give special emphasis to the affirmation that instinct, passions, sentiments, and appetites all may be transmitted, as illustrated in the case of a lady of Boston, who was accustomed to read everything she could secure relating to Napoleon during his triumphant career. Her son, born at that time, inherited the most decided martial tastes, and is so enthusiastic an admirer of Napoleon that he has covered the walls of his house with pictures of him and his troops.

—The Rev. S. H. Platt, De Kalb Avenue,
Methodist Episcopal Church, Brooklyn, New York

Life's circumstances had awarded Georgiana the glorious maternity Eliza Farnham had so passionately endorsed. But whereas Eliza had extolled motherhood as a general concept, for Georgiana motherhood was in the details. And from her observations she had arrived at several firm opinions:

Never run the risk of conception when you are sick or over-tired or unhappy; or when your husband is sick, or recovering from sickness, exhausted, or depressed, or when you are not in full sympathy with him, or when the children already yours claim for their welfare your entire strength and time. For the bodily condition of the child, its vigor and magnetic qualities, are much affected by the conditions ruling at this moment.

The faculties *actively used* by the mother during pregnancy, rather than those lying latent and part of her original character, will be found prominent in her offspring....Other things being equal, the children of youthful, immature parents will be inferior to those of the fully developed.

Georgiana's numerous convictions included the belief that a union favored by "amativeness," or love, produced a much superior child than otherwise: "*Could* it be necessary, or even possible, for a merely sensual act to originate a being like Margaret Fuller, or Hawthorne, or the author of Shakespeare's plays? He who replies in the affirmative is unbalanced and unnatural."

She further alleged that a mother's indulgence of "desires and fancies" influenced her unborn child: "It is very plain that if the pregnant woman used her *will* in denying herself that which she knew to be unwholesome, or in excess of sufficient, the child would be more likely to inherit self-control."

The mother was responsible, Mrs. Kirby argued, for her child's deficiencies:

> The unfurnished mind of the illiterate woman seizes on and retains the ugly or grotesque picture, which another rich in thought and experience would have dismissed at once. Thus we see club-feet, strabismus, and other defects almost confined to the lower orders of the people.
>
> Be this as it may, the mother should turn away *on principle* from the unpleasant object or circumstance, and occupy herself by an exercise of *her will* with something agreeable. If she acts thus, all will be safe.
>
> Habits of intoxication in either parent result in off-spring who prove to be *non compos mentis,* if not drivelling idiots. No wife should cohabit with an inebriate.

The father was not without responsibility in the health and welfare of the children, but for Mrs. Kirby his part lay more with the care and solicitude he tendered his wife. In Georgiana's observations, most farmers treated their brood mares better than their wives, the farmer being inclined to pamper his horse by freeing it from labor and releasing it into "a sunny pasture":

> But there is no considerate arrangement for the wife's walking in green meadows to drink in the beauties of nature, and absorb the invigorating sunlight when she has had as much exercise as is good for her. She cooks and scours, washes and irons, makes and mends,

churns, quilts, makes preserves, pickels [sic], rag mats, washes dishes three times a day, saves and contrives (than which nothing is so wearing on the mind), attends the meetings of her religious society, helping at their fairs and socials; it is probable she takes a boarder or two in summer, keeps up a limited correspondence with her family, and goes to bed every night so exhausted of her forces, that sleep has to be waited for, rising unrested to begin over again the dreary daily routine.

"It is the conscientious, self-sacrificing woman," concluded Mrs. Kirby, "who thus wears her life out so unnecessarily....Her maternal office was her first and highest. If she filled that well, she did a more important and profitable work than any that could fall to her husband."

Diligent observation convinced Mrs. Kirby that fathers transmitted almost nothing of themselves to their children:

I am acquainted with a gentleman conspicuous among his fellows for grace of soul and nobility of nature. He has the tenderness of a woman combined with masculine heroism. Of his six children not one equals the father. The mother, self-willed and external in character (though, of course, violently opposed to woman's rights and strong-minded women), had children much alike, and all like herself. A very faulty, but sympathetic woman has often finer children than those frigidly virtuous mothers who are never stirred to the depths by any event or consideration.

Georgiana collected examples of the consequences to a child born of a mother indulging her passions, or employing her intellect, or otherwise influencing her unborn child by her own behavior. Eliza Farnham had shared with her an anecdote Georgiana particularly liked:

In a remote hamlet in one of the then young Western States, Mrs. F became acquainted with a family which included nearly a dozen members...each and every one of these young men and women being in appearance and character below mediocrity, with one exception....a young girl about nineteen years old, who was so evidently and remarkably superior both in personal appearance and nature that it did not seem possible she could belong to the same family. Beside the heavy, coarse faces of her brothers and sisters, hers was angelic in its graceful contour, long-fringed lids and refined, expressive mouth....This girl, now the successful teacher of the district-school, filled her place in the always untidy, dilapidated household, unconscious of being an anomaly. She had made some effort to brighten the dingy walls, and here and there the uneven floor of the living-room was concealed by pretty rag-mats of her making....Mrs. F. was a long while in getting hold of any clue that would explain this phenomenon.

Finally, after insistent querying by Mrs. Farnham, the mother of this exceptional daughter confessed that she had, during the child's gestation, devotedly read and reread a small book of poetry, *The Lady of the Lake:*

> "I could think of nothing but that book...I wanted it so bad, and at night I couldn't sleep for thinking of it. At last I got up, and without making a bit of noise, dressed myself, and walked four miles to...where the peddler had told me he should stay that night...and bought the book, and brought it back with me, just as contented and satisfied as you can believe. I looked it over and through, put it under my pillow, and slept soundly till morning.
>
> "The next day I began to read the beautiful story. Every page took that hold of me that...perhaps you wouldn't believe it, but before Nelly was born, if you would but give me a word here and there, I could begin at the beginning, and say it clear through to the end. It appeared to me I was there with those people by the lakes in the mountains—with...Ellen...and the others. I saw Ellen's picture before me when I was milking the cow, or cooking on the hearth, or weeding the little garden. There she was, stepping about so sweetly in the rhyme that I felt it to be all true as the day, more true after I could repeat it to myself. And then when I found my baby grew into such a pretty girl, and so smart too, it seemed as if Providence had been ever so good to me again. But children are mysteries any way. I've wondered a thousand times why Nelly was such a lady, and why she loved to learn so much more than the other children. She has read to me ever since she was ten years old, and she's got quite a lot of books there, you see, ma'am. She's mighty fond of poetry, too."

For both Eliza and Georgiana, the significance of reading beautiful books and thinking beautiful thoughts was irrefutable.

Careful study offered Georgiana any number of lessons in heredity, on the transmission of characteristics from mother to child. The "results of unused talent" were clearly evident in the experience of a woman unhappily confined to a small room in a boardinghouse, whose child, born there, was timid and weak-minded. After the woman moved into her own home, which she was free to furnish and decorate, she bore another child in whom "firmness, courage, self-reliance, reasoning faculty" were markedly evident. "In after years the mother still remembered the pleasure she had had in the arrangement of their lovely home," Mrs. Kirby noted, "but she did not connect that fact with the sterling intellect and marked artistic ability of her fourth child (and second son), not withstanding that he was seen by all to be head and shoulders above the rest in all that makes a man."

There was the case, too, of the woman whose husband would give her no money, forcing her to sneak it from his pockets. Her children suffered in consequence: "Mrs. M had three boys, and they were the most inveterate liars. How could it be otherwise, when their mother spent half her time in eluding inspection... while she regularly searched Mr. M's pockets...."

Mrs. Kirby published her opinions and anecdotes on the consequences a mother's behavior has on her unborn offspring in a little book she titled *Transmission; or Variation of Character through the Mother.* Interestingly, nowhere in its pages does she mention her own children, or what effect her own behavior might have had on molding theirs. But the case of Eliza's daughter, little Mary Fitzpatrick, lamentably deceased at the tender age of two years, was one she could not resist including:

A very remarkably superior woman, but without quick, external perceptive faculties to give her insight into character, mistook a handsome, unprincipled brute for a man and gentleman. What she endured for six months after her marriage could not be written. When she found herself *enceinte,* for the sake of the child she sought refuge with an humble friend at a distance from her unhappy home. Being pinched for means, she earned money by her needle, endeavoring, at the same time, to banish from her memory the recollection of her late cruel experience.

Day after day this regal woman sat sewing with Elizabeth Browning's poems open on a chair beside her, committing to memory the most interior of those religious strains as she stitched, stitched in the solitude of the low-roofed cottage by the river. No exhilarating rides on horseback, such as had been her wont, no genial, social company, no brisk walks and happy communion with nature, were possible in her peculiar circumstances. She must forego the healthy, harmonious, external life of her past, and live solely within the inmost chambers of her soul.

At two years old the little girl born of these untoward conditions was lovely, large-eyed, thoughtful, considerate, and tender in her ways as any lady. "Where are your wings, Mary?" said a gentleman who noticed the radiant face at the mother's garden gate. For these seemed only necessary to prove her a seraph.

Alas! to her mother's infinite sorrow, she very soon departed to more blissful realms. The constantly repressed emotions of the mother, and her sedentary life, had caused an imperfect action of the lungs, and a low vital tone generally. Grief shortens the breathing as joy expands the lungs. Little Mary was extremely narrow-chested, with sloping shoulders, and hence quite unable to supply sufficient sustenance for so very large a brain, whose weight she bent under, and died, shortly after completing her second year, of acute hydrocephalus.

In 1877 S. R. Wells & Co. in New York published Mrs. Kirby's *Transmission* in a slender volume of sixty-eight pages. Five years later, the publisher, reorganized as Fowler & Wells, reissued a revised edition containing an additional twelve pages. Mrs. Kirby had expanded her observations to include a consideration of "kleptomania," concluding that a woman's "desire to get and keep would be harmless and justifiable as a temporary state of mind, if she were not pregnant....The selfish, grasping spirit increases on itself through generations of similar experience. On the same principle, the *remarkable* singer is the product of two or three generations of love of song."

She also added prescient comments on intemperance, warning that "nothing is more certain than that the desire for alcoholic drinks is inherited." She counseled "entire abstinence."

Mrs. Kirby also appended new concluding remarks:

> It has also been proved, to the simplest observation, that woman has the large balance of power in the formation of character, and it is for her to assume the responsibility. Genius is dependent on a combination of influences outside our control, but good sense, integrity, generosity, and chastity take their growth from thoughts, emotions, and *acts,* over which we have control to a very great extent. Let women take courage. The larger their responsibility, the nobler their reward.

Having taken up her pen, Georgiana was loathe to put it down again. She continued to write, with typical unrestraint, opinion pieces for the local newspaper in a style not seen since Eliza

Farnham had left the field. Famously critical of local educators, Mrs. Kirby described one teacher, called "Stovepipe," as having eyes like "a boiled codfish." Mr. Newell didn't impress her either: "Dr. Knight says that Mr. Newell does not spend his time in impressing upon the minds of his pupils that he is the most highly educated person in the world. This is extremely politic, inasmuch as he could scarcely expect to convince them, in a life-time, that such was the fact."

In 1886 Mrs. Kirby followed the revised edition of *Transmission* with fiction. *Amid Better Circumstances,* a novella about a child reluctantly given up at birth and happily reunited as an adult with his biological mother, provided a frame for Mrs. Kirby's opinions on "the influences of home, noble womanly character, self-sacrifice, music and love," as well as "the great subjects of temperance and religion."

Mrs. Kirby rarely missed a chance to let fly at religion. In *Amid Better Circumstances,* her fictional Mrs. Kennedy, an Irish emigrant, "was capable of taking a historic view of the church's position in the dark ages when her teachings were a little above the ignorance of the times." When Mrs. Kennedy's reunited son, Basil, says of Ireland, "I attributed all the poverty and ignorance to the national faith," she replies:

> It's easy, now, for me to see how the Catholic Church keeps grown up people ignorant, helpless children, telling them from childhood up that they must never dare to question any part of the creed, or to doubt the truth of any of the traditions of the church. Go to confession and to mass and you are sure of Heaven....

Briefly placing her characters in Ireland let Mrs. Kirby condemn English rule there:

> Why doctor, our ancestors were driven from their lands to the mountains, hunted like dogs, and starved, or only let return to work as laborers on the farms they owned. The English made a law that if a son would turn Protestant he might drive the rest of the family from the homestead and take possession. There was no law that would protect an Irishman's life, or his daughter's honor, and he might not own a horse worth more than £5, or the Sheriff could meet him, pay the £5 and take the animal that perhaps was worth £250, and they put taxes on everything. Even the Scotch and English Protestants

who came over to settle the lands of the murdered Irish complained that they were kept down by the trade laws—and they forbade us education and they degraded the peers of the land to whom the others looked up...and the most talented people left for other countries ....It's myself that always wondered they did not make the Irish hard and bitter and cruel like themselves by such terrible oppression.

And Georgiana wasn't done yet. Like Eliza, she had a life's story to tell, "years of experience," the title she gave her autobiography. She began with her birth in Bristol, to a mother mourning a husband lost at sea:

It is a bad beginning to be born of grief. It narrows the chest and makes the blood less buoyant and hopeful. Sometimes it affords a larger measure of thoughtfulness, but this is poor compensation for the loss of a natural gladness in one's existence.

In recounting her life in England and Canada, at Brook Farm, at Sing Sing, and the years before her decision to go West, Mrs. Kirby exhausted her energies. Taking up the pen had become painful to fingers crippled with arthritis. And it seemed enough to conclude with "in May, 1850, I left New York for California, where I have passed the remainder of my life."

With that, she closed the subject.

G. P. Putnam's Sons published *Years of Experience* in 1887. In reviewing, and quoting generously from its pages, the *Atlantic Monthly* summed Mrs. Kirby's book as "somewhat rude in its literary form" but "singularly attractive, both as the sketch of a forcible character, and as a series of silhouettes of American life in a turbulent mental period."

The *North American Review* praised it as well:

No thoughtful person can read this modest autobiography without interest and profit, as showing the course of a self-reliant and intellectual woman, thrown early in life upon her own endeavors, and bravely holding her own through all adversities and difficulties. It is not so much, however, a story of material as of intellectual and spiritual experience, gathered under outward circumstances and associations that impart to it special interest.

Alas, Georgiana had not the satisfaction of seeing her book in print, nor her life applauded by the press.

*Georgiana and her "little tanner" share a gravesite at the Odd Fellows Cemetery, Santa Cruz. Author's photo*

Mrs. Kirby died January 27, 1887, in her sixty-eighth year. The *San Francisco Chronicle* noted her death by summarizing her eventful life and concluded:

> Her mind and character were keenly analytical. She despised all sham and insincerity. She had the rare faculty of entering into the thoughts of others with an intuitive perception, and of sharing their sorrows through her great-hearted sympathy. All up and down this coast are men and women who, when they hear of her death, will remember her as one who aided them in time of trouble. She firmly believed that there is no death to the soul—that death is only a birth into a new experience.

The Kirbys were longtime Unitarians, and on Sunday, January 30, a memorial service was held in Santa Cruz's Unity Church. Flowers decorated the platform, the organist played, the choir sang, and Mrs. E. L. Watson of San Francisco, in a voice "clear and pleasing," eulogized:

> Death is as beautiful in its message to man as birth. A new soul entering on a new sphere of action is full of triumph. The chamber of death is a mountain of transformation. Nature is not satisfied until she finds greater opportunities for the soul.

For months our friend saw the coming change, and with a steady hand she made preparation to meet it. She felt that the grave was a bridge or chasm between this life and the other. Her heart had been filled with the strong conviction that she would dwell with the dear ones who had gone before. When the last days of her earthly existence were drawing to a close, she whispered to the dear ones, 'It is well.'

To which Eliza Farnham would have said, "Amen."

# THIRTY-THREE

# ...But Not Forgotten

Mrs. Farnham left her converts [to Spiritualism] here and departed for the East, where she left for that land she had so long believed herself to be familiar with; and if her views in life be correct, she can now hold converse with her friends who await to follow her. This belief will prove of little injury, excepting the additional expense to the Insane Asylum, that requires more room for its converts.

—Editor, *Stockton Herald,* 1866

On a hill south of the Hinds' place lived Joe Russell....His house was built in [the] early days by two women, Mrs. Kirby and Mrs. Farnham. The women wore bloomers when they built the house and were not considered nice women on that account.

—"My Early Childhood Memories," Sarah Elizabeth Gourley

Named for a Santa Cruz pioneer who devoted her life to the education, freedom and enfranchisement of all, the Georgiana Bruce Kirby Preparatory School is an independent coeducational secondary school serving the Santa Cruz community.

—Mission Statement, Georgiana Bruce Kirby Preparatory School

In March of 1868, one Mrs. Cora Daniels declared herself a conduit for a message from Eliza Farnham, deceased. Dr. Henry T. Child, of Philadelphia, leader of that city's circle of Spiritualists, recorded the "communication":

"Friends [declared the purported spirit of Mrs. Farnham], you may not recognize in this form the one who has shared your kind hospitalities, and revealed to you many of the aspirations of her spirit while it was trammeled with the bonds of the flesh; but I am constrained to present myself in this wise, that I may express to you the joy and gratification it is to me to be recognized by you again.

"I remember with pleasure the encouragement you gave me in times past, in reference to the thoughts and works in which I was engaged; and I feel that it will be agreeable to you to know that I realize now the possible fulfillment of all those plans which then were dreamily before me, and which I thought would not be realized in many years. I now see that these works are going steadily on, and that what I deemed almost impassable barriers to their realization are passing away."

Alas, no one who knew Mrs. Farnham would have recognized her in that form. Had the message been at least a little acerbic, or witty, or more eloquently expressive, Dr. Child and Mrs. Daniels might have made quite a case for Spiritualism. But the communication contained no hint of Mrs. Farnham's personal exuberance nor of her lively use of language. Dr. Child, who knew her, should have known that if Eliza Farnham had managed to speak from the "other side," she would not have missed the chance to amusingly describe who and what she saw there, or at least exult in the triumph of her afterlife predictions.

One bit Mrs. Daniels and Dr. Child got right: Eliza would have been working:

> "It has been my good fortune, in this world, to meet with a class of minds who are engaged in preparing and presenting plans for educating and uplifting the world. Our efforts are not only to remove the barriers to progress—cupidity and ignorance—but to implant within every human being the germs of thought that shall elevate them, and induce them to labor with the spirits for the regeneration of the world. We have organized a general plan."

In California, memories of both Eliza and Georgiana long survived. Writer Norick Neill revisited the women's accomplishments in an 1893 article for the *San Francisco Call*:

> Santa Cruz was in early days the home of several of the most brilliant minds California has ever possessed. This "charmed circle" of wit and intellect included Mrs. Eliza W. Farnham, authoress and philanthropist; [and] Georgiana B. Kirby, whose spicy articles have appeared in the leading magazines of the East and West....
>
> Mrs. Farnham's reputation was made by her work entitled "Woman and Her Era," which she wrote in Santa Cruz....Her personal history is full of romance and would itself make a novel of intensely interesting reading.

Unfortunately for the *Call*'s readers, and Eliza Farnham's memory, the writer got a lot of her "personal history" wrong. He claimed she "crossed the plains in 1848, only to find, on her arrival in the far West, that her husband was dead." A pity. Mrs. Farnham's voyage aboard the *Angelique* and her abandonment in Valparaiso, besides being factual, make a much more dramatic tale.

Norick Neill included William Fitzpatrick in his story, claiming, as had Fitzpatrick, that the Irishman helped secure the release of Napoleon from prison. The facts he gave regarding Fitzpatrick's involvement with Eliza are more easily verifiable:

> After a brief period of conjugal felicity Fitzpatrick gave way to his love of liquor. His jealousy for his wife was as fierce as it was unreasonable, and extended even to her much-prized books, many of which were pierced from cover to cover with Fitzpatrick's dagger. The result was that a judgment of divorce separated the two and Mrs. Fitzpatrick became Mrs. Farnham again.

Subscribing to the adage that a story worth telling is a story worth exaggerating, Neill declared that Mrs. Farnham, while serving as matron at the Stockton Insane Asylum, "was one day shocked at the appearance among the patients of Fitzpatrick, who had gone crazy from remorse and dissipation."

Of Georgiana, Neill not only wrote that she was descended from Scottish hero Robert the Bruce but that she and Mrs. Farnham arrived in Santa Cruz wearing bloomers to take possession of the property left by Thomas J. Farnham: "This property consisted of a small farm, which Mrs. Kirby, whose experience at Brook Farm now served her in good stead, aided Mrs. Farnham in tilling."

Georgiana's daughter Ora Bruce Kirby, upon reading Neill's article, declared it "recklessly patched together" and promptly penned a rejoinder:

> One of the most delightful bits of fanciful analogy is Norick Neill's theory that Miss Bruce's experience at Brook Farm was of such advantage to Mrs. Farnham in her amateur planting and plowing, for it happens, and the joke is historical, that one of the peculiarities of the Brook Farm venture was that none of this colony knew anything about farming at all, the head of the community being George Ripley, a literary man, simon pure....For practical duties in community labor Miss Bruce "did up" collars and etc., and helped keep the main house in order. The late Geo. Wm. Curtis used to hang out the collars and shirts on freezing days, sitting on a clothes basket between times to talk philosophy. By the way Miss Bruce was not descended from Robert Bruce, not that she was aware. This is probably Norickian evidence also....

Of Mrs. Kirby I need not write to a community which knew so well her long life filled with charity and good works. She was a natural reformer and though of a most sensitive and unaggressive nature, in any cause of principle or justice she was courageous and steadfast with an unwearied zeal, philanthropy was not only a theory but a living and doing thing....Her literary work was the pleasure of her later days.

I cannot fancy where those "spicy articles" were printed. Mrs. Kirby could no more have done a "spicy skit" than she could have told lies or 'damned facts.' She never learned the trick.

## Ora Kirby also set the record straight on Mrs. Farnham:

She had a noble, courageous soul, full of sympathy for all misery and misfortune. Her own life had been a hard one. An orphaned childhood, desperate struggles for an education, with a mind which far outran the plodding conservative gait set for women of her day, to whom original thought meant original sin, she had to make her way in the face of constant condemnation from the stupid and uneducated frontier communities where fate had tossed her fortunes. Yet through all her trials with a handsome, improvident selfish husband and later with a handsome, brutal drunken one, she bore herself with a pluck and pride which won respect even from those who did not respect her philosophies.

She was blessed above all with a keen sense of humor.

## Ora never knew William Fitzpatrick, but a longtime Santa Cruz resident had:

"All that stuff about Fitzpatrick is pure gammon" snorted the early day settler...Fitzpatrick was the biggest liar and rascal that ever lived. 'Handsome?' Yes, he was handsome, though not such a swell as Farnham and a smooth talker. As for all that stuff about the rescue of Napoleon I don't doubt Fitz told it. There is nothing he would stick at. A regular Barry Lyndon of an Irishman with no place for the truth in him, he was so full of lies and whiskey and brag. He was never one of the Potrero farm party, we would not of stood him, no, Mrs. Farnham had left the farm and gone to teaching in San Francisco to get some ready money, and there Fitzpatrick courted her and told her tales of all the fortune he had made and the care he would take of her. So she came down to Santa Cruz to be among her old friends for her wedding. But her friends knew Mr. Fitz and would not let any minister serve, but Fitz hunted up Clements, an Alcalde, of Soquel, and he married 'em, and then the trouble began.

Fitzpatrick was a drunkard and a blackguard. It was no time before he was abusing his wife. He beat her and threatened to blow her brains out with a pistol, scared her half to death until she had to leave him to save her life. It was not any jealousy, it was just cussedness and whiskey, and Fitz was skin tight full of both.

About the touching romance of Fitz meeting his wife in the Stockton asylum, that is another fairy tale, nor did his noble relatives send for him to reside in a castle in Spain. He died in Sacramento. I met him there one day in '75 or '76. A miserable dirty loafer came up and spoke to me on the street.

"I don't know you," I said, nor had I the least idea who the groggy, ragged wreck of a man was. "I am Fitzpatrick."

"Then I don't want to know you," and I marched off and left him.

Ora Bruce Kirby, Georgiana's firstborn, died two years after writing her letter of indignation, never having married. Georgiana's second son, Phillip, and her second daughter, Georgiana, both predeceased their mother. Cornelia married and bore one child, Margaret Bruce Brown, who married Richard Chalmers and named her only son Bruce.

Eliza Farnham's only surviving child, Charles, after studying drawing and music in Paris as a young man, briefly taught singing in New York. A "weakness of his throat" obliged him to give it up, and he "prepared himself as a writer," publishing several magazine articles and a biography of author Francis Parkman. Of himself he said, perhaps recollecting his mother's appraisal, that he was "deficient in driving ambition." He died in Florida in 1929 at the age of eighty-seven, never having married and without issue, and thus his brilliant mother's DNA died with him.

But both Eliza and Georgiana would be remembered through their words, delighting and confounding and surprising the occasional reader or scholar or publisher who chanced upon them.

In the 1940s, journalist Helen Beal Woodward, researching nineteenth-century women, discovered Farnham's *Woman and Her Era:*

> The originality of *Woman and Her Era* is so startling that one is puzzled by the temperateness of the reviews, which either shrugged it off with mild ridicule or murmured respectfully over it for a couple of paragraphs. Had the critics drowsed in those long dry stretches when Mrs. Farnham was crooning over history's famous females?

Were they lulled by the surface orthodoxy of her belief that Woman's sphere was Maternity, her place the Home? Or was "THE SUPERIORITY OF WOMAN," as Mrs. Farnham put it in her favorite capitals, simply lost in the shuffle of an age when every day dished up a fresh smorgasbord of revolutionary ideas? The women's movement might have been expected to welcome a book that spoke so highly of the sex, but it seems to have been cool to this one. Even Women's Righters, perhaps, did not want to be proved anything better than equal.

In the 1950s, W. David Lewis happened upon Mrs. Farnham's name while researching his doctoral dissertation on New York's early penitentiary system. Discovering her four years as matron of the women's division at Sing Sing and her fearlessly instituted major reforms in the face of constant criticism, Lewis fell under Eliza's spell. Not only did she receive a chapter in his book, he searched out the details of her life to provide a capsule biography to the editors of *Notable American Women.*

Eliza Farnham's contributions to American penology included the editing and publication of an American edition of Marmaduke Blake Sampson's *Criminal Jurisprudence Considered in Relation to Mental Organization.* Mrs. Farnham supplemented Sampson's work with her own notes, plus drawings of prisoners' heads to illustrate how, through phrenological examination, mental tendencies translate to behavior. The work remains significant today for the study of correctional history and the use of phrenology by some nineteenth-century reformers to explain criminal acts. With the addition of an index and introduction by W. David Lewis, the book was reprinted in 1973.

Author Madeleine B. Stern discovered Eliza Farnham while researching the life of Margaret Fuller for a biography E. P. Dutton published in 1942. When Ms. Stern became friends with Netherlands publisher Bob De Graaf, she offered him the opportunity to reprint Eliza's two travel books. With introductions by Ms. Stern, De Graaf published a facsimile edition of *Life in Prairie Land* in 1972 and of *California, In-Doors and Out* in 1973.

*Life in Prairie Land* is Mrs. Farnham's account of her pioneer years in Illinois, where she resided from 1835 to 1840, and in her husband's absence traveled about the Illinois countryside, often alone, drinking experience and scenery as if it were water and she a drowning woman. John Hallwas first read it in the early 1970s and found Mrs. Farnham's work "unique because of her feminist views" and "environmental concern." Hallwas, director of regional collections at Western Illinois University Libraries, further praised it as a "vivid account of early Illinois that combines the descriptive variety of travel literature, the self-characterization of autobiography, and the analytical depth of the extended essay," all held together by the "unique personality of its author." In 1988, the University of Illinois Press, in conjunction with the Illinois Center for the Book, reissued *Life in Prairie Land*, with an introduction by Dr. Hallwas.

It would be difficult to shine in any firmament containing Eliza Farnham's star, but Georgiana Kirby's autobiography, *Years of Experience*, glitters with adventure and social history. Her insightful observations on frontier Canada, Brook Farm, Sing Sing prison, and the anti-slavery movement, and her vivid account of teaching in the Midwest, fortunately caught the eye of New York's AMS Press, which, in 1971, reprinted it from the 1887 edition.

Captivated by Georgiana's *Years of Experience*, author Helen Smith Giffen spent several years researching Mrs. Kirby's life and writing her biography. Although never published in its complete form, the manuscript contributed significantly to *Georgiana, Feminist Reformer of the West*, in which the Santa Cruz County Historical Trust published, in 1987, Mrs. Kirby's Santa Cruz diary.

Helen Giffen, while writing Georgiana's biography, served as executive secretary and librarian to the Society of California Pioneers. In that capacity, in 1961, she received an inquiry from a Miss Gladys Tilden requesting information about any documents the society's library contained relating to Eliza Farnham. Ms. Giffen replied that she had a copy of Georgiana's *Years of Experience*, which "contains a good deal about her association with Mrs. Farnham at Sing Sing, but you no doubt have read that."

No doubt.

Gladys Tilden possessed a special interest in Georgiana and Eliza. The two women had known and admired and encouraged Gladys's grandmother, Maria Hecox, the promising young Santa Cruz student who had at seventeen married Dr. William Tilden of Chico. In 1861, when the Tildens moved from Chico to Stockton to oversee the State Insane Asylum, they had two sons. In 1864, the second son, Douglas, contracted scarlet fever and lost his hearing. He remained deaf throughout his life as a distinguished California sculptor. He and his wife had one daughter, Gladys, in 1900. At twenty-seven, Gladys Tilden moved to Paris, where she eventually became managing editor of the French *Vogue* magazine. She returned to California in 1935, after the death of her father. In 1949, in the midst of her career as an editor and writer, she began researching her famous father's life for a biography. And discovered Eliza Farnham. She promptly abandoned her plan to write the life of Douglas Tilden and determined instead to write Eliza's.

In 1959, Miss Tilden began, in earnest, to collect details of Eliza Farnham's life. With indefatigable dedication, she scoured books and newspapers, pored over periodicals, combed journals, scrutinized reel after reel of microfilm. Seeking the least mention, compiling lists of citations, she typed letter after letter to historical societies, to historians, to libraries across the country: "I am gathering biographical data on the celebrated Mrs. Eliza W. Farnham...."

Six years later she wrote a librarian in Milton, New York: "My research on Mrs. Farnham is completed as far as I can go at this time...I am working now on a bibliography, and if and when something is published I will send you a copy."

But in 1972, after thirteen years of sending out letters and seeking ever more information, she still had not finished her research. And, excepting a list of chapter heads and a title page, *This Singular Woman*, she had not yet written a word.

Nor did she ever.

After more than a decade in thrall to research rapture, a condition familiar to writers infatuated by history, Miss Tilden's literary intentions were quietly stolen by Alzheimer's disease.

There was this compensation: for nearly fifteen years, Gladys Tilden resided, in imagination, in the mid-nineteenth century, revisiting a remarkable time in the country's history and keeping company with two remarkable women—for Georgiana's life was inextricably linked to Eliza's. From the moment Eliza and Georgiana met at Horace Greeley's home, introduced by Margaret Fuller, each must have recognized the other as an incomparable companion of the mind. And so it proved. Their attachment survived Sing Sing's vicissitudes, individual and mutual disappointment, California's multiple insufficiencies, philosophical differences, time, and distance.

With a shared audacity of spirit and self-confidence, they defied accepted wisdom and relied on their own. At Sing Sing, they instructed imprisoned women, fettered by handcuffs and ignorance, to read, to aspire. In the face of ridicule, they fearlessly spoke out, in print and in person, on behalf of penal reform, abolition, women's rights. On California's frontier they championed intellect over ignorance, teaching an immigrant population—by book, precept, and example—to think, to question, to aim higher. They challenged the narrowness of religious doctrine, daringly mocked dogma, and boldly championed an inspiring belief in the unbounded potential of society and the human spirit.

And their legacy includes, not least, a valiant model of fortitude. Despite public and private calumny and bitter disappointments, these two intrepid reformers never lost hope.

"There is left us, at the worst," declared Mrs. Farnham, "one comfort—the only one which avails at times—the comfort of knowing that life *can bear*, and, in the end, throw off its burdens, or fit them to itself, and take joyously and carelessly to the sunshine again. You have seen such seasons, and been thrown thus upon yourself, I know. Try your strength again, now. We must be in the battle very soon, and then courage will lose its merit. They say the most arrant cowards become brave soldiers in the midst of the fire."

Eliza Farnham and Georgiana Kirby—extraordinary women of courage, accomplishment, adventure, and ideas—admirable, redoubtable, forces to be reckoned with—alive to an extraordinary time in American history. And they embraced those times fearlessly, challenging society in large ways and small, devoting themselves to making their world a better place, and most of all to their profound belief in the innate power, and wisdom, of—WOMEN.

Amen.

# Notes

## ABBREVIATIONS

Eliza W. Farnham   EWF
Georgiana B. Kirby   GBK
*California, In-Doors and Out   CI&O*
*My Early Days   MED*
*The Ideal Attained   IA*
*Years of Experience   YE*
*Woman and Her Era   W&HE*
*The Journal of Georgiana Bruce Kirby 1852–1860   GBK Journal*
*New York Times   NYT*
*New York Tribune   NYTr*
*San Francisco Alta California   AC*

## 1 – THIS SINGULAR WOMAN

**Mrs. Farnham, the celebrated matron of the Sing Sing Prison**: Mary E. Dewey, ed. *Life and Letters of Catharine M. Sedgwick* (New York: Harper & Bros., 1872), 312.

**Famed novelist Catharine Sedgwick**: Author of *Hope Leslie, Redwood, A New England Tale,* and *Married or Single,* Sedgwick also wrote instructional tales for youth, including *Live and Let Live* and *Poor Rich Man and Rich Poor Man.* She was praised for her rich descriptions of American history, geography, and culture.

**Among the privations and deteriorating influences**: Circular announcing California Association of American Women, New York, 2 February 1849 (in *CI&O*, 1972).

**thousands of impetuous young men**: For an exceptional overview of the gold rush, see J. S. Holliday's *Rush for Riches: Gold Fever and the Making of California* (Berkeley: University of California Press, 1999).

**Half of the houses in Monterey are empty**: *Boston Journal* letter in *NYTr,* 14 December 1848.

**the Farnhams determined to make their home in California**: EWF to Judge John W. Edmonds, 10 September 1845, Sing Sing: "Our California project grows daily. It is possible that Mr. Farnham may leave this season, in which case my departure would be deferred for a year, probably not longer...." James Roberts Gilmore Collection Ms. 37, Special Collections, Milton S. Eisenhower Library, The Johns Hopkins University.

**he contracted a fever and died**: Farnham died in San Francisco on 13 September 1848. The *Californian* reported, on 16 September 1848, the cause of death as "intermittent fever," the common name for malaria. Thomas Jefferson Farnham was the author of five books, most notably *Travels in the Great Western Prairies*, an account of his overland expedition from Peoria to Oregon in 1839, and *Travels in California*, its sequel for 1840. See also Charles B. Churchill, "Thomas Jefferson Farnham: An Exponent of American Empire in Mexican California," *Pacific Historical Review*, November 1991, LX, No. 4, 517–537. For various accounts of Farnham's Oregon expedition, see Le Roy R. and Ann W. Hafen, eds., *To the Rockies and Oregon, 1839–1842* (Glendale, Calif.: The Arthur H. Clark Co., 1955).

## 2 – SING SING PRISON

**a series of lectures she delivered in New York City**: *NYTr*, 7 November 1842: "Mrs. Farnham, a Western lady, proposes to give a Course of Eight Lectures to Ladies (only) at the Society Library, Broadway, commencing on Wednesday, at 11 a.m. Mrs. F has lectured in Baltimore, Troy and other Cities to large classes of her own sex, with decided approbation, and has the strongest testimonials to her ability and worth....Mrs. Farnham advertised her topics to include, "The Natural Position of Woman in the scale of being"; "Her present Physical Condition and the causes which have led her to it"; "Her present Mental Condition"; "The means of improving her Physical Condition or Physical Education"; "On Digestion and Dietetics"; "The True Natural Constitution of Woman"; "Mental Education and Training"; "On the treatment of Domestics, and the Duties which we owe to those in the humbler walks of life, in elevating and improving their condition."

**a sort of rebellion among the convicts**: *YE*, 190.

**an "intense curiosity to penetrate the innermost centre of the stained soul**: *MED*, 351.

**English penal reformer Elizabeth Fry**: Elizabeth Gurney Fry (1780–1845) became, in 1811, a minister in the Society of Friends, which believed in the spiritual equality of the sexes. As such, and in the tradition of Quaker women, she visited prisons. At London's Newgate Gaol she encountered starving, drunken, and unkempt women, imprisoned with their children. Religious conversion had been her purpose, but alleviation of suffering and the improvement of prison conditions became her mission. Principles advanced in Fry's 1827 treatise, "Observations in Visiting, Superintendence and Government for Female Prisoners," adopted by Eliza Farnham and employed by her at the women's division at Sing Sing prison, dominated women's prison reform in the United States. See Estelle B. Freedman's

*Their Sisters' Keepers: Prison Reform in America, 1830–1930* (Ann Arbor: University of Michigan Press, 1981).

**Horace Greeley roundly applauded**: *NYTr*, 18 March 1844.

**the name of the adjacent town**: The name Sing Sing originated from the Mohegan Indian word s*in-sing* or *sink-sink*, said to signify "stone upon stone." In 1901, after a boycott of prison-made goods hurt local business, the town changed its name to Ossining.

*Travels in California*: The *NYTr*, 1 March 1844, announced the second installment of Farnham's book as "just published by Saxton & Miles, 205 Broadway. It is very spirited, most spicy in its delineations of Spanish American character, and contains, we think, the latest and fullest accounts we have of California and the adjacent seas. It is to be completed in two more 25 cent. numbers."

**an impressive white marble building**: New York State Assembly Document 255, *Third Annual Report of the Executive Committee of the Prison Association of New-York*, 14 October 1847. Mount Pleasant Prison, or Sing Sing, as it was more commonly known, opened in 1826 to replace New York City's Newgate Prison, established in 1797. In 1839 the Mount Pleasant Female Prison opened at Sing Sing with women transferred there from the Bellevue asylum and Auburn prison.

**Mrs. Mary Anne Johnson, a lady admirably suited**: *YE*, 191. Mary Anne and her husband, Oliver Johnson, like Georgiana, were ardent abolitionists. Oliver Johnson is the author of *William Lloyd Garrison and His Times* (Boston: Houghton Mifflin, 1881).

**Margaret Fuller**: (1810–1850) Journalist, critic, teacher, lecturer; author of *Woman in the Nineteenth Century* and *Summer on the Lakes*; editor of transcendental *Dial*; *New York Tribune* foreign correspondent.

**there Miss Fuller introduced Mrs. Farnham**: *YE*, 190.

**As she was "so evidently fearless**: Ibid., 193.

**Although less than two weeks have elapsed**: *NYTr*, 11 April 1844.

**The prison reform measures instituted by**: *Second Report of the Prison Association of New York* (New York, 1846).

**The pulley, for example**: W. David Lewis, *From Newgate to Dannemora* (New York: Cornell University Press, 1965), 268. For additional details of Mrs. Farnham's career at Sing Sing, see Lewis's chapter, "The Ordeal of the Unredeemables," 157–177. See also "Report of the Prison Discipline Commission," *Third Annual Report of the Executive Committee of the Prison Association of New-York*.

**Stocks and chains**: Testimony of prisoners Lucy A. Price, Mary Tenyck, Eliza Hunt, and Phoebe Spires in New York State Assembly Document 255, *Third Annual Report of the Executive Committee of the Prison Association of New-York*, 14 October 1847, 59–60. A previous matron, Isabella Bard, testified to authorities that convicts were struck with "a small rattan over all their clothes." Although these practices were subsequently forbidden, matrons preceding Mrs. Farnham regularly employed such punishments as hair-cropping, mouth-gags, and solitary confinement on stinted rations; see *New York State Senate Document, 63$^{rd}$ Session* (1840), Vol. II, No. 48, 300.

**In New York friends of the new regime**: *YE*, 208.

**the Reverend John Luckey**: Interestingly, Luckey's autobiography, *Life in Sing Sing State Prison, as seen in a Twelve Years' Chaplaincy* (New York: N. Tibbals & Co., 1860), contains no mention of Eliza Farnham or their disagreements.

**a well-meaning, tight-skulled little chaplain**: *YE*, 190.

**self-educated intellectual**: Eliza's formal education consisted of one year at Nine Partners School (1831), and one year at the Albany Female Academy (1834). See Albany Academy to Tilden, 26 November 1962; J. Matthews to Tilden, 11 December 1961. BANC MSS Gladys Tilden Papers, The Bancroft Library.

**Religious, praying people**: *MED*, 73–74.

**Instead of spending half an hour each morning on Bible-reading**: *YE*, 193.

**If contact with, and the example of elevated**: "Annual Report of the Matron of Mt. Pleasant State Prison for Females, made in 1844," *Second Report of the Prison Association of New York*, 38–42.

***Life in Prairie Land* received the *Tribune*'s commendation**: For additional reviews see *Hunt's Merchant Magazine*, XV, July 1846, 123; *United States Magazine and Democratic Review*, Vol. 19, July 1846, 79; and *Knickerbocker Magazine*, July 1846, 70.

**Mrs. F. wields a vigorous pen**: *NYTr*, 2 June 1846.

**The phrenological principles**: For an excellent overview, see John D. Davies, *Phrenology, Fad and Science: A 19th-Century American Crusade* (New Haven, Conn.: Archon Books, 1971). Davies (p. 34), attests to phrenology's widespread acceptance:

"At one time the Fowler and Wells agency could list some twenty-six lecturers 'in the field'....A course of forty lectures in Boston in 1843 sometimes had audiences up to 3,000....In Philadelphia a congregation of 500 listened to twenty successive lectures; New York City had its own auditorium, Clinton

Hall, devoted to phrenology and its ancillary sciences. As early as 1838 it was cited as one of the indices of civilization that in Honolulu, along with sidewalks...there were lectures on phrenology at the Seaman's Institute."

Walt Whitman, then editor of the *Brooklyn Daily Eagle*, averred in the issue of 16 November 1846: "Phrenology, it must now be confessed by all men who have open eyes, has at last gained a position, and a firm one, among the sciences. It seems useless to deny this—and the only difference is as to the laying down of the dividing lines, and how distinctly and authoritatively they can be marked. Perhaps no philosophic revolutionisers ever were attacked with more virulence—struck with more sinewy arms, or greater perseverance—than Gall, Spurzheim, and the other early phrenologists....But the phrenologists withstood the storm and have gained the victory."

**My acknowledgments are due....Mr. Brady**: EWF, ed., *Rationale of Crime* (Montclair, N.J.: Patterson Smith, 1973), xxxviii.

**Fowler and Wells**: Madeleine B. Stern's *Heads & Headlines: The Phrenological Fowlers* (Norman: University of Oklahoma Press, 1971), provides an excellent history of the brothers and their publishing empire.

**We cannot too earnestly commend its facts**: *NYTr*, 11 November 1846.

**Some say that...Mr. Luckey, the Parson**: *Hudson River Chronicle*, 30 June 1846.

**The Prison House**: Ibid., 14 July 1846.

**John Bigelow**: Bigelow's subsequent achievements overshadowed his prison board appointment. In 1848 he became part owner and editor, with William Cullen Bryant, of the *New York Evening Post*. In 1861 he went to Paris as consul general under the Lincoln administration, and from 1865 to 1866 served as U.S. minister to France. In his later years, he wrote an analysis of French relations with the Confederate navy, two biographies, two books reflecting his devotion to Emanuel Swedenborg's philosophy; edited the works of Benjamin Franklin in ten volumes; and published a five-volume autobiography, *Retrospections of an Active Life*. See Margaret Clappe, *Forgotten First Citizen: John Bigelow* (Boston: Little, Brown & Co., 1947).

**The Parson remains**: EWF to John Bigelow, 20 July 1846. John Bigelow Papers. Manuscripts and Archives Division, The New York Public Library. Astor, Lenox and Tilden Foundations.

**Luckey aired his opposition:** *Hudson River Chronicle*, 22 September 1846. The *NYTr* (23 September 1846) withheld judgment: "We shall not follow the example of some of our contemporaries by taking sides in this controversy on the strength of ex parte statements and surmises, but shall wait patiently till both parties have told their story. Is not this fair? Some people are too much like the Judge who insisted on giving his opinion after listening to one of the parties only, alleging that it always confused and bothered him to hear both sides."

**You have seen the** *astonishing disclosures:* EWF to John Bigelow, 24 September 1846, Sing Sing. John Bigelow Papers. Manuscripts and Archives Division, The New York Public Library. Astor, Lenox and Tilden Foundations.

**Mrs. Farnham is herself a woman of ill fame:** *Hudson River Chronicle,* 11 August 1846.

**Do not entertain the idea:** Ibid.

**the Reverend Luckey declined to appear:** New York State Assembly Document 255, *Third Annual Report of the Executive Committee of the Prison Association of New-York,* 14 October 1847, 50.

**the prison is a sink of pollution:** *Hudson River Chronicle,* 11 August 1846.

**Thomas Jefferson Farnham had departed for California:** In New York, Farnham had met Lansford Hastings, who was lecturing there on California and organizing an emigration for 1846—which would include the Donner party he so fatally misled. See Dale Morgan, ed., *Overland in 1846: Diaries and Letters of the California–Oregon Trail* Vol. I (Lincoln: University of Nebraska Press, 1963), 40–41. Hastings to California pioneer John Marsh, 26 March 1845: "I brought a letter...for you, from your old friend T. J. Farnham Esq....Friend Farnham is doing everything in his power to increase the emigration to this far-famed region, and he is of the opinion that he will be able to bring, at least, three or four thousand from the State of New York alone."

Farnham's letter to Marsh, dated 6 July 1845, suggests plans for overthrowing California's Mexican government: "The excitement consequent on the admission of Texas into the Union must have time to abate. The winter of 46 will do. Next year will see me & my family—God willing, at your house.

"From 10 to 20 thousand emigrants will enter California next summer. There will then be population enough to authorize the step; & we shall have force enough for any Contingency."

### 3 – A RESTLESS WOMAN

**I must be glad to see you thrown so completely on yourself** All chapter 3 quotations are from *YE.* See also Carolyn Swift and Judith Steen, eds., *Georgiana, Feminist Reformer of the West: The Journal of Georgiana Bruce Kirby 1852–1860* (Santa Cruz, Calif.: Santa Cruz County Historical Trust, 1987), 3–10 (hereafter *GBK Journal*).

**Ezra Stiles Gannett**: Georgiana had fallen in with a noted Unitarian clergy-man. Gannett succeeded William Channing as pastor at Boston's Federal Street Church and was active in organizing the American Unitarian Association.

**Georgiana "decided on a fresh migration**: Brook Farm survived another three years after Miss Bruce's departure before collapsing into debt and dis-banding into its destiny as a charming and fascinating footnote to nineteenth-century social history. Founder George Ripley, who spent twenty years paying off its creditors, became a distinguished critic for the *New York Tribune* and founder of *Harper's New Monthly Magazine.*

## 4 – VALPARAISO

**Dr. Samuel Gridley Howe**: Pioneer in the education of the blind; estab-lished an innovative school in 1832; admitted Laura Bridgman in 1837 and became world-renowned for educating a deaf-blind child for the first time. Helen Keller came to the school in 1888. For a contemporary's description of the school, see George Combe, *Notes on the United States of America during a Phrenological Visit in 1838–9–40*, Vol. I (Edinburgh, 1851), 184–191.

**I have some hope that the situation may be suitable to Mrs. Farnham**: Eliza Robbins to Dr. S. G. Howe, 20 February 1848, New York. Samuel P. Hayes Research Library, Perkins School for the Blind, Watertown, Massachusetts. Eliza Robbins (1796–1853), socially well connected, was active in New York philanthropies, including the New York Prison Association.

**Mrs F is in every way worthy**: John D. Russ to S. G. Howe, 14 March 1848, New York. Samuel P. Hayes Research Library, Perkins School for the Blind.

**Dr. Howe offered Mrs. Farnham the position**: S. G. Howe to EWF, 20 April 1848, Boston. Samuel P. Hayes Research Library, Perkins School for the Blind.

**You cannot imagine how I long to see**: EWF to John Bigelow, 29 June 1848, Boston. John Bigelow Papers, New York Public Library. Manuscripts and Archives Division, The New York Public Library. Astor, Lenox and Tilden Foundations.

**Laura Bridgman**: For an excerpt from Dr. Howe's diary on her instruction, see Combe, 456–462. For recent biographies, see Elisabeth Gitter's *The Imprisoned Guest: Samuel Howe and Laura Bridgman, the Original Deaf-Blind Girl* (New York: Farrar, Straus & Giroux, 2001), and Ernest Freeberg's *The Education of Laura Bridgman: First Deaf and Blind Person to Learn Language* (Boston: Harvard University Press, 2001).

**The even vivacity of her disposition**: EWF, "Laura Bridgman," in *The Prisoners' Friend*, Vol. I, No. III, November 1848. *The Prisoners' Friend* began publication in January 1846. Published weekly on Wednesdays, subscriptions $1 per year, it devoted its pages to the abolition of capital punishment, the improvement of prison discipline, and various reform topics, such as antislavery works by Lydia M. Child.

**an attachment Laura felt keenly**: Maud Howe and Florence Howe Hall, *Laura Bridgman, Dr. Howe's Famous Pupil and What He Taught Her* (Boston: Little, Brown, & Co., 1903), 232.

**In subsequent issues of the *Tribune***: *NYTr*, 13 April and 18 April 1849.

**My proposed expedition**: EWF to Lydia Sigourney, 11 April 1849, New York. Manuscript Collection, Connecticut Historical Society.

*Angelique* **cleared for San Francisco**: *New York Herald*, 20 May 1849; *Baltimore Sun*, 21 May 1849.

**Windsor refused**: Numerous contemporary diaries attest to the perversity of ship captains on the California route in 1849. Oscar Lewis, *Sea Routes to the Gold Fields* (New York, 1949), observed, "If one accepts the evidence of the diaries, a startling new sidelight on the great migration becomes clear: nine out of ten of the ships that sailed for California were in charge of men who should not have been entrusted with the command of a rowboat."

Most passenger vessels, like the whalers that had established the Cape Horn passage to California, called at a South Atlantic port, usually Rio de Janeiro or St. Catherine's Island, to replenish supplies. St. Catherine's, reputed for its excellent water, offered a fine, uncrowded harbor with fewer delays than Rio.

**in consequence of the bad water**: EWF quotations this chapter, *CI&O*, 1–21.

**After rounding Cape Horn**: California-bound ships frequently put in at Valparaiso, Chile, for wood and water. Typically, the Cape Horn passage took as much as a month to accomplish, and the full voyage from eastern seaport to San Francisco consumed, on average, two hundred days.

**no mention from Eliza Farnham's pen**: The accounts of those traveling by sea generally included vivid descriptions of the voyage. Even the least of these, like Mary Ann Elliott's 1850 letter from Rio de Janeiro—"i have seen some things that i never could at home"—(Van Ness Family Papers, BANC MSS C-B 462, The Bancroft Library, University of California, Berkeley) remark the novelty of the adventure. Even the most prosaic voyage, such as Mrs. Farnham affirms was the *Angelique*'s, included rough seas and bone-chilling winds and not a little terror. A more harrowing experience that

Dolly Bates survived aboard the *Nonamtum*, however, challenges imagination: "Owing to the violent motion of the ship, I was compelled…to keep my berth, to prevent being dashed against the cabin walls…Oh, it was terrible to lie so many hours listening to the roaring of the storm without!…I knew not then the imminent danger impending from fire as well as water; for, the second morning after the commencement of the storm, smoke had been discovered between decks.…Obliged to vacate the cabin, which was filled to suffocation with gas…for five consecutive days and nights, I remained in a chair…lashed to the deck. It was quite cold, and often I was drenched with the water and spray that would dash…across the deck. Never can I forget those dreary days of suffering that I sat gazing…upon the boundless expanse of tossing, foam-crested billows." (Mrs. D. B. Bates, *Incidents on Land and Water* [New York: Arno Press, 1974], 18–21).

Even an ordinary voyage meant storms, fog, cold, and damp, like that encountered by the *Bengal,* on which Elizabeth Gunn sailed with her four children: "Such fogs I never saw or felt. Everything was damp; sheets so wet that when you got into bed it was just like 'taking a wet sheet,' only you took two instead of one and a pillow besides. And your clothes when you dressed were as damp as if they had been wrung out of water the night before…real 'Cape Horn weather;'.…A storm began which lasted ten days. The roaring of the sea was like a thousand dragons.…Such waves!.…We could not go to the table for two days, the ship rolled so.…One day I got tired of waiting for the steward to come for my plate after dinner…so I got up and ventured out…and bang I came up against the other wall. I put my plates down and got back, and into my berth, and I did not venture out again that day." (Anna Lee Marston, ed., *Records of a California Family* [San Diego, Calif.: Donald I. Segerstrom Memorial Fund, 1928], 106–108.)

See also Dr. John E. Pomfret's *California Gold Rush Voyages, 1848–1849: Three Original Narratives* (The Huntington Library, 1954).

**very hilly, with not a tree to be seen anywhere:** Marstan, *Records of a California Family,* 116.

### 5 – SAN FRANCISCO

**Our voyage was miserable:** *NYTr,* 14 February 1850.

**To all the lady passengers on board that vessel:** *CI&O,* 20.

**if that could properly be called shore:** Ibid., 22.

**Mary Jane Megquier:** Robert Glass Cleland, ed., *Apron Full of Gold: The Letters of Mary Jane Megquier from San Francisco, 1849–1856* (San Marino, Calif.: The Huntington Library, 1949), 33.

**This is not a town, it is a quagmire**: A. P. Nasatir, ed., *A French Journalist in the California Gold Rush: The Letters of Etienne Derbec*, (Georgetown, Calif.: The Talisman Press, 1964), 87.

**with mud above the knees**: Margaret De Witt, 14 January 1850, San Francisco. De Witt Family Papers, BANC MSS 73/163 The Bancroft Library, University of California, Berkeley.

**Bold-faced unfortunates**: *CI&O*, 23. Jacqueline Barnhart's *The Fair but Frail: Prostitution in San Francisco 1849–1900* (Reno: University of Nevada Press, 1986) estimates seven hundred prostitutes in San Francisco at this time.

**This, then, was California**: *CI&O*, 21.

**San Francisco's great fire of December 24**: The fire began on the eastern side of the plaza, spread rapidly in both directions, and consumed "a whole line of buildings...on Washington street, between Montgomery and Kearny streets." (Frank Soulé, et al., eds., *The Annals of San Francisco*, [New York: D. Appleton & Co., 1854]; reprint [Palo Alto, Calif.: Lewis Osborne, 1966]), 16.

**The glare grew bolder, the flames dashed**: *AC*, 24 December 1849.

**thirty thousand arrivals that year**: Holliday, *Rush for Riches*, 94.

**There is nothing pleasant**: Megquier, 28.

**I found things here just as I had heard**: Franklin Buck, *A Yankee Trader in the Gold Rush* (New York: Houghton Mifflin Co., 1930), 45.

**A furious wind was blowing**: Bayard Taylor, *Eldorado, or, Adventures in the Path of Empire*. (New York: G. P. Putnam, 1850); reprint (Berkeley, Calif.: Heyday Books, 2000), 44. This lively classic of western literature chronicles Taylor's travels in California as a correspondent for Horace Greeley's *New York Tribune*. An accomplished man of letters, Taylor (1825–1878) also published novels, poems, and accounts of his travels in the Middle East, China, India, and Japan.

**not a brick house in the place**: William Taylor, *California Life Illustrated* (New York: Carlton & Porter, 1858), 19.

**The combined influences of intemperance**: *AC*, 21 January 1850.

**Women are more in requisition than gold**: *NYTr*, 13 February 1850.

**foolish hope of obtaining**: *CI&O*, 23.

**a breach of contract to convey plaintiff**: *AC*, 18 January 1850.

**considerable scandal**: *NYTr,* 9 March 1850. Alas, the *Tribune's* correspondent did not elaborate further on the delicious details here alluded to, nor have they surfaced in any document yet discovered.

**the case went to the jury**: *AC,* 18 January 1850.

## 6 – SANTA CRUZ

**landed like bales of goods**: EWF quotations this chapter, *CI&O,* 41ff.

**Thomas Russell**: Leon Rowland's *Santa Cruz, The Early Years* (Santa Cruz, Calif.: Paper Vision Press, 1980) claims that Russell's brother, John, operated a tile factory at Mount Pleasant, near New York's Sing Sing prison, suggesting that Mrs. Farnham knew the Russells from her years as prison matron. A Thomas Russell listed in H. H. Bancroft's *Pioneer Register* is not likely the same man.

**William Anderson**: One of several signatories to a letter of gratitude written to Farnham from the City of Tepic, Republic of Mexico, 24 May 1840. Charles L. Camp, ed., "The Journal of a 'Crazy Man': Travels and Scenes in California from the Year 1834 to the American Conquest—The Narrative of Albert Ferdinand Morris," *California Historical Society Quarterly,* XV, No. 2 (June 1936), 239.

**indebted to Thomas Jefferson Farnham for his rescue**: The *Honolulu Polynesian* (June 1840) provides a contemporary report: "Disturbances in California, And outrage committed upon the rights of Foreigners." Farnham recounted the Monterey episode in his *Travels in California and Scenes in the Pacific Ocean* (New York, 1844). Hubert Howe Bancroft, *History of California,* Vol. IV, 1–41; Churchill, "Thomas Jefferson Farnham," 517–537; and Doyce B. Nunis, Jr., *The Trials of Isaac Graham* (Los Angeles: Dawson's Book Shop, 1967) address this event in detail. See also Donald Munro Craig's introduction to William Robert Garner's *Letters from California 1846–1847* (Berkeley: University of California Press, 1970). When Farnham returned to California in 1847, Garner, in a defamation of character suit, sued Farnham for calling him a "runaway Botany Bay English convict" and "a vile fellow" (*Travels in California,* 78). Farnham, personally unacquainted with Garner, had reiterated Isaac Graham's opinion, and had no substantive defense. Due to various delays, the case failed to come to trial before Farnham died in 1848.

**Farnham had organized the Peoria Company**: Thomas J. Farnham, *Travels in the Great Western Prairies…and in the Oregon Territory* (New York: Greeley & McElrath, 1843); reprint (Monroe, Ore.: Northwest Interpretive Association, 1983).

**Lower Oregon!**: T. J. Farnham, *Travels in California*, 1.

**the first of several books**: *Travels in the Great Western Prairies* (1841), *Travels in California* (1844); *History of Oregon Territory* (1844); *Mexico* (1846).

**a phrenologist had "read" his head**: Joseph Buchanan made the inspection in St. Louis, 8 October 1835, listing eighteen qualities possessed by Farnham, including, "A *moderate* degree of amorous emotion." Emphasis not added. (Joseph Buchanan, "Phrenological Opinion on the head of T. J. Farnham," Misc. Mss. Farnham, T. J., courtesy of The New-York Historical Society).

**Captain John Paty's ship, *Don Quixote***: "Journal of Captain John Paty, 1807–1868," *California Historical Society Quarterly*, XIV, No. 4 (December 1835), 321.

**a stout, sturdy backwoodsman**: T. J. Farnham, *Travels in California*, 67–73.

**In '36 he had a distillery**: H. H. Bancroft, Pioneer Register, Vol. III, *History of California* (San Francisco: The History Company), 763.

## 7 – TRIALS AND HUMILIATIONS

**To this gentleman**: EWF quotations this chapter, *CI&O*, 72–108.

**Catherine Bennett**: Eldest daughter of Mary and Vardamon Bennett, who had trekked overland with their family to Oregon in 1842 and the following year moved south to California. There Mary Bennett separated from her husband and commenced a lumbering business on land acquired near Graham's property.

**outraged his bride's mother**: Mary Bennett appealed to Thomas Larkin, alcalde at Monterey, as the nearest authority, to separate the two. Larkin wrote the justice of the peace at Santa Cruz, Jose Antonio Bolcoff, who replied that "Graham said they were well married and that he would not separate from the side of [Catherine] Bennett, that he would lose a thousand lives before he would give her up...." See Nunis, *The Trials of Isaac Graham*, for a complete account.

**NOTICE.—Whereas, my wife Catherine**: *AC*, 20 April 1850.

**The little community**: *CI&O*, 89. Possibly Mrs. Farnham didn't know that Graham had remarried without divorcing his first wife, or that his marriage to Catherine was invalid regardless, or perhaps Mrs. Farnham shared, out of gratitude, her husband's misplaced admiration for the old mountain man. In any event, Mrs. Farnham's sympathies represented the minority.

Earlier, in 1846, more than twenty Santa Cruz residents signed a petition against Graham, averring that he was "perpetually corrupting the peace in our vicinity and for the last six years has not ceased to invite or attempt revolutions, challenges for duels, assassinations, and disobedience of the law." (Nunis, *The Trials of Isaac Graham*, 46). In *CI&O* Mrs. Farnham asserts that Graham was arrested for aiding his son in the killing of Catherine's brother, but Nunis states, "Isaac Graham was never arrested as an 'accessory to the murder which his son committed.' There is no extant evidence to support [Mrs. Farnham's] allegation. Perhaps she confused Captain Graham's arrest for assault and battery in June 1850—a matter which resulted in a fine—with Jesse's case." (Ibid., 96).

**The road across these mountains**: Forebear of present-day Highway 17. See Stephen Michael Payne, *A Howling Wilderness: A History of the Summit Road Area of the Santa Cruz Mountains 1850–1906* (Santa Cruz, Calif.: Loma Prieta Publishing, 1978).

**unable to learn anything alarming respecting his solvency**: Ruckel may have made bad investments with Farnham's money. "During the troublous and exciting winter of 1849–50, speculation had gone beyond all bounds both in every kind of merchandise and in real estate. When the reaction came, prices fell nearly as much below the prime cost of goods as previously they had been above it....Real estate, when forced on the market, often did not fetch a tenth of its recent value. Added to this sudden collapse of prices, three great fires had helped to ruin many, and had affected indeed every inhabitant of the city in some measure prejudicially." (Soulé, *Annals of San Francisco*, 289).

**William Grove Deal**: See W. Taylor, *California Life Illustrated*, 104, 144. Deal was in San Jose on 29 March when Taylor visited there: "The doctor filled his seat in the Legislature during the week, and preached the Gospel to his fellow law-makers on the Sabbath."

**the state's first legislature at San Jose**: "...the seat of government was hawked about for years in a manner disgraceful to the state. Monterey, San Jose, Sacramento, and Vallejo all desired and made bids...." (Bancroft, *History of California*, Vol. V, 321–325). San Jose hosted as capital of California's government in 1850, with Vallejo and Benicia serving in 1852 and 1853; not until 1855 did the state government relocate permanently at Sacramento.

**She returned to Santa Cruz**: En route Mrs. Farnham and Anderson, on 2 April 1850, recorded a deed (Book A of Deeds, p.14, Santa Clara County Records) for property in Santa Clara County. She alludes to this land in a letter written from Santa Cruz, 15 November 1850: "I find property enough here to make myself and the boys independent if a little pains be taken to use it advantageously. There are about 200 acres of land at this place [she writes from Santa Cruz, but her property there, according to the deed of 1847, consisted of 2,000 acres, not 200; she may have referred to arable land] 200 at the Mission of St Josephs 12 miles from the Capital San Jose and from 300 to 500 in the near vicinity of the Capital....I suppose it may take two or three years to get things in such a shape that I could leave the country with safety. It is no easy thing for a woman to defend property here. She may get it more easily than any where else in Christendom but all things are so unsettled and baseless that when one has property one must be ever on the alert to see that it is not taken from them, a watch that it is not easy for a woman to keep up." (Fowler-Wells Collections, Collection of Regional History and University Archives, Cornell University, Ithaca, New York).

## 8 – SUMMER 1850

**It seemed to me a great step taken**: EWF quotations this chapter, unless otherwise noted, *CI&O*, 104–189.

**famous as the Bloomer**: Amelia Bloomer declared, "'Bloomerism,' 'Bloomerites,' and 'Bloomers' were the headings of many an article, item and squib; and finally some one—I don't know to whom I am indebted for the honor—wrote the 'Bloomer Costume,' and the name has continued to cling to the short dress in spite of my repeatedly disclaiming all right to it and giving Mrs. Miller's name as that of the originator or the first to wear such dress in public. Had she not come to us in that style, it is not probable that either Mrs. Stanton or myself would have donned it." (D. C. Bloomer, *Life and Writings of Amelia Bloomer* [New York: Schocken Books, 1975], 68.) The 'Bloomer costume' inspired various designations, including "Turkish" and "Albanian," possibly to conjure the idea of harem pants.

**Mr. Allen informed me that he had no objection to marriage**: Madeleine B. Stern, "Two Letters from The Sophisticates of Santa Cruz," Book Club of California *Quarterly News-Letter*, XXXIII, No. 3 (Summer 1968), 51–62.

**Susannah belonged to the Swine family**: EWF, *Life in Prairie Land*, 95.

## 9 – GEORDIE

**Horace Greeley loaned her the money**: *Santa Cruz Daily Sentinel*, 29 January 1887, quoting from the *San Francisco Chronicle*: "Horace Greeley loaned her the money to come here with. She returned it to him after she had earned it keeping house for J. B. Hill, in the Pajaro Valley....Mr. Greeley sent Miss

Bruce a receipt that, as a matter of curiosity, is kept in the family at Santa Cruz. He wrote that he did not expect the return of the money, but that it came at an opportune moment, as there was a young man whom he wanted to assist, and he loaned it to him to "go west."

**Isthmus of Panama**: See John Haskell Kemble, "The Panama Route to the Pacific, 1848–1869," *Pacific Historical Review* (March 1938), 1–13.

**Would to God I could describe**: Megquier, 21.

**We…reached the rapids**: A. Gaylord Beaman, ed., "Pioneer Letters," *Historical Society of Southern California Quarterly* (March 1939), 27–29.

**Mrs. Megquier visited the church at Gorgona**: Megquier, 21.

**Jessie Benton Fremont**: She planned to meet her husband in California. John C. Fremont, the famed "Pathfinder," had privately organized an expedition to cross the Rockies.

**I had a caution given me**: Jessie Benton Fremont, *A Year of American Travel: Narrative of Personal Experience* (San Francisco: Book Club of San Francisco, 1960), 31.

**A description…bearing any resemblance**: Emmeline Hubbard Day Journal, 1853–1856. BANC MSS 74/170, The Bancroft Library, University of California, Berkeley.

**I got along finely**: Beaman, "Pioneer Letters," 27–29.

**A lady from Maine**: B. Taylor, *Eldorado*, 24.

**There was nothing for it but to cling**: Mallie Stafford, *The March of Empire* (San Francisco: Geo. Spaulding & Co., 1884), 28–29.

**caught Sarah Brooks by surprise**: Sarah Merriam Brooks, *Across the Isthmus to California in '52* (San Francisco: C. A. Murdock & Co., 1894), 63.

**Georgiana found work in San Francisco**: Stern, "Two Letters," 60.

**As Colton observed**: Walter Colton, *The California Diary* (Oakland, Calif.: Biobooks, 1948), 207.

**arrival of Geordie**: *CI&O*, 158–166.

**the matter of the flour mill**: *Ibid.*, 167–168.

**Eliza wrote her friends, Orson and Lorenzo Fowler**: Stern, "Two Letters," 55–59.

**Especially any thing touching the Knocking Spirits**: In 1848, in Rochester, New York, young sisters Margaret and Kate Fox asserted that through a series of raps and knocks, in a playful attempt to communicate with the spirits of the dead, they summoned the spirit of Charles Haynes, who, rapping in reply, told them he had been killed and was buried in the basement of their home. When bones were discovered there, both the girls and their ghostly manipulations became a sensation. The belief that raps and knocks provided communication with those who had passed to the other side attracted adherents in staggering numbers. For a comprehensive overview of the impact, see Ann Braude, *Radical Spirits: Spiritualism and Women's Rights in Nineteenth-Century America* (Boston: Beacon Press, 1989).

**And so we gathered gradually our "plunder"**: *CI&O*, 169.

## 10 – AGRICULTURAL OPERATIONS

**concluded to enter upon "agricultural operations"**: EWF quotations this chapter, *CI&O*, 177–212.

**Worcester convention of 1850**: Although many in the women's rights movement saw the "color issue" as too divisive for the cause of women's rights, the Worcester Convention passed a resolution calling for "equality before the law, without distinction of sex or color."

**In 1843, she had debated**: A lengthy and lively exchange appeared in the *Brother Jonathan*, V, 24 June 1843; 15 and 29 July 1843. Mrs. Farnham denied Neal's accusation that she considered women inferior: "You say much of the *inferiority* which I have assumed of woman.—You misapprehend me—I acknowledge no inferiority....A *difference* I have assumed, but this does not *necessarily* imply *inferiority*."

**Georgiana wrote Charlotte Wells**: Stern, "Two Letters," 60.

## 11 – A LAST HOLIDAY

**The four adventurers set off**: The propriety of such an outing likely raised few eyebrows. Social conventions generally deteriorated with the trip west, as a male traveler crossing the Isthmus of Panama observed:

"On awakening, and sitting up in my cot, I was astonished to see a young woman sitting up also in the next cot to me, and fastening the back of her dress; while all around were upwards of a hundred men perhaps, in every stage of rising and dressing. My evident astonishment compelled me to observe to her that I thought it a very unpleasant predicament for a young lady to be placed in, and she replied that it was; but she had become accustomed to such inconveniences, having crossed the Isthmus several times!" J. Goldsborough Bruff, *Gold Rush: The Journals, Drawings, and Other Papers of J. Goldsborough Bruff, April 2, 1849–July 20, 1851* (New York: Columbia University Press, 1949), 513.

A boardinghouse keeper in the mines testified that conventions remained relaxed there:

"We have an open chamber...divided off by a cloth. The gentlemen occupy one end, Mrs. H—and daughter, your father and myself, the other. We have a curtain hung between our beds, but we do not take pains to draw it, as it is of no use to be particular here...." Walker D. Wyman, ed., *California Emigrant Letters* (New York: Bookman Associates, 1971), 147.

For Eliza's account of the strawberry excursion, see *CI&O*, 213–247.

**For a time he tanned leather at Astoria**: W. W. Elliott, *Santa Cruz County, Calif. Illustrated with Historical Sketch* (San Francisco: Wallace W. Elliott & Co., 1879); reprint (Santa Cruz, Calif.: The Museum of Art and History at The McPherson Center, 1997), 24–26.


## 12 – OBSERVATIONS

**In the accessions the state is constantly receiving**: EWF quotations this chapter, *CI&O*, 262–352.


## 13 – MARCH 23, 1852

**There is much belonging to the relation of marriage**: *IA*, 301.

**[My mother] married as her second husband:** Charles Farnham interview, "Information Concerning Charles H. Farnham." California State Library, Sacramento.

**one of the four men who rescued Louis Napoleon:** A French law of 1816 exiled the Bonapartes from France. Louis Napoleon, nephew of the emperor, spent his youth in Italy, Germany, and Switzerland. In Italy, he was connected with such revolutionary groups as the Carbonari. In 1836 he tried to overthrow the French monarchy of Louis Philippe, and in 1840 attempted a second insurrection, at Boulogne-sur-Mer. He was tried, sentenced to life imprisonment, and detained in the fortress of Ham. Fitzpatrick claimed to have aided the escape in 1846, when Napoleon walked out of the prison, disguised as a laborer, and went to England.

**There were many girls belonging**: GBK quotations this chapter, *GBK Journal*, 62–65.

**From November 1851, until the harvest of 1852**: "Watsonville Correspondence," *Santa Cruz Pacific Sentinel*, 15 September 1860.

**It was the 23ʳᵈ of March**: Marriage Certificate, Richard Kirby to Georgiana Bruce, Santa Cruz County Records.

**Georgiana didn't even dismount her horse**: Mary Hallock Foote, *A Victorian Gentlewoman in the Far West* (San Marino, Calif.: The Huntington Library, 1972), 144.

**deeds and promissory notes**: EWF to Thomas Russell, 23 March, 1852, Book I, Santa Cruz County Index to Deeds, p. 297; EWF to R. C. Kirby, 23 March 1852, Book I, Santa Cruz County Index to Deeds, p. 300; Santa Cruz County Records.

**California's Land Act of 1851**: See Bancroft, *History of California*, Vol. VI, 536–568. On 2 March 1853, Thomas Russell and EWF filed a claim before the Land Commission. Transcript No. 383SD, U.S. District Court of Appeal. The Bancroft Library. A deposition by Isaac Graham, 10 July 1855, confirmed Thomas J. Farnham's purchase.

**This is to certify**: Marriage Certificate, William Fitzpatrick to Eliza W. Farnham, Santa Cruz County Records.

**the Arcans and Briers**: See Frank F. Latta, *Death Valley '49ers* (Santa Cruz, Calif.: Bear State Books, 1979).

**destined for a terrible story**: *Santa Cruz Pacific Sentinel*, 20 March 1862.

## 14 – BABIES

**I am persuaded that it is better**: *IA*, 377.

**the thoughts that occupied her**: GBK quotations this chapter, *GBK Journal*, 61–82.

**It is the great wealth of our mortal life**: *IA*, 145.

**Luther Farnham**: See Santa Cruz County Probate Court Document No. 43, Petition by Luther Farnham for "Guardianship of the Minors C. H. and E. H. Farnham," 22 January 1853. The court approved Luther Farnham's sale of the land, in June, for $1,500 at auction to the highest bidder, who, interestingly, was William Fitzpatrick. Luther Farnham eventually became a leading citizen in Santa Cruz. In 1858 he was a member of a joint stock company organized for the purpose of constructing a turnpike road (*Santa Cruz Pacific Sentinel*, 24 April 1858), and in 1861 proprietor of the Exchange Hotel. In 1866 he listed his occupation as saloon keeper; in 1879 he was justice of the peace.

**Deborah Gannett**: *GBK Journal*, 103.

**It is a Godlike joy**: *IA*, 377.

**the first to greet man**: EWF, "Rights Of Women, Reply To Mr. Neal's Lecture. By Mrs. T. J. Farnham," *Brother Jonathan*, Vol. V, 24 June 1843.

**Mrs. F's dishonorable conduct**: Whatever financial imposition Eliza made upon the Kirbys is unfortunately not further revealed, although Georgiana clearly resented the debt of $2,000 and Eliza for causing it.

**Eliza quoted an authority who said that meant "music"**: James Redfield, author of *Outline of a New System of Physiognomy*. Mrs. Farnham corresponded with Redfield and quoted him extensively in Volume II of *Woman and Her Era*.

## 15 – HEARTACHE

**I knew there were feeling hearts**: *CI&O*, 18.

**I cannot forget the paroxysms**: Ibid., 19.

**If so terrible an experience**: *IA*, 176.

**Young Charlie, during one of Fitzpatrick's violent**: Charles Farnham interview.

**Rather a wearisome, hopeless time**: *GBK Journal*, 82.

**By the last mail I wrote you a note**: EWF to Parke Godwin, 25 June 1855, Santa Cruz. Bryant-Godwin Papers. Manuscripts and Archives Division, The New York Public Library. Astor, Lenox and Tilden Foundations.

**Adna Hecox**: The Hecox family emigrated to California in 1846. See Margaret M. Hecox, *California Caravan* (San Jose, Calif.: Harlan-Young Press, 1966). Adna Hecox, a lay minister, helped establish the first Methodist church in Santa Cruz. In 1850 the Reverend William Taylor arrived in Santa Cruz to organize the First Quarterly Conference. "They had also the best school, and the largest Sunday school, in the country. There were the Anthony, Case, Bennett, and Hecox families and others...." (W. Taylor, *California Life Illustrated*, 127).

**His sermon, though pronounced**: *CI&O*, 138.

**Eliza had given up on Fitzpatrick**: Apparently Fitzpatrick had left Santa Cruz, likely following Eddie's death. By mid-1854, he was in San Francisco, engaged in his trade of street contractor, grading and planking Broadway, between Dupont and Kearny (*AC*, 6 October 1854). In 1859 Fitzpatrick was arrested for assault and battery upon a Matthew Ryan and fined $600 (*San Francisco Daily Evening Bulletin*, 17 May, 14 June 1859).

**Since writing my last to you**: EWF to Parke Godwin, 11 August 1855, San Jose, California. Bryant-Godwin Papers.

**Our boy never grew better**: EWF, *Life in Prairie Land*, 163–65.

**I am hoping very earnestly**: EWF to Godwin, 11 August 1855.

**sent Charles to New York**: In his absence Mrs. Farnham petitioned the Santa Cruz probate court for a new guardian to collect rents and oversee her son's Santa Cruz County property. Luther Farnham, she testified, "has been absent a long time & not heard from & is not in correspondence with the family." Charles, "now residing in the State of New York...requires another and additional guardian." The court agreed to her request to name three guardians, including Richard Kirby (Petition for Appointment of Another Guardian of Minor Charles Farnham, 17 January 1856). On 6 February 1861, Charles, again a resident of Santa Cruz County, petitioned the court to reappoint his uncle, Luther Farnham, as his guardian (Santa Cruz County Probate Court Case No. 43).

**All hope of growth in Santa Cruz**: *GBK Journal*, 82–84.

## 16 – TICKETS AT THE DOOR

**San Francisco's Musical Hall**: Opened in July 1853 and, until destroyed by fire in January 1860, served as the city's premier public hall. Rebuilt as Platt's Music Hall in August 1860 and relocated to the east side of Montgomery, between Bush and Pine.

**Her style of reading was grave throughout**: *Daily California Chronicle*, 26 January 1856.

**a "free Lecture on Phrenology**: *St. Louis Argus*, 11 June 1840.

**It is well known to most of our readers**: Quoted in Davies, *Phrenology, Fad and Science*, 12.

**Orson S. Fowler**: See Stern, *Heads & Headlines;* also Davies, *Phrenology, Fad and Science*.

**introduced to his studious young sister:** *MED,* 418.

**I am the greatest Phrenologist ever lived***:* Kelly E. Burhans to Mary Wood Roberts, 17 January 1836. Letters of Kelly E. Burhans of Potters Hollow, N.Y. to his sister Mary Wood Roberts in Illinois, January 29, 1830–July 1, 1838. New York State Library.

**I am going the whole hog***:* Ibid., 10 January 1837.

**MRS. FARNHAM, a Western lady:** *NYTr,* 7 November 1842.

**Mr. Editor:—I have been so much pained:** *San Francisco Daily Evening Bulletin,* 23 January 1856.

**The second free lecture by Mrs. Farnham:** Ibid., 28 January 1856.

**Mr. King.—…Say to Mrs. Farnham:** Ibid.

**MRS. FARNHAM'S LECTURE LAST EVENING:** *Daily California Chronicle,* 30 January 1856.

## 17 – PRISON REPORT

**The State established a prison system:** See Bancroft, *History of California,* Vol. VI, 740ff, on crime and punishment; also Clinton T. Duffy, *The San Quentin Story* (New York: Pocket Books, 1951).

**There are nearly 400 men confined:** "Letter from Mrs. E. W. Farnham as to State Prison Matters," *Daily California Chronicle,* 9 February 1856.

**I too might speak "at random":** "Mrs. Farnham and the Ladies of San Francisco," *San Francisco Daily Evening News,* 11 February 1856.

**When another prison is to be erected:** *Daily California Chronicle,* 9 February 1856.

## 18 – SACRAMENTO AND BEYOND

**Monterey hosted the constitutional convention:** See Bancroft, *History of California,* Vol. VI, 251ff, for the state's political history.

**densely crowded with a very intelligent audience:** "Lecture by Mrs. Farnham," *Sacramento Daily Union,* 5 February 1856.

**legislative discussion the morning after Mrs. Farnham's appearance:** "From Seventh Session Legislature Notes," *Sacramento Daily Union,* 5 February 1856.

**with marked attention, pleasure, and we hope profit**: "The Lecture," Ibid., 9 February 1856.

**Her manner was mild and expressive**: "Free Lecture," *Sacramento Democratic State Journal,* 9 February 1856.

**I had the opportunity of listening**: *The American Phrenological Journal,* April 1856, quoted in Book Club of California *Quarterly News-Letter,* XXXIII, No. 3 (Summer 1968), 61.

**This lady lectured in Auburn**: "Mrs. Farnham," *Placer Herald,* 1 March 1856.

**Female lecturers.—Lately was chronicled**: *Nevada Journal,* 8 February 1856.

**Eliza did not disappoint her admirer:** Ibid., 1 March 1856.

**Dear Madam:—As very many persons:** "Mrs. Farnham's Lecture on Civilization," *Daily California Chronicle,* 23 April 1856.

**Mrs. Farnham promptly replied**: Ibid.

**the spiritual mania in san francisco**: *Sacramento Daily Union,* 13 February 1856.

**I accept the alleged phenomena:** *IA,* 391.

**In her "Women of the Pacific States" lecture**: *Daily California Chronicle,* 3 May 1856. On 9 February 1843 the *New York Tribune* published a letter from Mrs. Farnham in which she argued for property rights for women but against suffrage: "I have no desire that my sex should acquire political privileges, so called."

**The *lord* gave completely out**: Mrs. Farnham was undoubtedly referring to Santa Cruz's first Methodist minister, James W. Brier. For an account of the Briers' harrowing trip west, see William Manly Lewis, *Death Valley in '49* (San Jose: The Pacific Tree and Vine Co., 1894); reprint (Berkeley, Calif.: Heyday Books, 2001).

## 19 – THE FIRST BY A LADY

**Pacific Mail Steamship *John L. Stephens:*** *AC,* 5 July 1856.

**I have waited as long as it seems possible**: EWF to Joshua Dix, 28 August 1856. Dix, Edwards & Co. Papers, bMS Am 800.13. Houghton Library, Harvard University.

**Reviews, good ones**: *NYTr,* 20 November 1856.

**wrote the editor of the *Daily California Chronicle***: Reprinted in *Santa Cruz Pacific Sentinel,* 4 October 1856.

**Seventh Annual National Woman's Rights convention**: *NYTr*, 22 November 1856.

**her old friend, Mrs. Francis Wright**: EWF to Mrs. Francis Wright, 12 November 1842, New York. Department of Rare Books and Manuscripts, Boston Public Library.

**A general discussion of the wants of California**: *NYTr*, 2 December 1856.

**Life in Sing Sing Prison**: *NYTr*, 6 January 1857.

**While in Iowa, she met Colonel Vaughan**: EWF to John Beeson, 5 May 1857, New York, quoted in John Beeson, *A Plea for the Indians* (New York: J. Beeson, 1857), 134–138.

**a letter she received the following spring**: Ibid.

**I have always felt a deep interest in the Indian Race**: Ibid.

**only grown up children."** Dr. John Marsh, a Harvard graduate, Indian agent, and California pioneer, quoted in Albert L. Hurtado, *Indian Survival on the California Frontier* (New Haven, Conn.: Yale University Press, 1988), 74.

**Enclosed with this, is a story**: EWF to Joshua Dix, 31 July 1857. Dix, Edwards & Co. Papers.

**As I have not heard**: Ibid., EWF to Joshua Dix, 7 August 1857.

**The alleged fault**: Ibid., EWF to Joshua Dix, 15 August 1857.

**LETTER FROM MRS. FARNHAM:** *California Farmer*, San Francisco, 9 October 1857.

## 20 – WOMEN'S PROTECTIVE EMIGRATION SOCIETY

**The *Central America* was some two hundred miles off the Carolina coast**: Gary Kinder, *Ship of Gold in the Deep Blue Sea* (New York: Atlantic Monthly Press, 1998) relates the SS *Central America*'s harrowing final hours and the extraordinary story of how, 131 years later, visionary engineer Tommy Thompson recovered its gold.

**Sir: The extreme suffering and destitution**: *California Farmer*, 8 January 1858.

**The farmers are nearly all short of help**: "Employment in the West.— Extract from a Private Letter, dated Monmouth, Illinois, Nov. 15, 1857," *NYTr*, 25 November 1857.

**There are women who will hear and read**: "Woman and the Crisis," *NYTr*, 4 December 1857.

**organizing the Women's Protective Emigration Society**: *NYTr*, 6 December 1857. New York's population figures exploded during the 1850s, increasing 65 percent in a decade. Jobs disappeared with economic depression, reducing thousands to destitution and swelling the city's charity rolls. The Women's Protective Emigration Society was not the first organization to adopt the expedient of sending superfluous labor to the country. See Carl N. Degler, "The West as a Solution to Urban Unemployment," *New York History*, XXXVI (1955), 63–84.

**presented Richard Kirby with his third daughter**: *GBK Journal*, 109.

**forty women sponsored...Women's Protective Emigration Society**: *NYTr*, 31 December 1857.

**We dilate, mentally, if there be no audience present**: *California Farmer*, 8 January 1858.

**In my last I said a word about pictures**: Ibid., 5 February 1858.

**It was my inestimable privilege to share Mr. Hog's progress**: Ibid., 9 April 1858.

**Capital road is the Great Western**: Ibid., 7 May 1858.

**She wrote about politics, and the Kansas border war, about the British art exhibition, the weather, the generosity of a New Yorker**: Ibid., 5 February, 5 March, 9 April, 7 May 1858.

**You have heard of our great Revival**: Ibid., 7 May 1858.


## 21 – WOMAN'S APPROPRIATE SPHERE

**But I seek to establish a higher claim**: *W&HE*, Vol. I, 234.

**May 13, 1858, women's rights advocates convened their eighth national convention**: Due to the financial disruptions of late 1857, and the unavailability of many of the movement's leaders, the National Woman's Rights Convention planned for that year in New York City was postponed. (See Yuri Suhl, *Ernestine L. Rose and the Battle for Human Rights* [New York: Reynal and Company, 1957], 197.)

**Susan B. Anthony presided**: *History of Woman Suffrage, Vol. I, 1848–1861*, 668f.

**Thomas Wentworth Higginson**: Harvard Divinity School graduate, reformer, lecturer, and devoted abolitionist, Higginson later achieved fame for his twenty-five year correspondence with Emily Dickinson.

**Lucy Stone had organized, in *1850***: See Betsy Covington Smith, *Women Win the Vote* (Englewood Cliffs, N.J.: Silver Burdett Press, 1989); also Leslie Wheeler, "Lucy Stone: Radical Beginnings" in *Feminist Theorists: Three Centuries of Key Women Thinkers,* edited by Dale Spender (New York: Pantheon Books, 1983).

**Antoinette Brown Blackwell**: Wife of Samuel C. Blackwell, brother to Henry B. Blackwell, who had married Antoinette's Oberlin College friend Lucy Stone. The distinguished family included Elizabeth Blackwell, the first woman to graduate from medical school.

**One of Eliza's resolutions**: *NYTr,* 14 May 1858. For convention reportage, see the *New York Times,* 14 May 1858.

**It was a long speech Eliza made that night**: *History of Woman Suffrage, Vol. I, 1848–1861,* 669.

**I propose if nothing happens to hinder me**: EWF to Joshua Dix, 2 June 1858. Dix, Edwards & Co. Papers.

**Raritan Bay Union**: See Maud Honeyman Greene, "Raritan Bay Union, Eagleswood, New Jersey," *Proceedings of the New Jersey Historical Society,* 68, No. 1 (January 1950), 1–20.

**famed Grimke sisters**: Sarah (1792–1873) and Angelina (1805–1879) Grimke were among the first women to speak publicly in the United States, defying abuse and ridicule as early lecturers on abolitionism and women's rights.

**"The City of Perth Amboy"**: Henry David Thoreau to Sophia Thoreau, 1 November 1856. *The Correspondence of Henry David Thoreau,* edited by Walter Harding and Carl Bode (New York: New York University Press, 1958), 439–440.

**This is a lovely spot of retirement**: Henry C. Howells to Milo Adams Townsend, from Raritan Bay, Perth Amboy, 31 December 1854, in *Milo Adams Townsend and Social Movements of the Nineteenth Century,* edited by Peggy Jean Townsend and Charles Walker Townsend III. Historical Documents Collection. Beaver County History Online (www.bchistory.org), Beaver County, Pennsylvania.

**We have been having a visit from Mrs. Farnham**: Susan Lesley to Catherine Robbins, Eagleswood, Summer 1858. Mary L. Ames, ed., *Life and Letters of Peter and Susan Lesley,* Vol. I (New York: G. P. Putnam's Sons, 1909), 358–359.

**All Philanthropists and reformers**: *The Burlington Free Press* (weekly ed.), 4 June 1858. *Proceedings of the Free Convention Held at Rutland, Vt., July 25th, 26th, and 27th, 1858* (Boston: J. B. Yerrington and son, 1858).

**medley of people...of heterodox notions**: "Radicals in Council," *NYT*, 29 June 1858.

**Spiritualists dominated the convention**: "The Reformers' Free Convention," *NYTr*, 29 June 1858.

**We must first ascertain the truth**: *Proceedings of the Free Convention Held at Rutland*, 34.

**If the convention was not called**: Ibid.

**My friend, Mrs. Rose**: Ibid.

**The most sacred and important right**: Ibid., 9.

**Eliza Farnham spoke on Saturday afternoon**: Ibid., 67–69.

**She began with the announcement**: "The Reformers' Free Convention," *NYTr*, 29 June 1858.

**I believe that to-day, with the force of the truths I have**: *Proceedings of the Free Convention Held at Rutland*, 69.

**One of the queerest conventions on record**: *Brooklyn Daily Times*, 29 June 1858, "The Radicals in Council," in *I Sit and Look Out: Editorials from the Brooklyn Daily Times by Walt Whitman*, edited by Emory Holloway and Vernolian Schwarz (New York: Columbia University Press, 1932), 45–46.

**but he informs me that he has no arrangement**: EWF to Joseph L. Warren, 19 July 1858. Joseph L. Warren Papers, BANC MSS C-B 418, The Bancroft Library, University of California, Berkeley.

**The Cause and Cure of Evil**: *NYT*, 2 September 1858.

**About 1,500 persons were present**: *NYTr*, 21 September 1858.

## 22 – SELDOM THE BEST INTELLECTS

**Ora was a most troublesome child**: GBK quotations this chapter, *GBK Journal*, 69–90.

**John Sheridan Zelie, the Congregationalist pastor**: Elliot, *Santa Cruz County*, 69.

**There was a supper, a post-office, and a "grab-bag" for entertainment:** The 'post-office' Mrs. Kirby mentions was likely a variation on the charming fund-raiser hosted by the church-building women of Nevada City, reported on by Charles Ferguson. The activity not only collected funds for a good cause but presumably relieved the local express company of otherwise undeliverable letters:

"Miss Bowers kept the 'post-office' at that bazaar, and no sooner than a fellow got inside, after paying two dollars entrance fee, than he was notified by the pleasant postmistress that there was a letter in the office for him. I was young and felt quite flattered when notified by that young lady, in her most winsome manner, that she had in her official keeping a letter for me. I stepped up and received a letter at her hands, and was in the act of returning her gracious smile...when she said, in the sweetest of womanly accents, "Two dollars and fifty cents." I paid it with alacrity. When I opened it I found it to be written in Dutch or Indian, not a word of which could I make out. I was not wise enough to keep the joke to myself, but must go and tell her. "Dear me, how stupid I was," said she; "but here is your letter," handing me another. I was innocent enough to receive it, when the same sweet seductive voice repeated: "Two dollars and a half," and I again discharged my obligation to the post-office without shedding a tear." Charles D. Ferguson, *California Gold Fields* (Oakland, Calif.: Biobooks, 1948), 105.

### 23 – TO G. B. K.

**Eliza's autobiographical manuscript:** Eliza Farnham, for reasons known only to herself, changed the names of people and places in her book. Her brother Kelly is "John"; Thomas Jefferson Farnham is "Mr. Harrington"; her beloved sister Mary, interestingly, retains her name. Eliza identifies the childless middle-aged couple with whom she spent her abusive childhood only as "Uncle John" and "Aunt Phebe" Smalley, fictitious names possibly chosen because they were not strangers to the Burhans family. In the book, a hired boy, a blood nephew of "Aunt," says of Eliza's mother: "She was a Quaker, though; for my aunt says she was, and I guess she knows." The implication, clearly, is that Mary Wood Burhans was known to the family. Eliza retorts, "The bad Quaker is your aunt—she's no relation of mine nor my mother's."

On another occasion, a member of a canal-surveying expedition says, "I shall go in and see more of your—what is it?—your aunt?" Eliza retorts: "No, sir," I replied, indignantly; "she is not my aunt at all; I call her so because I can't bear to call her mother, though I am her adopted daughter. She is no relation of mine."

It is probably irrelevant to make much of Eliza's repeated protest that she is unrelated to this "aunt," but she was likely connected to the couple through the uncle. He is good to her, despite his failure to protest his wife's mistreatment, and Eliza clearly is fond of him. She described "Uncle John" as a man of about fifty, balding, inclined to stoutness, possessing a gentle temperament. Impoverished and uneducated as a youth, he had gone to sea and in the early years of the War of 1812 been taken prisoner. He had got exchanged and fled to western New York where, industrious and enterprising, he became the respected owner of a large property. Eliza would remember him as happiest on winter nights, sitting in a large chair angled toward the hearth, smoking his pipe and telling stories by the fire. Eliza had his sympathy, for which she was grateful, but never his intervention. His domestic life was subjugated by his marriage of twenty years to a woman better educated than he, handsome in her earlier years, well-bred, intelligent, and spirited.

Researcher Gladys Tilden was convinced that the connection was the uncle. In Eliza's book, uncle "John Smalley" is appointed postmaster. Pitt Petri's *Postal History of Western New York* names James Wood (whom Tilden concluded was Mary Wood Burhans' brother) as being appointed postmaster to Woods Hollow (later Wales Hollow), Wales Township, Erie County, Pennsylvania, at a time and location consistent with references in *MED* (Tilden to Ridgway McNallie, Buffalo and Erie County Public Library, 3 May 1964. BANC MSS 89/229, Gladys Tilden Papers.)

**In one of the first scenes**: *MED,* 56ff.

**Eliza Burhans was born November 17, 1815**: Samuel Burhans, Jr., *Burhans Genealogy* (New York: privately printed, 1894), 193.

**When Eliza was just four**: Mary Wood Burhans died in 1820. Eliza remembered her mother's death in her first book (*Life in Prairie Land,* 229).

**At six, Eliza was sent off**: Until age fifteen, Eliza labored on a dairy farm in western New York, and yearned for the education each year promised and each year denied. There was no going home, for her father died when she was twelve. When she at last realized her so-called aunt and uncle would never send her to school, she wrote her father's brother that if he didn't come for her she would run away—and finally was rescued from a loveless home and servitude.

**I had ever a dread**: *MED,* 21.

**Had I loved, and been loved**: Ibid., 41.

**Kelly paid her tuition for a year at a Quaker boarding school**: Kelly Burhans to Mary Roberts, 12 April 1832, Cincinnati. Letters of Kelly E. Burhans.

**when she was eighteen, a year at the Albany Female Academy:** Albany Academy for Girls to Tilden, 26 November 1962: "In an old account book...we found a record of Kelly Burhans, a patron, who was billed for tuition in 1834 and again in 1836." (BANC MSS 89/229, Gladys Tilden Papers.)

**she was still in New York City, writing and lecturing:** *NYTr,* 21 May 1859.

**Mrs. F.'s views on the question of woman are peculiar:** Ibid., 23 May 1859.

**Her remarks referred to woman and her organic traits:** Ibid., 25 May 1859.

**Judge Edmonds...embrace of spiritualism:** Ibid., 23 May 1859.

**Mrs. F will not return to Cal.:** *GBK Journal,* 88.

## 24 – A SPIRITUALIST SEASON

**Here I am at last after three years absence:** EWF to Joshua Dix, 9 August 1859, Santa Cruz. Dix, Edwards & Co. Papers.

**Mrs. Farnham has returned to Cal:** *GBK Journal,* 24 September 1859. GBK quotations this chapter, *GBK Journal,* 91–94.

**It was also very uncomfortable:** EWF to Joshua Dix, 9 August 1859, Santa Cruz. Dix, Edwards & Co. Papers.

**I find myself so straitened:** EWF to Joseph L. Warren, 24 July 1859. Joseph L. Warren Papers.

**Dr. Rawson:** Asa Warren Rawson was a physician in "declining health" at this time (Elliot, *Santa Cruz County,* 83).

**I was much pleased with the enthusiasm:** *Santa Cruz News,* 9 September 1859.

**asked to speak on politics:** Ibid., 21 September 1859.

**creating "a great sensation" in Santa Cruz:** *AC,* 28 August 1859.

**at the request of the Society of Spiritualists:** *Santa Cruz News,* 31 August 1859.

**Sarah Moore Clarke:** In 1858, Edward C. Kemble described Mrs. Clarke as "an estimable lady and accomplished writer" who edited her paper "with much ability....Mrs. Clarke now resides in San Leandro and, we are pained to add, is slowly passing away under the ravages of her disease." (Kemble, *History of California Newspapers;* reprint: Los Gatos, Calif.: Talisman Press, 1962). Mrs. Clarke died in 1880, age 60 (*AC,* 17 April 1880).

**It was the first news I had of B & A's failure:** EWF to Joshua Dix, 7 September 1859. Dix, Edwards & Co. Papers.

**if nothing can be done in the use of electricity for her:** Georgiana, Eliza, and much of the general public at this time believed in the therapeutic powers of electric and magnetic fields. Various so-called galvanic devices utilizing electromagnetism and other forms of electricity were invented and touted for their magical powers to cure a wide variety of diseases. See Edward B. Foot, *Plain Home Talk and Medical Common Sense* (New York: Murray Hill Publishing Co., 1884).

**Eliza wrote William Lloyd Garrison:** EWF to William Lloyd Garrison, 25 September 1859, San Francisco. William Lloyd Garrison Papers, Boston Public Library.

**more followed, as well as a series on the history of African slavery:** *Santa Cruz News*, 28 September; 5, 12, 19 October; 2, 9, 16 November; 21 December 1859.

**Last evening the Hall of the Sons of Temperance:** *San Francisco National*, reprinted in *Santa Cruz News*, 16 October 1859.

**LECTURE.—All of our readers will be interested:** *Santa Cruz News*, 21 December 1859.

## 25 – EXALTED POSSIBILITIES

**Never were such exalted possibilities:** *Santa Cruz News*, 27 January 1860.

**"The News" still continues:** *GBK Journal*, 94.

**By 1860, the Kirby tannery numbered:** *Santa Cruz Pacific Sentinel*, 17 August 1860.

**Women who give undue attention to dress:** *Santa Cruz News*, 20 April 1860.

**A train had been stopped:** *Santa Cruz Pacific Sentinel*, 18 November 1859.

**We prate loudly:** Ibid., 3 February 1860.

**No wonder that while they look:** *Santa Cruz News*, 27 January 1860.

**A notice of Santa Cruz:** *AC*, 30 August 1860.

**No one need be deterred:** *Santa Cruz News*, 22 June 1860.

**Mental and moral idleness is the cause of gossip:** *Santa Cruz News*, 29 June 1860.

**Died of starvation at Santa Cruz, the Santa Cruz News**: Quoted in *GBK Journal*, 108. Slocum moved to San Jose, where, according to the *Santa Cruz Pacific Sentinel* (3 August 1860), he bought an existing newspaper, the *San Jose Telegraph*, subsequently renamed the *San Jose Mercury*.

**Mr. Editor:—Will you give the following statement**: *Santa Cruz Pacific Sentinel*, 18 October 1860.

**Thanks to our neighbor for his offer**: Ibid., 25 October 1860.

## 26 – STOCKTON

**Every building from Center to El Dorado Street**: Martin V. Covert, *Stockton Album through the Years* (Stockton, Calif.: privately printed, 1959), 135.

**Doctor Ryer had pointed out**: George H. Tinkham, *A History of Stockton* (San Francisco, Calif.: W. M. Hinton, 1880), 275.

**It appears from the tables**: Ibid.

**Forty-two patients...insane from intemperance**: Ibid., 276.

**Supposed cause" for confinement**: "Table First, An Exhibit of Patients received in, continuing, and discharged from the Asylum," California State Archives document GP1:373–374, Stockton State Hospital.

**Stockton's newspaper noted her appointment**: *San Joaquin Republican*, 16 April 1861. See also *AC*, 16 April 1861; *San Francisco Evening Bulletin*, 17 April 1861; and the *Sacramento Daily Bee*, 19 April 1861.

**The appointment is one well deserved**: *Santa Cruz Pacific Sentinel*, 25 April 1861.

**For the current year, ending June 30th, 1861**: *San Francisco Daily Times*, 18 April 1861.

**The mad house—its construction**: Ibid.

**more than four hundred patients**: Ninth Annual Report of the Trustees for the Insane Asylum, for the Year 1861, Appendices to the Journal of the Legislature, 1862, 14. California State Archives.

**Inmates represented twenty-two states and twenty-three foreign countries**: Stockton State Hospital document GP1:373–374, California State Archives.

**The Matron...will be with the female patients**: Rules and Regulations of the Insane Asylum of California, Ninth Annual Report of the Trustees for the Insane Asylum, for the Year 1861, 71. California State Archives.

**insanity induced by "dissatisfaction with her boarding house"**: Report of the State Hospital Committees on the Condition of the Insane Asylum, March 1862, Senate and Assembly Journal Appendix, 1862, 6. California State Archives.

**The more carefully I inquire into the condition of the Asylum**: Report of the Resident Physician, Ninth Annual Report of the Trustees for the Insane Asylum, for the Year 1861, 24. California State Archives.

**These cesspools had become rather numerous**: Report of the Special Committee to Visit the State Insane Asylum (November 1861), 9. Senate and Assembly Journal Appendix, 1862.

**The evils of idleness:** Report of the Resident Physician, 26.

**a series of flag "incidents":** Delmar M. McComb, Jr., *Beat! Beat! Beat!: A History of Stockton During the Civil War* (Stockton, Calif.: privately printed, 1965), 17ff.

**every Union man, and there are few or no others**: *Stockton Daily Republican,* 14 May 1861.

**A flagpole that had recently been erected atop the steeple**: Tinkham, 278.

**ASYLUM FARM.—Among the most thrifty**: *Stockton Daily Independent,* 3 April 1862.

**In the portion of the Asylum occupied by the female patients**: Report of the Special Committee to Visit the State Insane Asylum (November 1861), 7; Report of Assembly Committee on State Hospitals relative to The State Insane Asylum, April 1862. Senate and Assembly Journal Appendix, 1862. California State Archives.

**"senseless and unreasoning babble":** Report of the Special Committee to Visit the State Insane Asylum (November 1861), 3.

**In May Mrs. Farnham was in San Francisco**: *San Francisco Evening Bulletin,* 17 May 1862.

**People have a position if they belong to a Church**: EWF, "A Lecture on the Philosophy of Spiritual Growth Delivered at Platt's Hall May 18, 1862" (San Francisco: Valentine & Co: Commercial Steam Printing Establishment, 1862), 10.

**In June she lectured in Santa Cruz:** *Santa Cruz Pacific Sentinel,* 13 June 1862.

**But let the "talking-wires" span free soil:** *CI&O,* 507.

**boarded the steamer *Sonora* for Panama**: *San Francisco Daily Herald and Mirror,* 21 August 1862.

## 27 – GETTYSBURG

**Charles to France to study drawing and music:** Charles Farnham interview. On 7 April 1864, Charles Farnham signed, at the American Consulate in Nice, France, a document authorizing Richard Kirby to sell his Santa Cruz property, recorded 15 October 1864, Vol. I, Powers of Attorney, 44. Santa Cruz County Records.

**Should our unhappy war be continued:** *NYT,* 29 April 1861.

**Dr. Bellows enjoyed the distinction as President of the Sanitary Bureau:** Stanton, *History of Woman Suffrage,* Vol. 2, 88. See also Charles J. Stille, *History of the United States Sanitary Commission* (Philadelphia: J. B. Lippincott Co., 1866).

**far-off California generously sending more than $400,000:** For an account of California's support of the U.S. Sanitary Commission, see Robert J. Chandler's "The Soldier's Friend: The United States Sanitary Commission" in *The Far-Westerner,* The Quarterly Bulletin of the Stockton Corral of Westerners, Stockton, Calif., XXXVI (Fall/Winter 1995), 5–32.

**On that day they organized the Women's National Loyal League:** That the same women who were praised for this effort were derided for suffrage was not forgotten by them, nor forgiven:
"The leading Journals vied with each other in praising the patience and prudence, the executive ability, the loyalty, the patriotism of the women of the League, and yet these were the same women, who when demanding civil and political rights, privileges, and immunities for themselves, had been uniformly denounced as 'unwise,' 'imprudent,' 'fanatical,' 'impracticable.' During the six years they held their own claims in abeyance to the slaves of the South, and labored to inspire the people with enthusiasm for the great measures of the Republican party, they were highly honored as 'wise, loyal, and clear-sighted.' But again when the slaves were emancipated and they asked that women should be recognized in the reconstruction as citizens of the Republic, equal before the law, all these transcendent virtues vanished like dew before the morning sun. And thus it ever is so long as woman labors to second man's endeavors and exalt *his sex* above her own, her virtues pass unquestioned; but when she dares to demand rights and privileges for herself, her motives, manners, dress, personal appearance, character, are subjects for ridicule and detraction." (Stanton, *History of Woman Suffrage,* Vol. II, 51).

**through an amendment to the U.S. Constitution:** The League eventually collected some 400,000 signatures. In 1865, with the passage of the Thirteenth Amendment, abolishing slavery, the League disbanded.

**I consider women a great deal superior to men:** Stanton, *History of Woman Suffrage,* Vol. II, 59.

**First organized as the Harmonial Benevolent Society:** Emma Hardinge, *Modern American Spiritualism* (New York: University Books, 1970), 273ff.

**After my only brother and every male relative:** Henrietta Stratton Jaquette, ed., *South After Gettysburg: Letters of Cornelia Hancock from the Army of the Potomac, 1863–1865,* (Philadelphia: University of Pennsylvania Press, 1937), 2.

**Every hour was bringing tidings:** Ibid., 3.

**Every barn, church, and building:** Ibid., 4.

**I am very tired tonight:** Ibid., 7.

**Eliza wrote Georgiana:** *San Francisco Spiritualist,* 22 August 1874, 178.

**We have been two days on the field:** Jaquette, *South After Gettysburg,* 8ff.

**Eliza had developed a cough, a bad cough:** Charles Farnham told his interviewer that his mother died "a year after the battle of Gettysburg, having contracted consumption through exposure on the field where she was a nurse."

**Girls who sewed umbrellas at six to eight cents:** James A. Frost, "The Home Front in New York During the Civil War," in *New York History* (Proceedings of the New York State Historical Society, 1961), 273–297.

**The Broadway saloons with their so-called pretty waiter-girls:** Ibid., 282.

**draft riots of July 1863:** In consequence of the large conscription of poor Irish immigrants to fight a war they blamed blacks for, New York City witnessed one of the deadliest race riots in American history. (See Frost, "The Home Front in New York During the Civil War").

## 28 – THE GREAT WORK

**In the afternoon I devoted myself to reading:** Ames, *Life and Letters of Peter and Susan Lesley,* Vol. II, 86.

**she had permitted Mrs. Day...to publish excerpts:** *Hesperian,* December 1860; March 1861; March, April, May 1862.

**all but completed her "great work" in California:** Several passages in Volume II of *Woman and Her Era* are dated 1860. In New York, Mrs. Farnham, in a final review of her manuscript, added asterisked notes dated 1862, 1863, and 1864.

Eliza Farnham bequeathed, in the two-volume *Woman and Her Era,* her self-acclaimed "great work," a veritable banquet of potential dissertations to women's studies programs. To make a starting point, interested scholars need only address the claim made for the work by its publisher:

"The author's treatment of the subject differs from that of writers who have heretofore, in broken and fragmentary dissertations, attempted a description of Woman's 'Rights, Duties and Sphere.' 'Woman and Her Era' is in no true sense a treatise upon the 'Rights of Woman,' neither a homily upon her 'duties,' nor yet a discussion of her 'proper sphere.' Its purpose is deeper and broader than all these. It is a calm, candid, thoroughly rational and fundamental inquiry into the NATURE OF WOMAN—a considerate and exhaustive analysis by Woman, of her own exalted nature and office, and the relations, responsibilities, privileges, duties and possibilities consequent thereupon.

"The work takes the highest ground yet claimed for Woman, viz.: *her innate superiority.*

"In support of this startling position the author does not sentimentalize or argue merely, but critically examines every leading point, with a purpose toward absolute demonstration. The analysis is made *seriatim,* beginning with the Organic Statement, which will have to be sharply handled and very closely dissected to be successfully controverted. Following this we have the Religious, Esthetic, Historical and Intellectual divisions into which the subject naturally falls. The work closes by setting forth the Divine Purpose in the higher endowment of Woman, viz., the performance of a Divine Artistic Maternity—the very noblest service, the author claims, that can be rendered to humanity by any earthly being.

"The book has a powerful appeal to Woman, not simply as its subject, but as its subject made illustrious by the treatment she receives, and by the measure and character of the responsibility shown to be hers in the strictly natural woman-offices.

"In its faithful trust in the sufficiency of Woman's nature to vindicate the dignity of Woman, lies one of the brightest characteristics and chief elements of strength in this important work."

**An early review from the *Chicago New Covenant:* Reprinted in *IA.*

**The *New York Tribune* also reviewed it favorably**: 20 February 1864.

**The *New York Atlas* liked it**: Reprinted in *IA.*

**A review in *Life Illustrated* glowed**: Ibid.

**The *San Francisco Daily Times* added its compliments**: Ibid.

**READY TO-DAY: A BOOK FOR THE CENTURY!**: *NYTr,* 9 April 1864.

**laudatory reviews continued to roll in for** *Eliza Woodson*: Reprinted in an advertisement, *NYTr*, 23 April 1864. The retitling of Mrs. Farnham's childhood autobiography resulted in a misidentification of Eliza's middle name, historians mistaking the W. for Woodson. In *Notable American Women* (Cambridge: Harvard University Pres, 1971), Dr. W. David Lewis corrected the error by identifying Mrs. Farnham as Eliza Wood Burhans Farnham.

**Many of these women have proved the noblest possibilities:** *W&HE*, Vol. I, 251–52.

**Or, if very amiable and gentle:** Ibid., 282.

**success in any position is warrant for taking it:** Ibid., 310.

**Wherever Woman as Thinker, Worker, Artist, Reformer:** Ibid., 311.

**I write in the hope of being read by Women:** Ibid., 110.

**the ROUND TABLE has at last found a work:** *NYTr*, 30 April 1864.

**the** *New York Tribune* **criticized it, too:** *NYTr*, 7 May 1864.

**A review in the** *Continental Monthly*: "Literary Notices," *Continental Monthly: Devoted to Literature and National Policy,* Vol. 6, No. 1 (July 1864), 117–118.

**The** *San Francisco Evening Bulletin* **quoted passages:** 15 June 1864.

**A devastating review in** *Harper's New Monthly Magazine*: "Literary Notices," *Harper's New Monthly Magazine,* Volume 29, Issue 169 (June 1864), 130.

**the** *Atlantic Monthly* **took a turn:** "Reviews and Literary Notices," *The Atlantic Monthly: A Magazine of Literature, Art, and Politics,* Vol. XIV (September 1864), 388.

## 29 – UNFALTERING AND FEARLESS

**About a year since Eliza W. Farnham laid down her weary head:** *History of Woman Suffrage,* Vol. 2, 906.

*The Ideal Attained:* Like *Woman and Her Era,* Mrs. Farnham's novel is also as yet unaddressed by scholars, and equally rich with possibility. *The Ideal Attained* not only portrays Mrs. Farnham's ideas on the progression of human development, it occupies a unique position in California fiction as one of the earliest depictions of gold rush society, uniquely told from a female perspective. Among her predictions for the state's future is this:

"I have no fear…but ultimately there will be found here the grandest outgrowth and illustration of the Republican Idea. For where should all the men of a State come up to that standard so naturally and uniformly, as in such a land and clime, which neither pampers nor impoverishes—neither enervates nor stints? Depend upon it...there will one day throng these plains and hills and valleys, the noblest people on the globe. Art will flourish, because the love of the Beautiful will grow into all souls, and wealth will nourish it with culture and refinement. There will be a sound and perfect physical life—free from the lassitude of the warmer climates and from the destroying diseases engendered in our Atlantic colds and heats....The Yankee sharpness and assiduity were a valuable root on which to engraft the heedless largeness of the Western soul; the two may be several generations in blending into a harmonious and beautiful one, but they will ultimately." (p. 270)

**Whoever lives to see the twentieth century ushered in**: *IA*, 271.

**Maggie Voorhees had been with her**: Gladys Tilden, indefatigable researcher, established that Margaret Voorhees was the sister of Catherine Sinclair, one of California's pioneer theatrical producers. "As Mrs. Kirby indicates [in her Journal]..., the Voorhees family returned to New York in the winter of 1859–60. There they took a house in 35th Street near Fifth Avenue, and in New York directories B. F. Voorhees is listed as being in business, in Wall Street....Meanwhile, Catherine Sinclair, still embroiled with her ex-husband, Edwin Forrest, was living on Staten Island. Mrs. Farnham was living on Staten Island during the winter of 1863–64 while finishing her "great work," *Woman and Her Era*...and it seems quite possible that she and Mrs. Sinclair may have taken the ferry over to New York to see the Voorhees family, when Mrs. Farnham died suddenly." (Gladys Tilden to Helen Giffen, Society of California Pioneers, 8 December 1967. Gladys Tilden Papers.)

**"Anyone in attendance," wrote one who was**: *Santa Cruz Sentinel*, 21 January 1865, Letter, signed "H" (identified by Gladys Tilden as John S. Hittell).

**Mrs. Eliza W. Farnham, well-known throughout the nation**: *NYT*, 18 December 1864.

**The *New York Daily Tribune* further reported**: 19 December 1864.

**I believe not only that death is no termination**: *IA*, 166–167.

**the assassination of President Lincoln**: Of the Civil War, still in progress as *Woman and Her Era* went to press, Mrs. Farnham tucked in one last optimistic footnote:
"How grandly has our nation withstood the shock and strain of Civil War, since these words were written, more than three years ago. To what moral grandeur will she tower, when final victory, now [February, 1864] near at hand, is hers, and she stands before her own and the world's Conscience,

cleansed of her Great Sin; commended to God and the universal heart by her faithfulness. We need not fear henceforth to commit the cause of Woman to her keeping." (Vol. II, 451)

**"Mrs. Farnham's great fiction"..."No common novel":** *NYTr*, 22 April, 13 May 1865.

**[Eleanore Bromfield] was frank to a daring degree:** *IA,* 358.

**Does not the world, because you are a man:** Ibid., 223–224.

**Depend upon it...there will one day throng these plains:** Ibid., 270.

**I have mourned through endless summer days:** Ibid., 158–160.

**Susan Anthony...visited Eliza Farnham's grave:** Ida Husted Harper, ed., *Life and Work of Susan B. Anthony,* Vol. II (Indianapolis: Hollenbeck Press, 1898), 252.

## 30 – SWEET RECOLLECTION

**This is one of the most beautiful places:** Quoted in George Willis Cooke, "Brook Farm," *The New England Magazine* (December 1897), 392. For a history of social associationism and the roots of Brook Farm, see also William B. Shaw, "A Forgotten Socialism," *The New England Magazine*, Vol. 14, No. 6 (August 1893), 773.

**Whatever might be said of:** Ibid., 407.

**An Old Landmark Gone:** *Santa Cruz Sentinel,* 30 May 1868.

**In spite of our much vaunted climate:** GBK, "Letter from California," *National Anti-Slavery Standard,* 25 December 1869, XXX, No. 34, 2. The *National Anti-Slavery Standard,* printed from 1840–1872, was a publication of the American Anti-Slavery Society. The AASS was founded in Philadelphia on 4 December 1833, at a meeting attended by sixty-two abolitionist delegates representing eleven states.

**I should not have ventured:** *YE,* 91. Mrs. Kirby devoted several chapters of her autobiography to her experiences at Brook Farm (pp. 89–189), incorporating much of the material written for the *Overland Monthly* and three subsequent articles published in *Old and New:* "Before I Went to Brook Farm," February 1871; "Reminiscences of Brook Farm," April 1871; September 1871; May 1872.

**Mrs. Kirby's article:** GBK, "My First Visit to Brook Farm," 9–19.

**a more pure, more lovely, more divine state of society**: Cooke, "Brook Farm," 391.

**It was objected to by some**: *YE*, 91.

**promised just the spiritual hospitality**: Ibid., 90.

**No one could have been more out-of-place than he**: Ibid., 102. Hawthorne's *Blithedale Romance* is an imaginative account of Brook Farm.

**...not one man...who would kill any animal larger than a chicken**: Ibid., 136.

## 31 – FIGHTING FOR SUFFRAGE

**California.—The advocacy of woman's rights began in Santa Cruz county**: *History of Woman Suffrage*, Vol. 3, 765.

**For nearly a score of years after the great incursion**: Ibid., 750–751.

**the first statewide California woman's suffrage organization**: *History of Woman Suffrage*, Vol. 3, 749–766, summarizes California's part in the national effort to gain the vote for women.

**Sarah Wallis**: As a semi-literate nineteen-year-old immigrant to California in 1844, wife of Allen Montgomery, Sarah learned to write at Sutter's Fort, courtesy of Eliza Gregson (see "The Gregson Memoirs," *California Historical Society Quarterly* 19 (June 1940), 113–143). Abandoned by Montgomery, she married Talbot Green in 1849, a respected and wealthy man discovered in 1851 to be an absconding bank clerk and bigamist. In 1854 Sarah married Joseph Wallis, who became a state senator in 1862. In 1856 Sarah Wallis had taken ownership in her own name of Mayfield Farm (in present-day Palo Alto), where she and her husband built an elegant home and entertained lavishly. In 1877 President Ulysses S. Grant attended a party at Mayfield Farm. (See Dorothy Regnery, "Pioneering Women—Portraits of Sarah," *The Californian*, Magazine of the California History Center Foundation, Vol. 8, No. 2 [December 1986], 6–9).

**Laura de Force Gordon**: Born in Pennsylvania in 1838. After marrying Charles H. Gordon, she traveled west with him by wagon to Nevada in 1867 and later settled in California. Laura Gordon gave occasional public lectures, and in February 1868 she delivered in San Francisco a call for equal rights for women, one of the first such public appeals made in the West. In 1873 she began publishing and editing the *Stockton Weekly Leader*, with such success that it soon became a daily. In 1875 she moved the paper to Sacramento and a year later she sold it. From 1875 to 1878 she edited the *Oakland Daily Democrat*. While covering the 1877–78 session of the state legislature for her paper, Gordon lobbied for a bill to admit women to the practice of law in California. Denied admission to the Hastings College of Law in San Francisco, she and Clara Foltz, who also had applied, instituted a suit against the school, argued their case jointly before the state Supreme Court, and won. In February 1885 she was admitted to practice before the U.S. Supreme Court. She died in Lodi, California, in 1907.

**Mrs. Laura de Force Gordon**: *Santa Cruz Sentinel,* 18 February 1870.

**It is the opinion of very many of the best men**: Ibid.

**Mrs. Kirby lives in Santa Cruz. Progressive woman**: Ibid., 7 May 1870.

**He "ordered me to make a written apology**: Ibid., 2 April 1870.

**mistook a cellar door for her bedroom door**: Ibid., 15 October 1870.

**The year 1871 was an election year in California**: In June 1871 Romualdo Pacheco received the Republican party nomination for lieutenant governor, and Newton Booth the nomination for governor. Both were elected. In 1875, when Newton Booth was elected to the U.S. Senate, Pacheco became governor of California, the only Hispanic to serve in that office.

**The general sentiment of the large audience**: *Santa Cruz Sentinel,* 12 August 1871.

**Miss Anthony was less successful in nearby Watsonville**: *Watsonville Pajaronian,* 10 August 1871.

**The popularity of this estimable lady**: *Santa Cruz Sentinel,* 12 August 1871.

**For more than a quarter of a century**: Ibid., 26 August 1871.

**I feel somewhat depressed in appearing before you**: Ibid.

**Under the civil law women had certain rights**: Ibid.

**Richard Kirby chaired the meeting**: Ibid., 30 September 1871.

**Convinced that what she had done was proper**: Ibid.

**If any doubt existed as to the really low opinion men entertain**: Ibid., 23 December 1871.

**Will a Lady Ever be President?**: Ibid., 6 January 1872.

**I must close by saying that if John Dimon**: Ibid., 17 February 1872.

**I was much disappointed after reading the article of Mrs. Kirby**: Ibid., 24 February 1872.

**This settles the question of the right of suffrage**: Ibid., 1 April 1872.

**Richard Kirby...visited England**: Ibid., 17 February 1872; 1 June 1872.

**third annual farmers club fair, the Kirbys' daughter**: Ibid., 25 October 1873.

**the Santa Cruz Temperance Union**: Ibid., 21 March 1874.

**anti-liquor crusade**: Ibid.

**mainly an eloquent and forcible plea for mental and moral courage**: Ibid., 1 May 1875.

**an institution—you felt she might put you on a list**: Foote, *A Victorian Gentlewoman*, 141. Mrs. Foote's visit to Santa Cruz is included in Wallace Stegner's Pulitzer Prize–winning novel, *Angle of Repose*, based on her life, with the character Mrs. Elliot representing Georgiana Kirby.

**The Kirbys were called rich**: Ibid., 142–143.


## 32 – A MOTHER'S INFLUENCE

**It is my wish to impress on women the grave truth**: GBK, *Transmission; or Variation of Character through the Mother* (New York: Fowler & Wells, 1882), 5. GBK quotes this chapter, *Transmission*, 1882 edition, 11–80.

**We would give special emphasis**: Reprinted in GBK, *Transmission*, 1877 edition.

**Famously critical of local educators**: "Mrs. Kirby on School Matters," *Santa Cruz Sentinel*, 9 April 1881.

**Amid Better Circumstances**: Published serially, *Santa Cruz Surf*, beginning 17 June 1886.

**Mrs. Kennedy, an Irish emigrant, was capable of taking a historic view**: *Santa Cruz Surf*, 2 September 1886.

**Why doctor, our ancestors were driven from their lands**: Ibid., 28 August 1886.

**It is a bad beginning to be born of grief**: *YE*, 2.

**in May, 1850, I left New York for California, where I have passed the remainder of my life**: Ibid., 315.

**somewhat rude in its literary form**: "Two American Memoires," *The Atlantic Monthly*, Vol. 60, No. 357 (July 1887), 127–129.

**No thoughtful person can read this modest autobiography without interest**: "Book Reviews and Notices," *North American Review*, Vol. 145, No. 370 (September 1887), 339–340.

**Her mind and character were keenly analytical**: Quoted from the *San Francisco Chronicle* in *Santa Cruz Daily Sentinel*, 29 January 1887.

**a memorial service was held in Santa Cruz**: Ibid., 1 February 1887.

**Santa Cruz's Unity Church**: Mrs. Kirby's long campaign for a Unitarian minister for Santa Cruz was answered in 1866 when the Rev. Charles G. Adams arrived and organized Unity Church.

## 33 – ...BUT NOT FORGOTTEN

**We had pointed to us the former residence of Mrs. Farnham**: "Trip to Santa Cruz," by the editor of the *Stockton Herald*, *Santa Cruz Daily Sentinel*, 2 June 1866.

**On a hill south of the Hinds' place**: Sarah Elizabeth Gourley, "My Early Childhood Memories," *Santa Cruz County History Journal*, No. 2 (The History Museum of Santa Cruz County, 1995), 74.

**Named for a Santa Cruz pioneer**: In 1994 Seagate technology executive Ken Wing and Murray Walker, a music teacher from New York interested in innovative and accessible education, founded an independent, coeducational secondary school in Santa Cruz and named it in honor of Georgiana Bruce Kirby.

**Friends, you may not recognize in this form**: "Phenomenal Facts.—Mrs. Eliza W. Farnham," *Banner of Progress*, 17 May 1868.

**Santa Cruz was in early days**: Norick Neill, "Santa Cruz's Interesting Literary History.—A Circle of Intellect," *San Francisco Call*, 11 June 1893; reprinted in the *Santa Cruz Daily Sentinel*, 13 June 1893.

**One of the most delightful bits of fanciful analogy**: Ora Bruce Kirby, *Santa Cruz Surf*, 16 June 1893. Miss Kirby also erred, in small details, stating, for example, that Thomas J. Farnham died in the spring of 1849, rather than September 1848; and that Ruckel owed Mrs. Farnham $14,000.

**All that stuff about Fitzpatrick is pure gammon**: Ibid.

**He died in 1929**: "Charles Haight Farnham, scholar and author, died in a hospital here [Daytona Beach, Florida] of pneumonia today at the age of 87. He had lived here in virtual seclusion for years, spending his time writing an encyclopedia of the fine arts, which he recently completed." (*NYT*, 27 February 1929).

**The originality of *Woman and Her Era* is so startling:** Helen Beal Woodward, *The Bold Women* (New York: Farrar, Straus and Young, 1953), 341.

**Mrs. Farnham's contribution to penal history:** W. D. Lewis, *From Newgate to Dannemora*, 157–177.

***Notable American Women:*** W. David Lewis, "Eliza Wood Burhans Farnham," in *Notable American Women*, 598–600.

**Mrs. Farnham supplemented Sampson's work:** EWF, *Rationale of Crime.*

**a vivid account of early Illinois:** John Hallwas, Introduction to *Life in Prairie Land*, by E. W. Farnham, University of Illinois Press edition, xv.

**Although never published in its complete form:** According to Ms. Griffen, Georgiana's great-grandson "wished me to put in material that I did not consider would do the biography any good, and I have never published it." Helen S. Giffen to Gladys Tilden, 7 November 1961. Gladys Tilden Papers.

**Ms. Giffen replied that she had a copy of Georgiana's *Years of Experience*:** Ibid.

**Miss Tilden's literary intentions:** In 1975 she resumed research on her father, but never wrote his biography either. In 1988 she became a ward of Alameda County. She died in 1995.

**There is left us, at the worst:** *IA*, 219.

# Bibliography

## BOOKS

Ames, Mary L., ed. *Life and Letters of Peter and Susan Lesley.* 2 volumes. New York: G. P. Putnam's Sons, 1909.

Bancroft, Hubert Howe. *History of California.* San Francisco: The History Company, 1884–1890. Reprint. Santa Barbara: W. Hebberd, 1963.

Barnhart, Jacqueline. *The Fair but Frail: Prostitution in San Francisco 1849–1900.* Reno: University of Nevada Press, 1986.

Bates, Mrs. D. B. *Incidents on Land and Water, or Four Years on the Pacific Coast.* Boston: E. O. Libby & Co., 1858. Reprint. New York: Arno Press, 1974.

Beeson, John. *A Plea for the Indians.* New York: J. Beeson, 1857. Reprint. Fairfield, Wash.: Ye Galleon Press, 1982.

Bloomer, D. C. *Life and Writings of Amelia Bloomer.* New York: Schocken Books, 1975.

Braude, Ann. *Radical Spirits: Spiritualism and Women's Rights in Nineteenth-Century America.* Boston: Beacon Press, 1989.

Brooks, Sarah Merriam. *Across the Isthmus to California in '52.* San Francisco: C. A. Murdock & Co., 1894.

Bruff, J. Goldsborough. *Gold Rush: The Journals, Drawings, and Other Papers of J. Goldsborough Bruff, April 2, 1849–July 20, 1851.* New York: Columbia University Press, 1949.

Buck, Franklin. *A Yankee Trader in the Gold Rush.* New York: Houghton Mifflin Co., 1930.

Burhans, Samuel Jr. *Burhans Genealogy.* New York: privately printed, 1894.

Cleland, Robert Glass, ed. *Apron Full of Gold: The Letters of Mary Jane Megquier from San Francisco, 1849–1856.* San Marino, Calif.: The Huntington Library, 1949.

Colton, Walter. *Three Years in California.* New York: A. S. Barnes & Co., 1850. Reprint, *The California Diary.* Oakland, Calif.: Biobooks, 1948.

Combe, George. *Notes on the United States of North America during a Phrenological Visit in 1838-9-40,* Vol. I. Edinburgh, 1851. Reprint. New York: Arno Press, 1974.

Covert, Martin V. *Stockton Album through the Years.* Stockton, Calif.: privately printed, 1959.

Davies, John D. *Phrenology, Fad and Science: A 19th-Century American Crusade.* New Haven, Conn.: Archon Books, 1971.

Dewey, Mary E., ed., *Life and Letters of Catharine M. Sedgwick.* New York: Harper & Bros.,1872.

Elliott, W. W. *Santa Cruz County, Calif. Illustrated with Historical Sketch.* San Francisco: Wallace W. Elliott & Co., 1879. Reprint. Santa Cruz, Calif.: The Museum of Art and History at The McPherson Center, 1997.

Farnham, Eliza W. *California, In-doors and Out; or, How we Farm, Mine, and Live generally in the Golden State.* New York: Dix, Edwards & Co., 1856. Reprint. Nieuwkoop, Netherlands: B. De Graaf, 1972.

Farnham, Eliza W. *Life in Prairie Land.* New York: Harper & Bros., 1846. Reprint. Urbana: University of Illinois Press, 1988.

Farnham, Eliza W. *My Early Days.* New York: Thatcher & Hutchinson, 1859.

Farnham, Eliza W. *The Ideal Attained.* New York: C. M. Plumb & Co., 1865.

Farnham, Eliza. W. *Woman and Her Era.* 2 volumes. New York: A. J. Davis & Co., 1864.

Farnham, Eliza W., ed. *Rationale of Crime, Marmaduke B. Sampson's "Treatise on Criminal Jurisprudence Considered in Relation to Cerebral Organization."* Reprint. Montclair, N.J.: Patterson Smith, 1973.

Farnham, Thomas J. *Life, Adventures and Travels in California.* New York: numerous early editions, 1844–1855. Reprint. *Travels in California.* Oakland, Calif.: Biobooks, 1947.

Farnham, Thomas J. *Travels in the Great Western Prairies...and in the Oregon Territory.* New York: Greeley & McElrath, 1843. Reprint. Monroe, Ore.: Northwest Interpretive Association, 1983.

Ferguson, Charles D. *California Gold Fields.* Oakland, Calif.: Biobooks, 1948.

Foote, Edward B. *Plain Home Talk and Medical Common Sense.* New York: Murray Hill Publishing Co., 1884.

Foote, Mary Hallock. *A Victorian Gentlewoman in the Far West.* San Marino, Calif.: The Huntington Library, 1972.

Freedman, Estelle B. *Their Sisters' Keepers: Prison Reform in America, 1830–1930.* Ann Arbor: University of Michigan Press, 1981.

Fremont, Jessie Benton. *A Year of American Travel: Narrative of Personal Experience.* San Francisco: Book Club of San Francisco, 1960.

Garner, William Robert. *Letters from California 1846–1847.* Introduction by Donald Munro Craig. Berkeley: University of California Press, 1970.

Hafen, Le Roy R. and Ann W., eds., *To the Rockies and Oregon, 1839–1842.* Glendale, Calif.: The Arthur H. Clark Co., 1955.

Harding, Walter and Carl Bode, eds. *The Correspondence of Henry David Thoreau.* New York: New York University Press, 1958.

Hardinge, Emma. *Modern American Spiritualism.* Reprint. New York: University Books, 1970.

Harper, Ida Husted, ed. *Life and Work of Susan B. Anthony,* Vol. II. Indianapolis: Hollenbeck Press, 1898.

Hecox, Margaret M. *California Caravan.* San Jose, Calif.: Harlan-Young Press, 1966.

Holliday, J. S. *Rush for Riches: Gold Fever and the Making of California.* Berkeley: University of California Press, 1999.

Holloway, Emory and Vernolian Schwarz, eds. *I Sit and Look Out: Editorials from the Brooklyn Daily Times by Walt Whitman, ed.* New York: Columbia University Press, 1932.

Howe, Maud and Florence Howe Hall. *Laura Bridgman, Dr. Howe's Famous Pupil and What He Taught Her.* Boston: Little, Brown, & Co., 1903.

Hurtado, Albert L. *Indian Survival on the California Frontier.* New Haven, Conn.: Yale University Press, 1988.

Jaquette, Henrietta Stratton, ed. *South After Gettysburg: Letters of Cornelia Hancock from the Army of the Potomac, 1863–1865.* Philadelphia: University of Pennsylvania Press, 1937.

Kemble, Edward C. *History of California Newspapers.* Reprint. Los Gatos, Calif.: Talisman Press, 1962.

Kinder, Gary. *Ship of Gold in the Deep Blue Sea.* New York: Atlantic Monthly Press, 1988.

Kirby, Georgiana B. *Amid Better Circumstances.* Serially, *Santa Cruz Surf,* 1886.

Kirby, Georgiana B. *Transmission; or Variation of Character Through the Mother.* New York: S. R. Wells & Co., 1877. Reissued. New York: Fowler & Wells, 1882.

Kirby, Georgiana Bruce. *Years of Experience: An Autobiographical Narrative.* New York: AMS Press, 1971.

Latta, Frank F. *Death Valley '49ers.* Santa Cruz, Calif.: Bear State Books, 1979.

Lewis, Oscar. *Sea Routes to the Gold Fields.* New York, 1949.

Lewis, W. David. *From Newgate to Dannemora: The Rise of the Penitentiary in New York, 1796–1848.* New York: Cornell University Press, 1965.

Luckey, John. *Life in Sing Sing State Prison, as seen in a Twelve Years' Chaplaincy.* New York: N. Tibbals & Co., 1860.

McComb, Delmar M. Jr. *Beat! Beat! Beat!: A History of Stockton During the Civil War.* Stockton, Calif.: privately printed, 1965.

Marston, Anna Lee, ed. *Records of a California Family: Journals and Letters of Lewis C. Gunn and Elizabeth LeBreton Gunn.* San Diego, Calif.: Donald I. Segerstrom Memorial Fund, 1928.

Meyrick, Henry. *Santa Cruz & Monterey Illustrated Handbook.* San Francisco: San Francisco News Publishing Co., 1880.

Morgan, Dale, ed. *Overland in 1846: Diaries and Letters of the California–Oregon Trail.* 2 volumes. Lincoln: University of Nebraska Press, 1963.

Nasatir, A. P., ed. *A French Journalist in the California Gold Rush: The Letters of Etienne Derbec.* Georgetown, Calif.: The Talisman Press, 1964.

Nunis, Doyce B. Jr. *The Trials of Isaac Graham.* Los Angeles: Dawson's Book Shop, 1967.

Payne, Stephen Michael. *A Howling Wilderness: A History of the Summit Road Area of the Santa Cruz Mountains 1850–1906.* Santa Cruz, Calif.: Loma Prieta Publishing, 1978.

Petri, Pitt. *Postal History of Western New York.* Buffalo, N.Y.: P. Petri, 1960.

Pomfret, Dr. John E. *California Gold Rush Voyages, 1848–1849: Three Original Narratives.* San Marino, Calif.: The Huntington Library, 1954.

*Proceedings of the Free Convention Held at Rutland, Vt., July 25th, 26th, and 27th, 1858.* Boston: J. B. Yerrington and Son, 1858.

Rowland, Leon. *Santa Cruz, The Early Years: The Collected Historical Writings of Leon Rowland.* Santa Cruz, Calif.: Paper Vision Press, 1980.

Soulé, Frank, et al., eds. *The Annals of San Francisco.* New York: D. Appleton & Co., 1854. Reprint. Palo Alto, Calif.: Lewis Osborne, 1966.

Stafford, Mallie. *The March of Empire*. San Francisco: Geo. Spaulding & Co., 1884.

Stanton, Elizabeth Cady, Susan B. Anthony, and Matilda Joslyn Gage, eds., *History of Woman Suffrage*, Vol. 1, 2, 3. New York: Arno and The New York Times, 1969.

Stern, Madeleine B. *Heads & Headlines: The Phrenological Fowlers*. Norman: University of Oklahoma Press, 1971.

Stille, Charles J. *History of the United States Sanitary Commission*. Philadelphia: J. B. Lippincott Co., 1866.

Swift, Carolyn and Judith Steen, eds. *Georgiana, Feminist Reformer of the West: The Journal of Georgiana Bruce Kirby 1852–1860*. Santa Cruz, Calif.: Santa Cruz County Historical Trust, 1987.

Suhl, Yuri. *Ernestine L. Rose and the Battle for Human Rights*. New York: Reynal & Company, 1959.

Taylor, Bayard. *Eldorado, or, Adventures in the Path of Empire*. New York: G. P. Putnam, 1850. Reprint. Berkeley, Calif.: Heyday Books, 2000.

Taylor, William. *California Life Illustrated*. New York: Carlton & Porter, 1858.

Tinkham, George H. *A History of Stockton*. San Francisco, Calif.: W. M. Hinton, 1880.

Townsend, Peggy Jean and Paul Walker Townsend III. *Milo Adams Townsend and Social Movements of the Nineteenth Century*. Historical Documents Collection. Beaver County History Online (www.bchistory.org), Beaver County, Pennsylvania.

Woodward, Helen Beal. *The Bold Women*. New York: Farrar, Straus and Young, 1953.

Wyman, Walker D., ed. *California Emigrant Letters*. New York: Bookman Associates, 1971.

**ARTICLES**

*American Phrenological Journal*, April 1856, in Book Club of California *Quarterly News-Letter*, XXXIII, No. 3, Summer 1968.

Beaman, A. Gaylord, ed. "Pioneer Letters," *Historical Society of Southern California Quarterly*, March 1939.

"Book Reviews and Notices," *North American Review*, Vol. 145, No. 370, September 1887.

Camp, Charles L., ed. "The Journal of a 'Crazy Man': Travels and Scenes in California from the Year 1834 to the American Conquest—The Narrative of Albert Ferdinand Morris," *California Historical Society Quarterly*, XV, No. 2, June 1936.

"Case of Laura Bridgman," *American Phrenological Journal*, September 1841.

Chandler, Robert J. "The Soldier's Friend: The United States Sanitary Commission," *The Far-Westerner*, The Quarterly Bulletin of the Stockton Corral of Westerners, Stockton, California, XXXVI, Fall/Winter 1995.

Churchill, Charles B. "Thomas Jefferson Farnham: An Exponent of American Empire in Mexican California," *Pacific Historical Review*, LX, No. 4, November 1991.

Cooke, George Willis. "Brook Farm," *The New England Magazine*, Dec. 1897.

Degler, Carl N. "The West as a Solution to Urban Unemployment," *New York History*, XXXVI, 1955.

Farnham, E. W. "A Lecture on the Philosophy of Spiritual Growth Delivered at Platt's Hall May 18, 1862." San Francisco: Valentine & Co: Commercial Steam Printing Establishment, 1862.

Farnham, E. W. "Laura Bridgman," *The Prisoners' Friend*, Vol. I, No. III, November 1848.

Farnham, E. W. Letter to Georgiana Bruce Kirby from Gettysburg. *San Francisco Spiritualist*, 22 August 1874.

Farnham, Mrs. T. J. "Rights Of Women, Reply To Mr. Neal's Lecture," *Brother Jonathan*, Vol. V, 24 June 1843; 15 July 1843; 29 July 1843.

Frost, James A. "The Home Front in New York During the Civil War," *New York History*, Proceedings of the New York State Historical Society, 1961.

Gourley, Sarah Elizabeth. "My Early Childhood Memories," *Santa Cruz County History Journal*, No. 2, The History Museum of Santa Cruz County, 1995.

Greene, Maud Honeyman. "Raritan Bay Union, Eagleswood, New Jersey," *Proceedings of the New Jersey Historical Society*, 68, No. 1, January 1950.

*Hesperian Magazine*, Vol. 5, 6, 8.

*Hunt's Merchant Magazine*, Vol. XV, July 1846.

"Journal of Captain John Paty, 1807–1868," *California Historical Society Quarterly*, XIV, No. 4, December 1835.

Kemble, John Haskell. "The Panama Route to the Pacific, 1848–1869," *Pacific Historical Review*, March 1938.

Kirby, Georgiana B. "Before I Went to Brook Farm," *Old and New*, February 1871.

Kirby, Georgiana B. "Letter from California," *National Anti-Slavery Standard*, XXX, No. 34, 25 December 1869.

Kirby, Georgiana B. "My First Visit to Brook Farm," *Overland Monthly*, Vol. 5, No. 1, July 1870.

Kirby, Georgiana B. "Reminiscences of Brook Farm," *Old and New*, April 1871.

Kirby, Georgiana B. "Reminiscences of Brook Farm," *Old and New*, September 1871.

Kirby, Georgiana B. "Reminiscences of Brook Farm," *Old and New*, May 1872.

*Knickerbocker Magazine*, Vol. XLVIII, July 1846.

Lewis, W. David. "Eliza Wood Burhans Farnham." In *Notable American Women: 1607–1950: A Biographical Dictionary*. Cambridge: Harvard University Press, 1971.

"Literary Notices," *Continental Monthly: Devoted to Literature and National Policy*, Vol. 6, No. 1, July 1864.

"Literary Notices," *Harper's New Monthly Magazine*, Vol. 29, No. 169, June 1864.

"Phenomenal Facts.—Mrs. Eliza W. Farnham," *Banner of Progress*, 17 May 1868.

Regnery, Dorothy. "Pioneering Women—Portraits of Sarah," *The Californian*, Magazine of the California History Center Foundation, Vol. 8, No. 2, December 1986.

"Reviews and Literary Notices," *The Atlantic Monthly: A Magazine of Literature, Art, and Politics*, Vol. XIV, September 1864.

Shaw, William B. "A Forgotten Socialism," *The New England Magazine*, Vol. 14, No. 6, August 1893.

Stern, Madeleine B. "Two Letters from The Sophisticates of Santa Cruz," Book Club of California *Quarterly News-Letter*, XXXIII, No. 3, Summer 1968.

"Table First, An Exhibit of Patients received in, continuing, and discharged from the Asylum...", Document GP1:373–374, Stockton State Hospital. California State Archives.

"Two American Memoires." *The Atlantic Monthly*, Vol. 60, No. 357, July 1887.

*United States Magazine and Democratic Review*, Vol. 19, July 1846, and Vol. 20, January 1847.

## NEWSPAPERS

*Alta California*

*Baltimore Sun*

*Californian*

*Daily California Chronicle*

*California Farmer*

*Honolulu Polynesian*

*Hudson River Chronicle*

*Nevada Journal*

*New York Herald*

*New York Times*

*New York Tribune*

*Placer Herald*

*Sacramento Daily Bee*

*Sacramento Daily Union*

*Sacramento Democratic State Journal*

*San Francisco Call*

*San Francisco Daily Evening Bulletin*

*San Francisco Daily Evening News*

*San Francisco Daily Herald and Mirror*

*San Francisco Daily Times*

*San Francisco Evening Bulletin*

*San Francisco Herald*

*San Francisco Spiritualist*

*San Joaquin Republican*

*Santa Cruz (Pacific) Daily Sentinel*

*Santa Cruz News*

*Santa Cruz Surf*

*St. Louis Argus*

*Stockton Daily Independent*

*Stockton Daily Republican*

*Watsonville Pajaronian*

## UNPUBLISHED DOCUMENTS, PAPERS, REPORTS

John Bigelow Papers. Manuscripts and Archives Division, The New York Public Library. Astor, Lenox and Tilden Foundations.

Bryant-Godwin Papers. Manuscripts and Archives Division, The New York Public Library. Astor, Lenox and Tilden Foundations.

Buchanan, Joseph. "Phrenological Opinion on the head of T. J. Farnham," Misc. Mss. Farnham, T. J., courtesy of The New-York Historical Society.

Letters of Kelly E. Burhans of Potters Hollow, N.Y. to his sister Mary Wood Roberts in Illinois, January 29, 1830–July 1, 1838. New York State Library.

Emmeline Hubbard Day Journal, 1853–1856. BANC MSS 74/170 c, The Bancroft Library, University of California, Berkeley.

De Witt Family Papers. BANC MSS 73/163 c, The Bancroft Library, University of California, Berkeley.

Dix, Edwards & Co. Papers. bMS Am 800.13, Houghton Library, Harvard University.

Farnham, Charles interview. "Information Concerning Charles H. Farnham." California State Library, Sacramento.

Farnham, E. W., to Mrs. Francis Wright, 12 November 1842, New York. Department of Rare Books and Manuscripts, Boston Public Library.

Farnham, E. W., to Lydia Sigourney, 11 April 1849, New York. Manuscript Collection, Connecticut Historical Society.

Fowler-Wells Collections. Collection of Regional History and University Archives, Cornell University, Ithaca, New York.

William Lloyd Garrison Papers. Boston Public Library.

James Roberts Gilmore Collection Ms. 37, Special Collections, Milton S. Eisenhower Library, The Johns Hopkins University.

S. G. Howe Correspondence, Samuel P. Hayes Research Library, Perkins School for the Blind, Watertown, Massachusetts.

New York State Senate Document, 63rd Session (1840), Vol. II, No. 48.

Ninth Annual Report of the Trustees for the Insane Asylum, for the Year 1861, Appendices to the Journal of the Legislature, 1862. California State Archives.

Report of Assembly Committee on State Hospitals relative to The State Insane Asylum, April 1862. Senate and Assembly Journal Appendix, 1862. California State Archives.

Report of the Resident Physician, Ninth Annual Report of the Trustees for the Insane Asylum, for the Year 1861. California State Archives.

Report of the Special Committee to Visit the State Insane Asylum (November 1861). Senate and Assembly Journal Appendix, 1862. California State Archives.

Report of the State Hospital Committees on the Condition of the Insane Asylum, March 1862. Senate and Assembly Journal Appendix, 1862. California State Archives.

Rules and Regulations of the Insane Asylum of California. Ninth Annual Report of the Trustees for the Insane Asylum, for the Year 1861. California State Archives.

Santa Cruz County Probate Court Case No. 43.

Santa Clara County Records. Book A of Deeds.

Santa Cruz County Records. October 1864, Vol. I, Powers of Attorney, 44.

Santa Cruz County Records. Marriage Certificate, Richard Kirby to Georgiana Bruce.

Santa Cruz County Records. Marriage Certificate, William Fitzpatrick to Eliza W. Farnham.

Santa Cruz County Records. Santa Cruz County Index to Deeds, Book I, Eliza W. Farnham to Thomas Russell, March 23, 1852; Eliza W. Farnham to R. C. Kirby, March 23, 1852.

Second Report of the Prison Association of New York. New York, 1846.

Stockton State Hospital document GP1:373–374, California State Archives.

Third Annual Report of the Executive Committee of the Prison Association of New-York, 14 October 1847. New York State Assembly document 255.

Gladys Tilden Papers. BANC MSS 89/229c, The Bancroft Library, University of California, Berkeley.

U.S. District Court of Appeal Transcript No. 383SD. The Bancroft Library, University of California, Berkeley.

Van Ness Family Papers. BANC MSS C-B 462, The Bancroft Library, University of California, Berkeley.

Joseph L. Warren Papers. BANC MSS C-B 418, The Bancroft Library, University of California, Berkeley.

# Acknowledgments

The research contribution of Gladys Tilden to this work is, in a word, immeasurable. Citations she compiled during more than a decade of industriously seeking Eliza Farnham's name in New York, Illinois, and California newspapers provided an invaluable dimension to a work that would have been impoverished by their absence.

Without archivists and librarians, of course, Miss Tilden's remarkable effort would have been lost. My gratitude to The Bancroft Library for preserving and making available the Gladys Tilden Papers is boundless. At The Bancroft, I wish chiefly to acknowledge David Kessler, who for more than five years has assisted my every request both expeditiously and graciously.

The miracle of interlibrary loan does not just assist historical research; for those of us residing in rural communities it makes it possible. To the Amador County Library I am hugely indebted for years of unflagging effort by Mary Anne Spurlock, and then her successor, Trudy Ann Vimini, to obtain for me one obscure request after another and another and another.

Librarians and historians throughout the country have assisted this work, and I particularly thank David Smith for practicing "guerrilla librarianship" at the New York Public Library. I am indebted as well to Ken Stuckey of the Samuel P. Hayes Research Library, Perkins School for the Blind; to Kathleen A. Correia at the California State Library; to Beth Graham at the California Historical Society; and to Genevieve Troka at the California State Archives. Dr. Robert Chandler kindly provided a copy of Mrs. Farnham's Gettysburg letter and for several years has cheered this effort.

For their individual encouragement and assistance I also thank eminent gold rush historian J. S. Holliday; California author James D. Houston; Gary Kurutz, Principal Librarian, Special Collections, California State Library; Madeleine Stern; John E. Hallwas; Santa Cruz Museum of Art and History archivist Rachel McKay; and Lynn Bonfield. Barbara Dudley of Rensselaerville has my gratitude for generously taking me on a wild, foggy drive to Potter Hollow to see Eliza's birthplace and for sharing the Kelly Burhans correspondence. I thank Dr. W. David Lewis for "blessing" this project way back in 1997 and delightfully declaring that "any friend of Eliza's is a friend of mine." To Dr. Kevin Starr, State Librarian of California, I am most grateful, and happily indebted, not only for his interest in this book, but for his generous and perceptive contribution to it.

By no means least is my heartfelt appreciation to Malcolm Margolin of Heyday Books and Dr. Terry Beers at Santa Clara University for the enthusiasm and dedication to California history that make books like this possible. My gratitude to the production staff at Heyday is boundless, most particularly to Jeannine Gendar, for her improving editorial eye and artful editorial hand.

And to family—most particularly my husband, Dan, whose belief and support never waver—as well as friends, acquaintances, and not a few strangers whose ears I talked off with tales of Eliza, my great gratitude for many years of kind indulgence.

# Index

# A CALIFORNIA LEGACY BOOK

Santa Clara University and Heyday Books are pleased to publish the California Legacy series, vibrant and relevant writings drawn from California's past and present.

Santa Clara University—founded in 1851 on the site of the eighth of California's original twenty-one missions—is the oldest institution of higher learning in the state. A Jesuit institution, it is particularly aware of its contribution to California's cultural heritage and its responsibility to preserve and celebrate that heritage.

Heyday Books, founded in 1974, specializes in critically acclaimed books on California literature, history, natural history, and ethnic studies.

Books in the California Legacy series appear as anthologies, single author collections, reprints of important books, and original works. Taken together, these volumes bring readers a new perspective on California's cultural life, a perspective that honors diversity and finds great pleasure in the eloquence of human expression.

*Series editor:* Terry Beers
*Publisher:* Malcolm Margolin
*Advisory committee:* Stephen Becker, William Deverell, Charles Faulhaber, David Fine, Steven Gilbar, Ron Hansen, Gerald Haslam, Robert Hass, Jack Hicks, Timothy Hodson, James Houston, Jeanne Wakatsuki Houston, Maxine Hong Kingston, Frank LaPena, Ursula K. Le Guin, Jeff Lustig, Tillie Olsen, Ishmael Reed, Alan Rosenus, Robert Senkewicz, Gary Snyder, Dr. Kevin Starr, Richard Walker, Alice Waters, Jennifer Watts, Al Young.

Thanks to the English Department at Santa Clara University and to Regis McKenna for their support of the California Legacy series.

SCU

CALIFORNIA
LEGACY

# OTHER CALIFORNIA LEGACY BOOKS

*Mark Twain's San Francisco*
Edited with a New Introduction by Bernard Taper

*Storm* George R. Stewart

*Dark God of Eros: A William Everson Reader*
Edited with an Introduction by Albert Gelpi

*920 O'Farrell Street: A Jewish Girlhood in San Francisco* Harriet Lane Levy

*Under the Fifth Sun: Latino Literature from California* Edited by Rick Heide

*The Journey of the Flame* Walter Nordhoff

*California: A Study of American Character* Josiah Royce

*One Day on Beetle Rock* Sally Carrighar

*Death Valley in '49* William Lewis Manly

*Eldorado: Adventures in the Path of Empire* Bayard Taylor

*Fool's Paradise: A Carey McWilliams Reader*
Foreword by Wilson Carey McWilliams

*November Grass* Judy Van der Veer

*Lands of Promise and Despair: Chronicles of Early California, 1535–1846*
Edited by Rose Marie Beebe and Robert M. Senkewicz

*The Shirley Letters: From the California Mines, 1851–1852*
Louise Amelia Knapp Smith Clappe

*Unfinished Message: Selected Works of Toshio Mori*
Introduction by Lawson Fusao Inada

*Unfolding Beauty: Celebrating California's Landscapes*
Edited with an Introduction by Terry Beers

If you would like to be added to the California Legacy mailing list, please send your name, address, phone number, and email address to:

California Legacy Project, English Department
Santa Clara University, Santa Clara, CA 95053

For more on California Legacy titles, events, or other information, please visit www.californialegacy.org.

# About the Author

JoAnn Levy is the author of the now-classic *They Saw the Elephant: Women in the California Gold Rush.* Her first work of fiction, *Daughter of Joy: A Woman of the West Novel of gold rush San Francisco,* won the 1999 Willa Award for Best Historical Fiction. A second novel, *For California's Gold,* received the prize in 2001 after debuting at the National Archives in Washington, D.C., where Levy spoke in honor of Women's History Month and California's statehood sesquicentennial. She is a frequent speaker on behalf of the gold-rushing women she discovered in nearly a decade of research, and she has been featured in numerous television documentaries. She lives and writes in Sutter Creek, in the heart of California's gold country.